Shojo Beat

pping on Roses

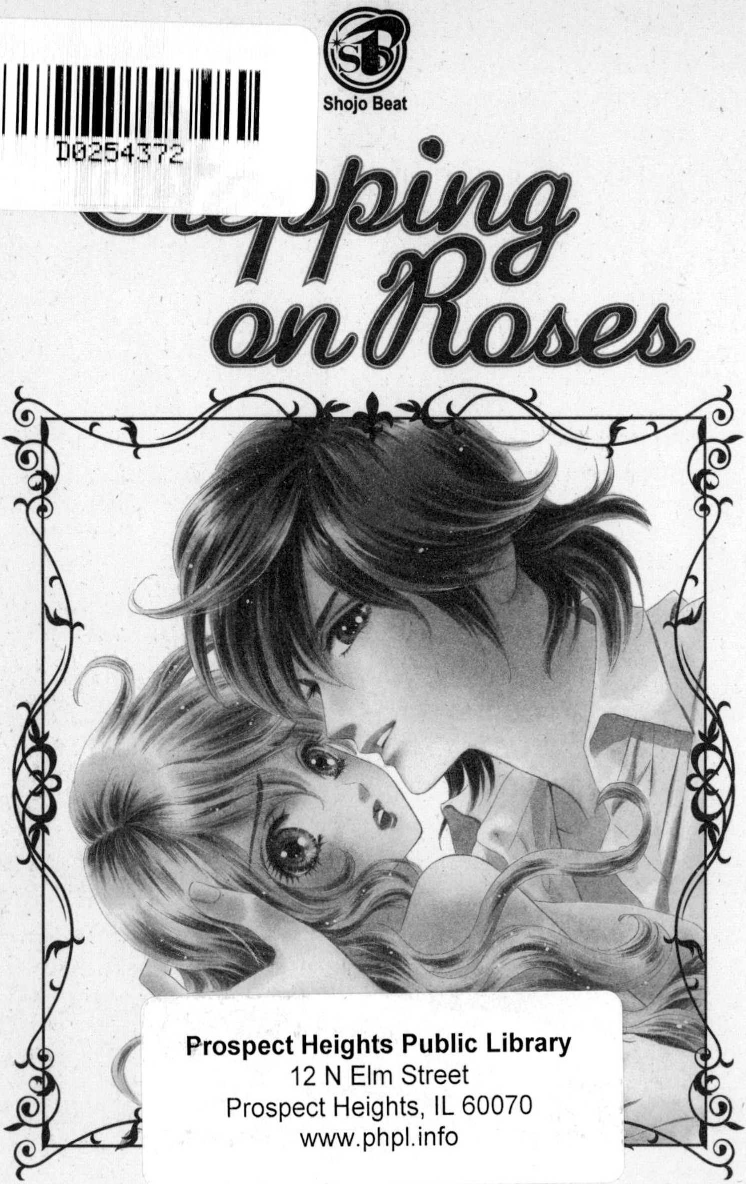

Vol. 1

Story & Art by

Rinko Ueda

Stepping on Roses

Volume 1
CONTENTS

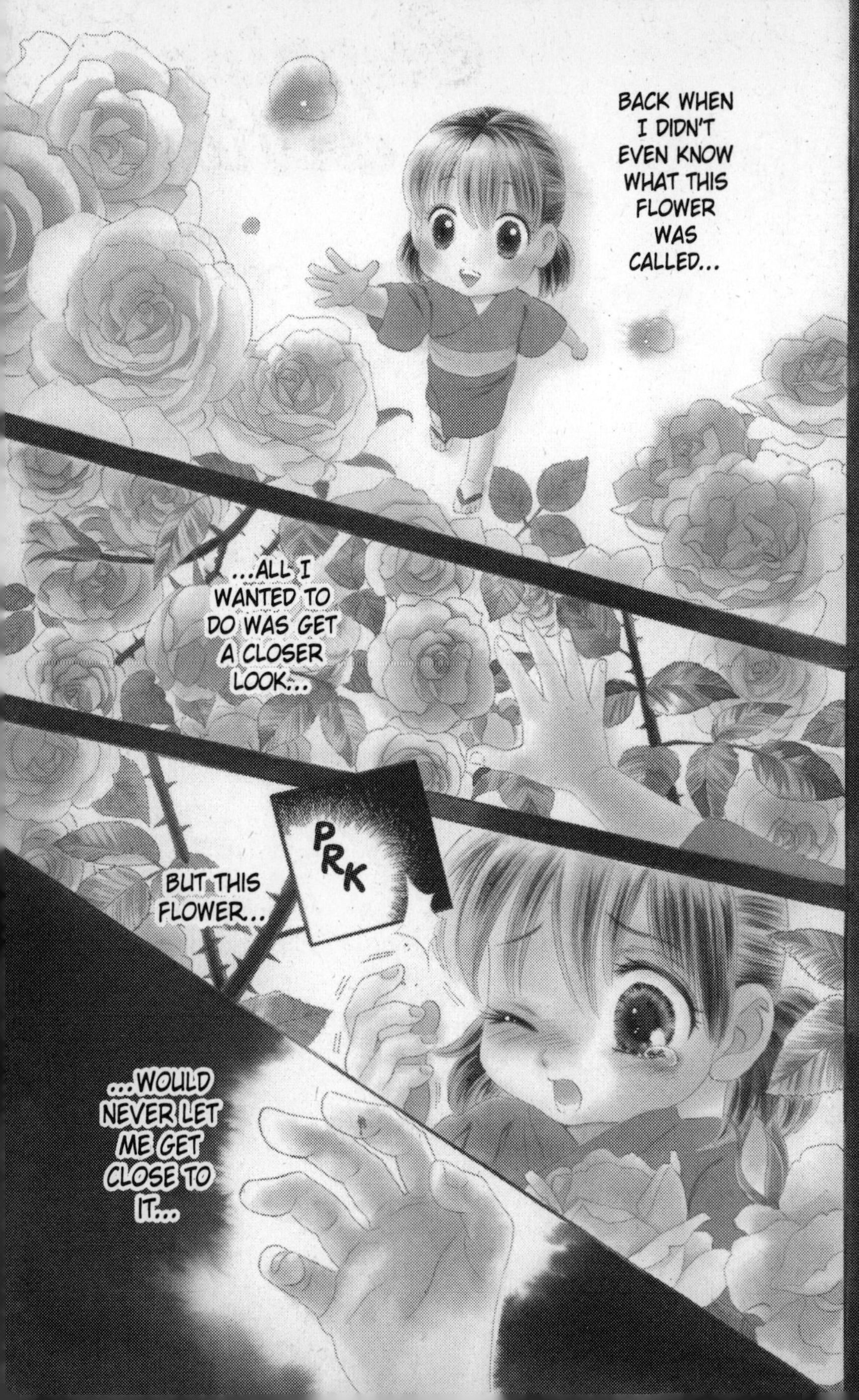
BACK WHEN I DIDN'T EVEN KNOW WHAT THIS FLOWER WAS CALLED...
...ALL I WANTED TO DO WAS GET A CLOSER LOOK...
PRK
BUT THIS FLOWER...
...WOULD NEVER LET ME GET CLOSE TO IT...

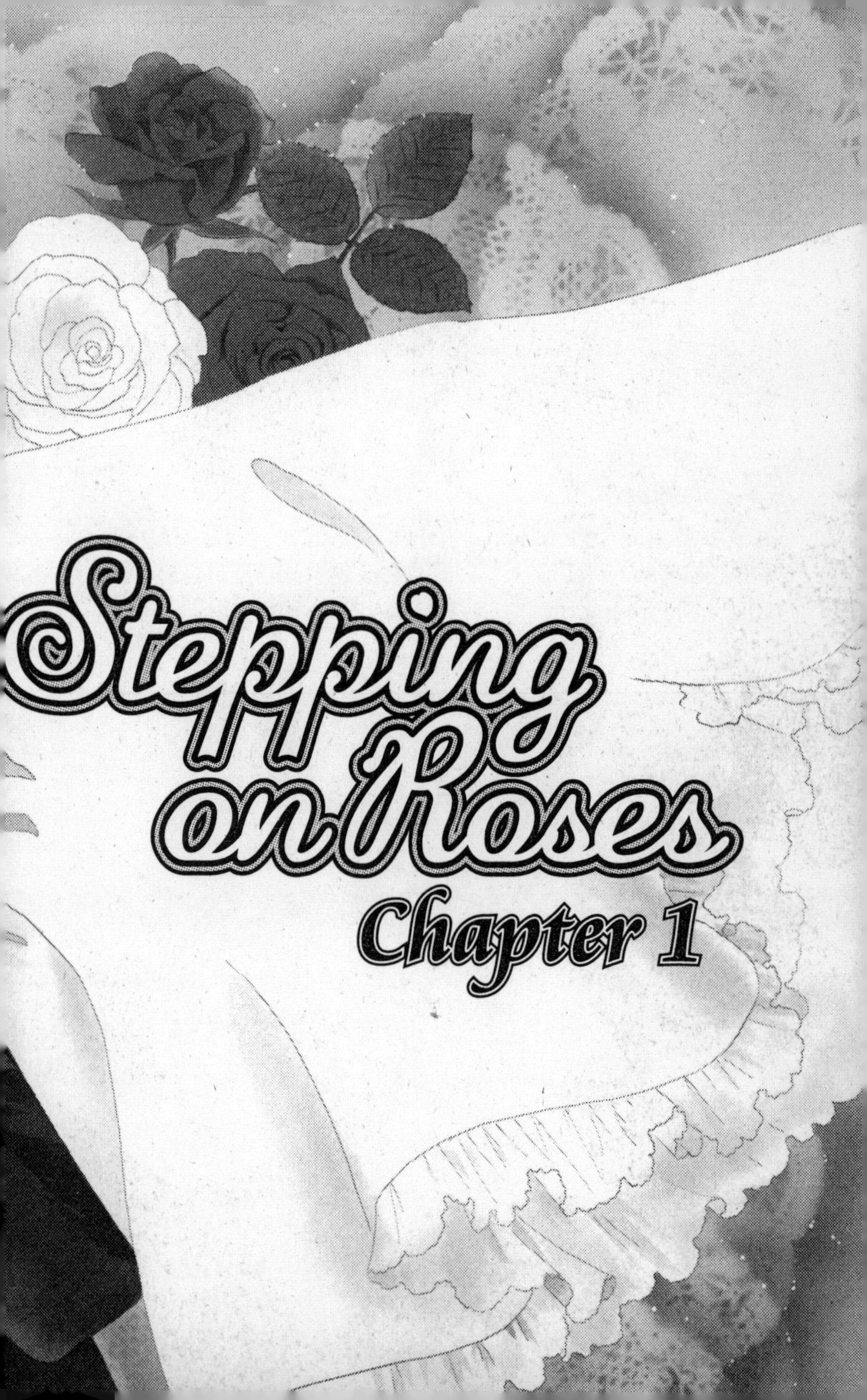
Stepping on Roses
Chapter 1

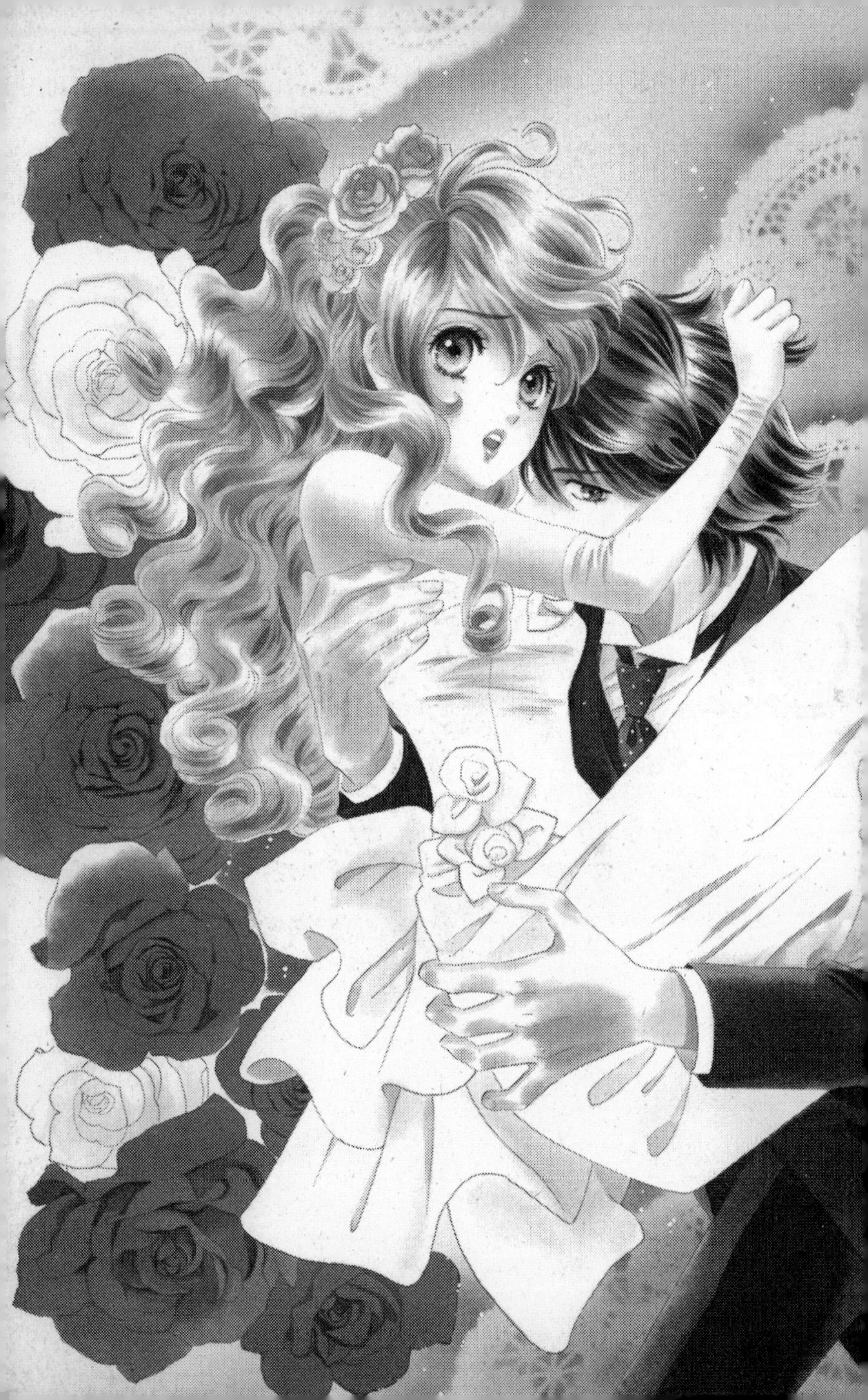

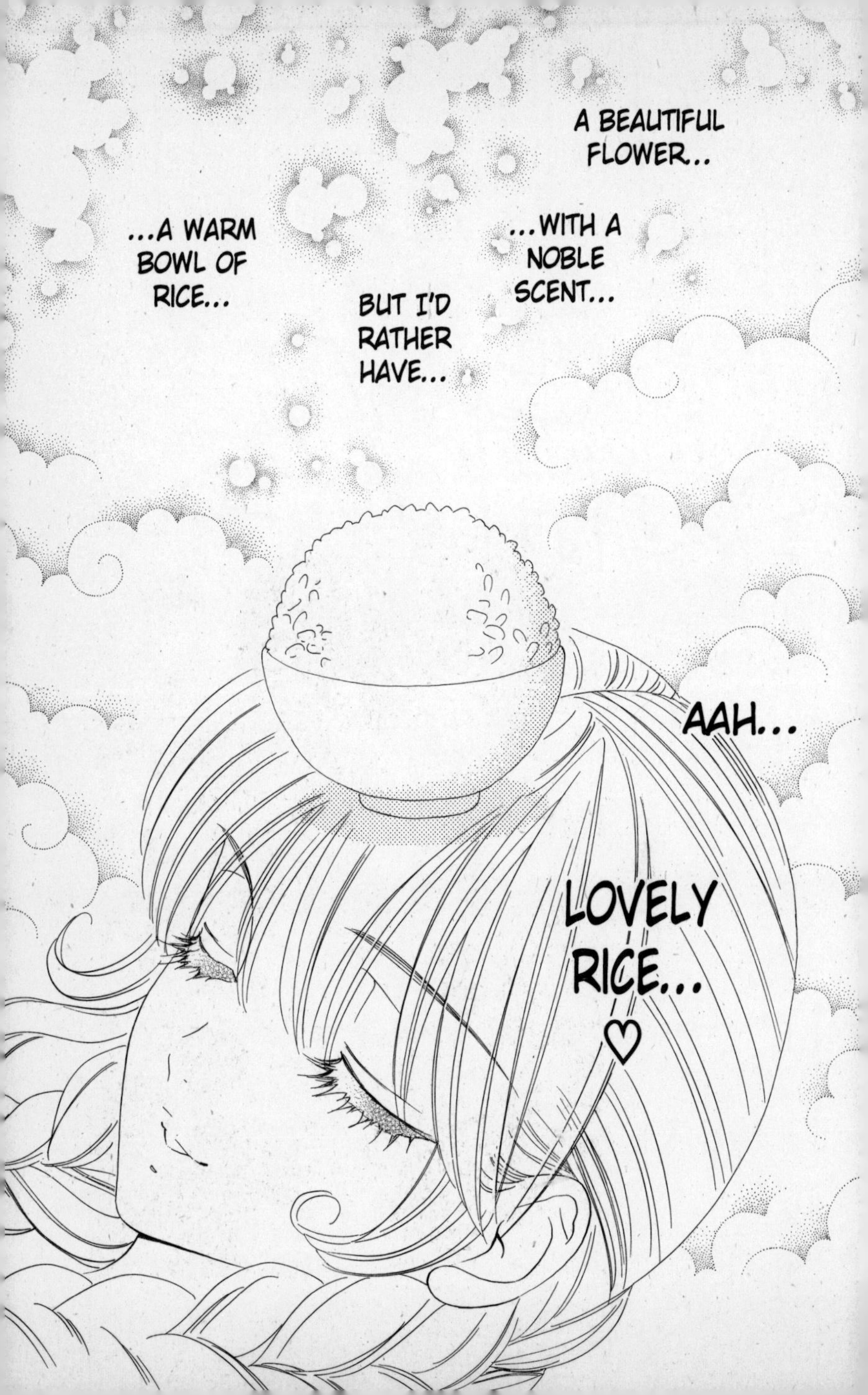
A BEAUTIFUL FLOWER...
...WITH A NOBLE SCENT...
BUT I'D RATHER HAVE...
...A WARM BOWL OF RICE...
AAH...
LOVELY RICE... ♡

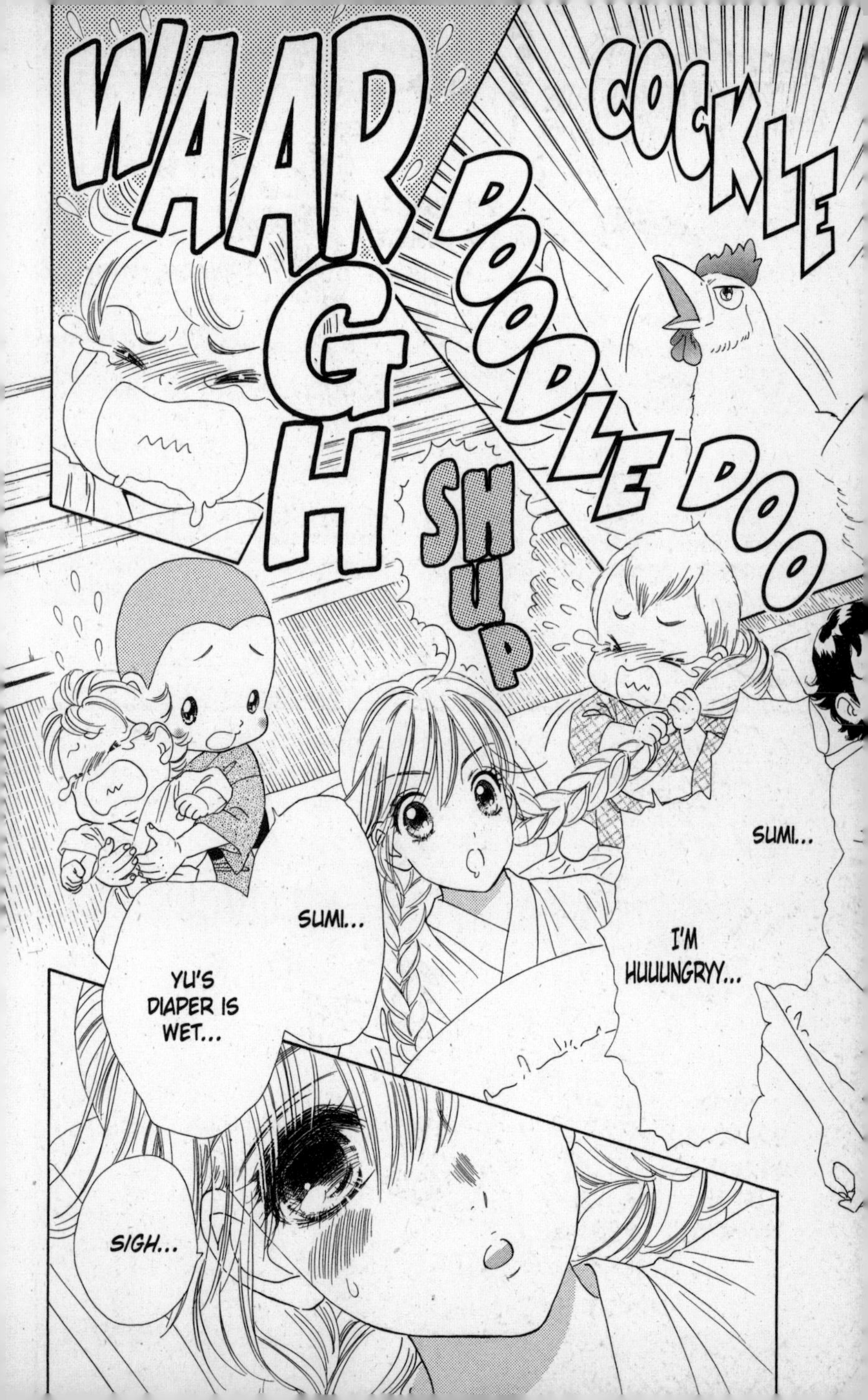

COCKLE DOODLE DOO
WAARGH
SHUP
SUMI...
I'M HUUUNGRYY...
SUMI...
YU'S DIAPER IS WET...
SIGH...

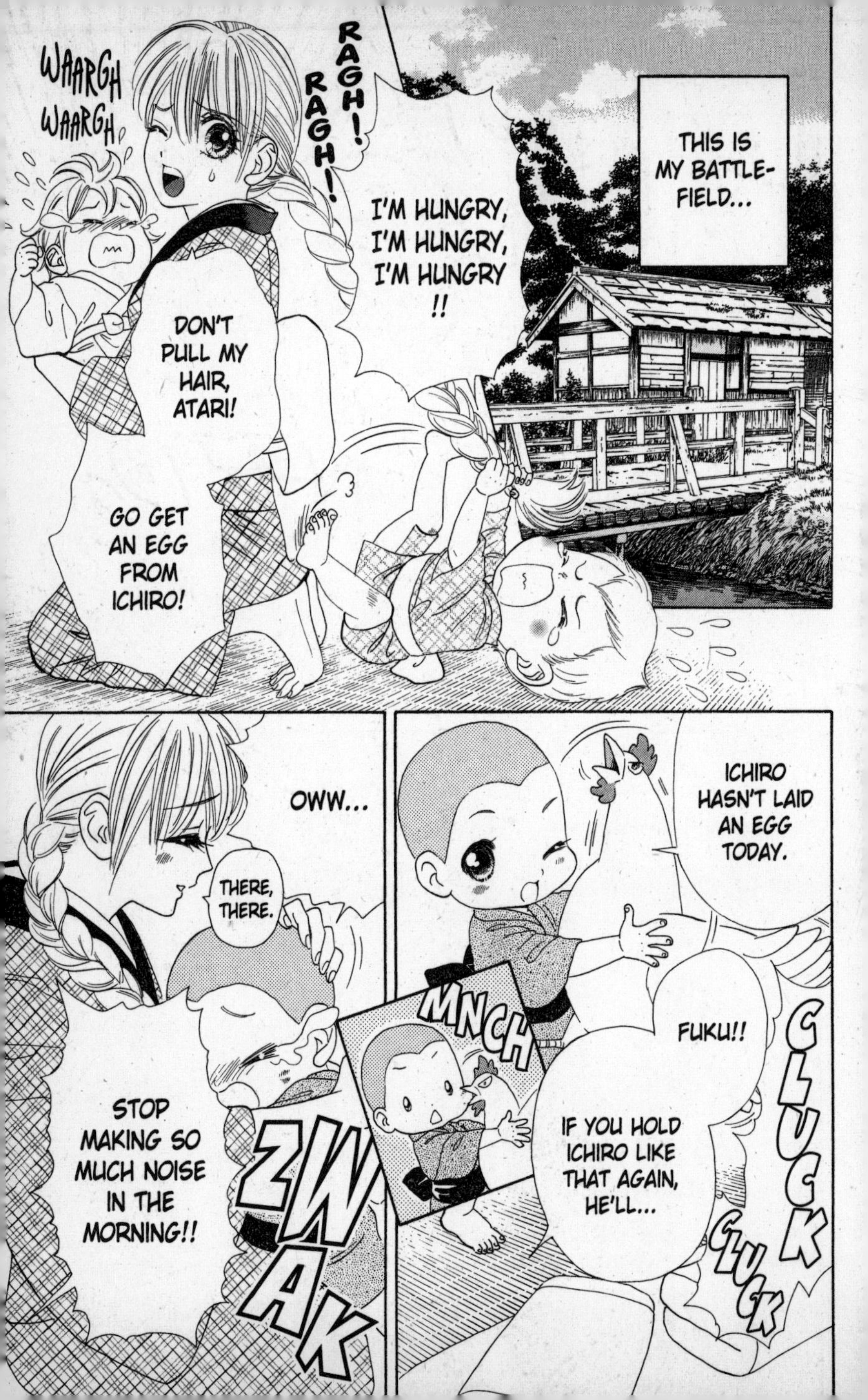
THIS IS MY BATTLE-FIELD...
RAGH!
RAGH!
I'M HUNGRY, I'M HUNGRY, I'M HUNGRY!!
WAARGH WAARGH
DON'T PULL MY HAIR, ATARI!
GO GET AN EGG FROM ICHIRO!
ICHIRO HASN'T LAID AN EGG TODAY.
FUKU!!
CLUCK
CLUCK
MNCH
IF YOU HOLD ICHIRO LIKE THAT AGAIN, HE'LL...
OWW...
THERE, THERE.
ZWAK
STOP MAKING SO MUCH NOISE IN THE MORNING!!

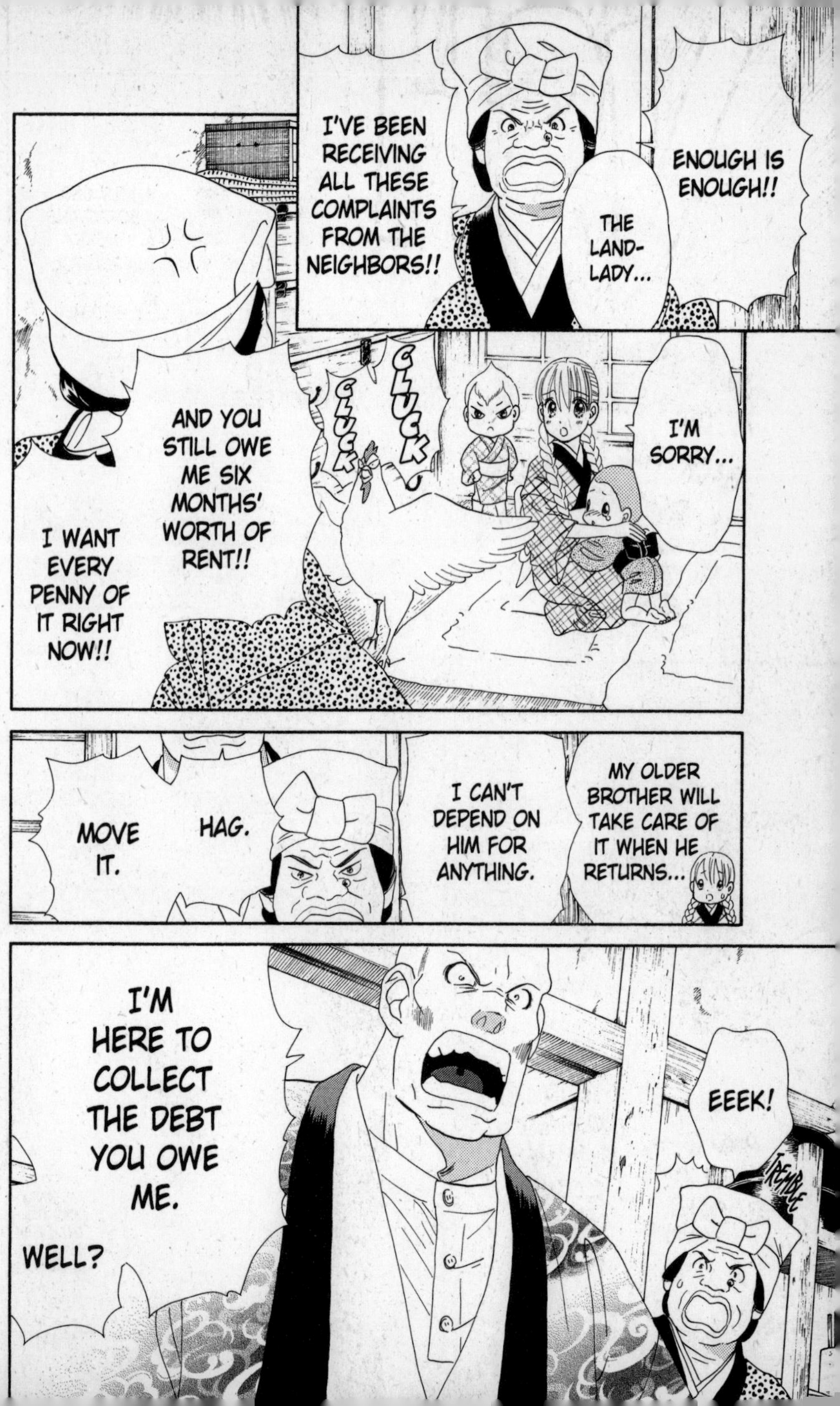
ENOUGH IS ENOUGH!!
THE LAND-LADY...
I'VE BEEN RECEIVING ALL THESE COMPLAINTS FROM THE NEIGHBORS!!
I'M SORRY...
CLUCK
CLUCK
AND YOU STILL OWE ME SIX MONTHS' WORTH OF RENT!!
I WANT EVERY PENNY OF IT RIGHT NOW!!
MY OLDER BROTHER WILL TAKE CARE OF IT WHEN HE RETURNS...
I CAN'T DEPEND ON HIM FOR ANYTHING.
HAG.
MOVE IT.
EEEK!
TREMBLE
I'M HERE TO COLLECT THE DEBT YOU OWE ME.
WELL?

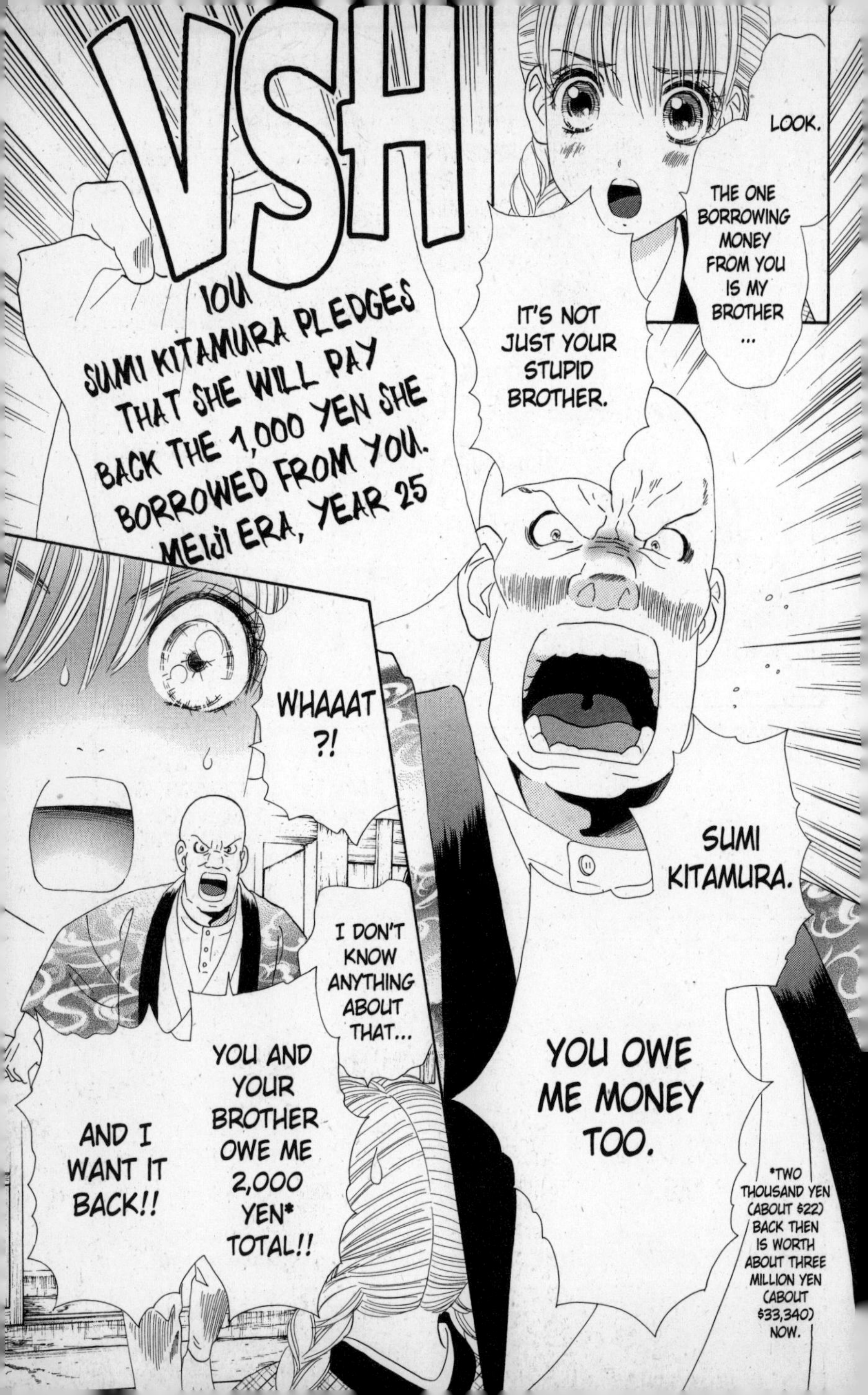
LOOK.
THE ONE BORROWING MONEY FROM YOU IS MY BROTHER...
VSH
IOU
SUMI KITAMURA PLEDGES THAT SHE WILL PAY BACK THE 1,000 YEN SHE BORROWED FROM YOU.
MEIJI ERA, YEAR 25
IT'S NOT JUST YOUR STUPID BROTHER.
SUMI KITAMURA.
YOU OWE ME MONEY TOO.
WHAAAT ?!
I DON'T KNOW ANYTHING ABOUT THAT...
YOU AND YOUR BROTHER OWE ME 2,000 YEN* TOTAL!!
AND I WANT IT BACK!!
*TWO THOUSAND YEN (ABOUT $22) BACK THEN IS WORTH ABOUT THREE MILLION YEN (ABOUT $33,340) NOW.

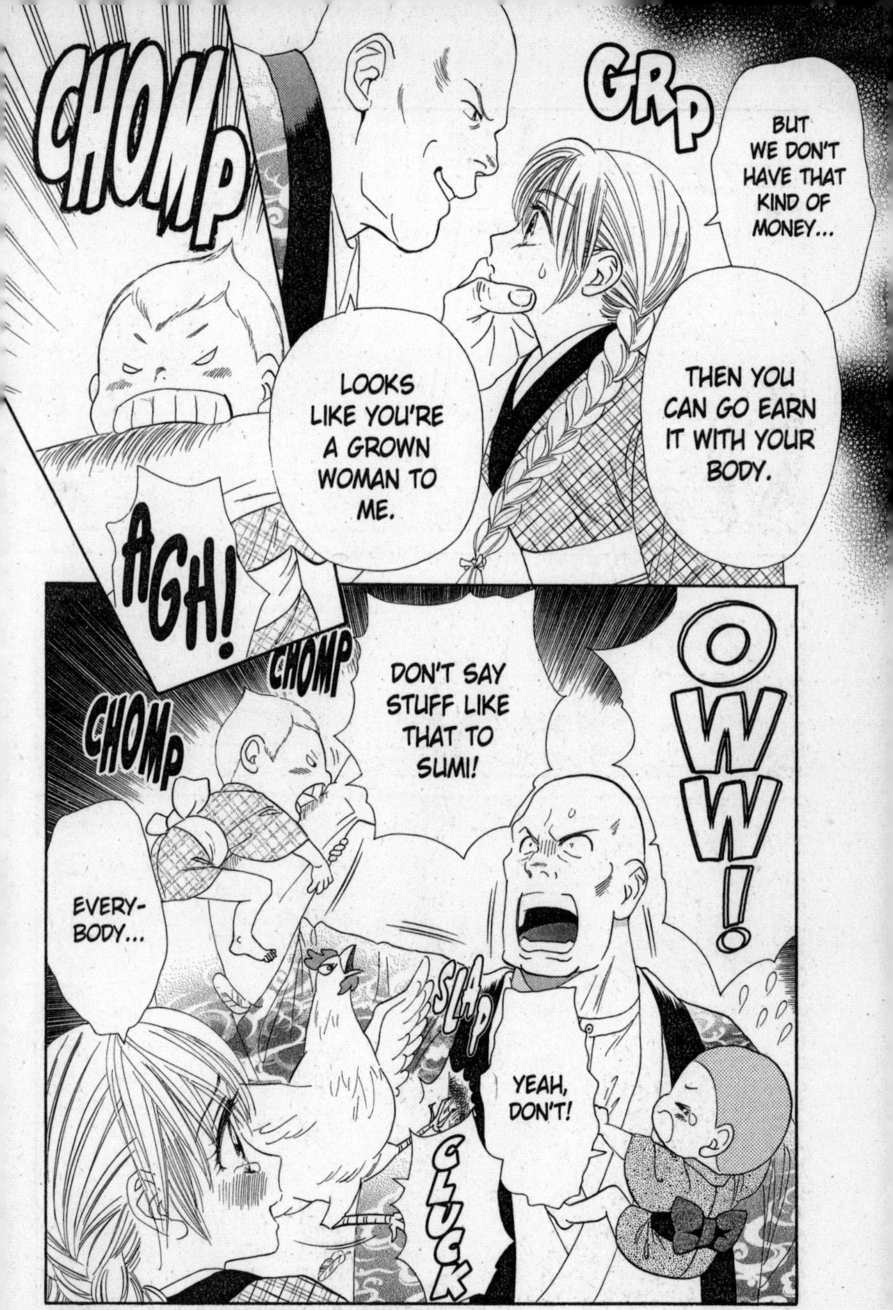
GRP
BUT WE DON'T HAVE THAT KIND OF MONEY...
THEN YOU CAN GO EARN IT WITH YOUR BODY.
LOOKS LIKE YOU'RE A GROWN WOMAN TO ME.
CHOMP
AGH!
OWW!
DON'T SAY STUFF LIKE THAT TO SUMI!
CHOMP
CHOMP
SLAP
YEAH, DON'T!
CLUCK
EVERY-BODY...

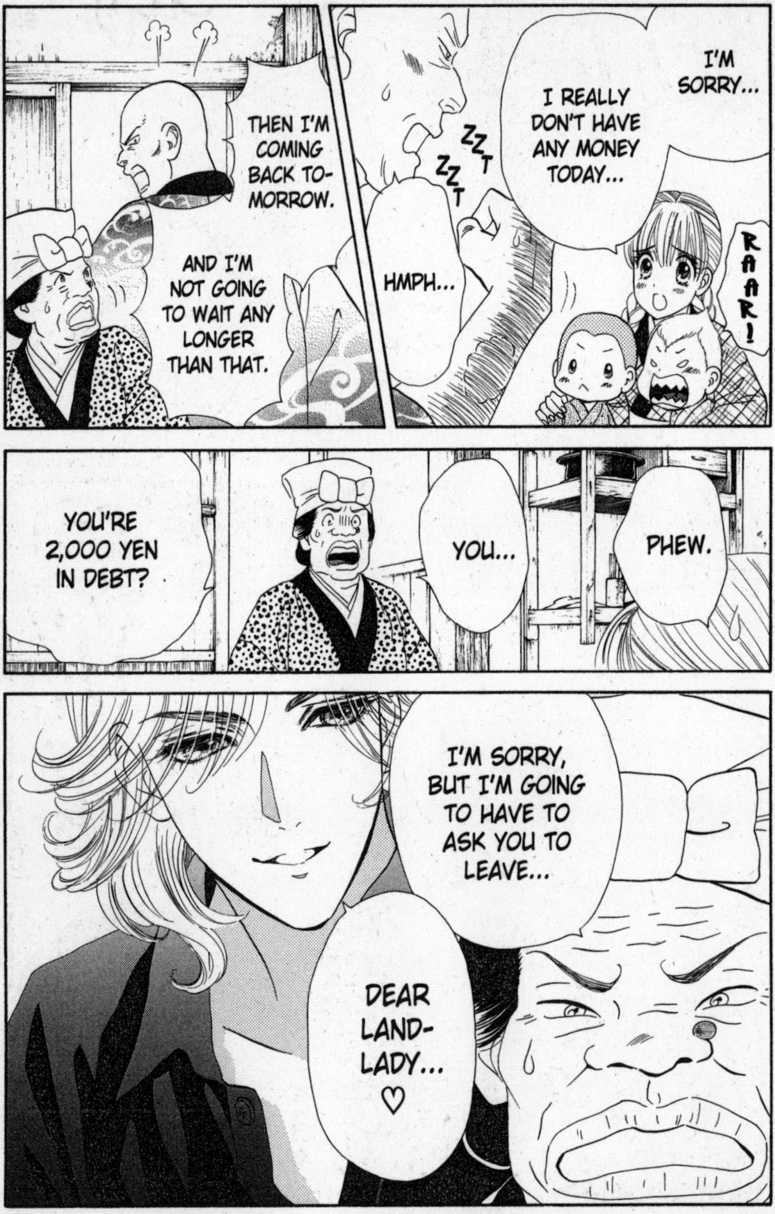
I'M SORRY...
I REALLY DON'T HAVE ANY MONEY TODAY...
RAAR!
ZZT
ZZT
HMPH...
THEN I'M COMING BACK TO-MORROW.
AND I'M NOT GOING TO WAIT ANY LONGER THAN THAT.
PHEW.
YOU...
YOU'RE 2,000 YEN IN DEBT?
I'M SORRY, BUT I'M GOING TO HAVE TO ASK YOU TO LEAVE...
DEAR LAND-LADY... ♡

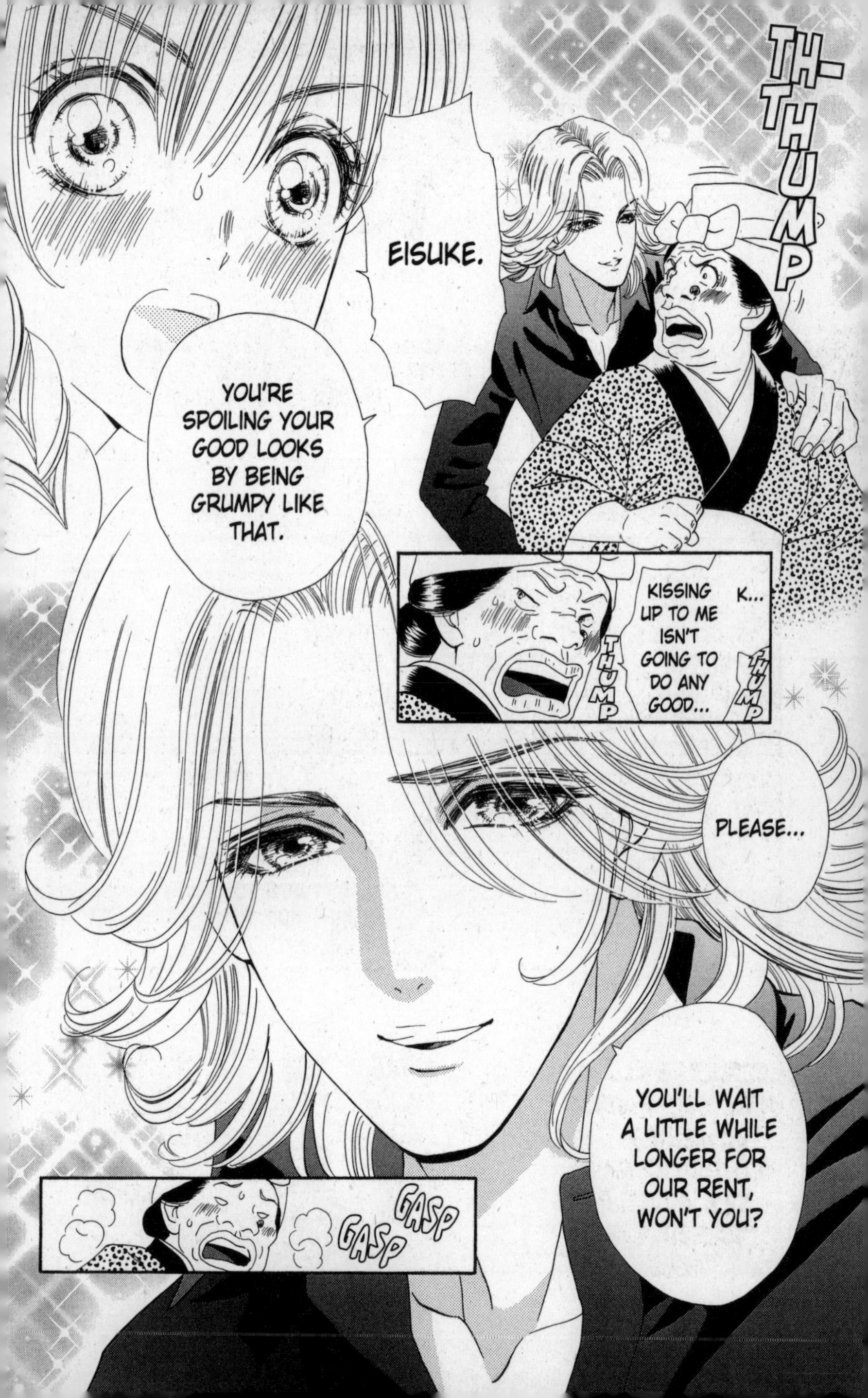
TH-THUMP
EISUKE.
YOU'RE SPOILING YOUR GOOD LOOKS BY BEING GRUMPY LIKE THAT.
K...
KISSING UP TO ME ISN'T GOING TO DO ANY GOOD...
THUMP
THUMP
PLEASE...
YOU'LL WAIT A LITTLE WHILE LONGER FOR OUR RENT, WON'T YOU?
GASP
GASP

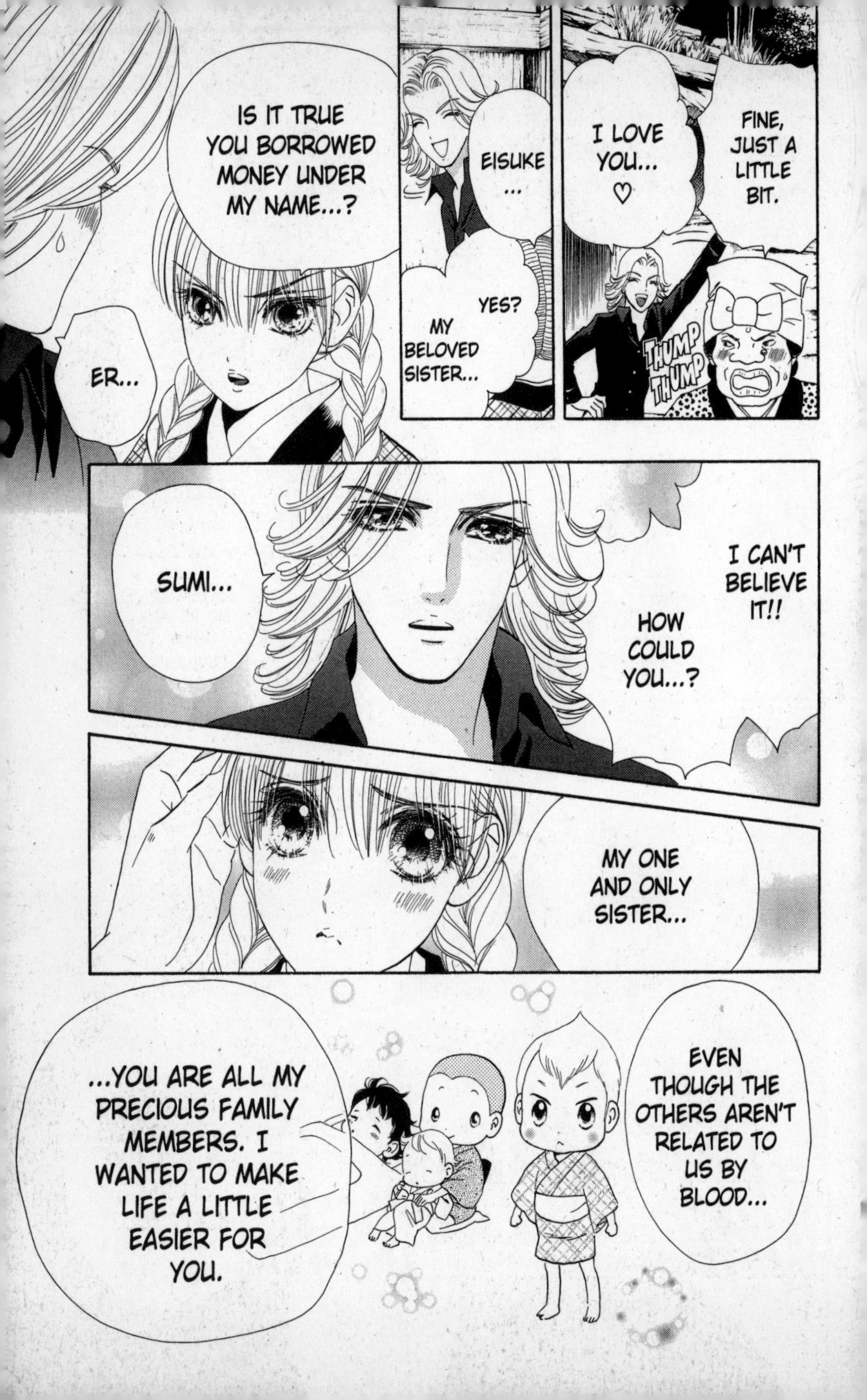
FINE, JUST A LITTLE BIT.
I LOVE YOU... ♡
THUMP THUMP
EISUKE...
YES?
MY BELOVED SISTER...
IS IT TRUE YOU BORROWED MONEY UNDER MY NAME...?
ER...
I CAN'T BELIEVE IT!!
HOW COULD YOU...?
SUMI...
MY ONE AND ONLY SISTER...
EVEN THOUGH THE OTHERS AREN'T RELATED TO US BY BLOOD...
...YOU ARE ALL MY PRECIOUS FAMILY MEMBERS. I WANTED TO MAKE LIFE A LITTLE EASIER FOR YOU.

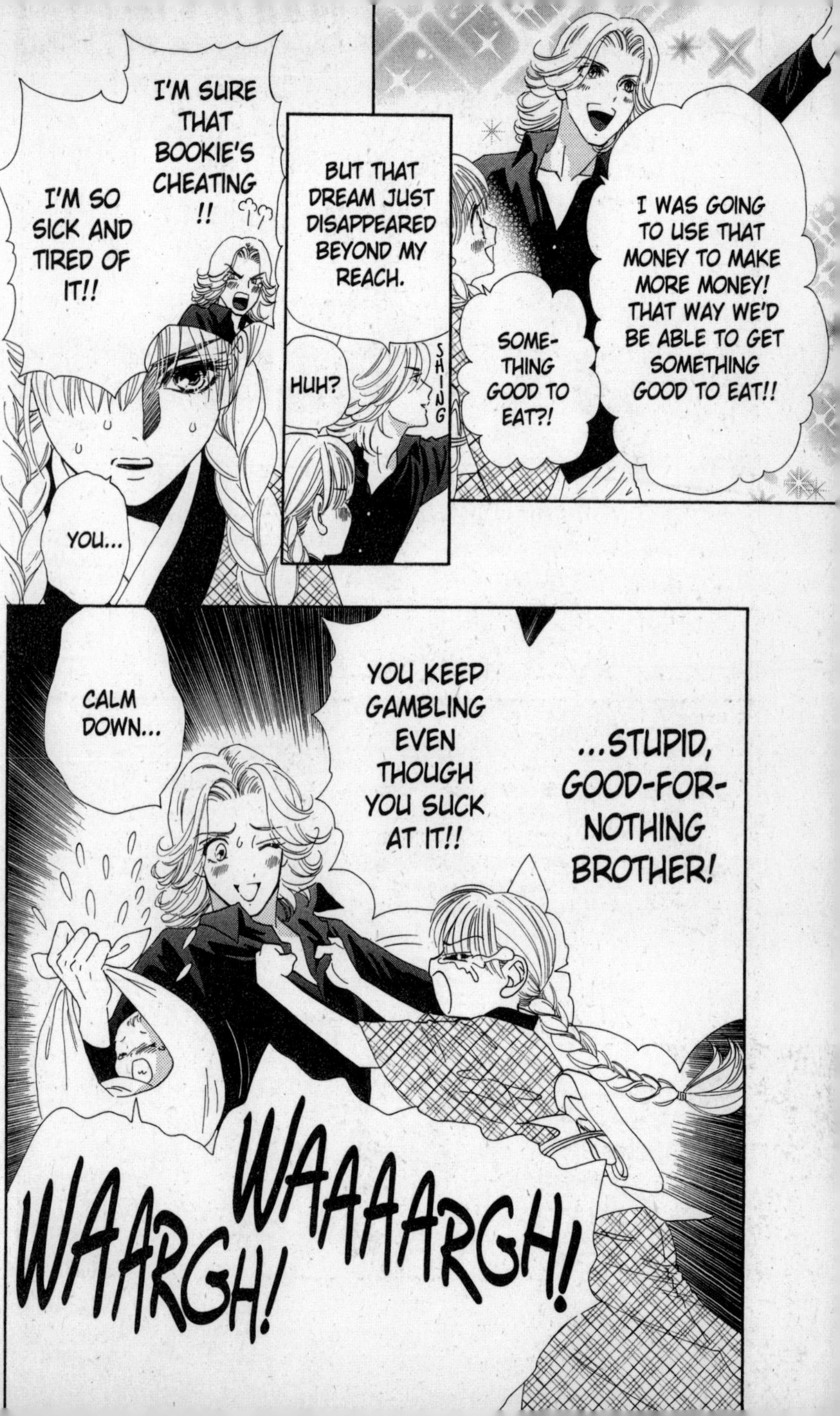
I WAS GOING TO USE THAT MONEY TO MAKE MORE MONEY! THAT WAY WE'D BE ABLE TO GET SOMETHING GOOD TO EAT!!
SOME-THING GOOD TO EAT?!
BUT THAT DREAM JUST DISAPPEARED BEYOND MY REACH.
SHING
HUH?
I'M SURE THAT BOOKIE'S CHEATING!!
I'M SO SICK AND TIRED OF IT!!
YOU...
...STUPID, GOOD-FOR-NOTHING BROTHER!
YOU KEEP GAMBLING EVEN THOUGH YOU SUCK AT IT!!
CALM DOWN...
WAAAARGH!
WAARGH!

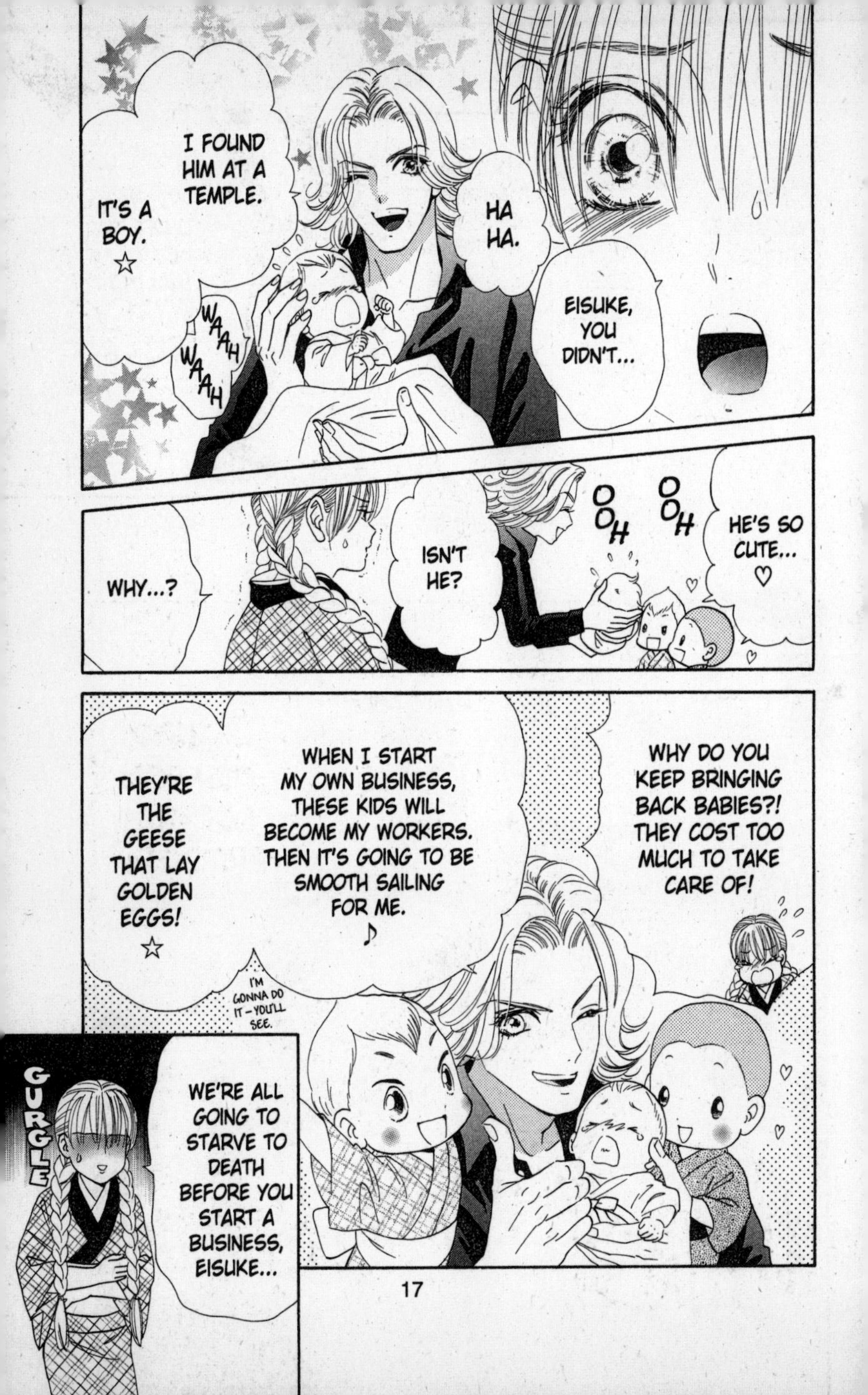
EISUKE, YOU DIDN'T...
HA HA.
I FOUND HIM AT A TEMPLE.
IT'S A BOY. ☆
WAAAH WAAAH
HE'S SO CUTE... ♡
OOH OOH
ISN'T HE?
WHY...?
WHY DO YOU KEEP BRINGING BACK BABIES?! THEY COST TOO MUCH TO TAKE CARE OF!
WHEN I START MY OWN BUSINESS, THESE KIDS WILL BECOME MY WORKERS. THEN IT'S GOING TO BE SMOOTH SAILING FOR ME. ♪
THEY'RE THE GEESE THAT LAY GOLDEN EGGS! ☆
I'M GONNA DO IT—YOU'LL SEE.
GURGLE
WE'RE ALL GOING TO STARVE TO DEATH BEFORE YOU START A BUSINESS, EISUKE...

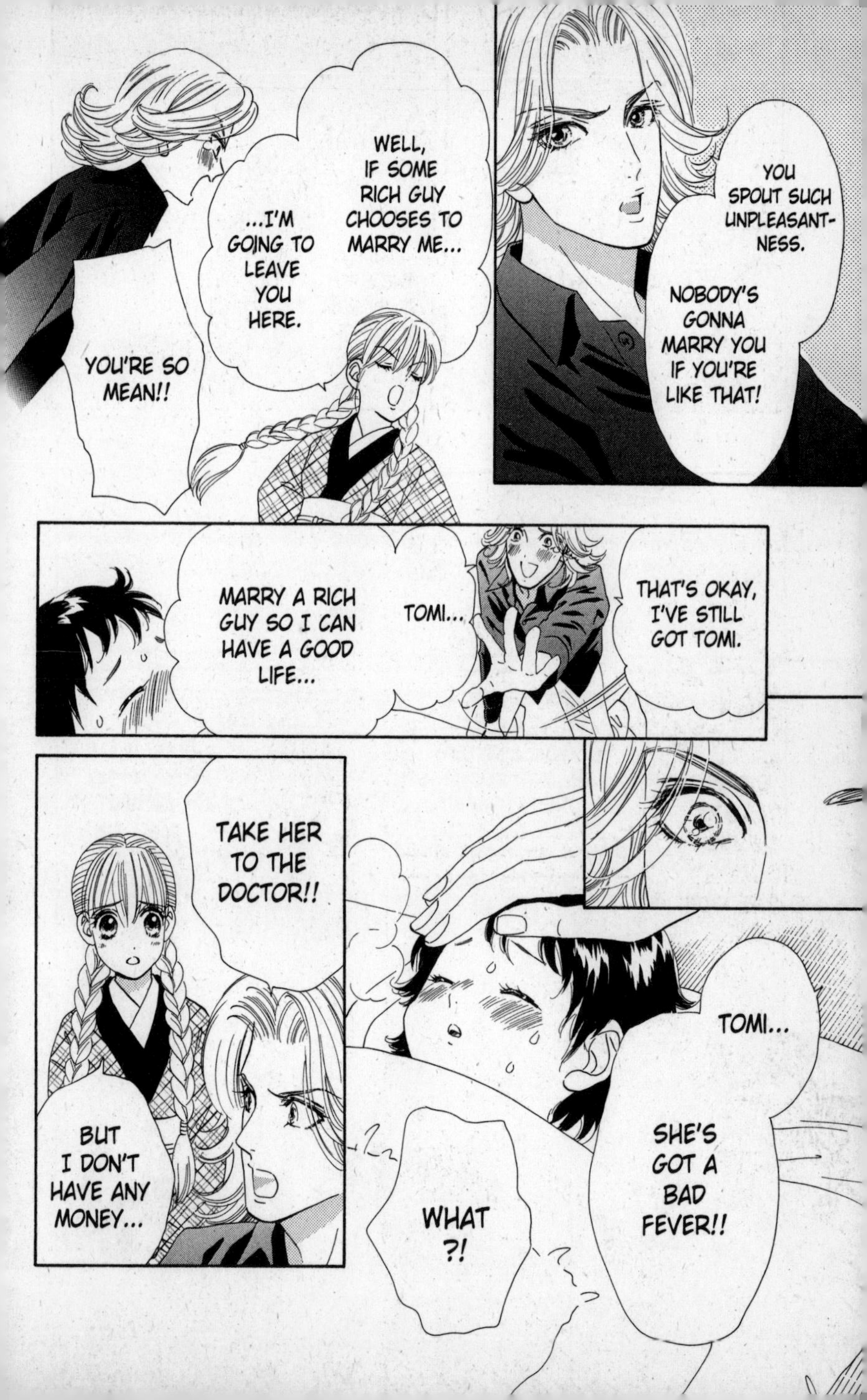
YOU SPOUT SUCH UNPLEASANT-NESS.
NOBODY'S GONNA MARRY YOU IF YOU'RE LIKE THAT!
WELL, IF SOME RICH GUY CHOOSES TO MARRY ME...
...I'M GOING TO LEAVE YOU HERE.
YOU'RE SO MEAN!!
THAT'S OKAY, I'VE STILL GOT TOMI.
TOMI...
MARRY A RICH GUY SO I CAN HAVE A GOOD LIFE...
TOMI...
SHE'S GOT A BAD FEVER!!
WHAT ?!
TAKE HER TO THE DOCTOR!!
BUT I DON'T HAVE ANY MONEY...

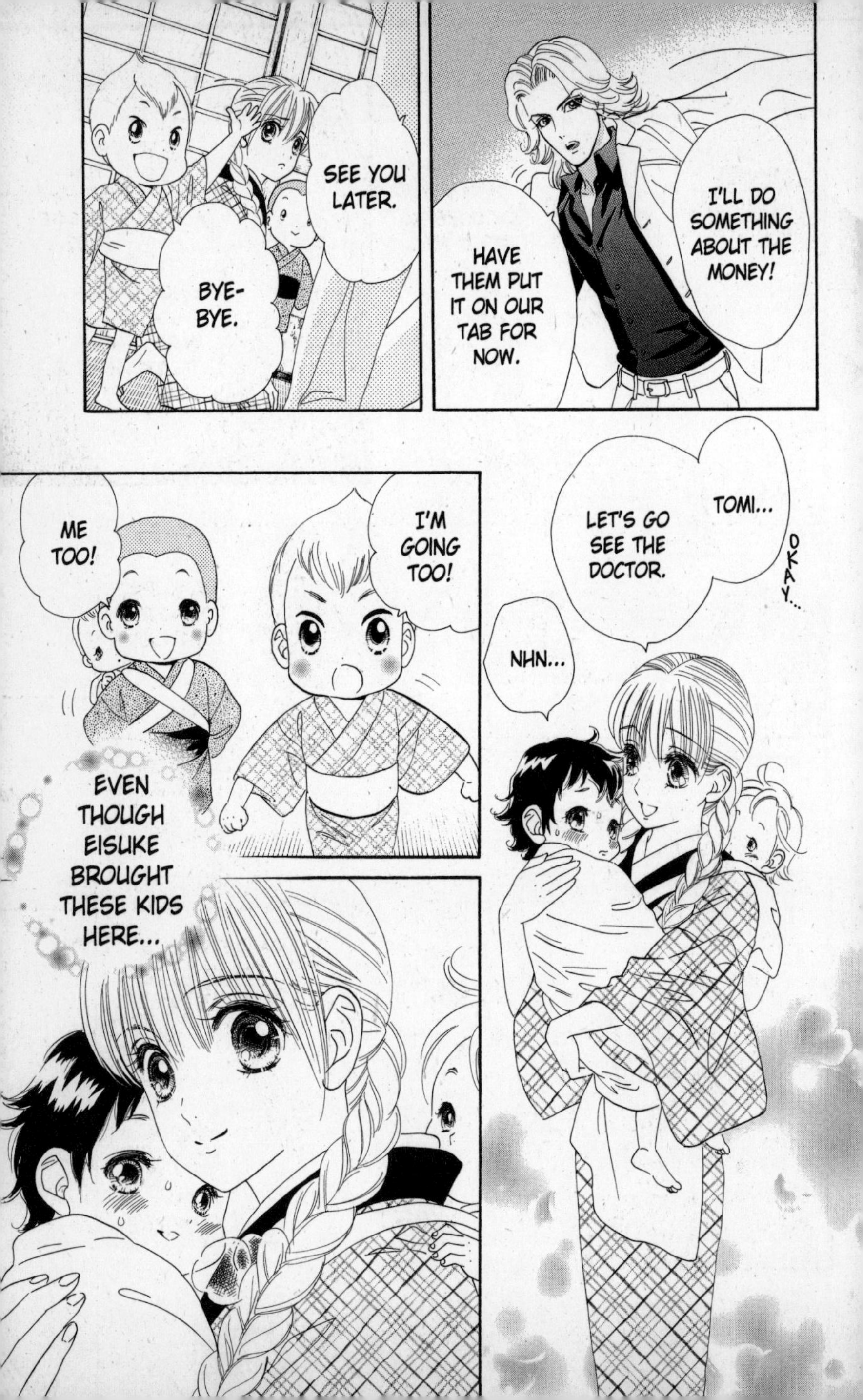
I'LL DO SOMETHING ABOUT THE MONEY!
HAVE THEM PUT IT ON OUR TAB FOR NOW.
SEE YOU LATER.
BYE-BYE.
TOMI...
LET'S GO SEE THE DOCTOR.
OKAY...
NHN...
I'M GOING TOO!
ME TOO!
EVEN THOUGH EISUKE BROUGHT THESE KIDS HERE...

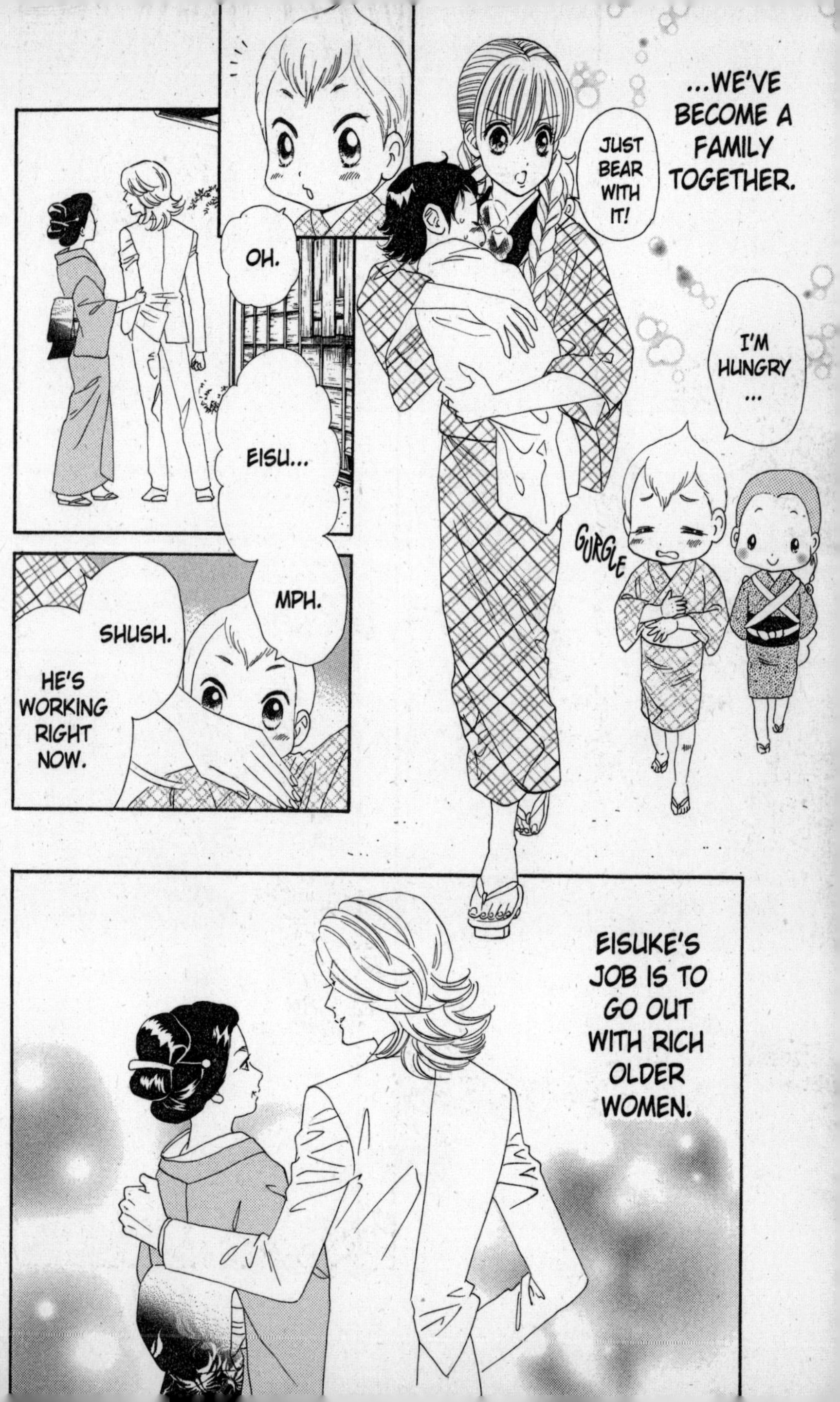
...WE'VE BECOME A FAMILY TOGETHER.
JUST BEAR WITH IT!
I'M HUNGRY...
GURGLE
OH.
EISU...
MPH.
SHUSH.
HE'S WORKING RIGHT NOW.
EISUKE'S JOB IS TO GO OUT WITH RICH OLDER WOMEN.

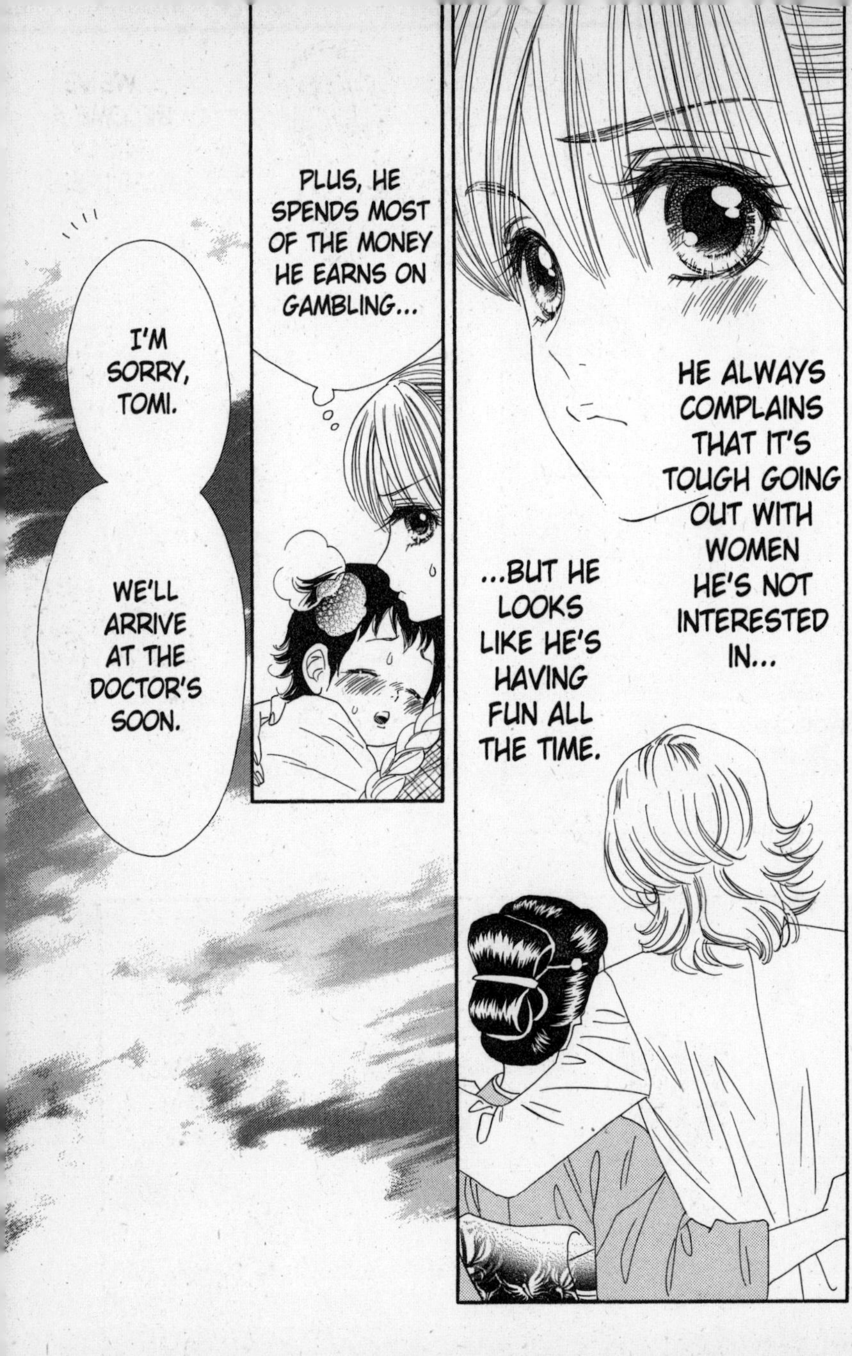
HE ALWAYS COMPLAINS THAT IT'S TOUGH GOING OUT WITH WOMEN HE'S NOT INTERESTED IN...
...BUT HE LOOKS LIKE HE'S HAVING FUN ALL THE TIME.
PLUS, HE SPENDS MOST OF THE MONEY HE EARNS ON GAMBLING...
I'M SORRY, TOMI.
WE'LL ARRIVE AT THE DOCTOR'S SOON.

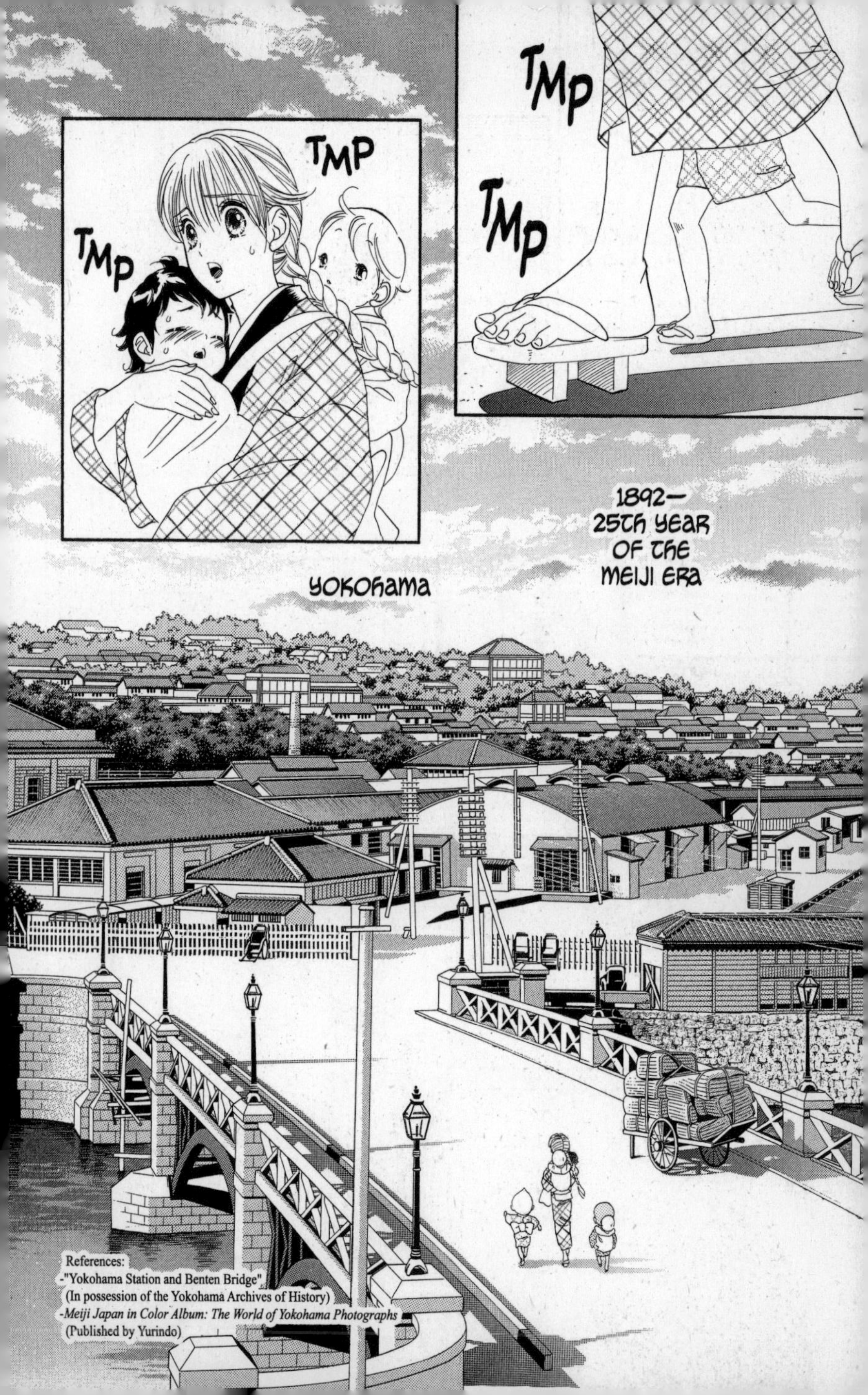
TMP
TMP
TMP
TMP
1892—
25TH YEAR
OF THE
MEIJI ERA
YOKOHAMA

References:
-"Yokohama Station and Benten Bridge"
(In possession of the Yokohama Archives of History)
-*Meiji Japan in Color Album: The World of Yokohama Photographs*
(Published by Yurindo)

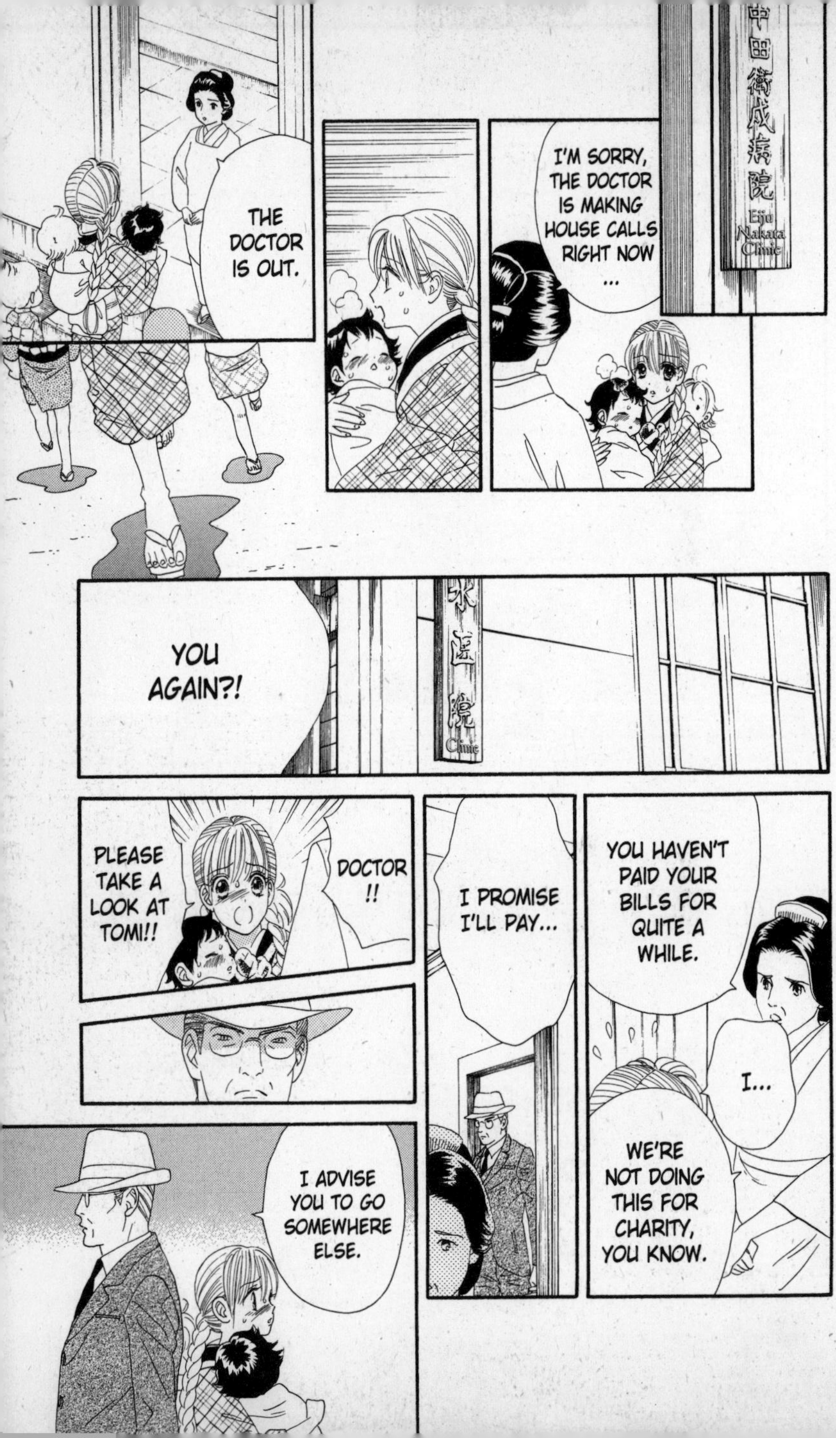
Eiju Nakata Clinic
I'M SORRY, THE DOCTOR IS MAKING HOUSE CALLS RIGHT NOW ...
THE DOCTOR IS OUT.
YOU AGAIN?!
Clinic
YOU HAVEN'T PAID YOUR BILLS FOR QUITE A WHILE.
I...
WE'RE NOT DOING THIS FOR CHARITY, YOU KNOW.
I PROMISE I'LL PAY...
DOCTOR !!
PLEASE TAKE A LOOK AT TOMI!!
I ADVISE YOU TO GO SOMEWHERE ELSE.

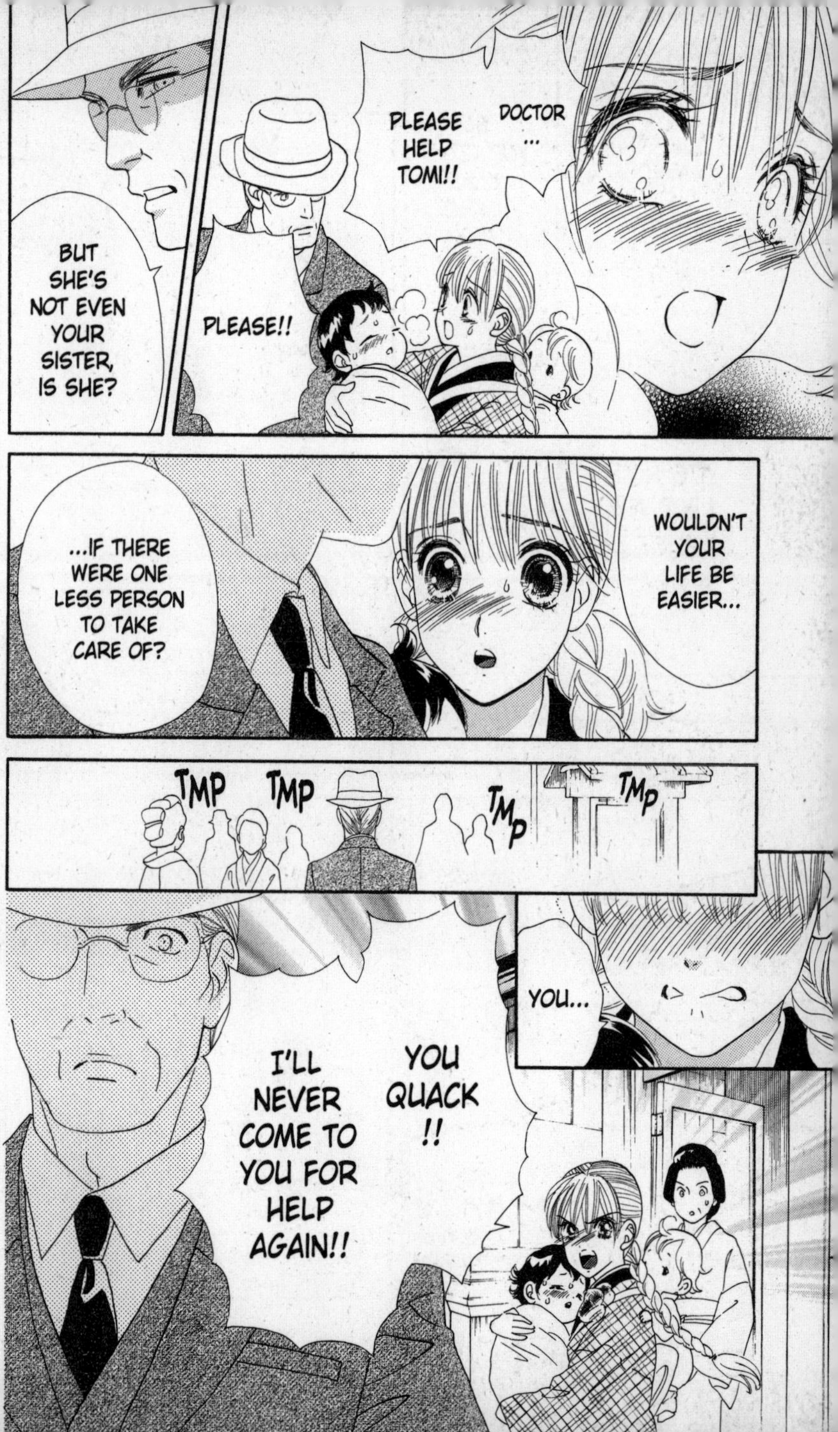
DOCTOR ...
PLEASE HELP TOMI!!
PLEASE!!
BUT SHE'S NOT EVEN YOUR SISTER, IS SHE?
WOULDN'T YOUR LIFE BE EASIER...
...IF THERE WERE ONE LESS PERSON TO TAKE CARE OF?
TMP
TMP
TMP
TMP
YOU...
YOU QUACK!!
I'LL NEVER COME TO YOU FOR HELP AGAIN!!

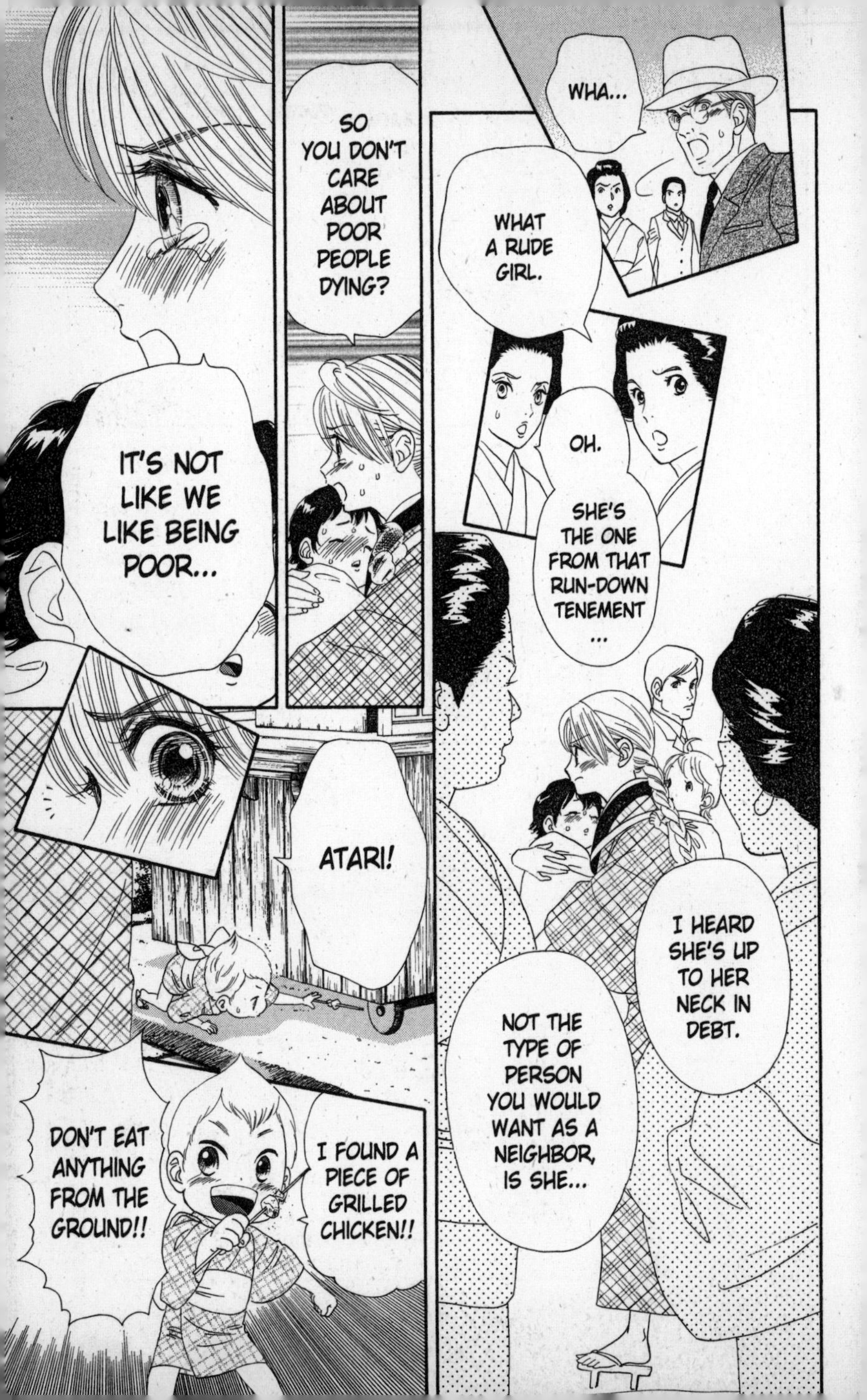
WHA...
WHAT A RUDE GIRL.
OH.
SHE'S THE ONE FROM THAT RUN-DOWN TENEMENT...
I HEARD SHE'S UP TO HER NECK IN DEBT.
NOT THE TYPE OF PERSON YOU WOULD WANT AS A NEIGHBOR, IS SHE...
SO YOU DON'T CARE ABOUT POOR PEOPLE DYING?
IT'S NOT LIKE WE LIKE BEING POOR...
ATARI!
I FOUND A PIECE OF GRILLED CHICKEN!!
DON'T EAT ANYTHING FROM THE GROUND!!

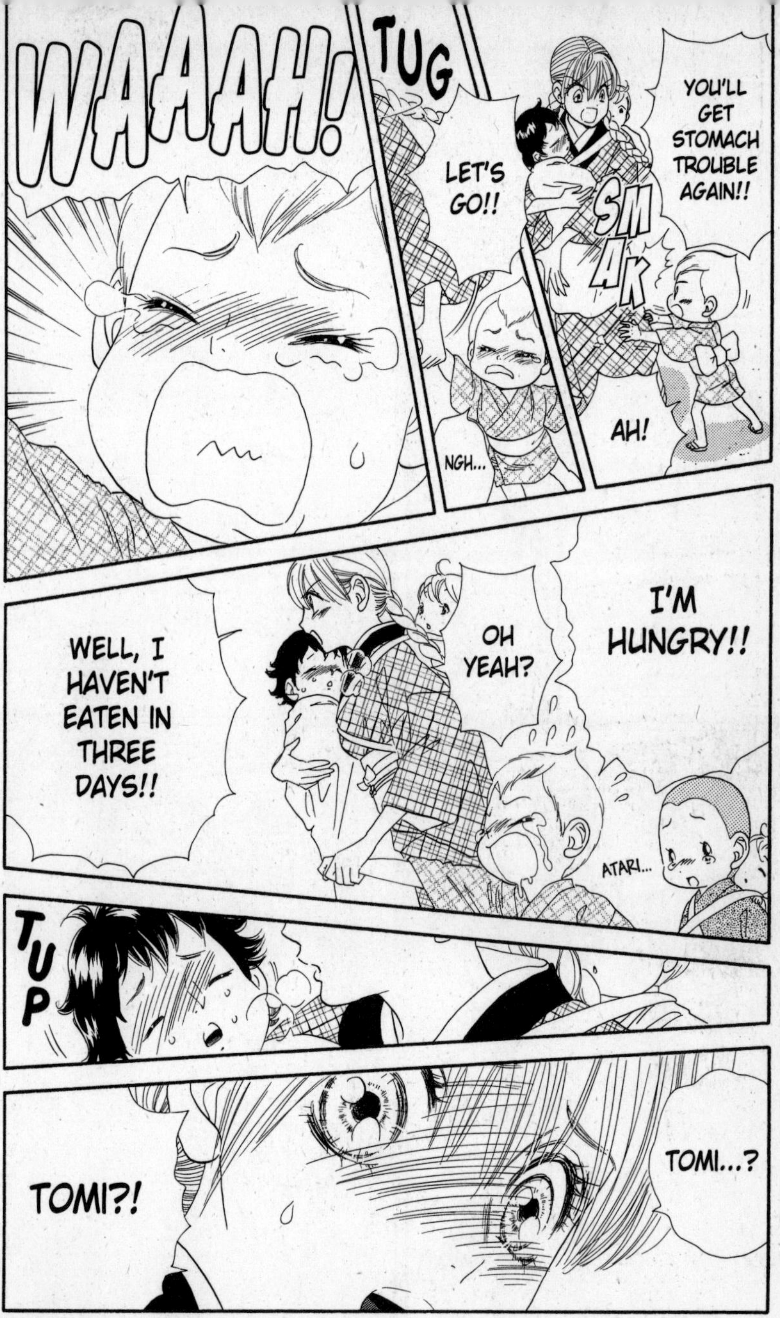
YOU'LL GET STOMACH TROUBLE AGAIN!!
SMAK
AH!
TUG
LET'S GO!!
NGH...
WAAAH!
I'M HUNGRY!!
OH YEAH?
WELL, I HAVEN'T EATEN IN THREE DAYS!!
ATARI...
TUP
TOMI...?
TOMI?!

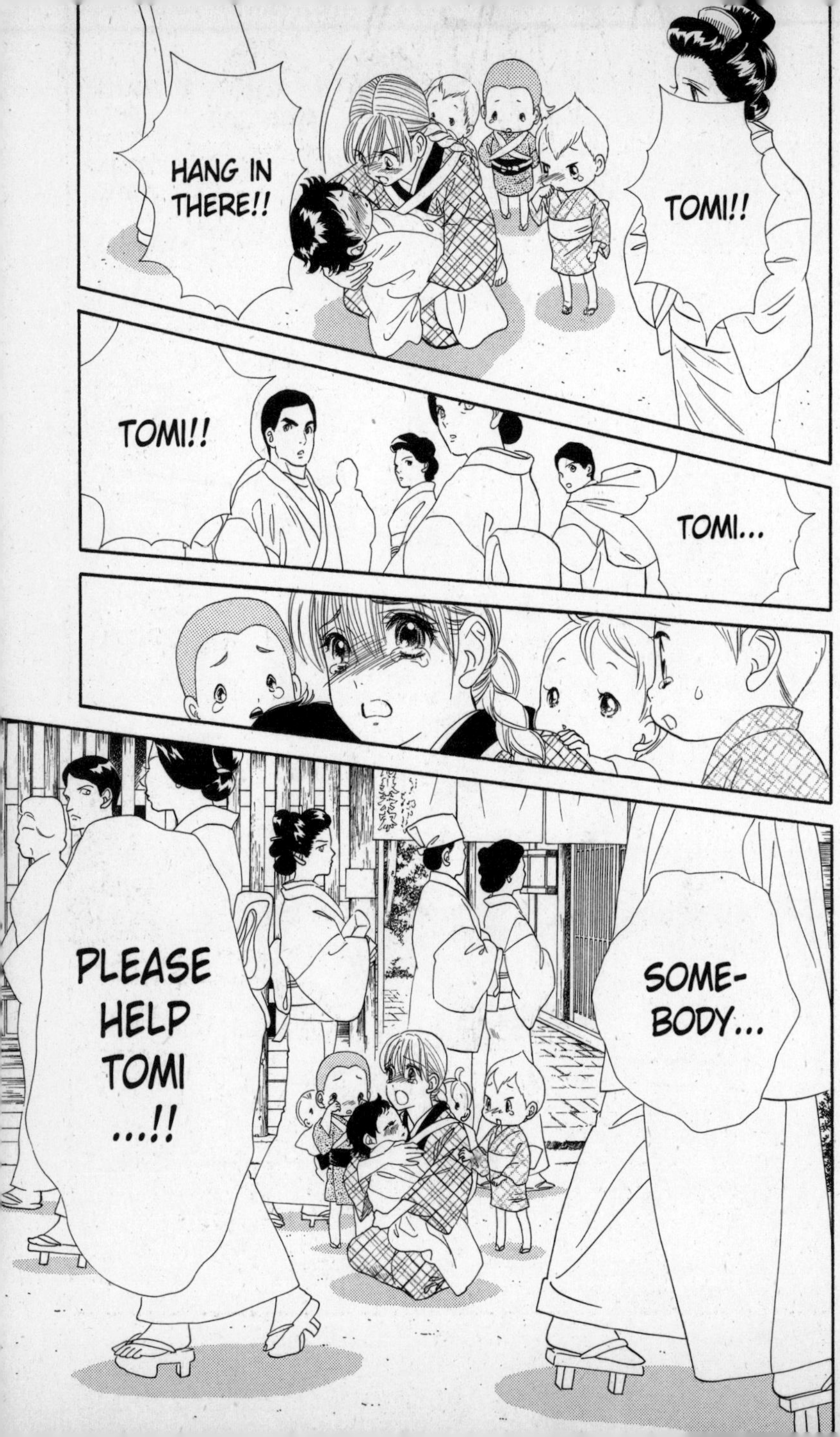
TOMI!!
HANG IN THERE!!
TOMI...
TOMI!!
SOME-BODY...
PLEASE HELP TOMI ...!!

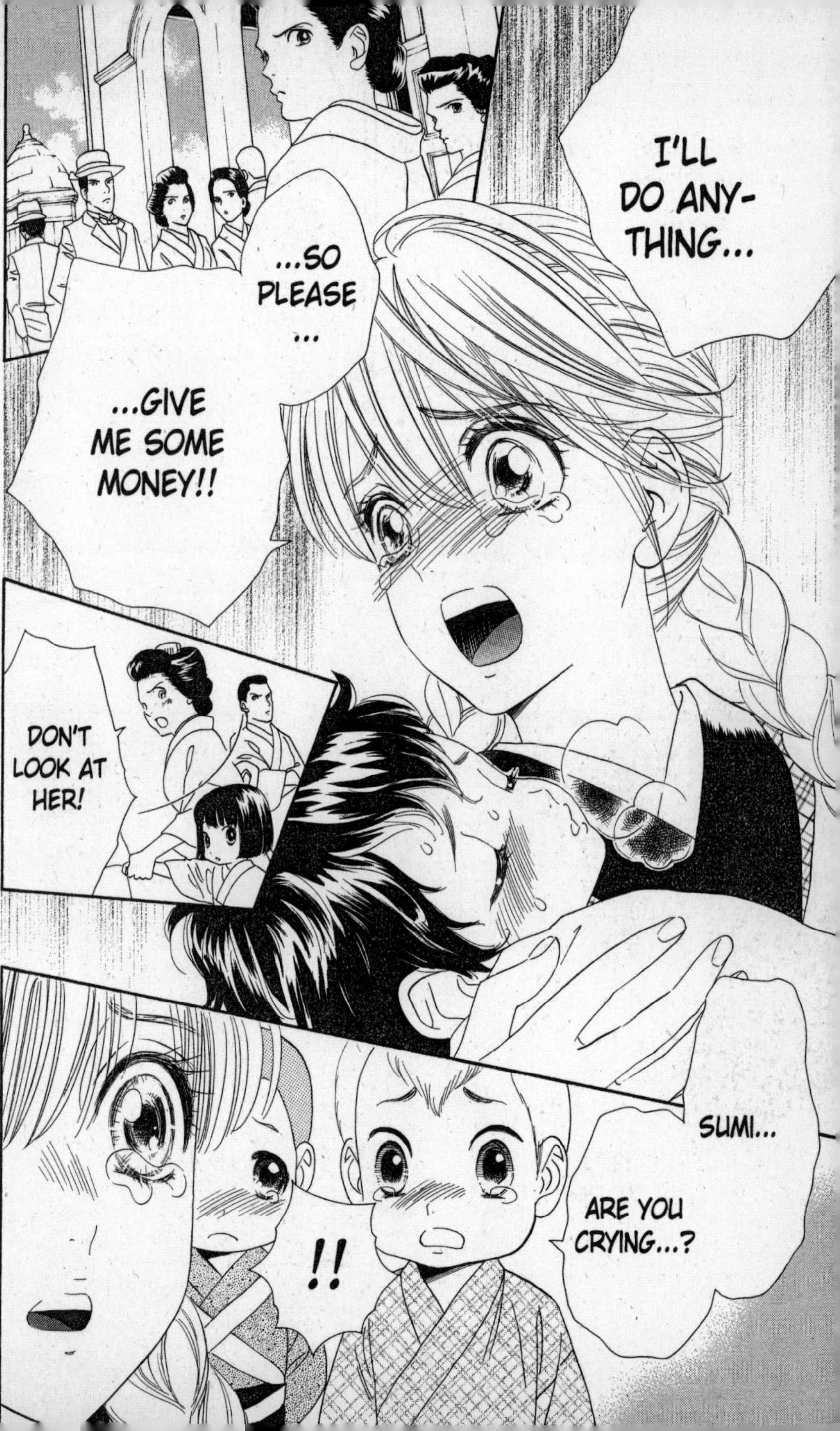
I'LL DO ANY-THING...
...SO PLEASE ...
...GIVE ME SOME MONEY!!
DON'T LOOK AT HER!
SUMI...
ARE YOU CRYING...?
!!

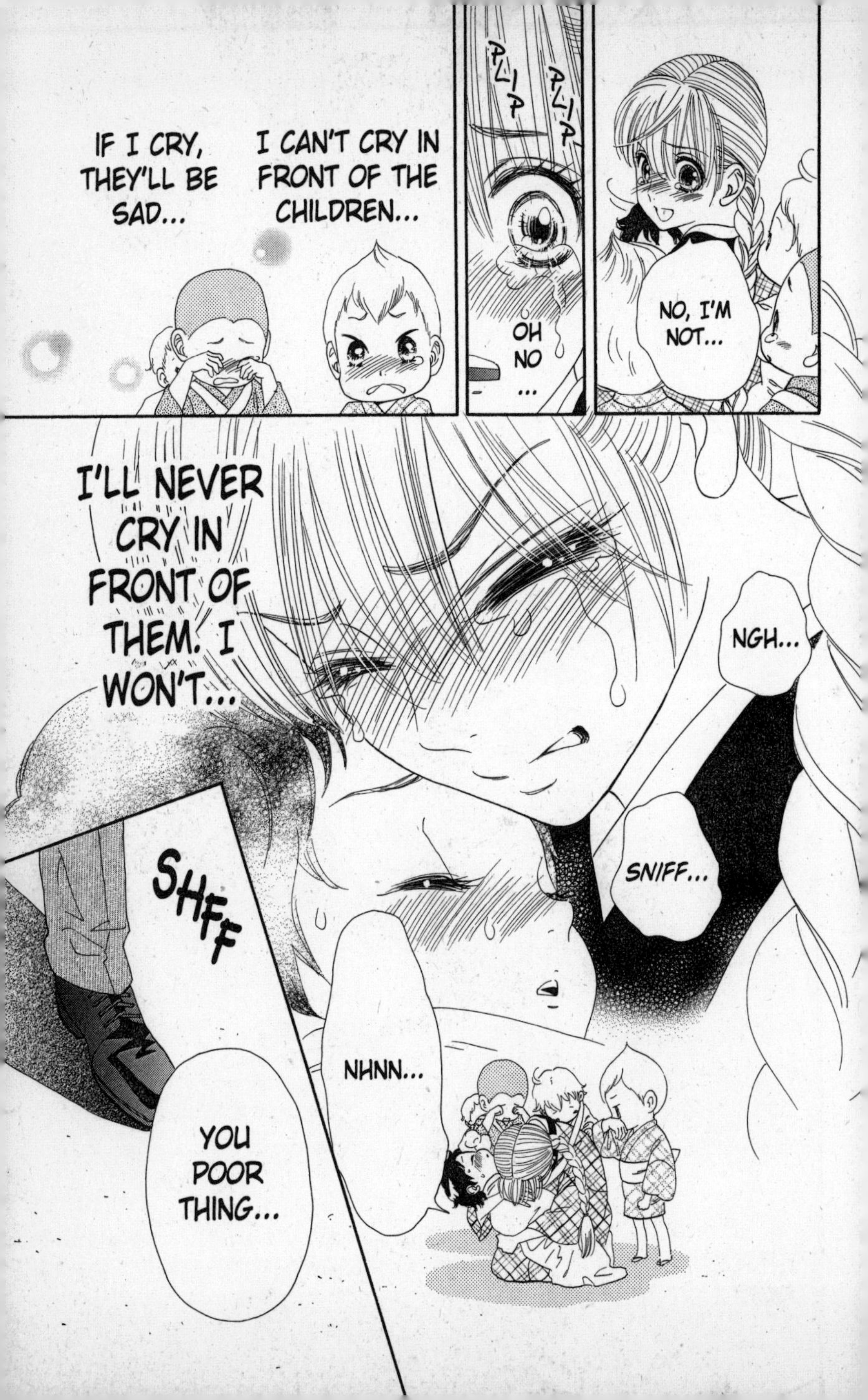
NO, I'M NOT...
PLIP
PLIP
OH NO ...
I CAN'T CRY IN FRONT OF THE CHILDREN...
IF I CRY, THEY'LL BE SAD...
NGH...
I'LL NEVER CRY IN FRONT OF THEM. I WON'T...
SNIFF...
NHNN...
SHFF
YOU POOR THING...

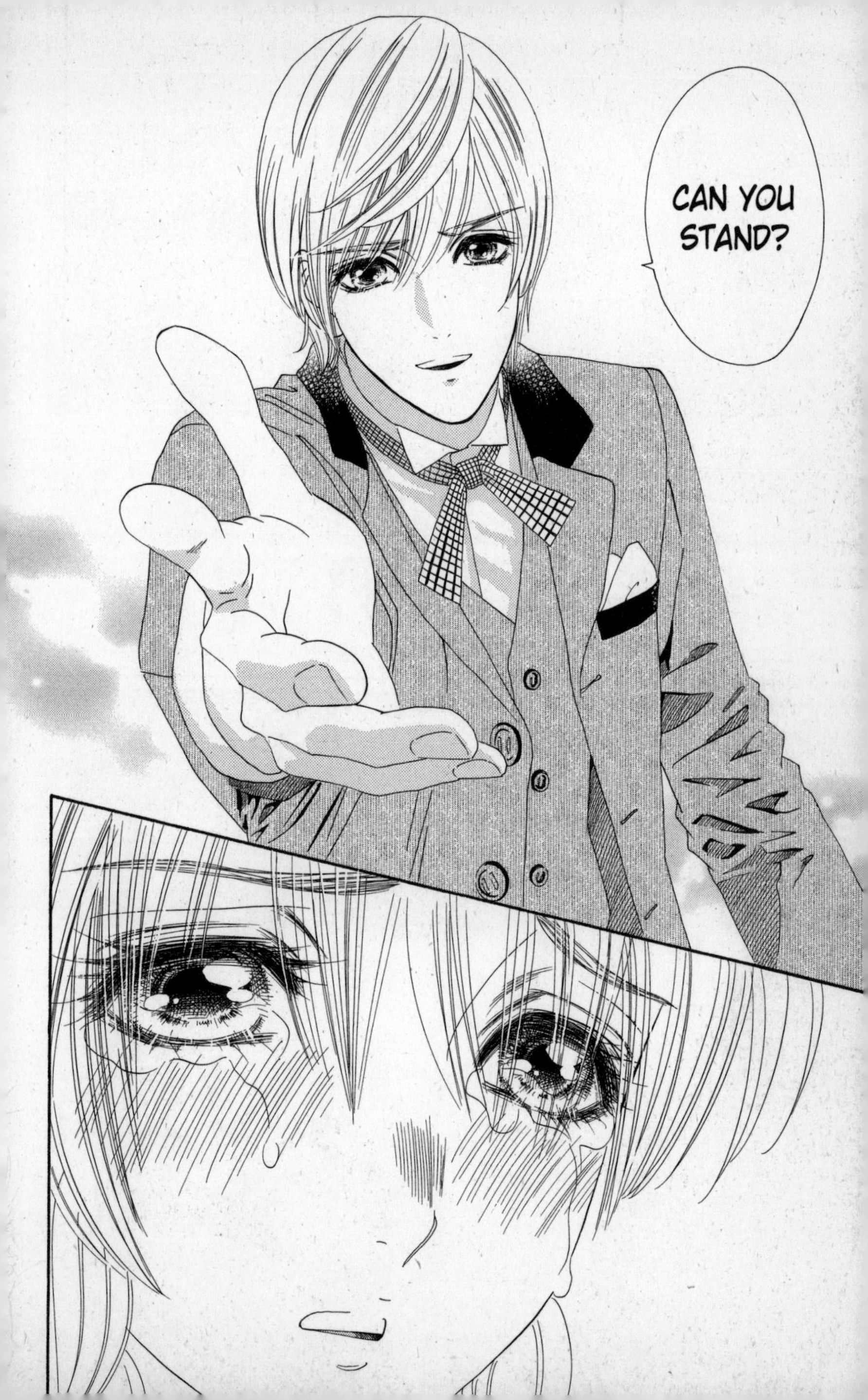
CAN YOU STAND?

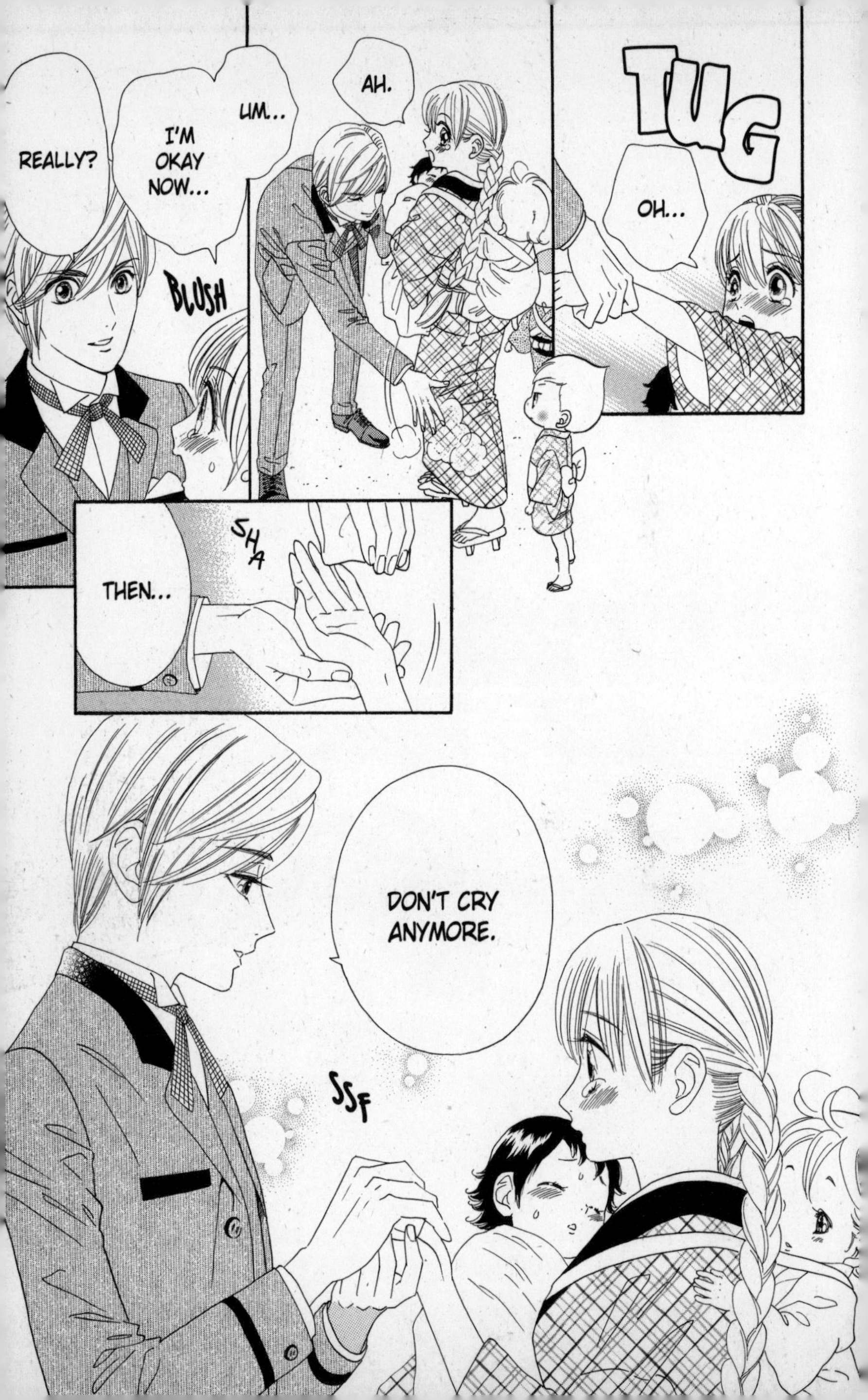
TUG
OH...
AH.
UM...
I'M OKAY NOW...
BLUSH
REALLY?
SHA
THEN...
DON'T CRY ANYMORE.
SSF

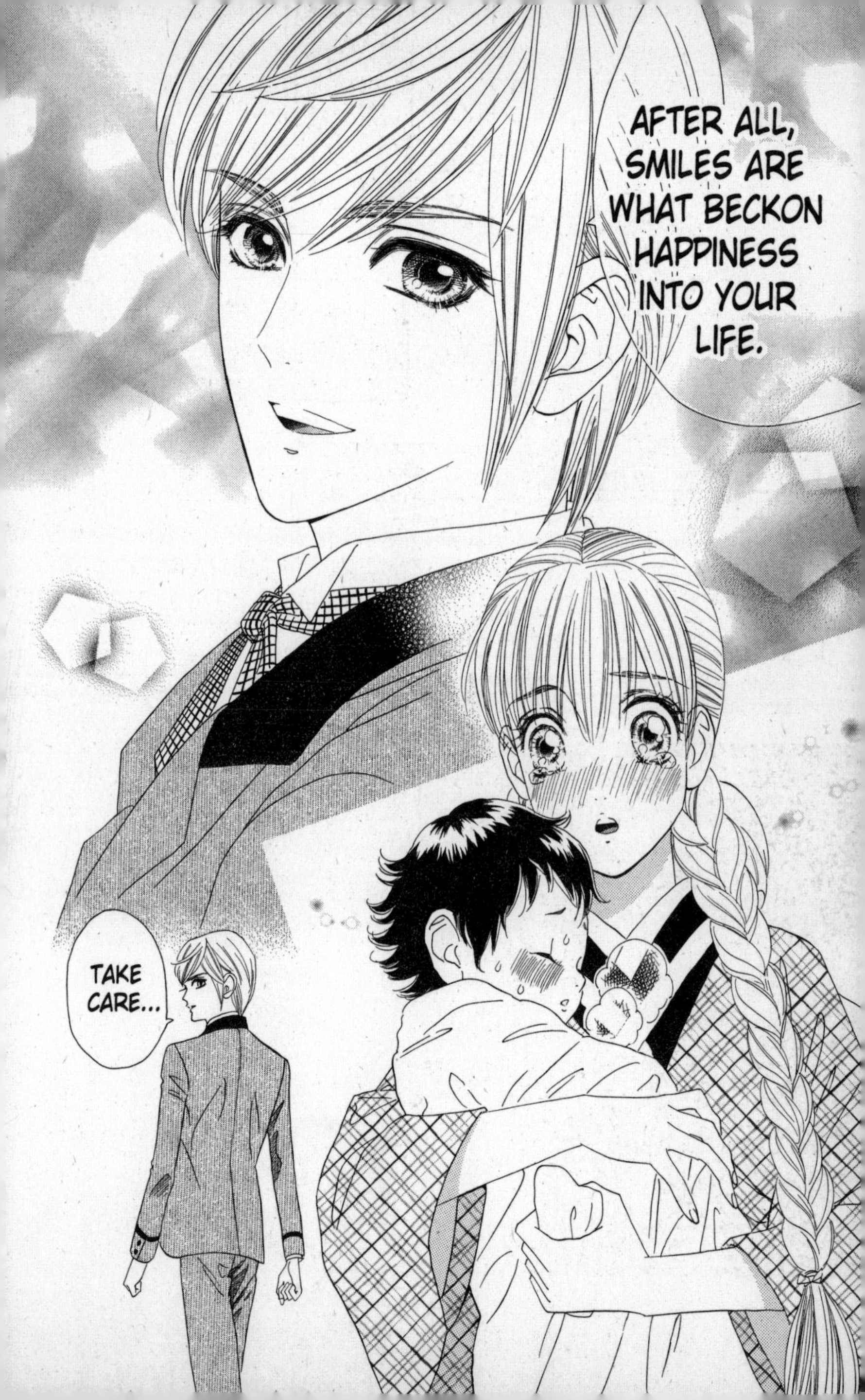
AFTER ALL, SMILES ARE WHAT BECKON HAPPINESS INTO YOUR LIFE.
TAKE CARE...

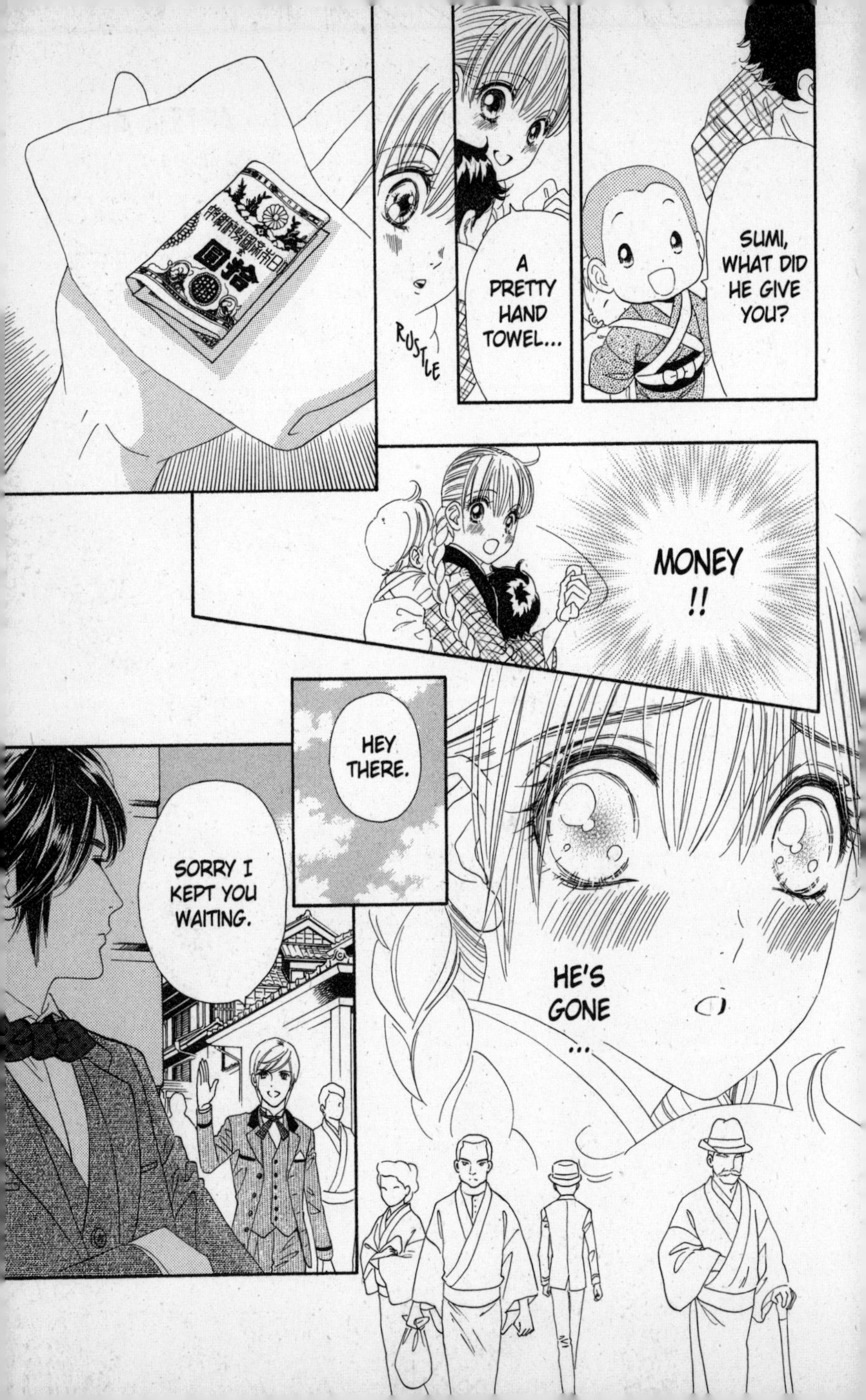
SUMI, WHAT DID HE GIVE YOU?
A PRETTY HAND TOWEL...
RUSTLE
MONEY !!
HE'S GONE ...
HEY THERE.
SORRY I KEPT YOU WAITING.

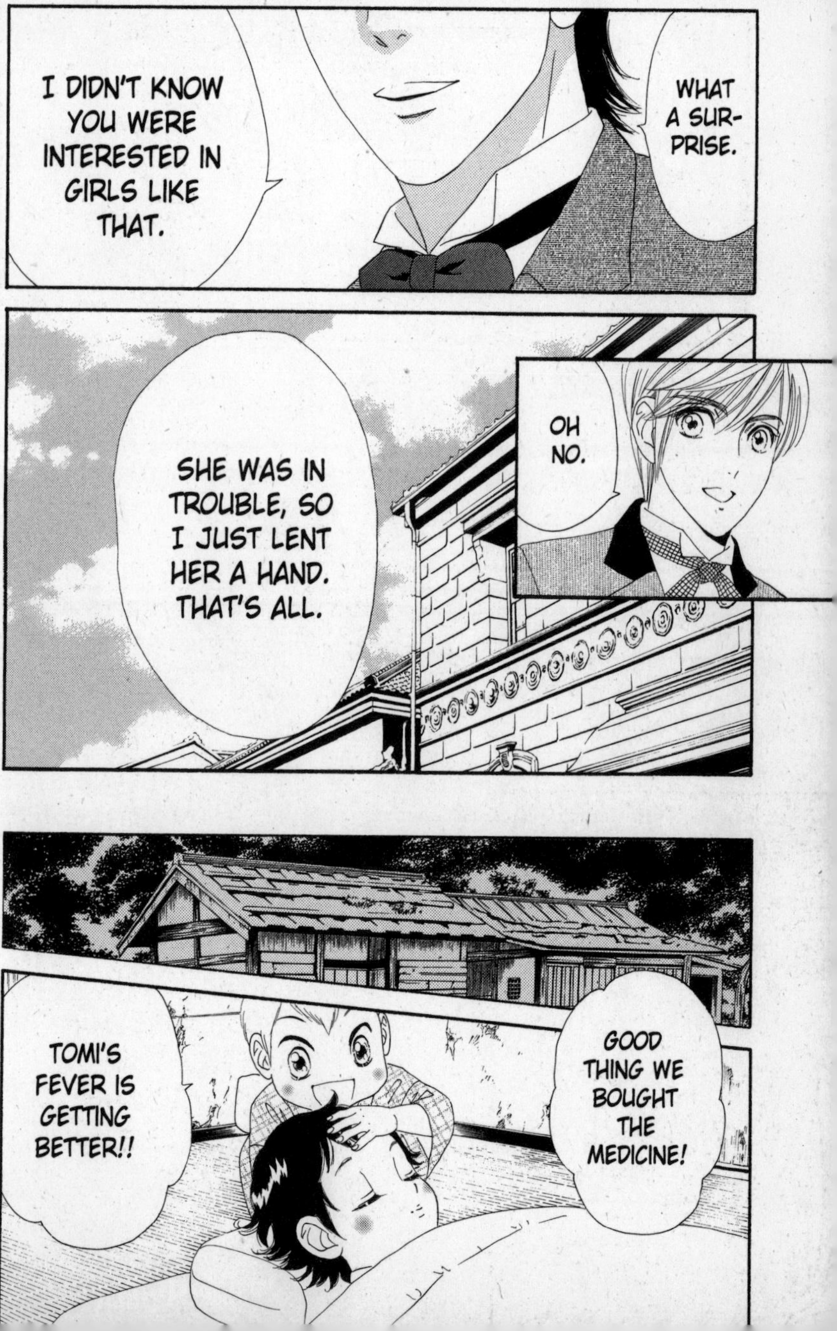
WHAT A SURPRISE.
I DIDN'T KNOW YOU WERE INTERESTED IN GIRLS LIKE THAT.
OH NO.
SHE WAS IN TROUBLE, SO I JUST LENT HER A HAND. THAT'S ALL.
GOOD THING WE BOUGHT THE MEDICINE!
TOMI'S FEVER IS GETTING BETTER!!

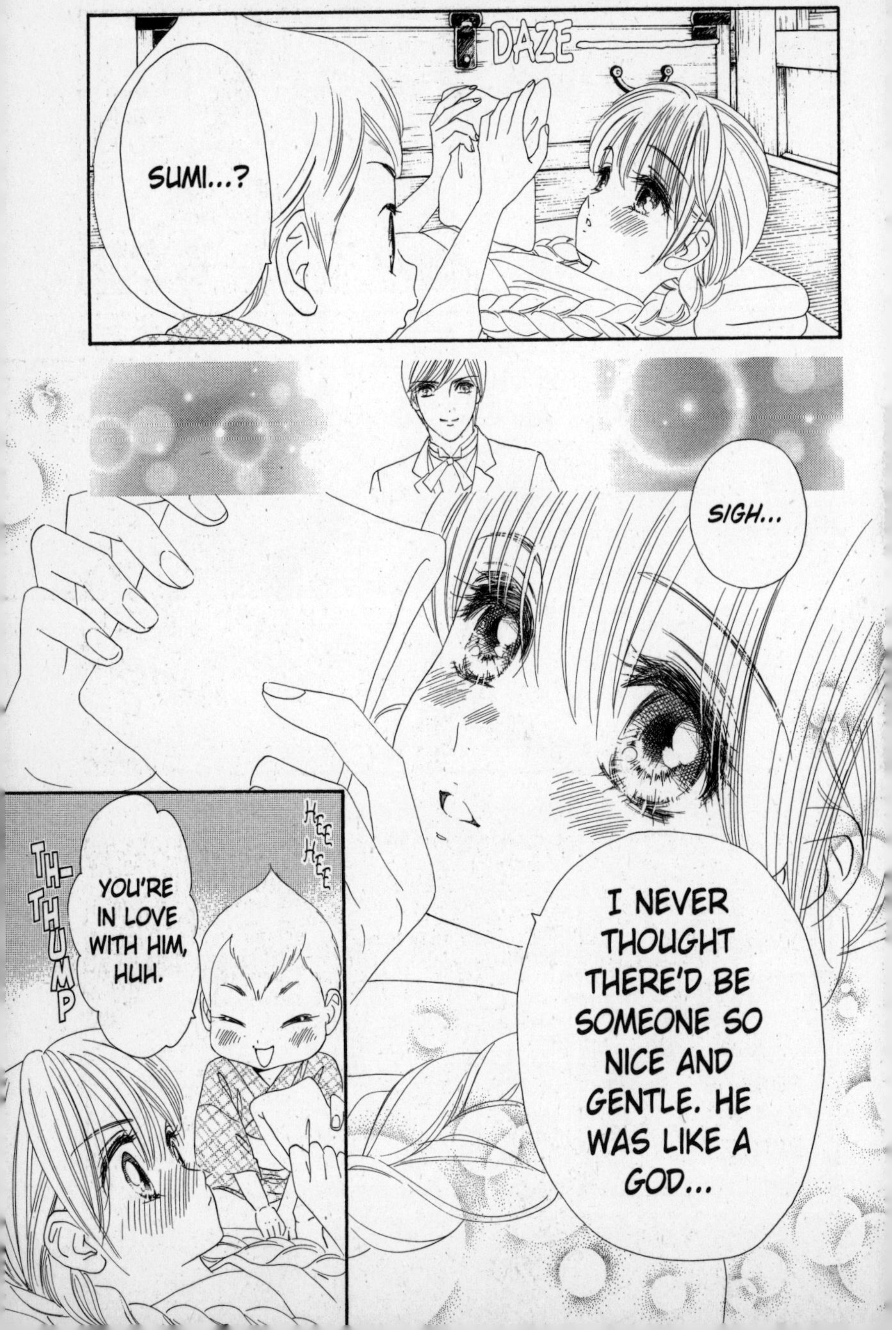
DAZE
SUMI...?
SIGH...
I NEVER THOUGHT THERE'D BE SOMEONE SO NICE AND GENTLE. HE WAS LIKE A GOD...
HEE HEE
TH-THUMP
YOU'RE IN LOVE WITH HIM, HUH.

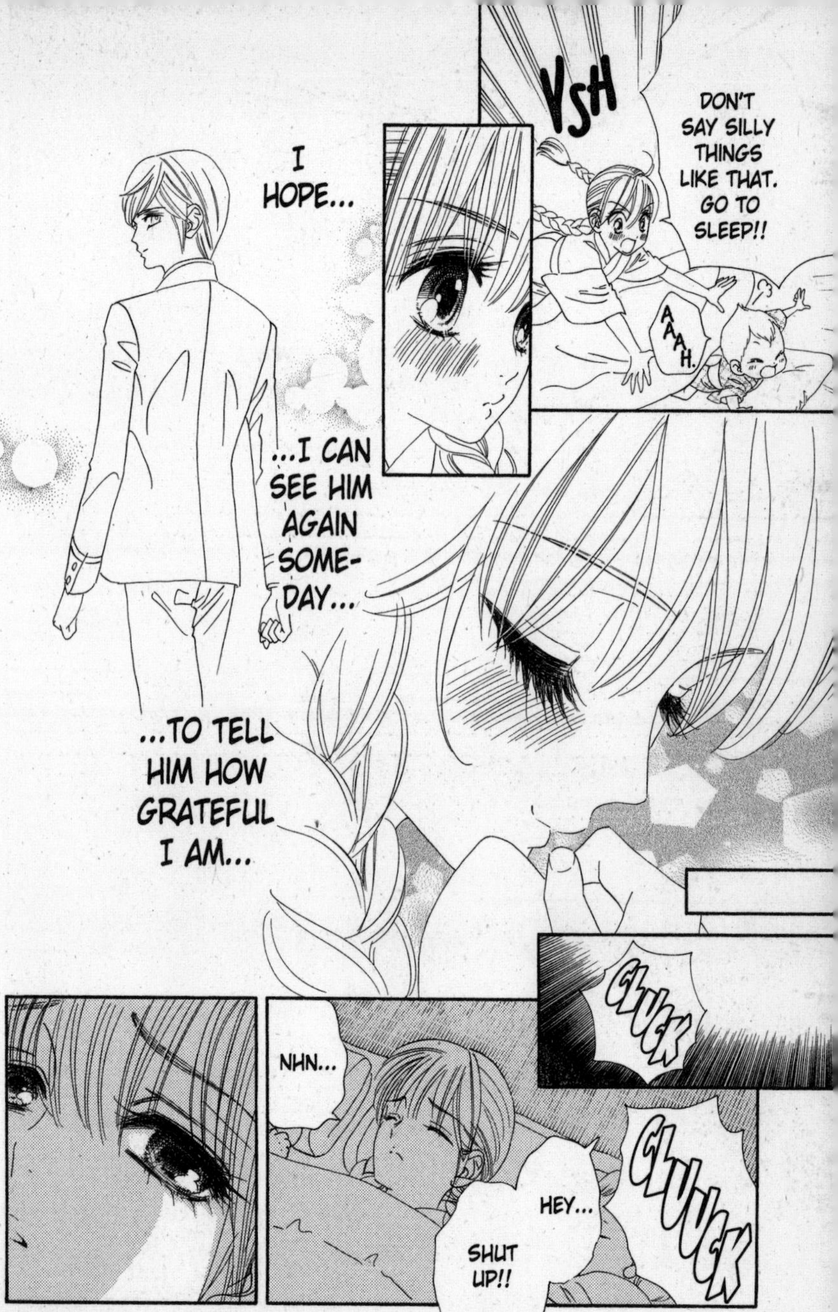
YSH
DON'T SAY SILLY THINGS LIKE THAT. GO TO SLEEP!!
AAAH.
I HOPE...
...I CAN SEE HIM AGAIN SOME-DAY...
...TO TELL HIM HOW GRATEFUL I AM...
CLUCK
CLUUCK
NHN...
HEY...
SHUT UP!!

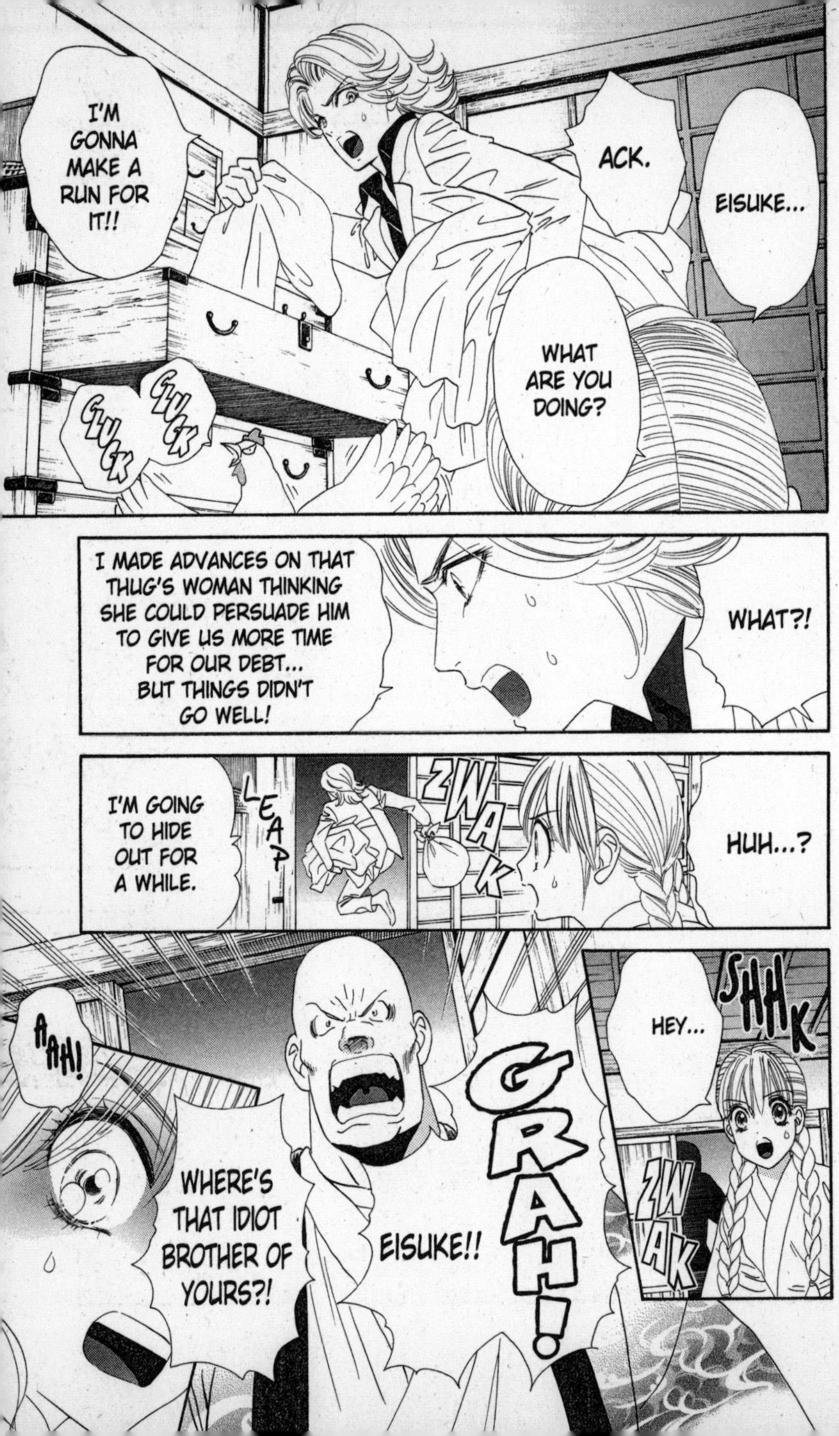
EISUKE...
ACK.
WHAT ARE YOU DOING?
I'M GONNA MAKE A RUN FOR IT!!
CLUCK
CLUCK
WHAT?!
I MADE ADVANCES ON THAT THUG'S WOMAN THINKING SHE COULD PERSUADE HIM TO GIVE US MORE TIME FOR OUR DEBT... BUT THINGS DIDN'T GO WELL!
HUH...?
ZWAK
LEAP
I'M GOING TO HIDE OUT FOR A WHILE.
SHHK
HEY...
ZWAK
GRAH!
EISUKE!!
WHERE'S THAT IDIOT BROTHER OF YOURS?!
AAH!

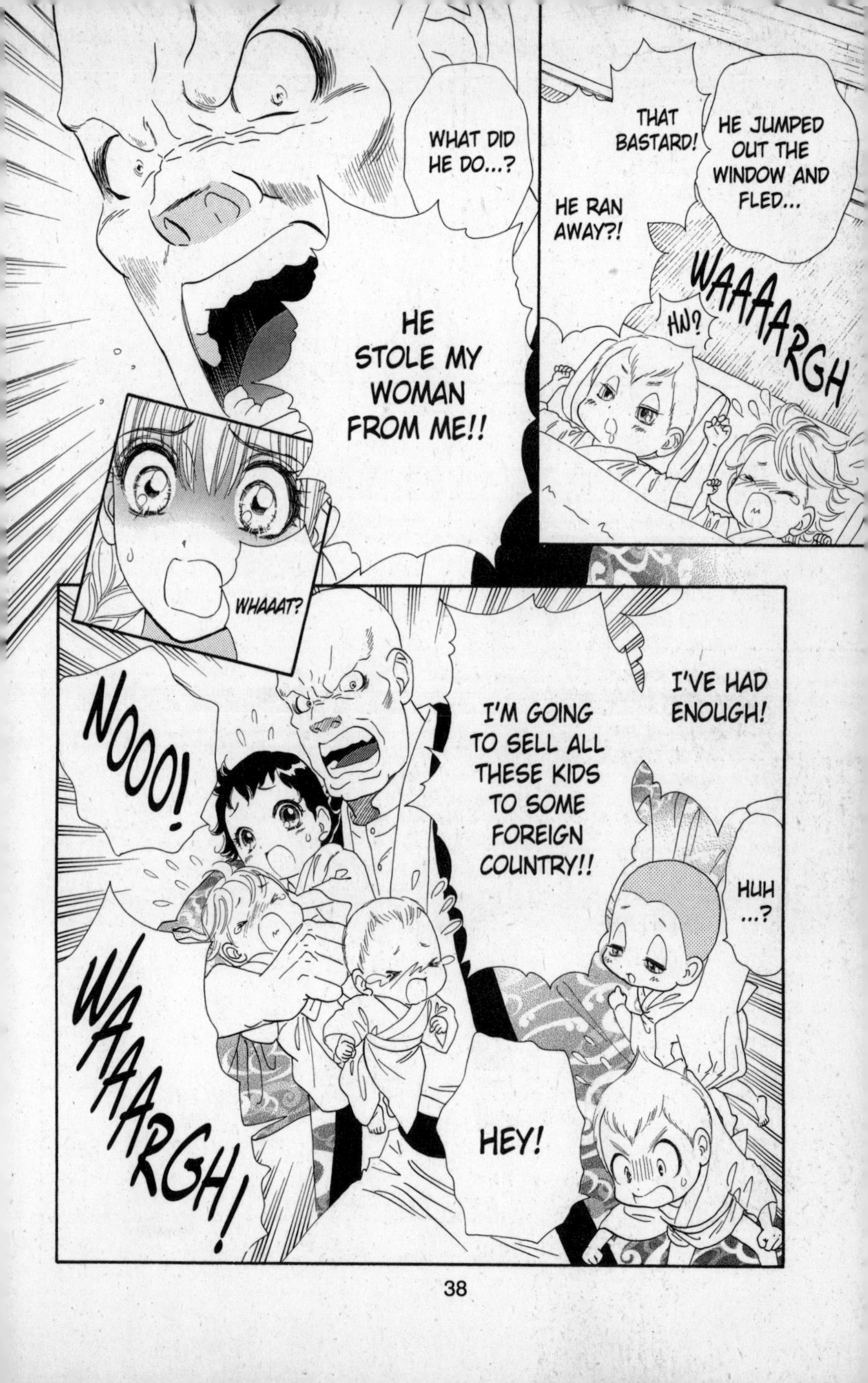
HE JUMPED OUT THE WINDOW AND FLED...
THAT BASTARD!
HE RAN AWAY?!
WAAAARGH
HN?
WHAT DID HE DO...?
HE STOLE MY WOMAN FROM ME!!
WHAAAT?
I'VE HAD ENOUGH!
I'M GOING TO SELL ALL THESE KIDS TO SOME FOREIGN COUNTRY!!
HUH ...?
NOOO!
HEY!
WAAAARGH!

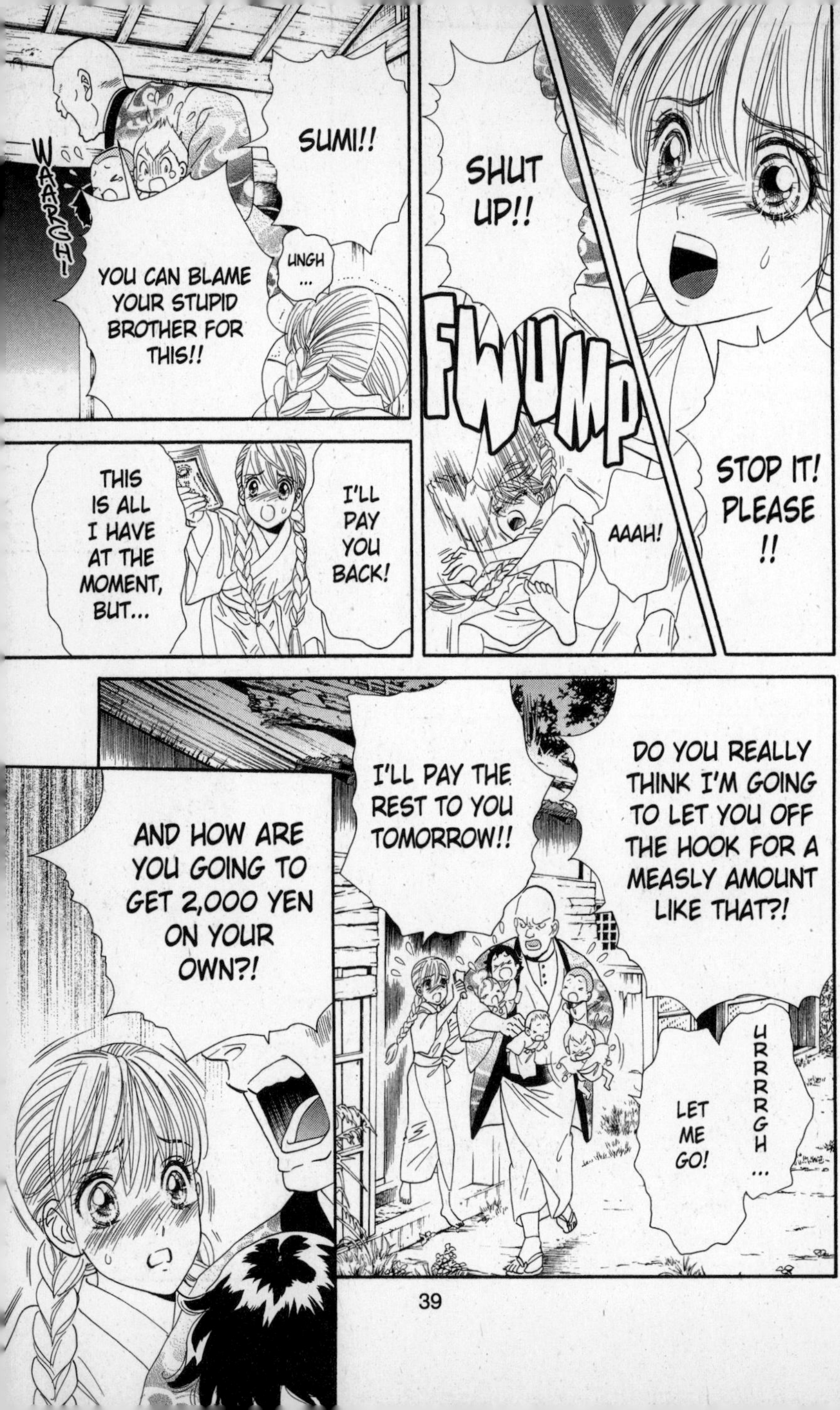
STOP IT! PLEASE!!
SHUT UP!!
FWUMP
AAAH!
SUMI!!
UNGH...
YOU CAN BLAME YOUR STUPID BROTHER FOR THIS!!
WAAARGH!
I'LL PAY YOU BACK!
THIS IS ALL I HAVE AT THE MOMENT, BUT...
DO YOU REALLY THINK I'M GOING TO LET YOU OFF THE HOOK FOR A MEASLY AMOUNT LIKE THAT?!
I'LL PAY THE REST TO YOU TOMORROW!!
URRRRGH...
LET ME GO!
AND HOW ARE YOU GOING TO GET 2,000 YEN ON YOUR OWN?!

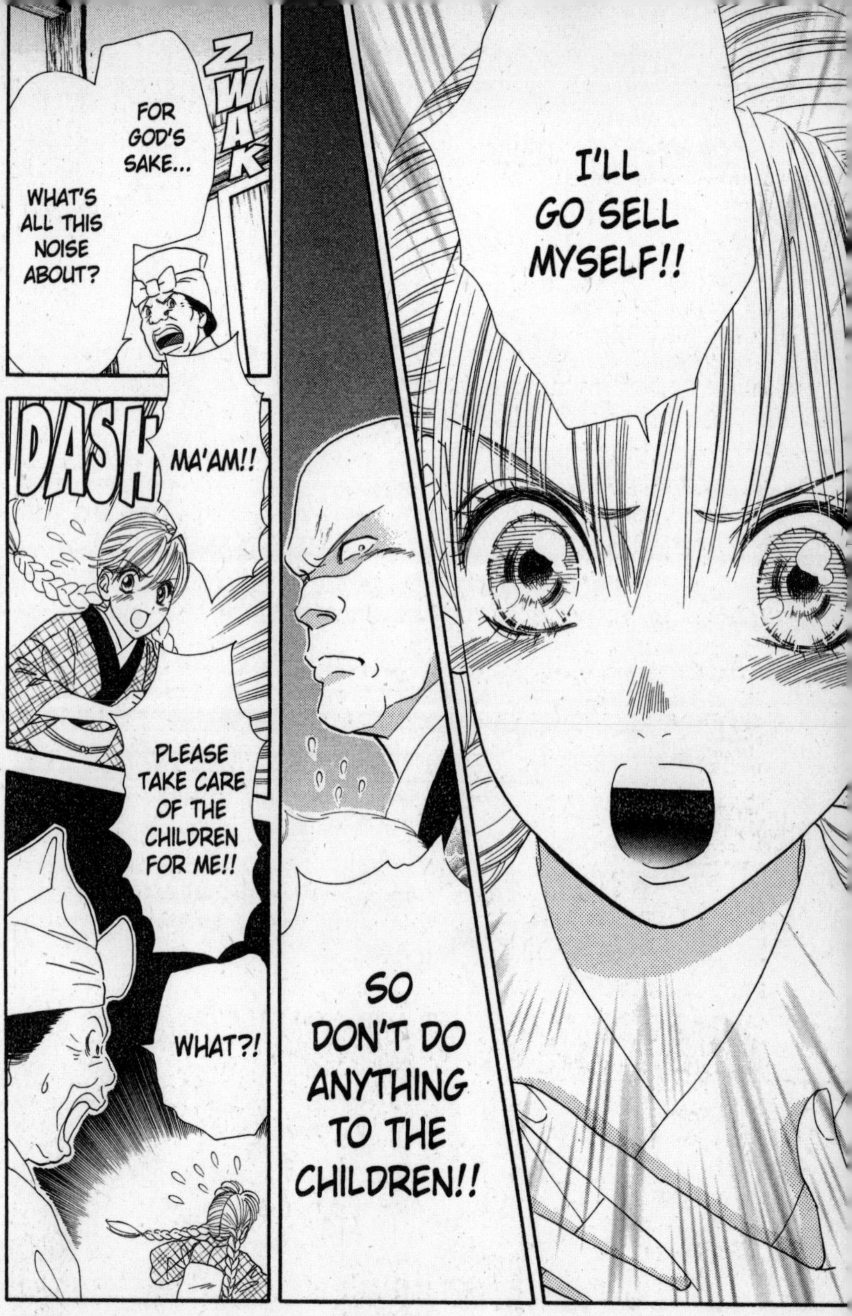
I'LL GO SELL MYSELF!!
SO DON'T DO ANYTHING TO THE CHILDREN!!
ZWAK
FOR GOD'S SAKE...
WHAT'S ALL THIS NOISE ABOUT?
MA'AM!!
DASH
PLEASE TAKE CARE OF THE CHILDREN FOR ME!!
WHAT?!

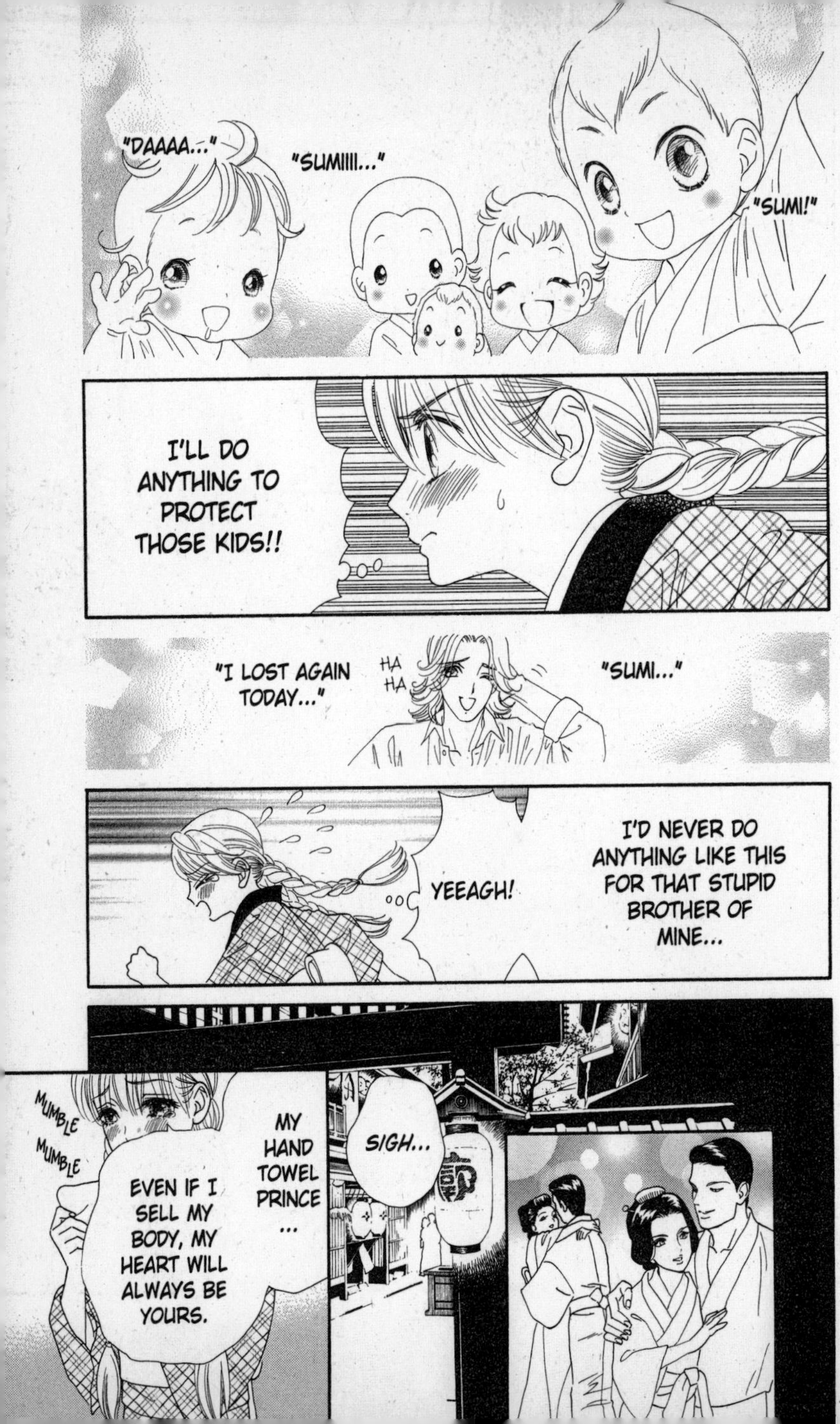
"SUMI!"
"SUMIIII..."
"DAAAA..."
I'LL DO ANYTHING TO PROTECT THOSE KIDS!!
"SUMI..."
HA HA
"I LOST AGAIN TODAY..."
I'D NEVER DO ANYTHING LIKE THIS FOR THAT STUPID BROTHER OF MINE...
YEEAGH!
SIGH...
MY HAND TOWEL PRINCE...
EVEN IF I SELL MY BODY, MY HEART WILL ALWAYS BE YOURS.
MUMBLE MUMBLE

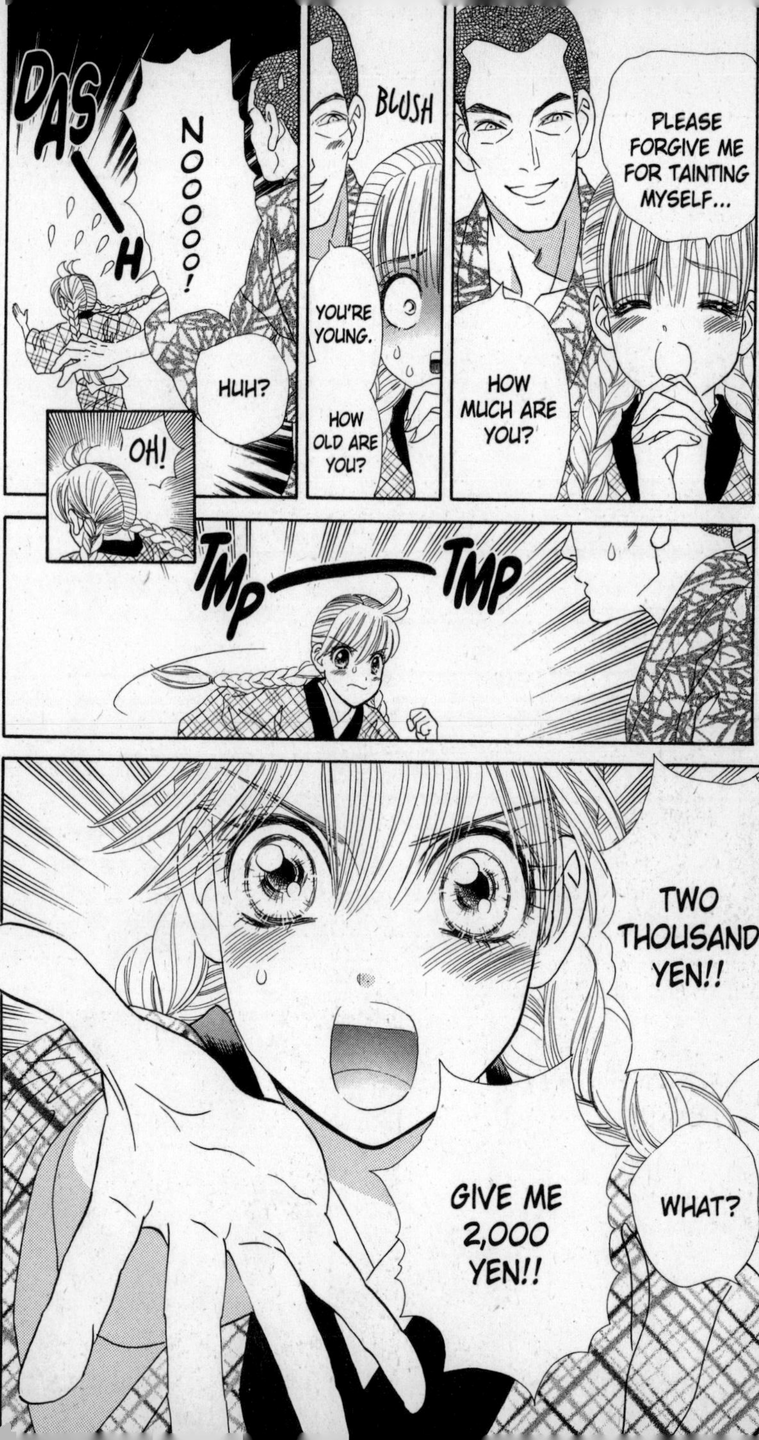
PLEASE FORGIVE ME FOR TAINTING MYSELF...
HOW MUCH ARE YOU?
BLUSH
YOU'RE YOUNG.
HOW OLD ARE YOU?
NOOOOOO!
DASH
HUH?
OH!
TMP—TMP
TWO THOUSAND YEN!!
GIVE ME 2,000 YEN!!
WHAT?

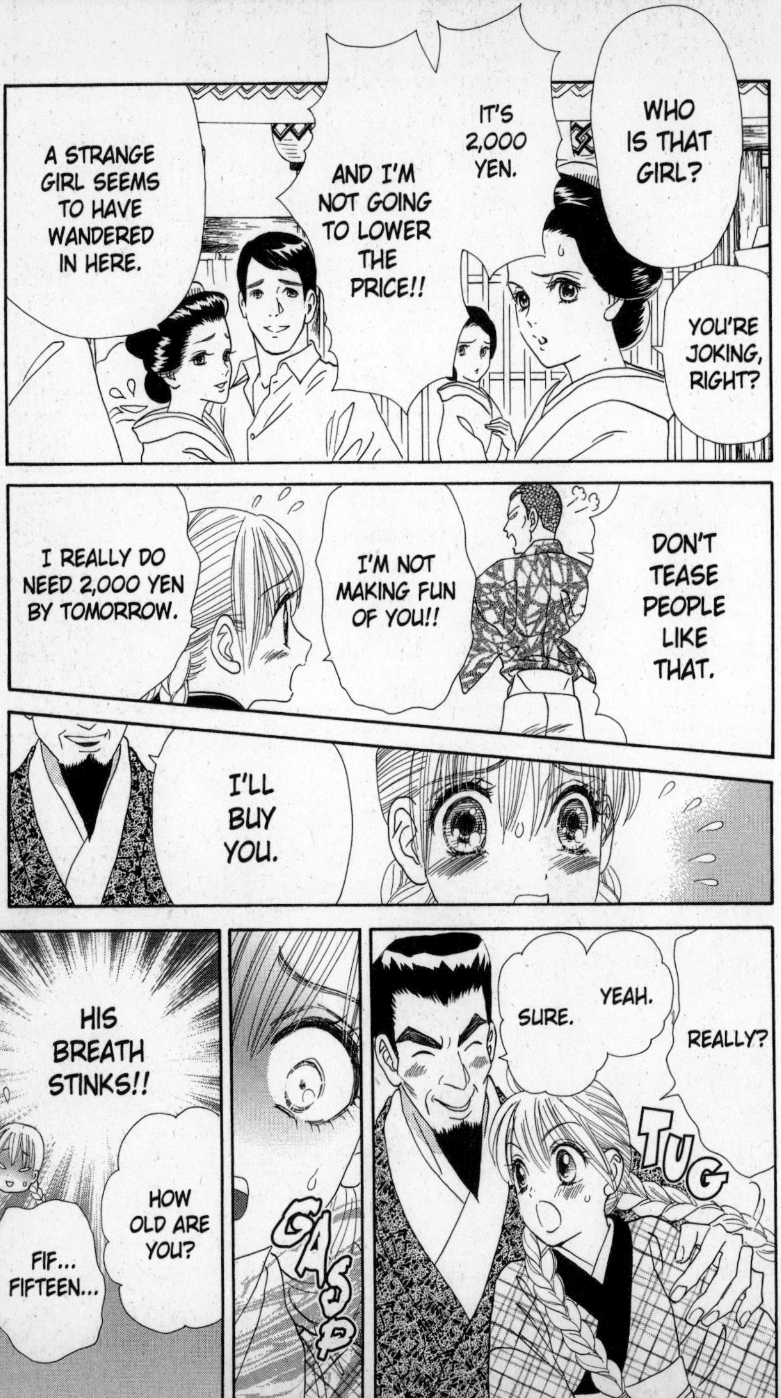
WHO IS THAT GIRL?
YOU'RE JOKING, RIGHT?
IT'S 2,000 YEN.
AND I'M NOT GOING TO LOWER THE PRICE!!
A STRANGE GIRL SEEMS TO HAVE WANDERED IN HERE.
DON'T TEASE PEOPLE LIKE THAT.
I'M NOT MAKING FUN OF YOU!!
I REALLY DO NEED 2,000 YEN BY TOMORROW.
I'LL BUY YOU.
REALLY?
YEAH.
SURE.
TUG
GASP
HIS BREATH STINKS!!
HOW OLD ARE YOU?
FIF... FIFTEEN...

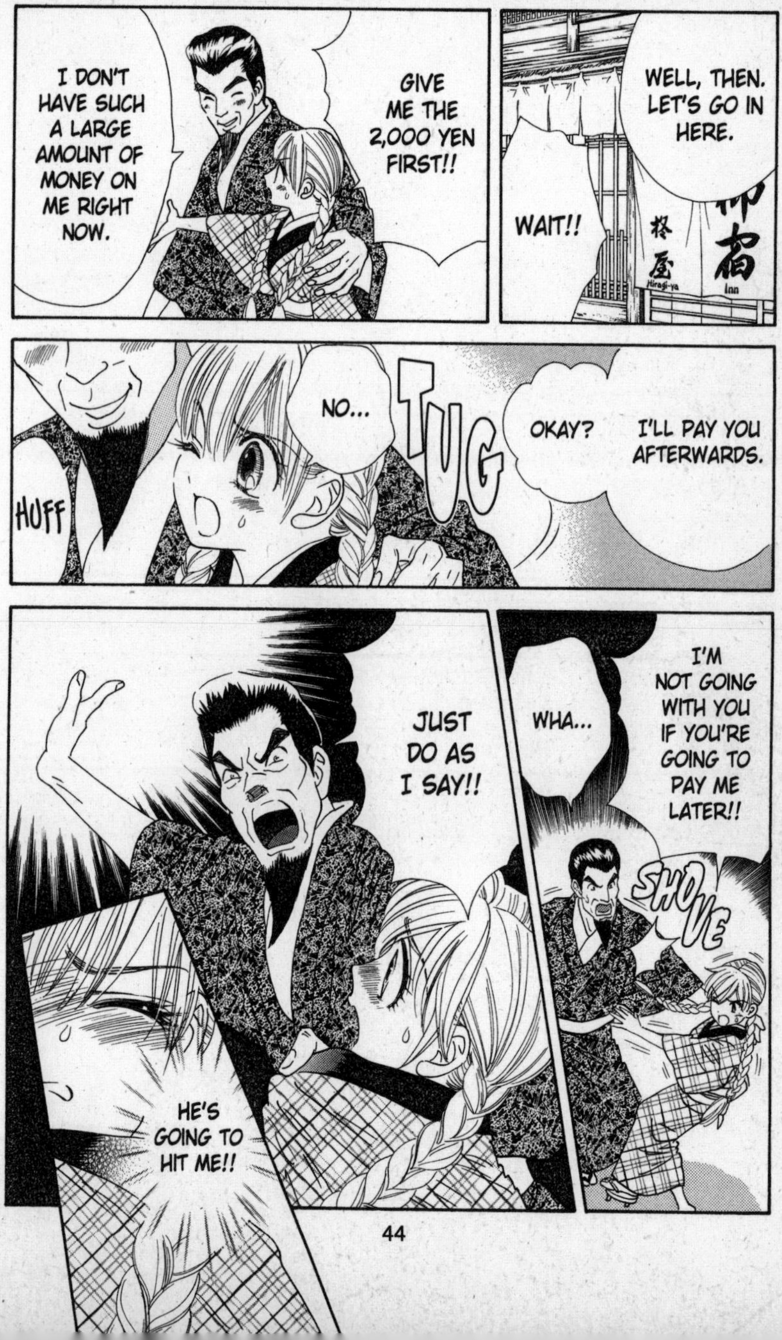
WELL, THEN. LET'S GO IN HERE.
WAIT!!
Hiragi-ya
Inn
GIVE ME THE 2,000 YEN FIRST!!
I DON'T HAVE SUCH A LARGE AMOUNT OF MONEY ON ME RIGHT NOW.
I'LL PAY YOU AFTERWARDS.
OKAY?
TUG
NO...
HUFF
I'M NOT GOING WITH YOU IF YOU'RE GOING TO PAY ME LATER!!
WHA...
SHOVE
JUST DO AS I SAY!!
HE'S GOING TO HIT ME!!

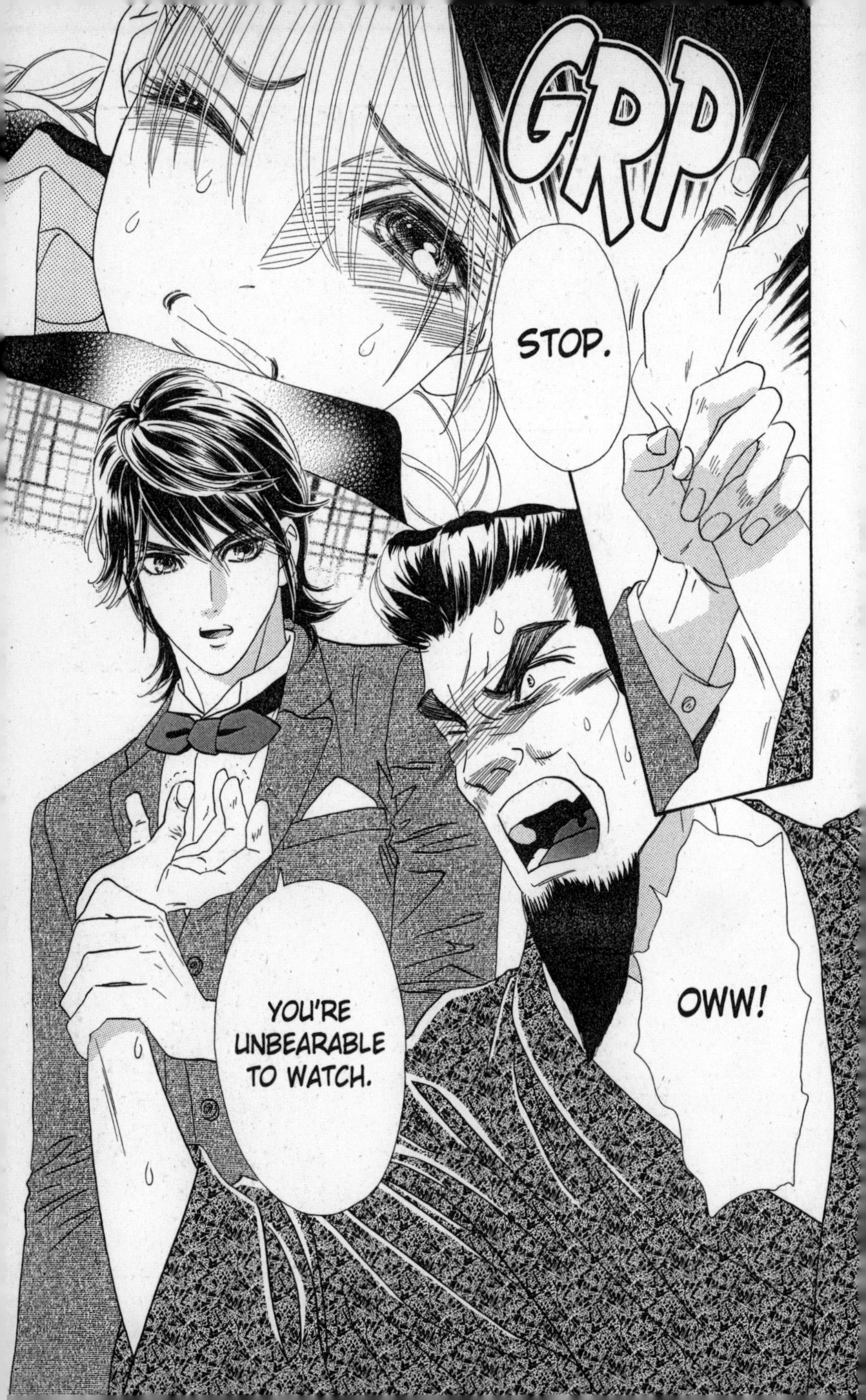
GRP
STOP.
OWW!
YOU'RE UNBEARABLE TO WATCH.

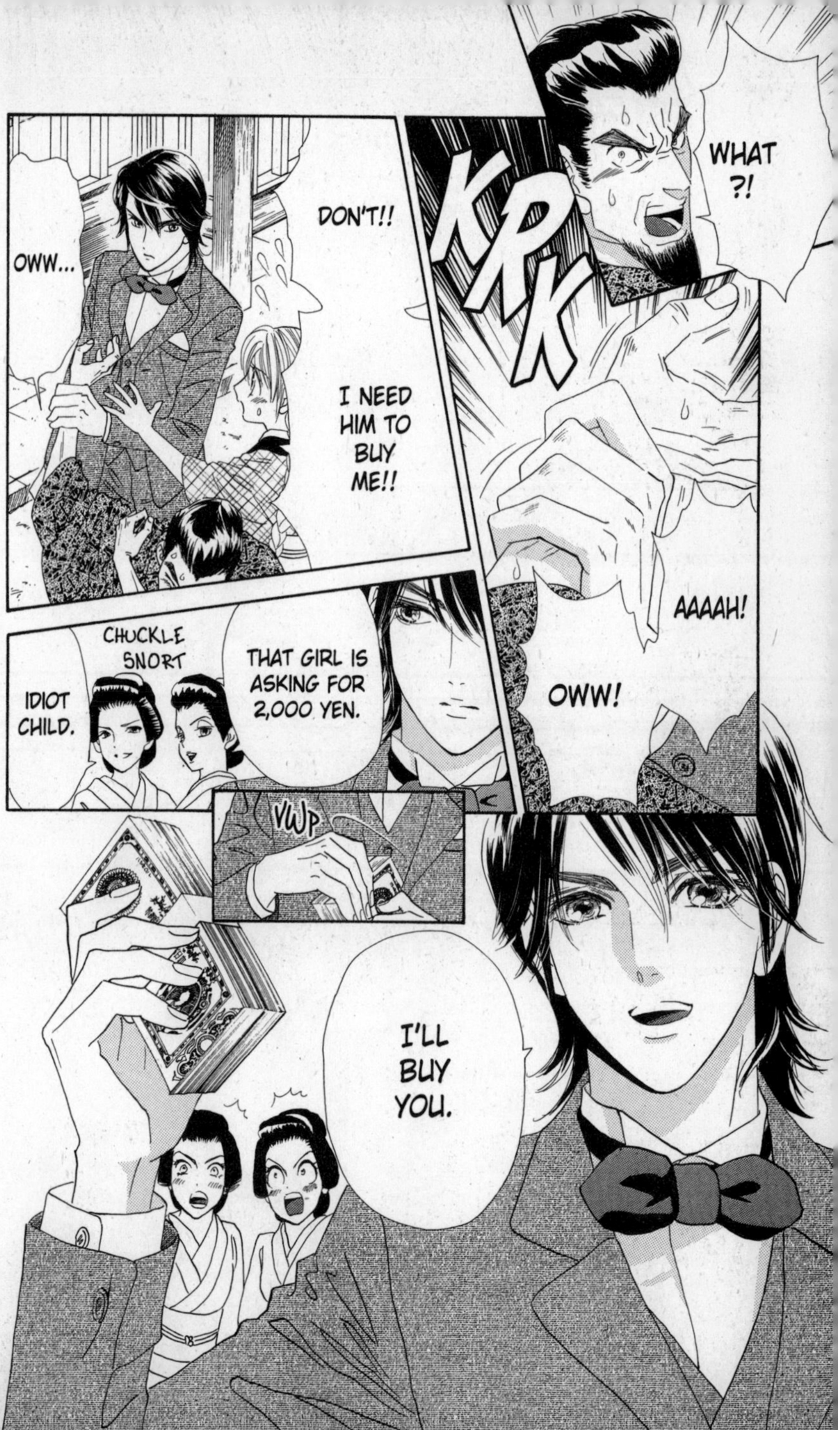
WHAT ?!
KRK
AAAAH!
OWW!
DON'T!!
OWW...
I NEED HIM TO BUY ME!!
THAT GIRL IS ASKING FOR 2,000 YEN.
CHUCKLE SNORT
IDIOT CHILD.
VWP
I'LL BUY YOU.

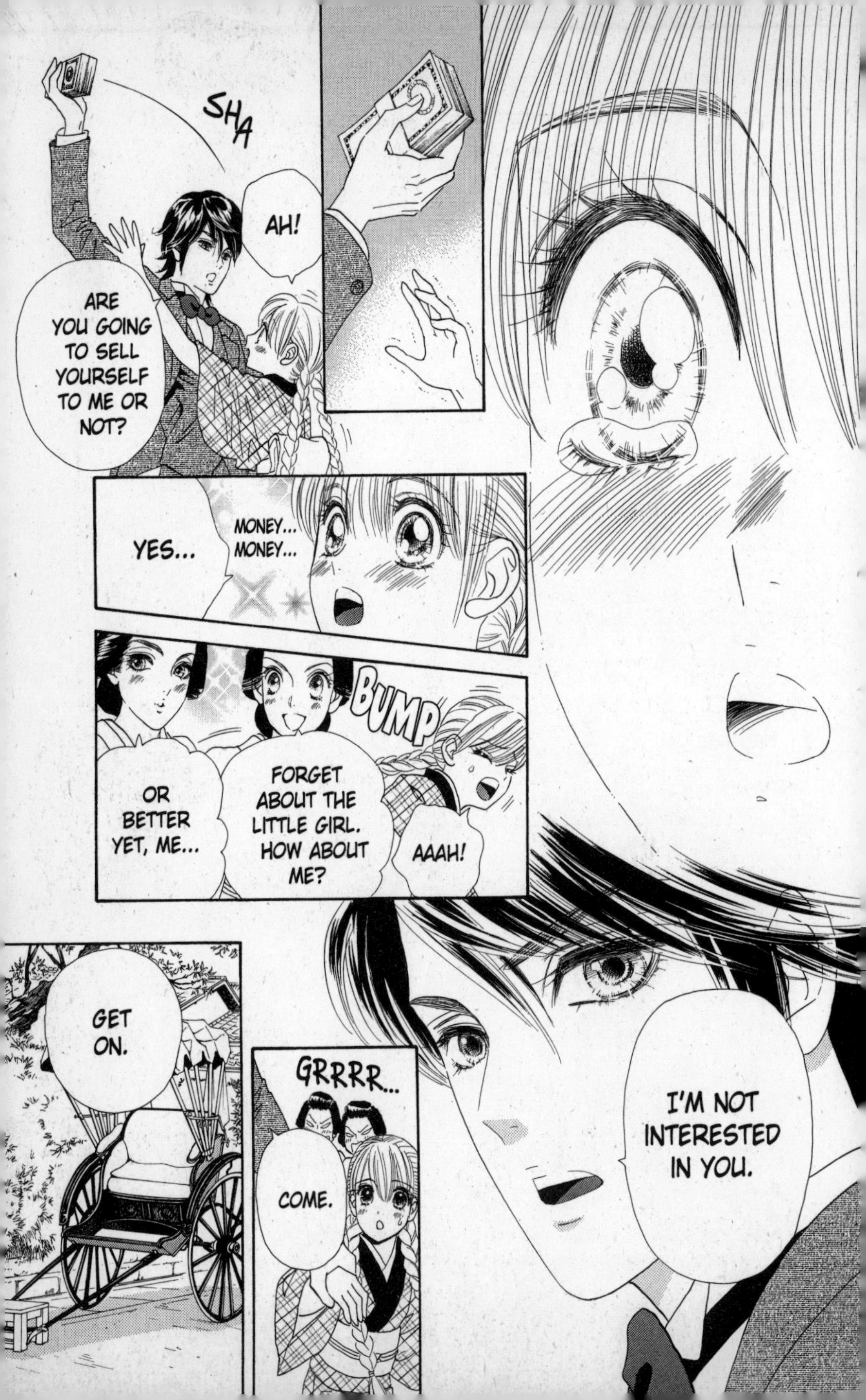
SHA
AH!
ARE YOU GOING TO SELL YOURSELF TO ME OR NOT?
MONEY... MONEY...
YES...
BUMP
AAAH!
FORGET ABOUT THE LITTLE GIRL. HOW ABOUT ME?
OR BETTER YET, ME...
I'M NOT INTERESTED IN YOU.
GRRRR...
COME.
GET ON.

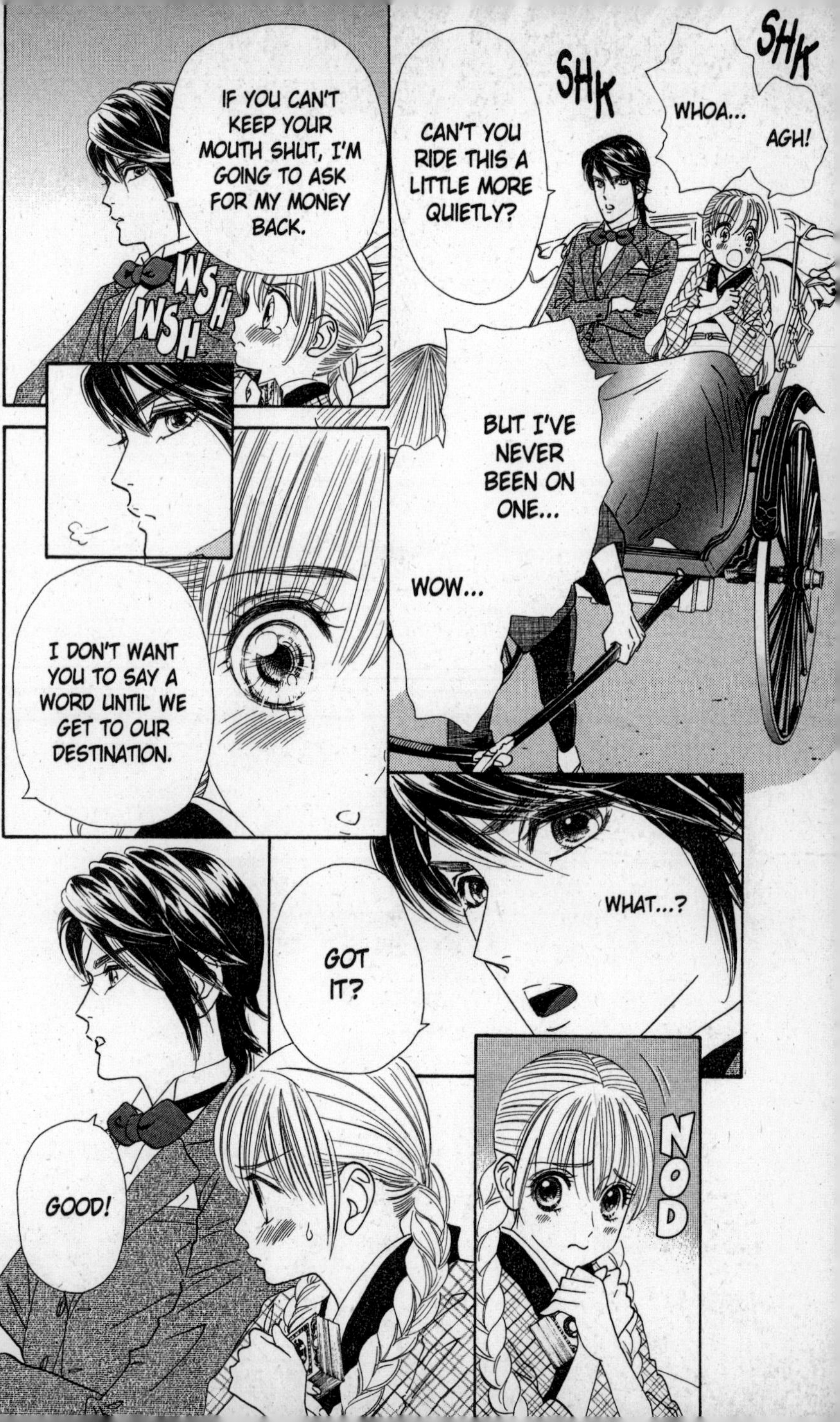
SHK
WHOA...
AGH!
SHK
CAN'T YOU RIDE THIS A LITTLE MORE QUIETLY?
BUT I'VE NEVER BEEN ON ONE...
WOW...
IF YOU CAN'T KEEP YOUR MOUTH SHUT, I'M GOING TO ASK FOR MY MONEY BACK.
WSH WSH
I DON'T WANT YOU TO SAY A WORD UNTIL WE GET TO OUR DESTINATION.
WHAT...?
GOT IT?
NOD
GOOD!

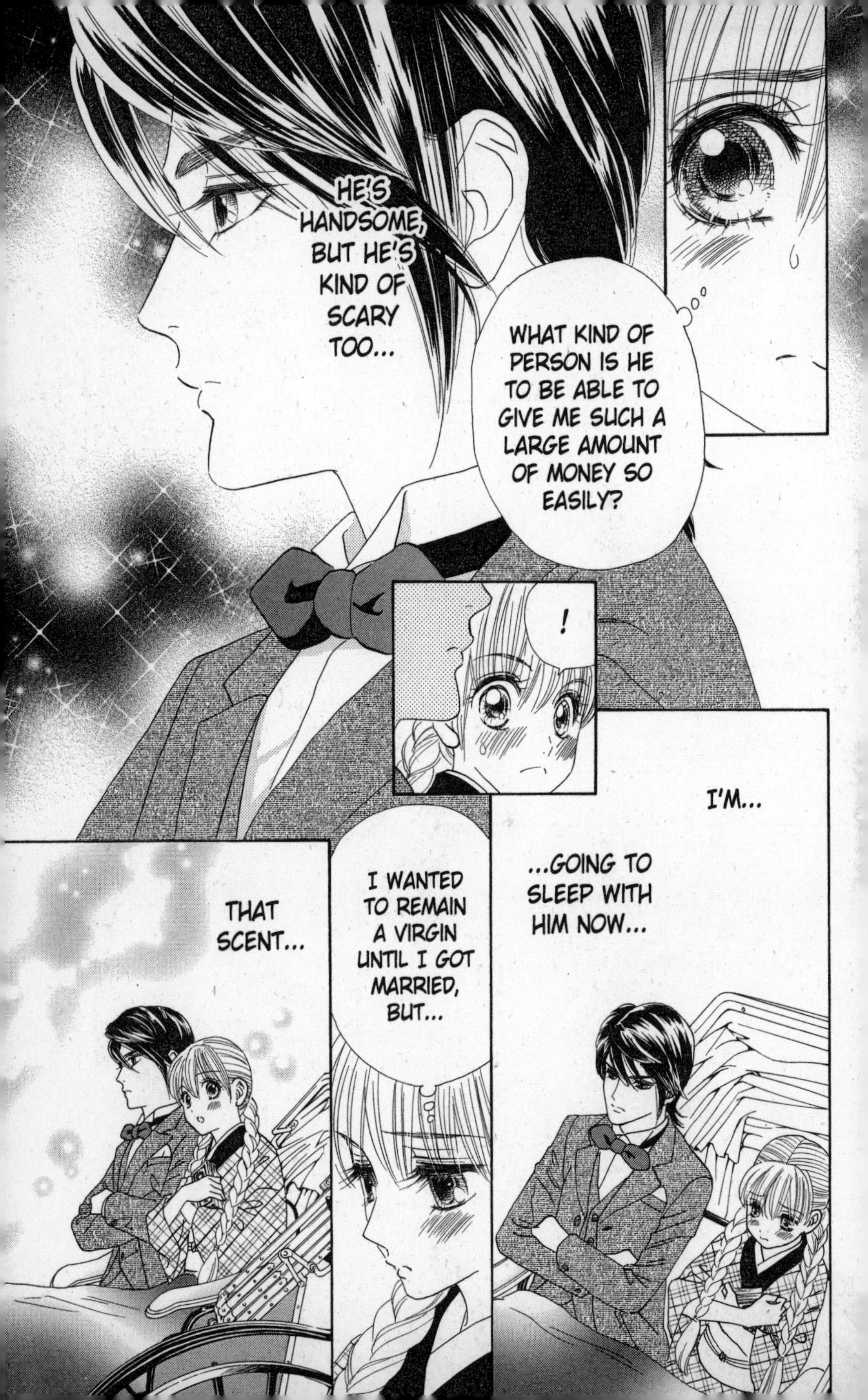
WHAT KIND OF PERSON IS HE TO BE ABLE TO GIVE ME SUCH A LARGE AMOUNT OF MONEY SO EASILY?
HE'S HANDSOME, BUT HE'S KIND OF SCARY TOO...
!
I'M...
...GOING TO SLEEP WITH HIM NOW...
I WANTED TO REMAIN A VIRGIN UNTIL I GOT MARRIED, BUT...
THAT SCENT...

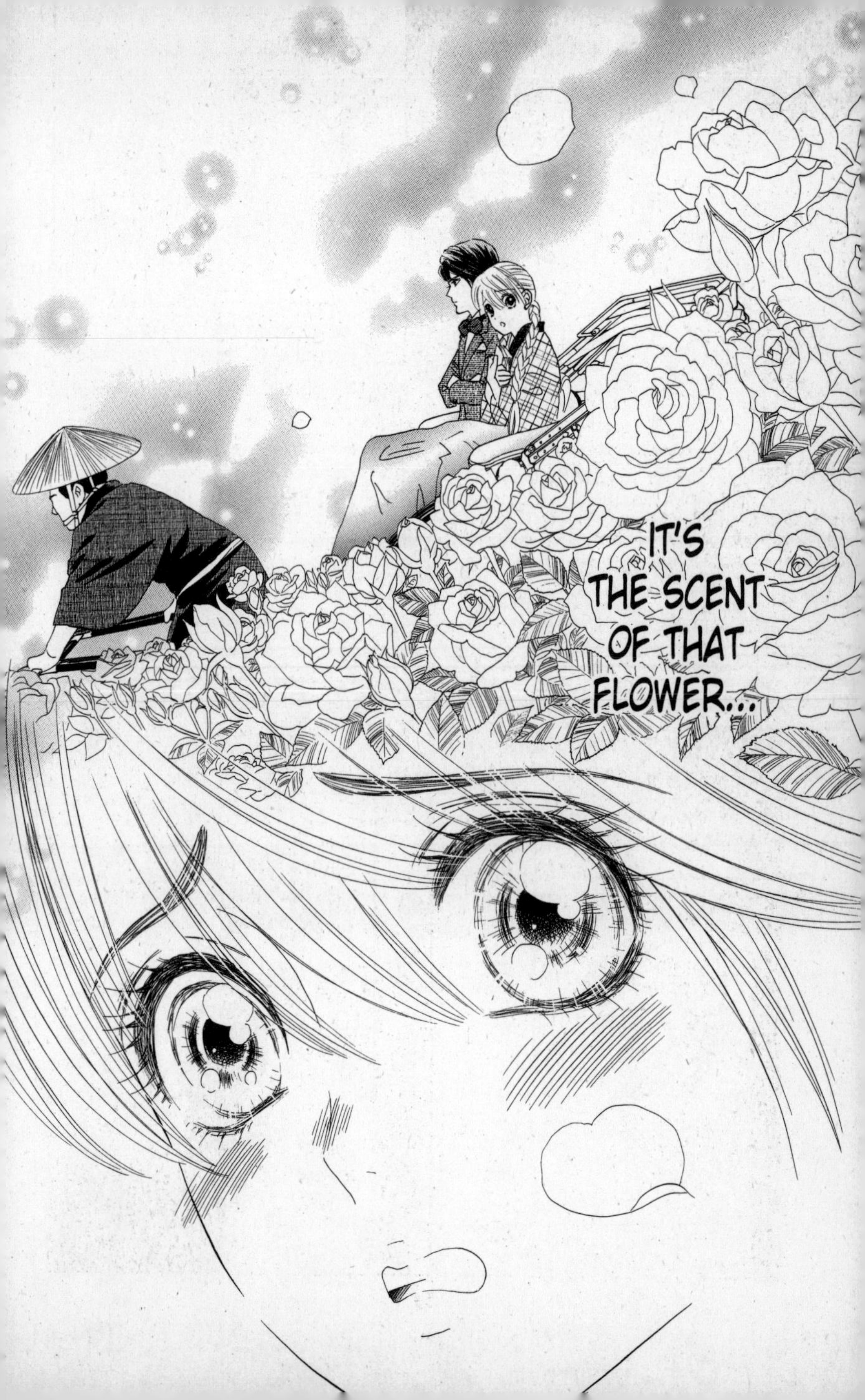
IT'S THE SCENT OF THAT FLOWER...

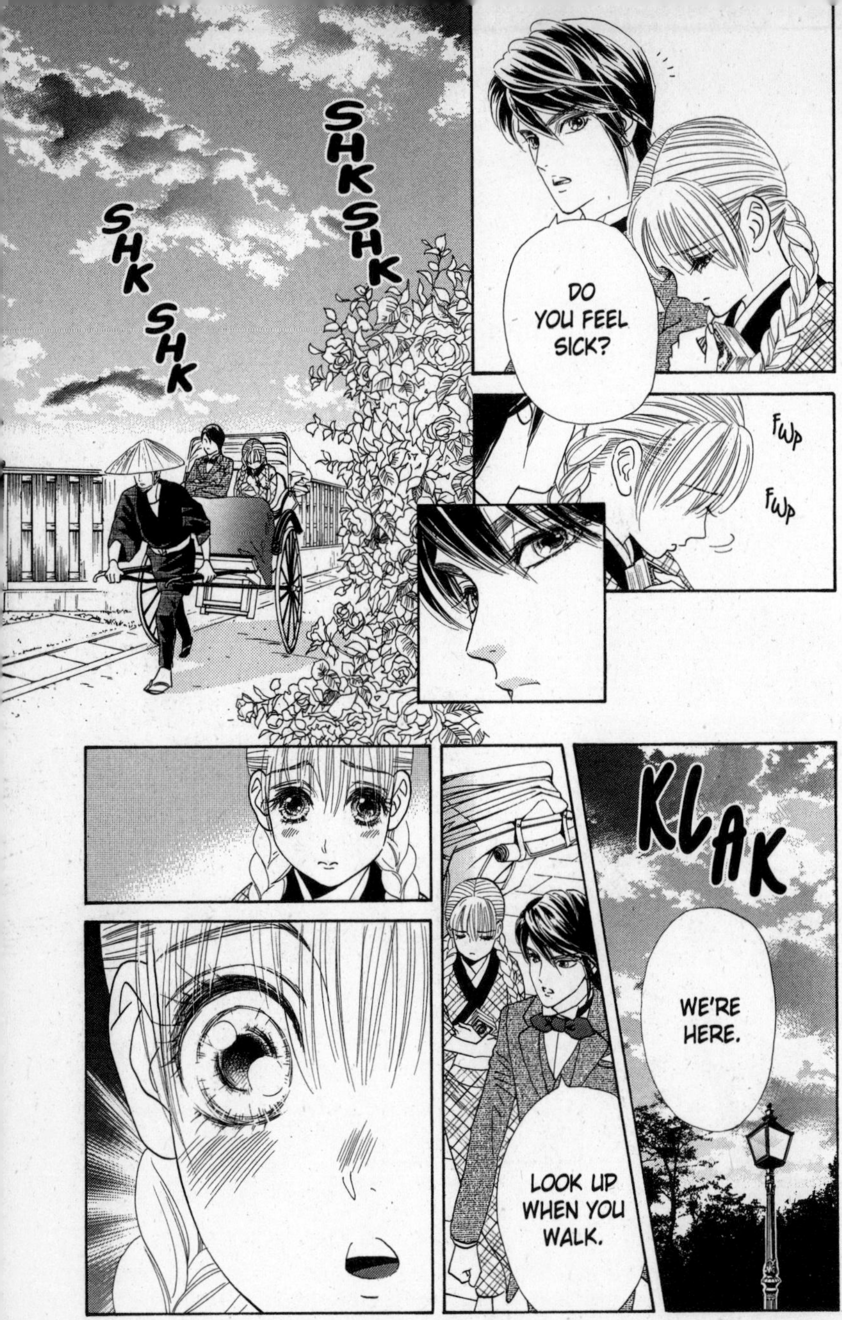
DO YOU FEEL SICK?
FWP
FWP
SHK SHK
SHK SHK
KLAK
WE'RE HERE.
LOOK UP WHEN YOU WALK.

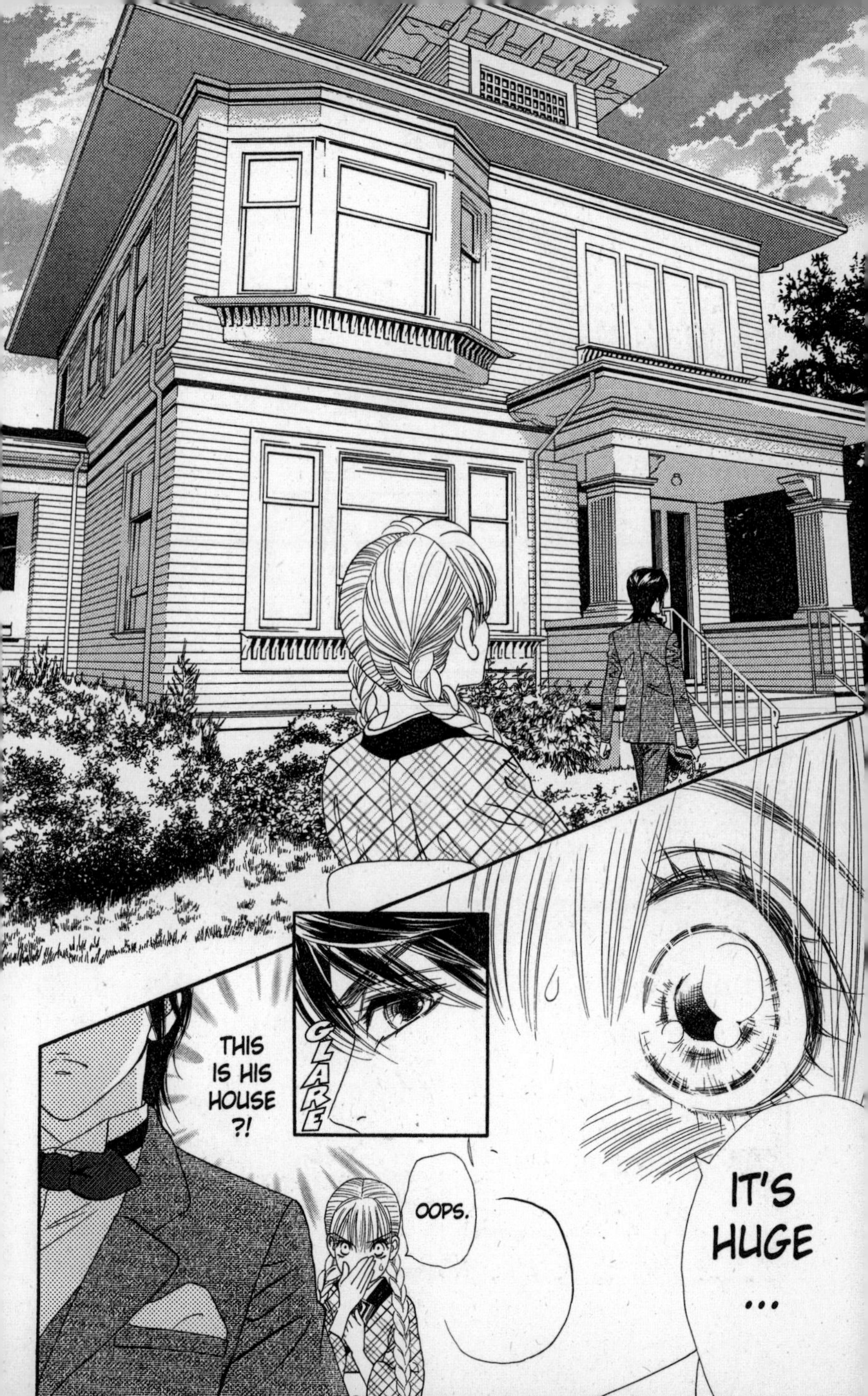
IT'S HUGE ...
GLARE
THIS IS HIS HOUSE ?!
OOPS.

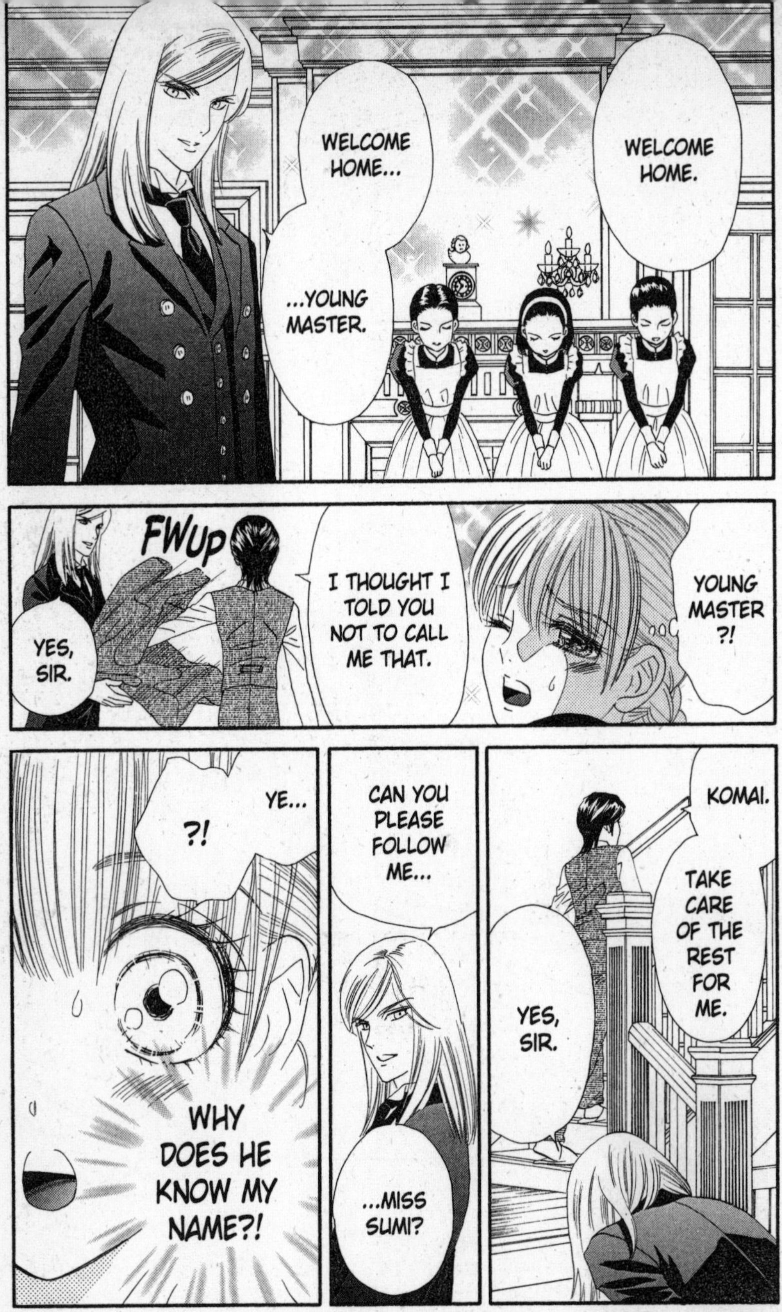
WELCOME HOME.
WELCOME HOME...
...YOUNG MASTER.
YOUNG MASTER?!
I THOUGHT I TOLD YOU NOT TO CALL ME THAT.
FWUP
YES, SIR.
KOMAI.
TAKE CARE OF THE REST FOR ME.
YES, SIR.
CAN YOU PLEASE FOLLOW ME...
...MISS SUMI?
YE...
?!
WHY DOES HE KNOW MY NAME?!

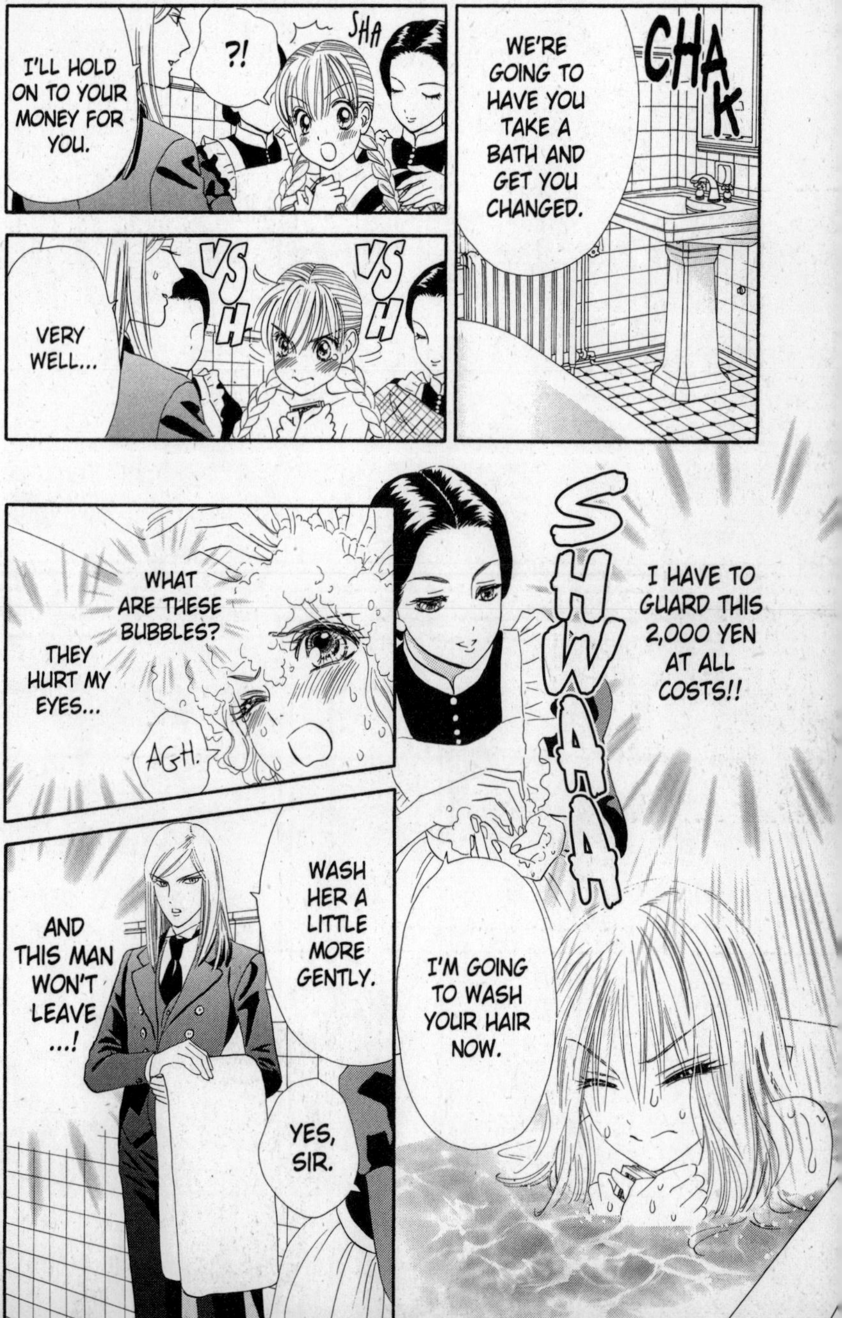
CHAK
WE'RE GOING TO HAVE YOU TAKE A BATH AND GET YOU CHANGED.
SHA
?!
I'LL HOLD ON TO YOUR MONEY FOR YOU.
VSH VSH
VERY WELL...
SHWAAA
I HAVE TO GUARD THIS 2,000 YEN AT ALL COSTS!!
I'M GOING TO WASH YOUR HAIR NOW.
WHAT ARE THESE BUBBLES?
THEY HURT MY EYES...
AGH.
WASH HER A LITTLE MORE GENTLY.
YES, SIR.
AND THIS MAN WON'T LEAVE ...!

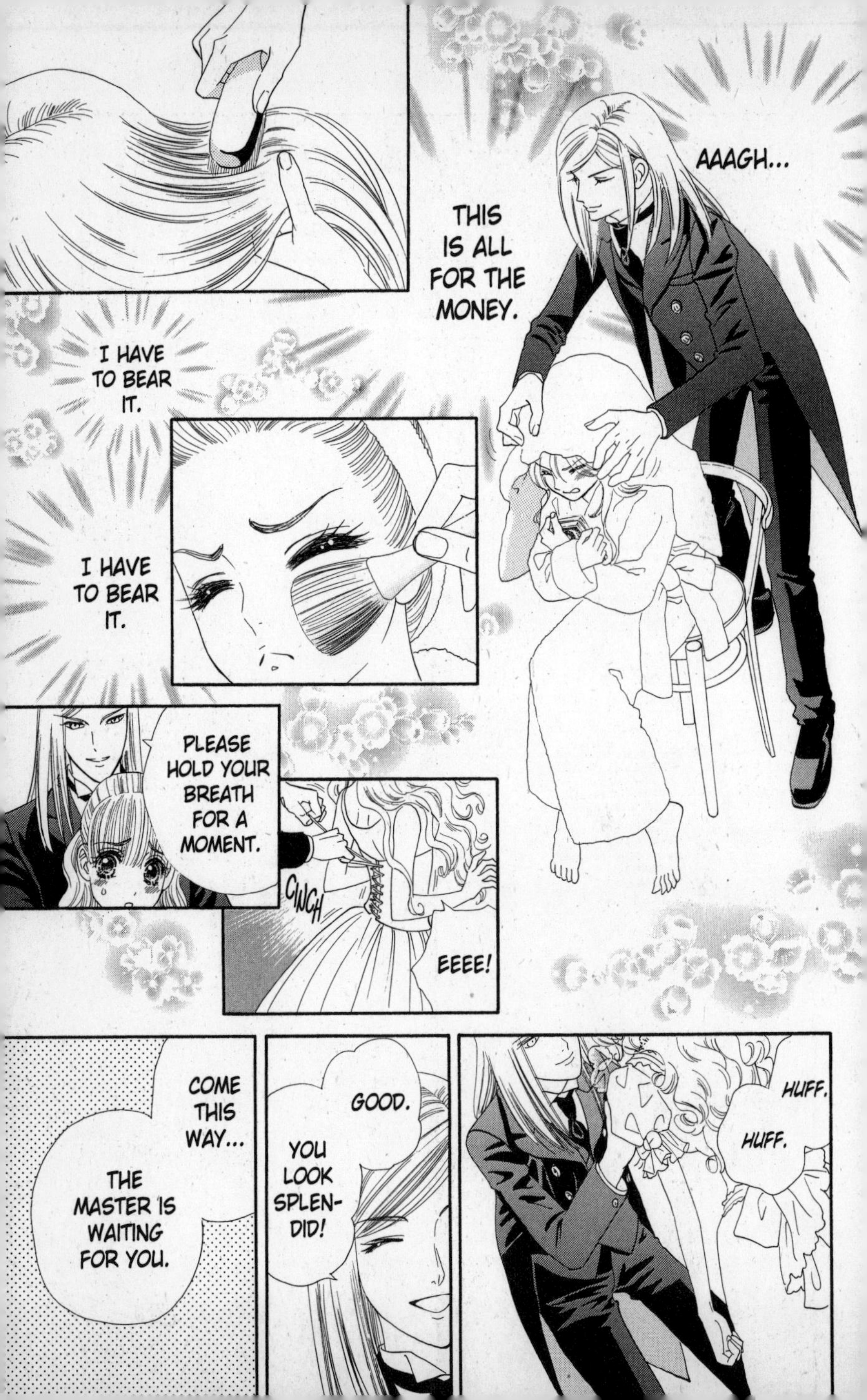
AAAGH...
THIS IS ALL FOR THE MONEY.
I HAVE TO BEAR IT.
I HAVE TO BEAR IT.
PLEASE HOLD YOUR BREATH FOR A MOMENT.
CINCH
EEEE!
HUFF.
HUFF.
GOOD.
YOU LOOK SPLEN-DID!
COME THIS WAY...
THE MASTER IS WAITING FOR YOU.

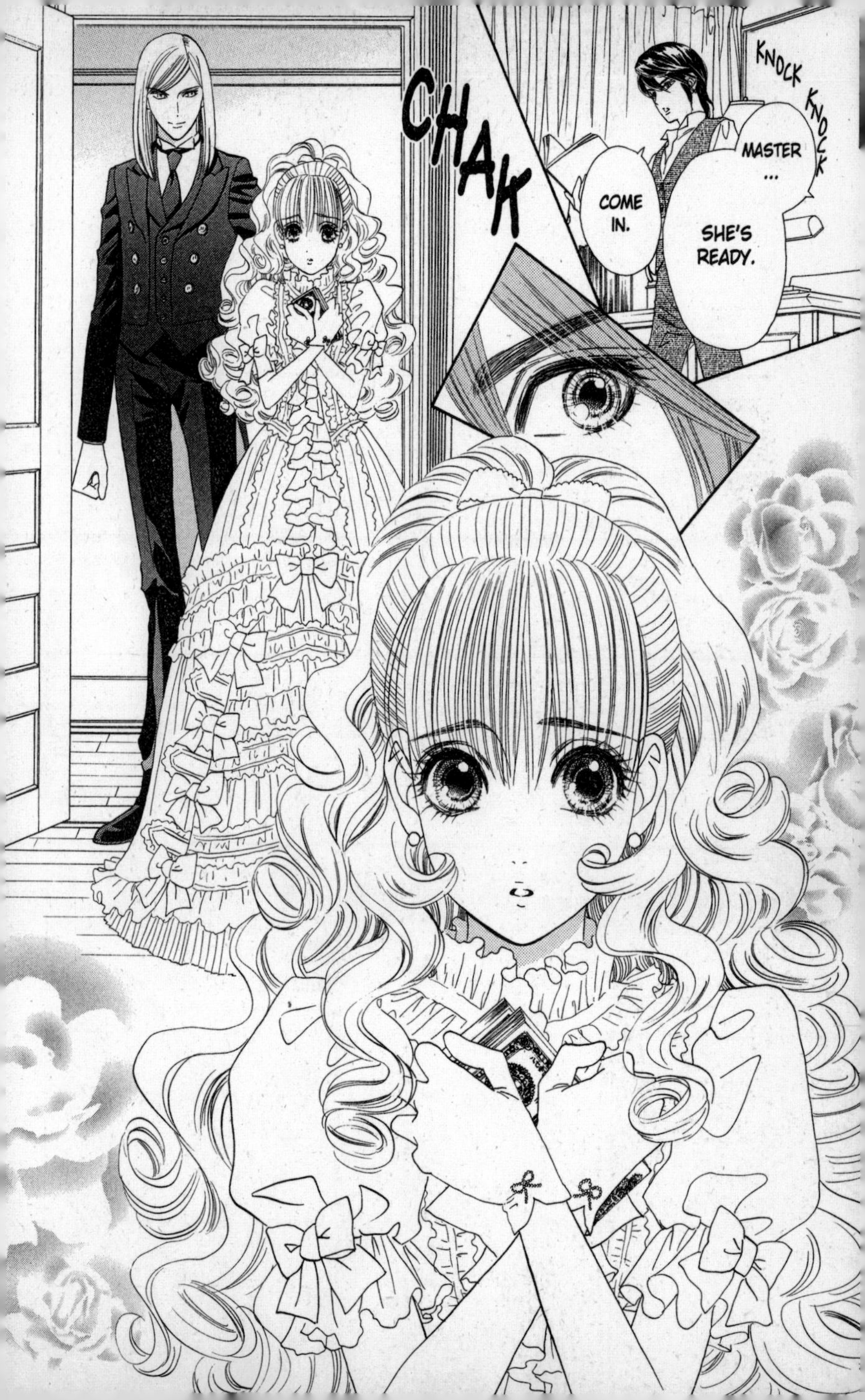
KNOCK KNOCK
MASTER ...
SHE'S READY.
COME IN.
CHAK

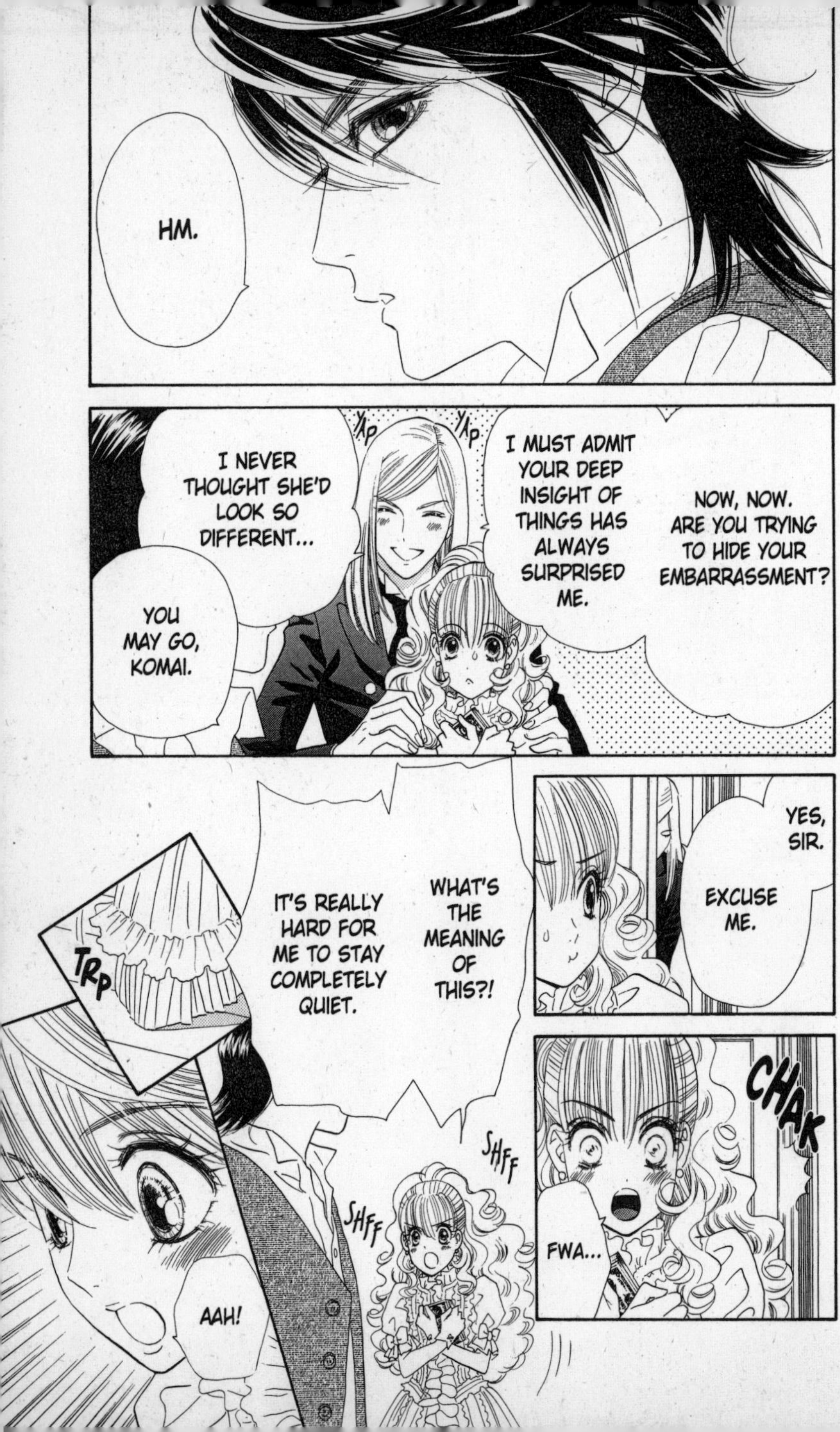
HM.
NOW, NOW. ARE YOU TRYING TO HIDE YOUR EMBARRASSMENT?
I MUST ADMIT YOUR DEEP INSIGHT OF THINGS HAS ALWAYS SURPRISED ME.
YAP
YAP
I NEVER THOUGHT SHE'D LOOK SO DIFFERENT...
YOU MAY GO, KOMAI.
YES, SIR.
EXCUSE ME.
CHAK
FWA...
WHAT'S THE MEANING OF THIS?!
IT'S REALLY HARD FOR ME TO STAY COMPLETELY QUIET.
TRP
SHFF
SHFF
AAH!

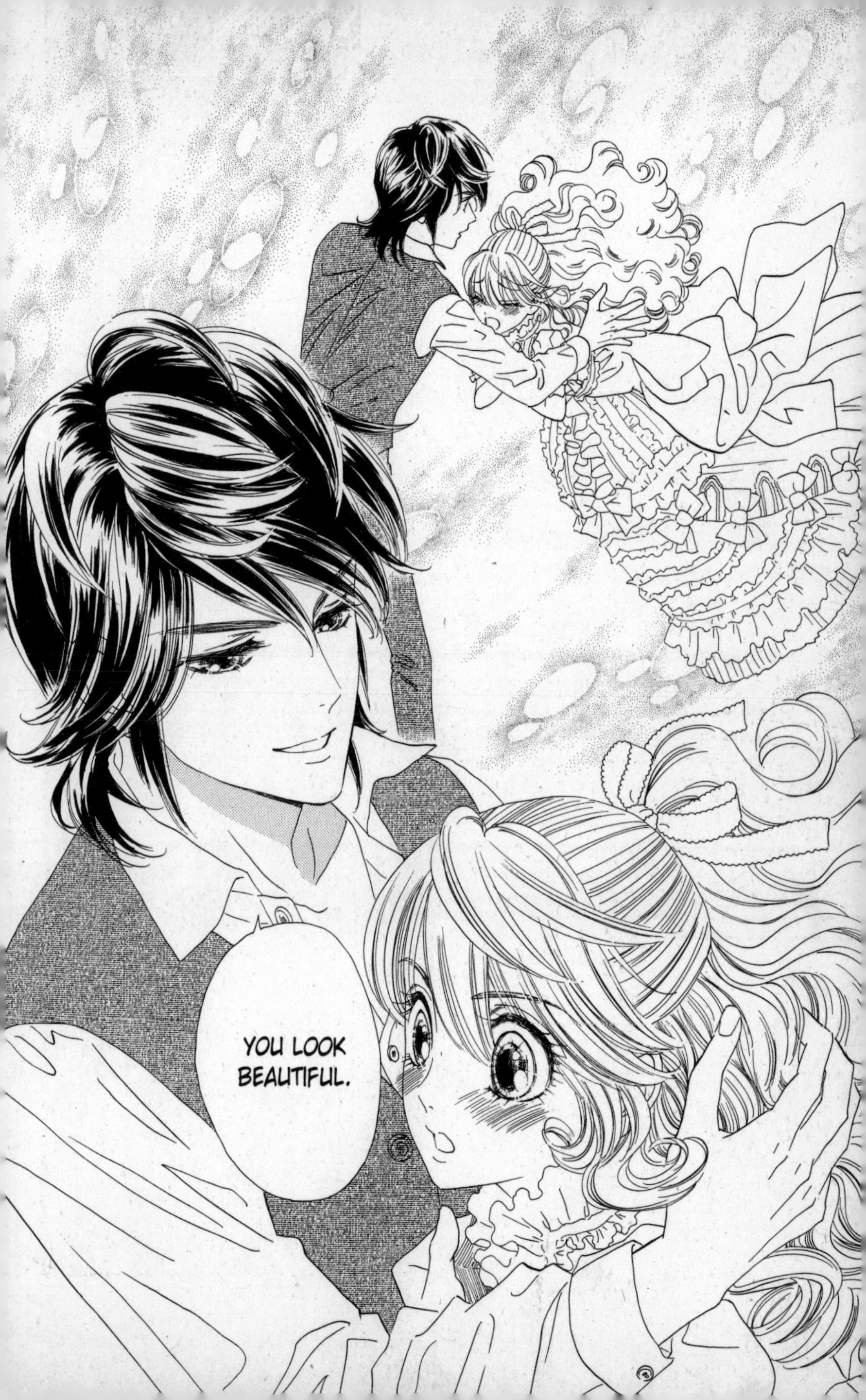
YOU LOOK BEAUTIFUL.

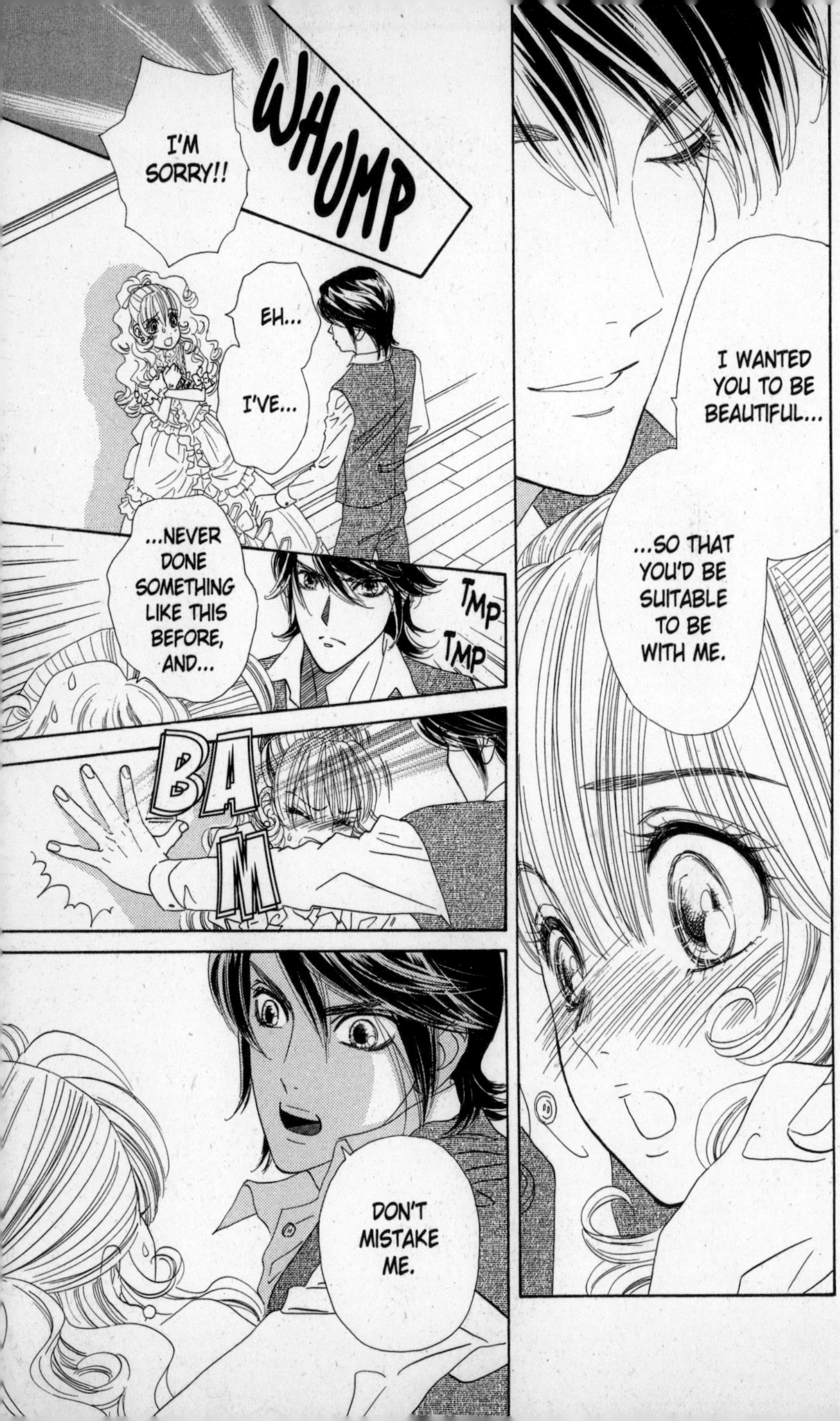
I WANTED YOU TO BE BEAUTIFUL...
...SO THAT YOU'D BE SUITABLE TO BE WITH ME.
WHUMP
I'M SORRY!!
EH...
I'VE...
...NEVER DONE SOMETHING LIKE THIS BEFORE, AND...
TMP TMP
BAM
DON'T MISTAKE ME.

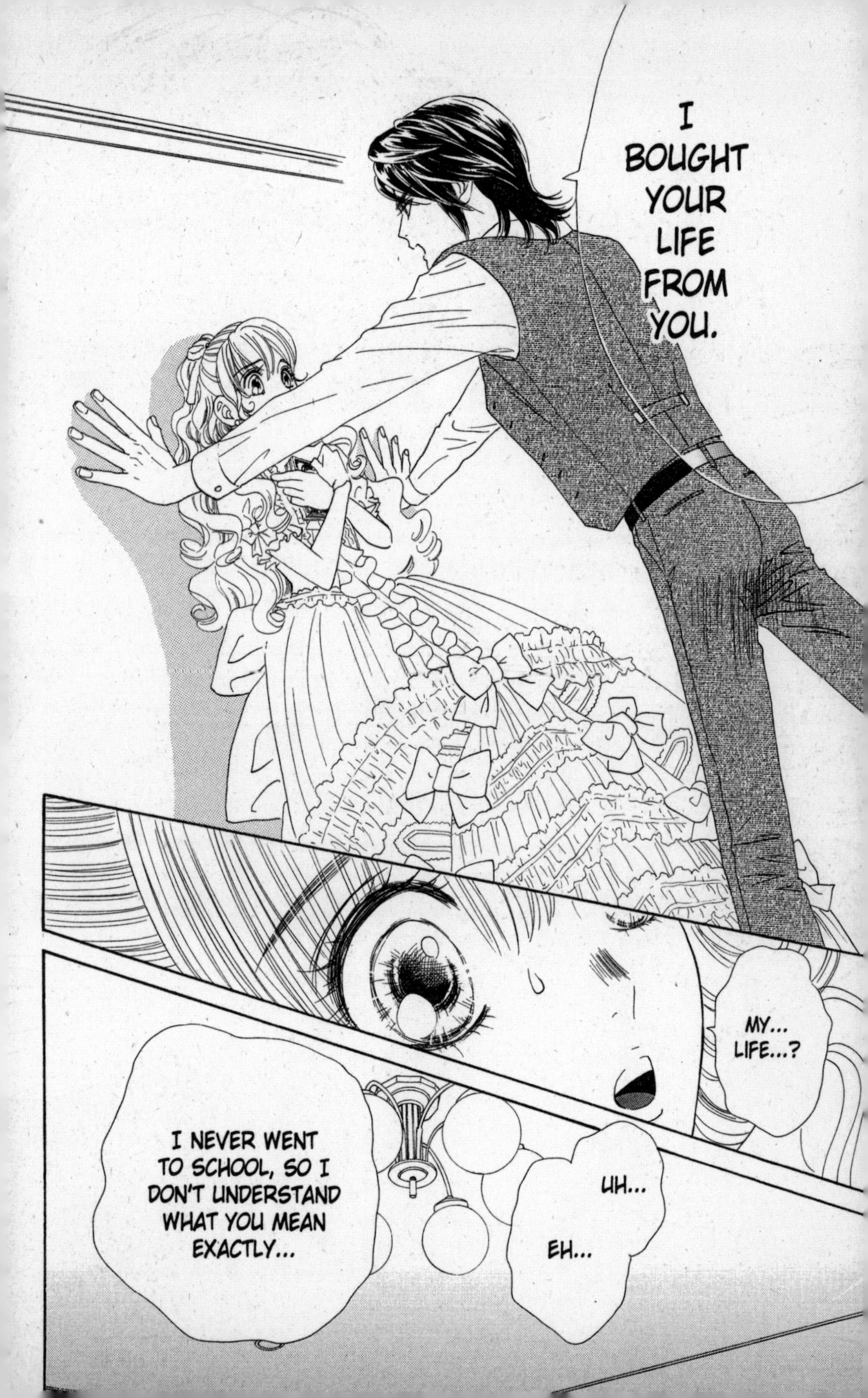
I BOUGHT YOUR LIFE FROM YOU.
MY... LIFE...?
UH...
EH...
I NEVER WENT TO SCHOOL, SO I DON'T UNDERSTAND WHAT YOU MEAN EXACTLY...

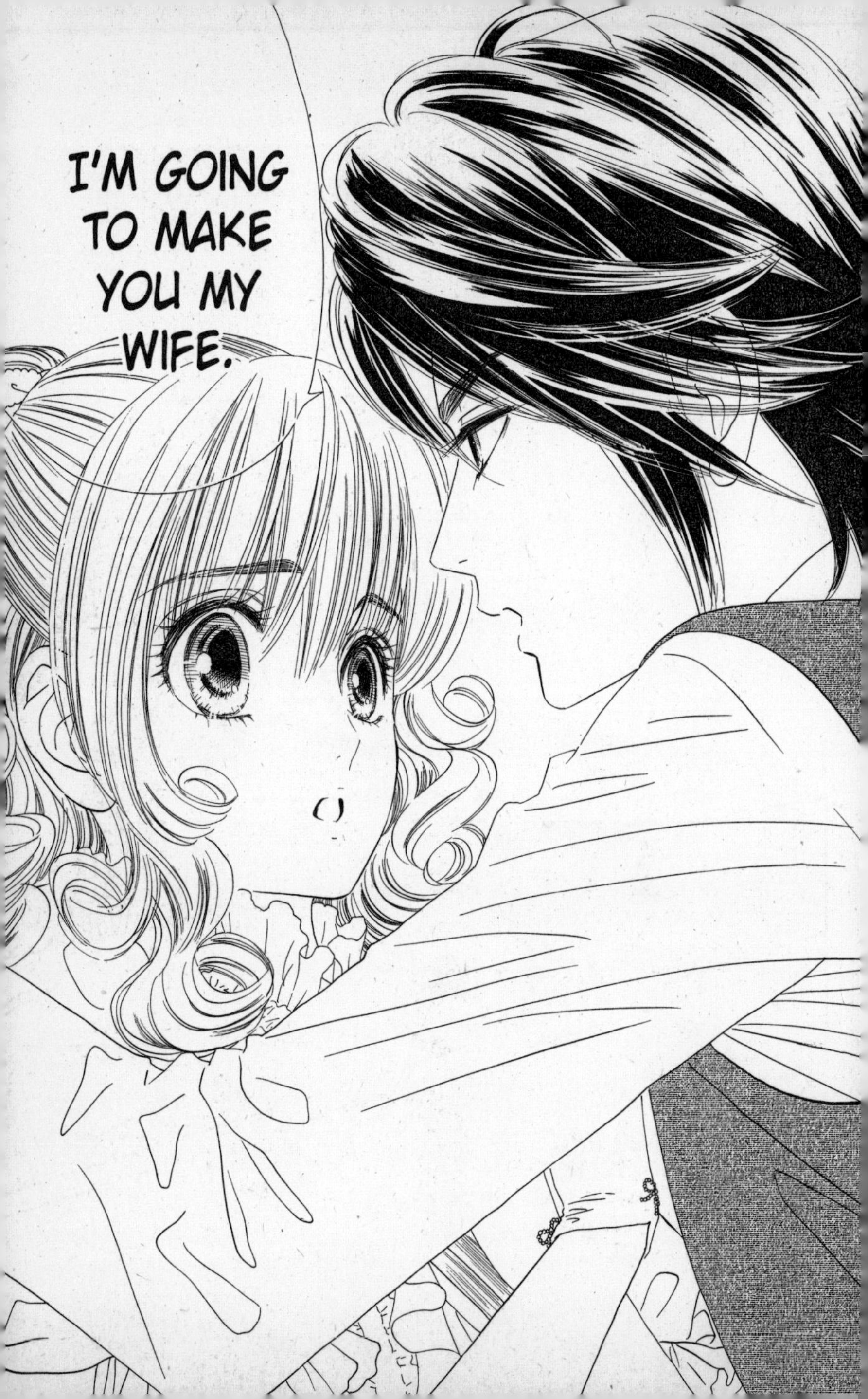
I'M GOING TO MAKE YOU MY WIFE.

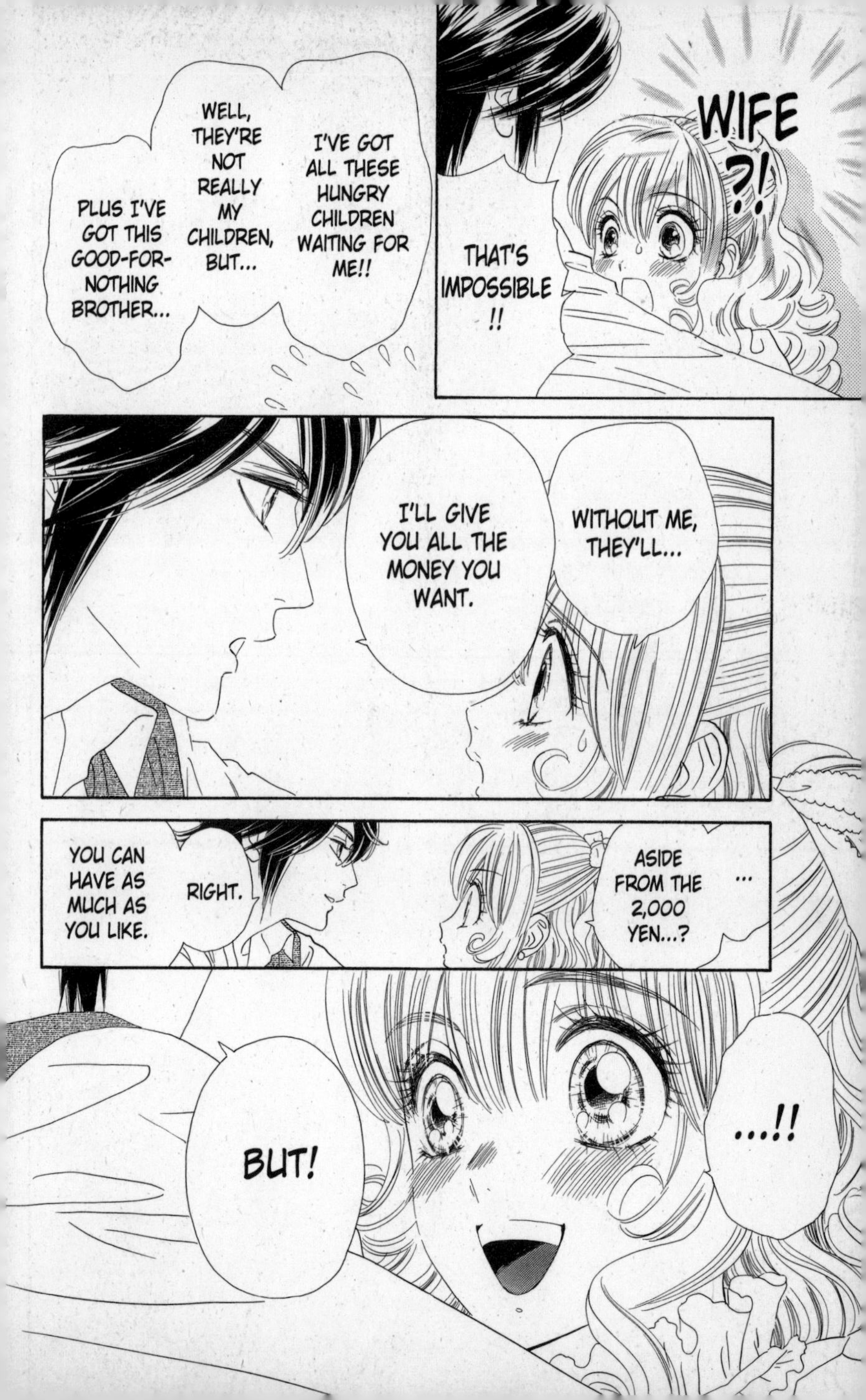
WIFE?!
THAT'S IMPOSSIBLE!!
I'VE GOT ALL THESE HUNGRY CHILDREN WAITING FOR ME!!
WELL, THEY'RE NOT REALLY MY CHILDREN, BUT...
PLUS I'VE GOT THIS GOOD-FOR-NOTHING BROTHER...
WITHOUT ME, THEY'LL...
I'LL GIVE YOU ALL THE MONEY YOU WANT.
...
ASIDE FROM THE 2,000 YEN...?
RIGHT.
YOU CAN HAVE AS MUCH AS YOU LIKE.
...!!
BUT!

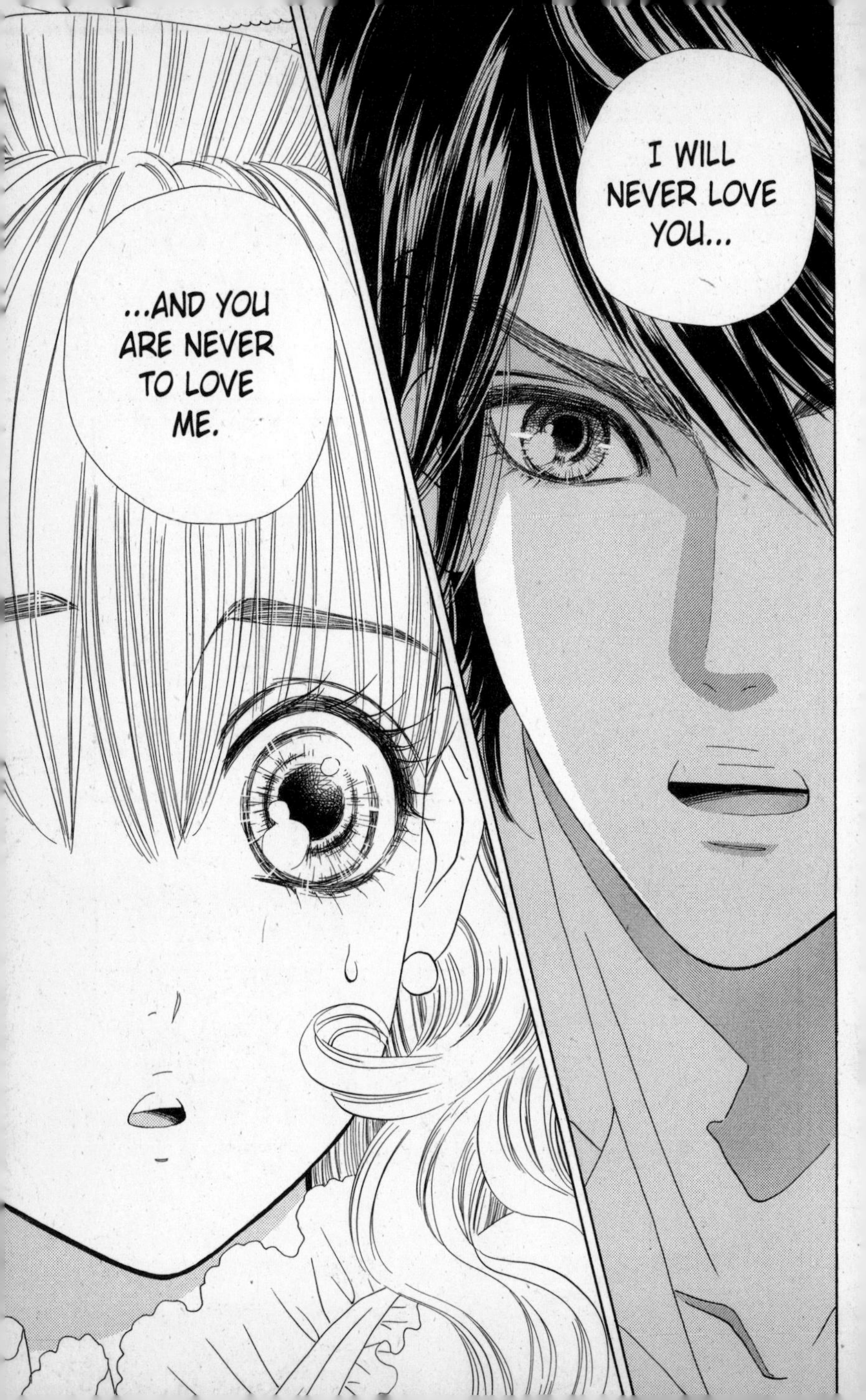
I WILL NEVER LOVE YOU...
...AND YOU ARE NEVER TO LOVE ME.

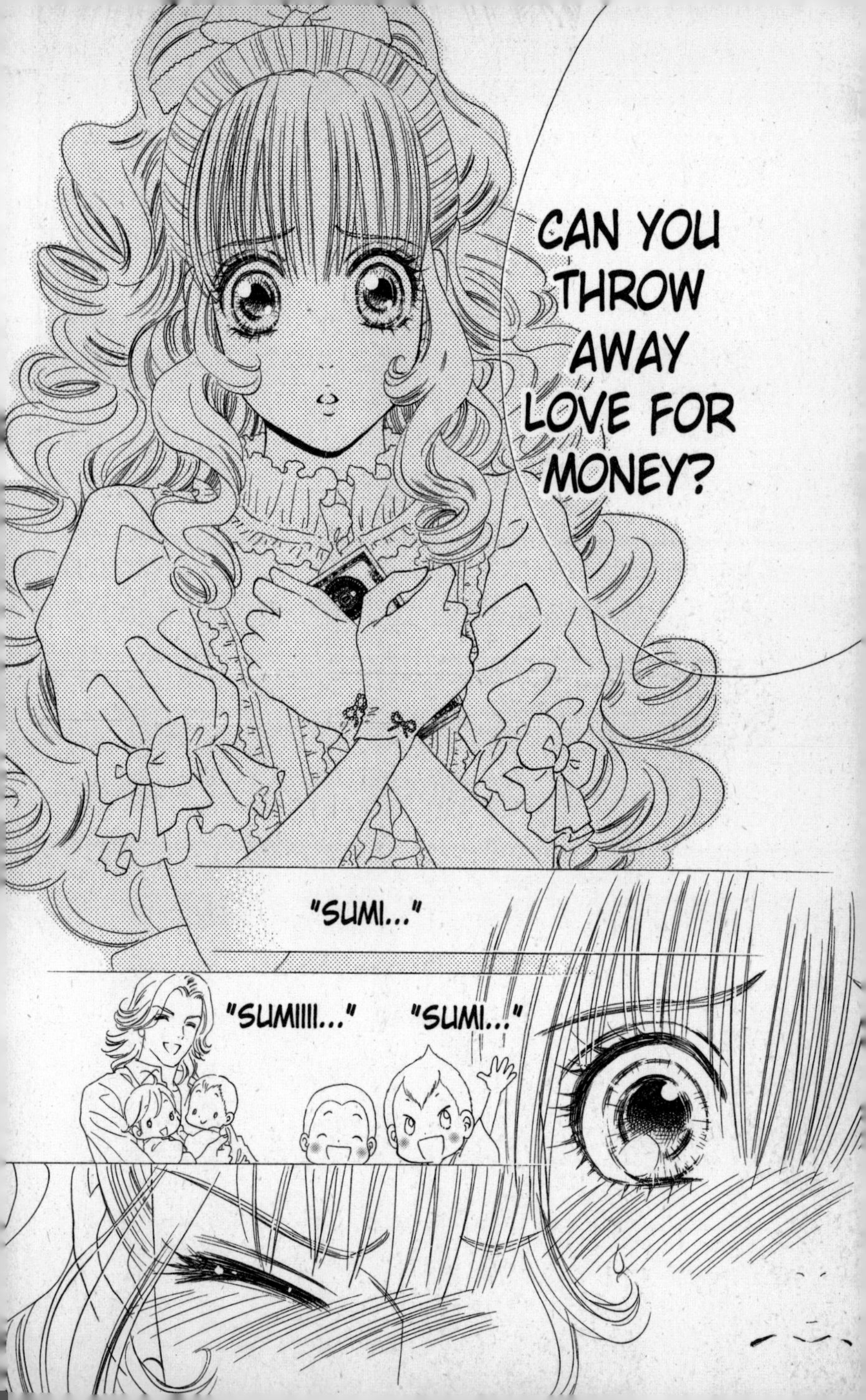
CAN YOU THROW AWAY LOVE FOR MONEY?
"SUMI..."
"SUMI..."
"SUMIIII..."

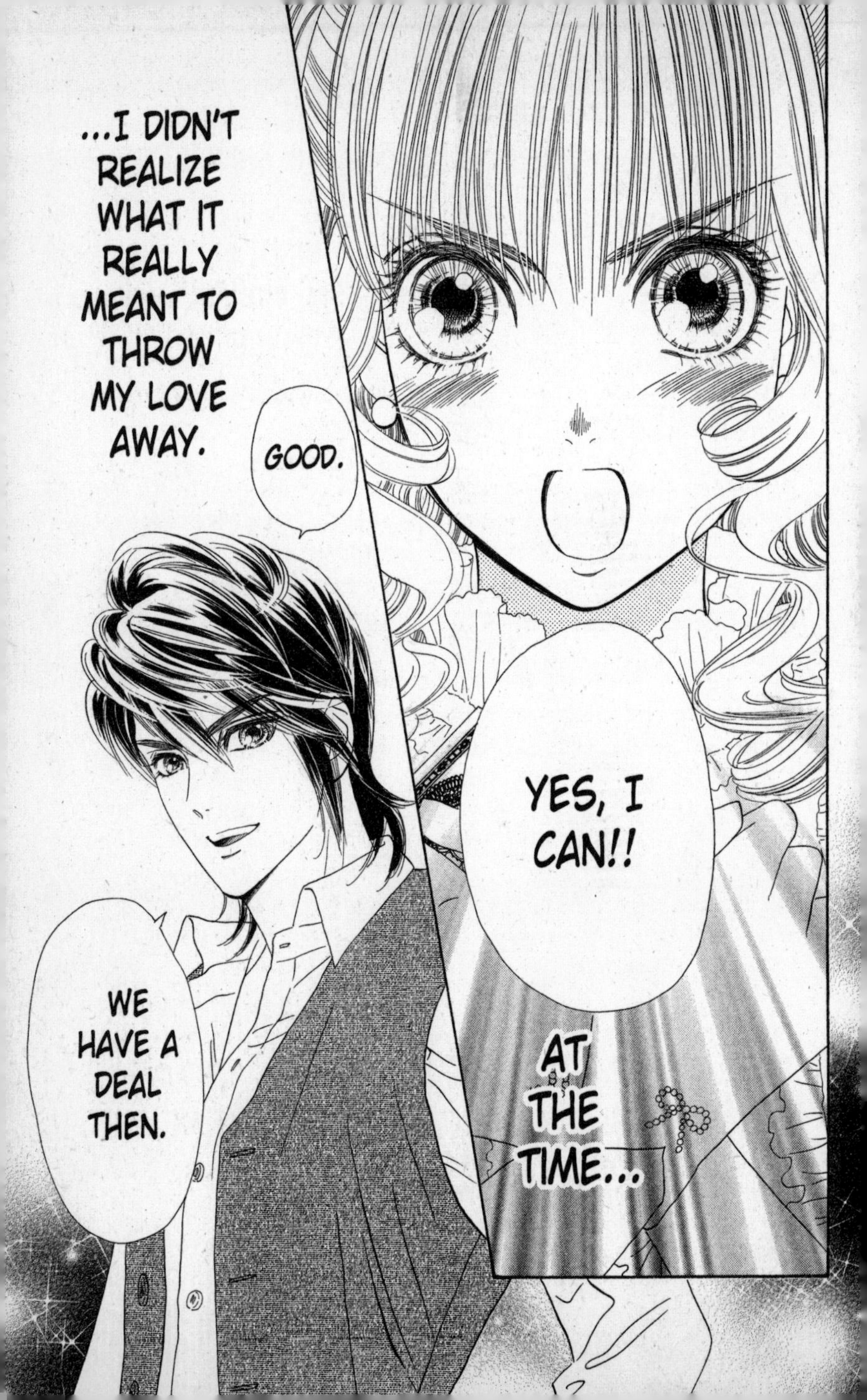
YES, I CAN!!
AT THE TIME...
...I DIDN'T REALIZE WHAT IT REALLY MEANT TO THROW MY LOVE AWAY.
GOOD.
WE HAVE A DEAL THEN.

GREETINGS

No.

HELLO! IT'S UE-RIN...!!

Date · ·

IT'S BEEN A WHILE SINCE MY LAST SERIES. FOR THIS NEW SERIES, I WAS GIVEN ONE REQUEST FROM THE CHIEF EDITOR: "I WANT TO READ SOMETHING GORGEOUS." GORGEOUS...?! MY LAST SERIES, *TAIL OF THE MOON*, WAS ABOUT THE LIVES OF NINJA WHO WORKED IN THE SHADOWS, AND THEY WERE FAR FROM BEING GORGEOUS. IS THAT WHY...?

WHENEVER I CREATE A MANGA STORY, I START BY COMING UP WITH ALL THE VARIOUS HUMAN RELATIONSHIPS IN IT. THEN I DECIDE ON A HISTORICAL PERIOD THOSE RELATIONSHIPS WOULD LOOK NATURAL IN. FOR *STEPPING ON ROSES*, I DIDN'T MIND WHAT PERIOD THE STORY WAS SET IN AS LONG AS THE FAKE MARRIAGE DIDN'T LOOK UNREAL.

I DECIDED TO CHOOSE THE SPECTACULAR TIME OF THE MEIJI ERA FOR ITS FEELING OF CIVILIZATION AND ENLIGHTENMENT SINCE I'D NEVER DRAWN THAT TIME PERIOD BEFORE. I CAME UP WITH THE MAIN CHARACTER, HER OPPOSITE PLAYER, HIS FRIEND, THE STUPID ELDER BROTHER AND THE CHILDREN FAIRLY QUICKLY. I WAS ALSO ABLE TO GET A ROUGH IDEA OF HOW THE STORY WOULD TURN OUT AFTER THIS AND THAT.

← THIS WAS THE TOUGH PART.

WE DECIDED WHAT ISSUE OF THE MAGAZINE THE SERIES WOULD START IN, AND I THOUGHT, "OKAY, I'M READY FOR ANYTHING..." BUT THEN I NOTICED SOMETHING IMPORTANT!

"I HAVEN'T COME UP WITH THE TITLE YET...!!"
"I HAVEN'T DECIDED ON THE NAMES OF THE CHARACTERS YET EITHER...!!"

THE STORY IS IMPORTANT, BUT THE SERIES TITLE AND THE NAMES OF THE CHARACTERS ARE EQUALLY IMPORTANT!!
SO WHAT DID UE-RIN DO DURING THIS SITUATION?!

TO BE CONTINUED...

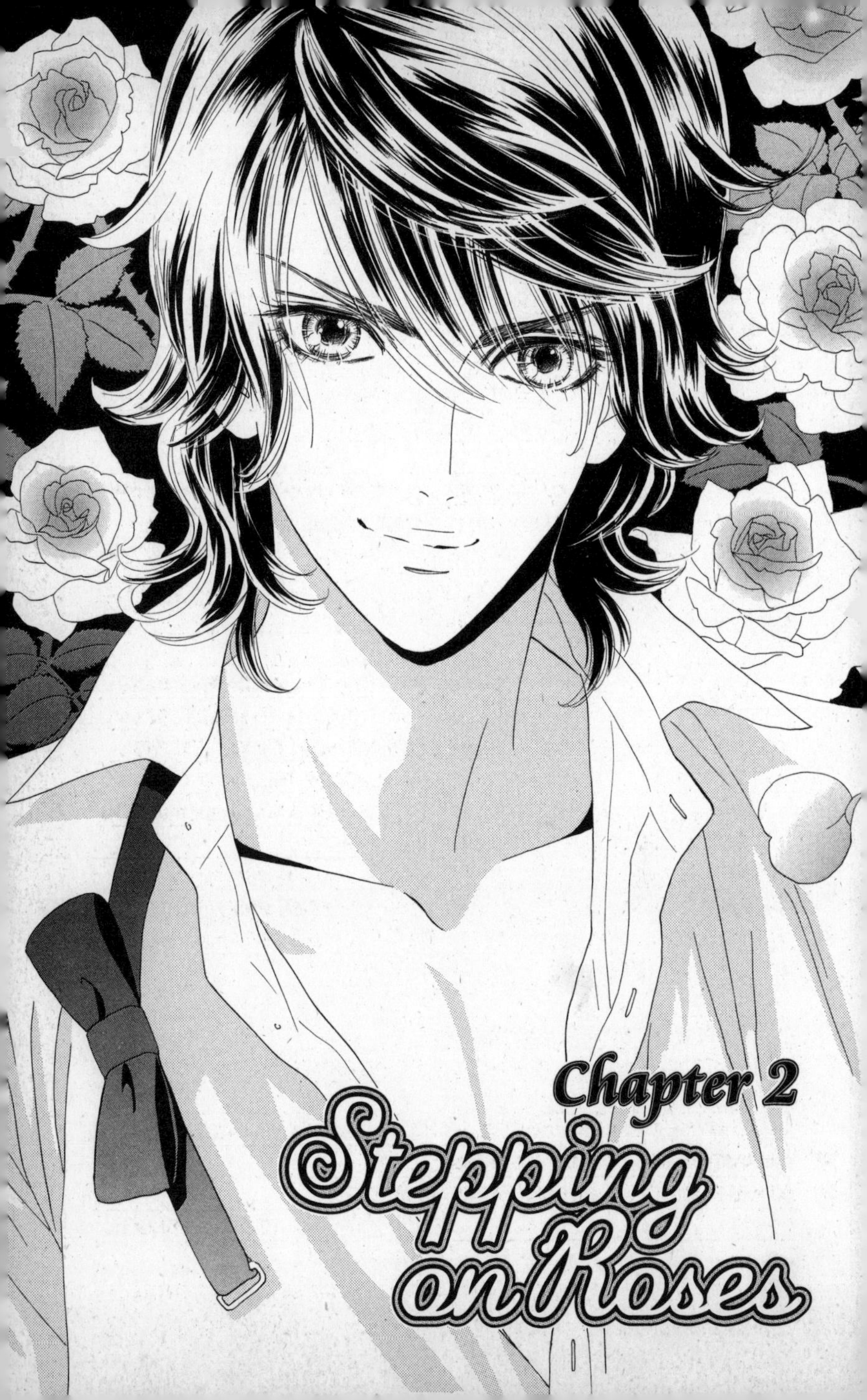
Chapter 2
Stepping on Roses

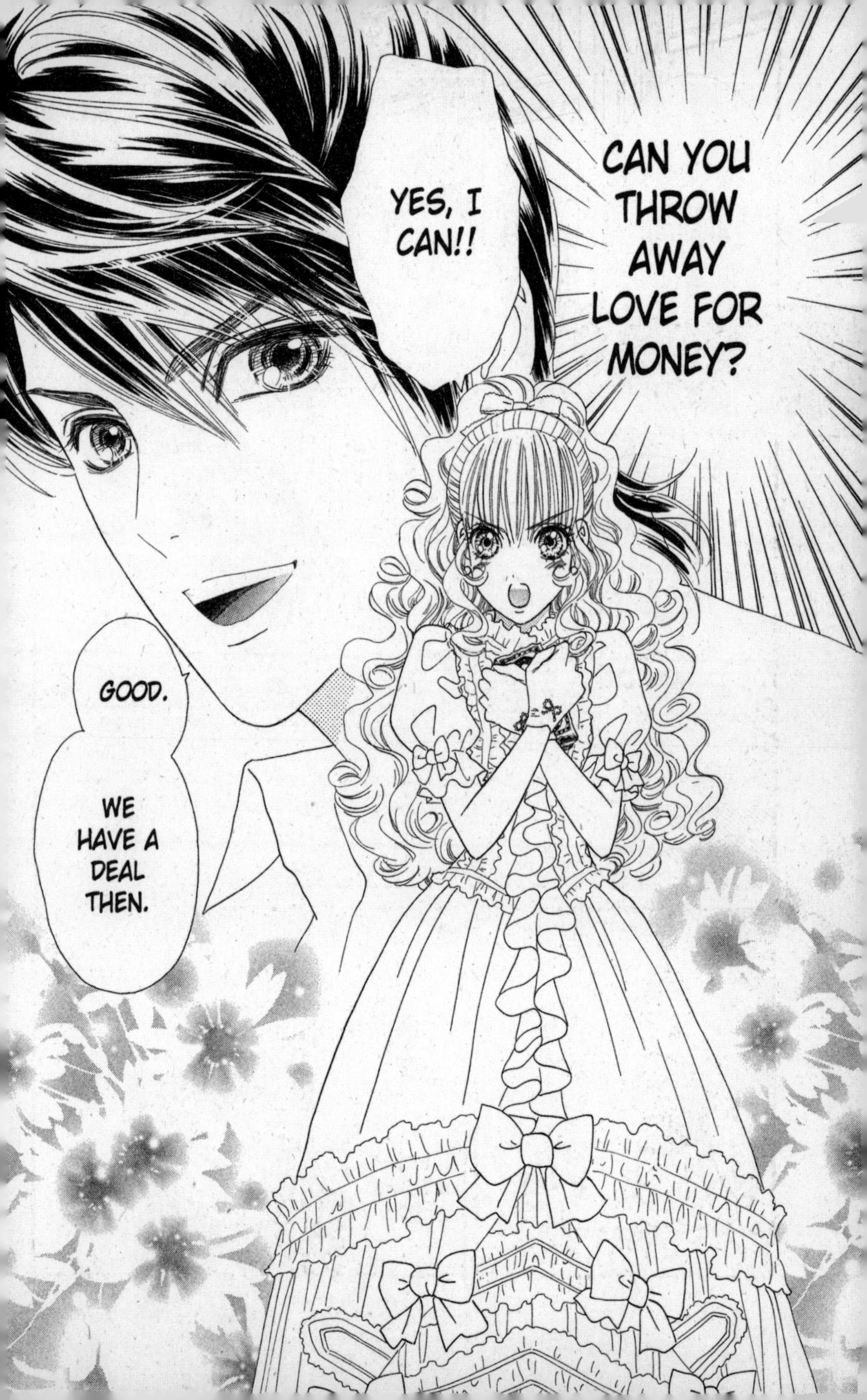
CAN YOU THROW AWAY LOVE FOR MONEY?
YES, I CAN!!
GOOD.
WE HAVE A DEAL THEN.

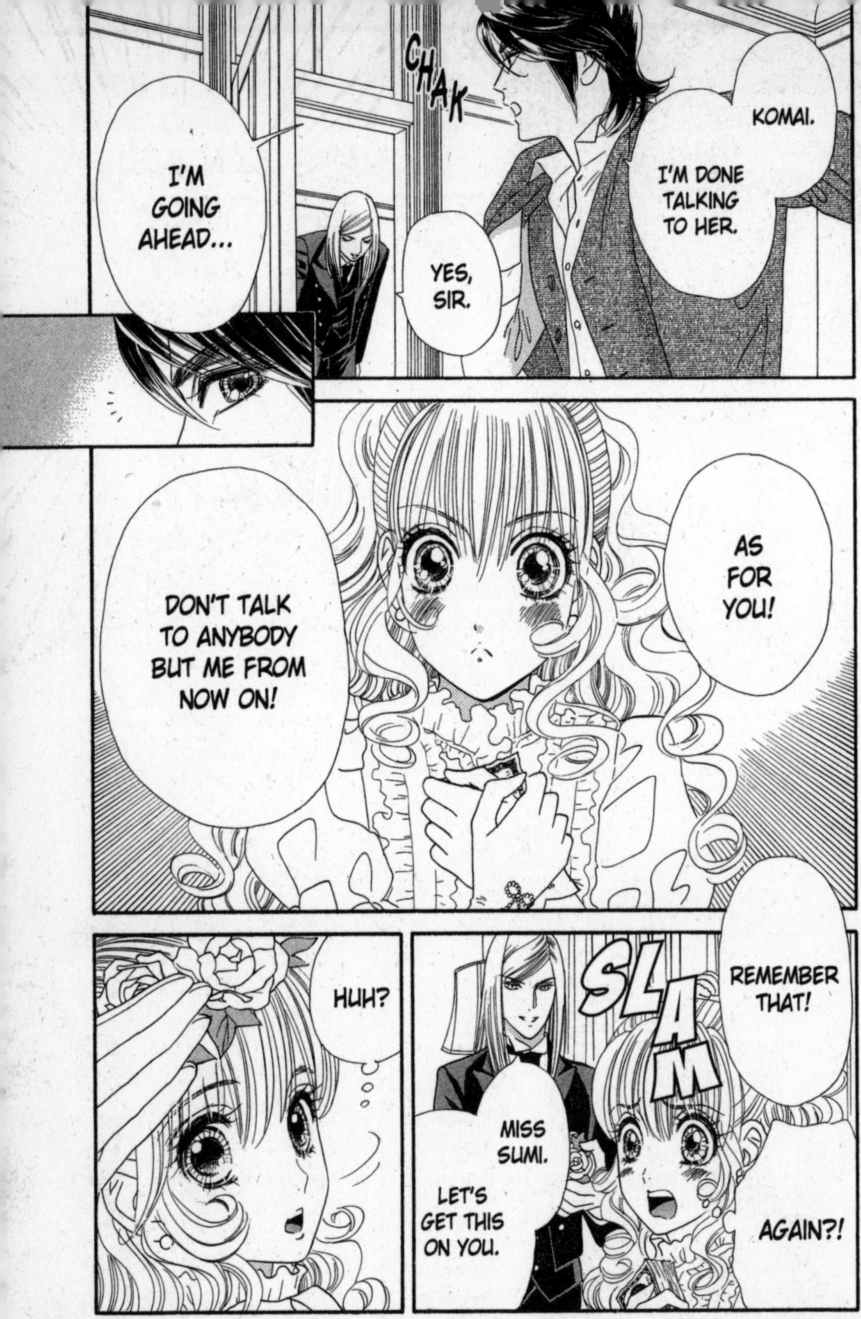
CHAK
KOMAI.
I'M DONE TALKING TO HER.
YES, SIR.
I'M GOING AHEAD...
AS FOR YOU!
DON'T TALK TO ANYBODY BUT ME FROM NOW ON!
REMEMBER THAT!
SLAM
MISS SUMI.
LET'S GET THIS ON YOU.
AGAIN?!
HUH?

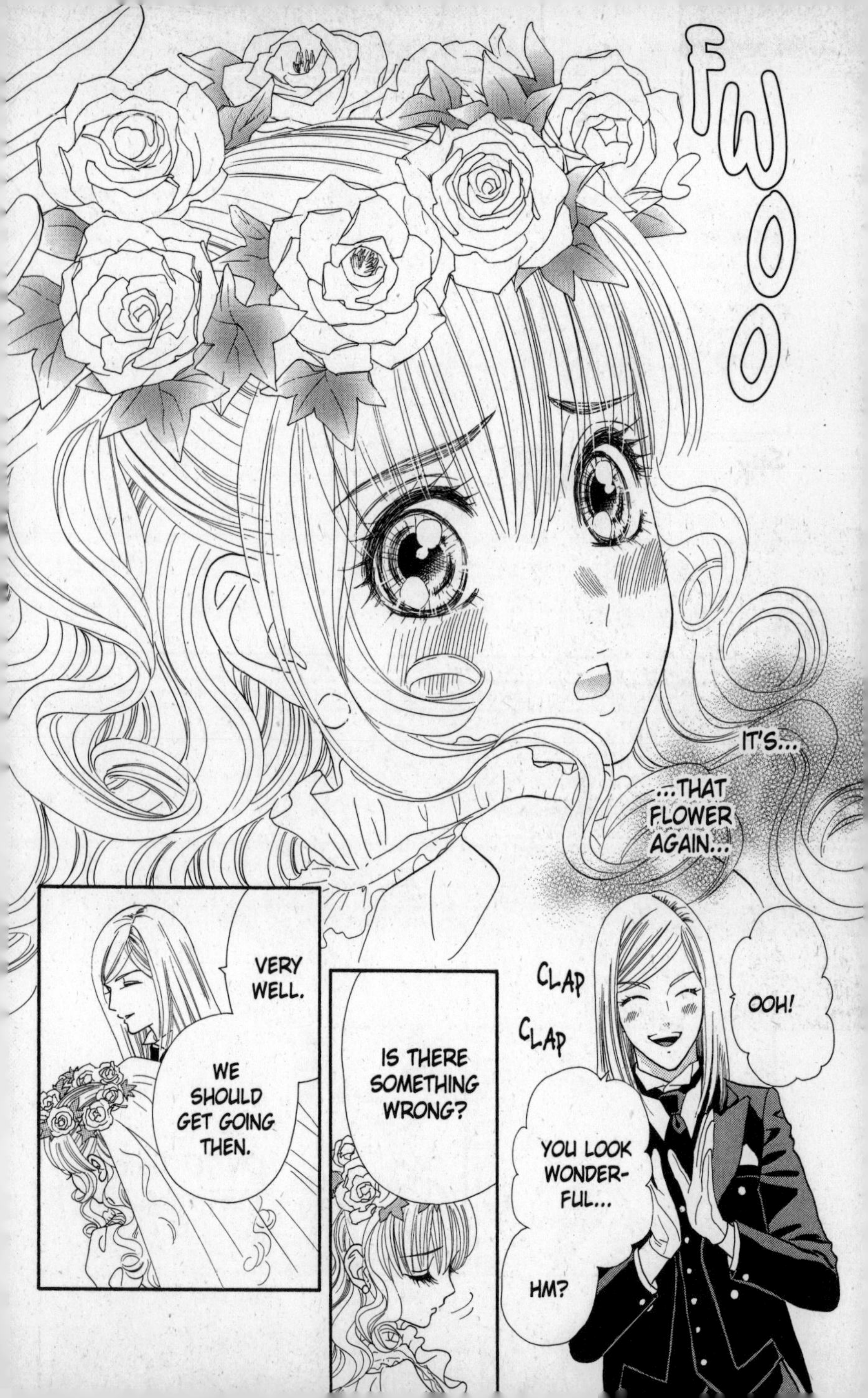
FWOO
IT'S...
...THAT FLOWER AGAIN...
OOH!
CLAP CLAP
YOU LOOK WONDERFUL...
HM?
IS THERE SOMETHING WRONG?
VERY WELL.
WE SHOULD GET GOING THEN.

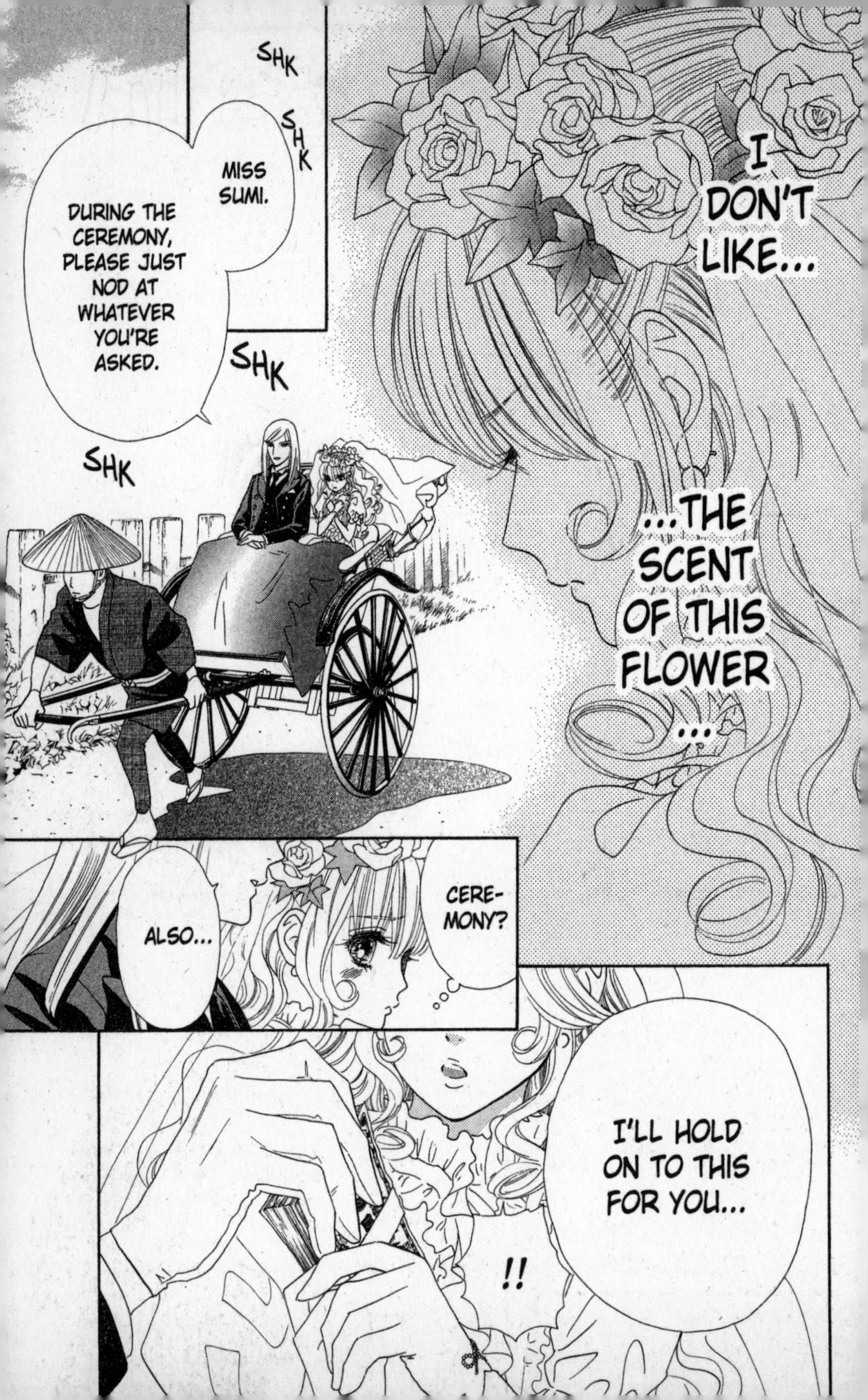

I DON'T LIKE...
...THE SCENT OF THIS FLOWER...
SHK
SHK
MISS SUMI.
DURING THE CEREMONY, PLEASE JUST NOD AT WHATEVER YOU'RE ASKED.
SHK
SHK
CERE-MONY?
ALSO...
I'LL HOLD ON TO THIS FOR YOU...
!!

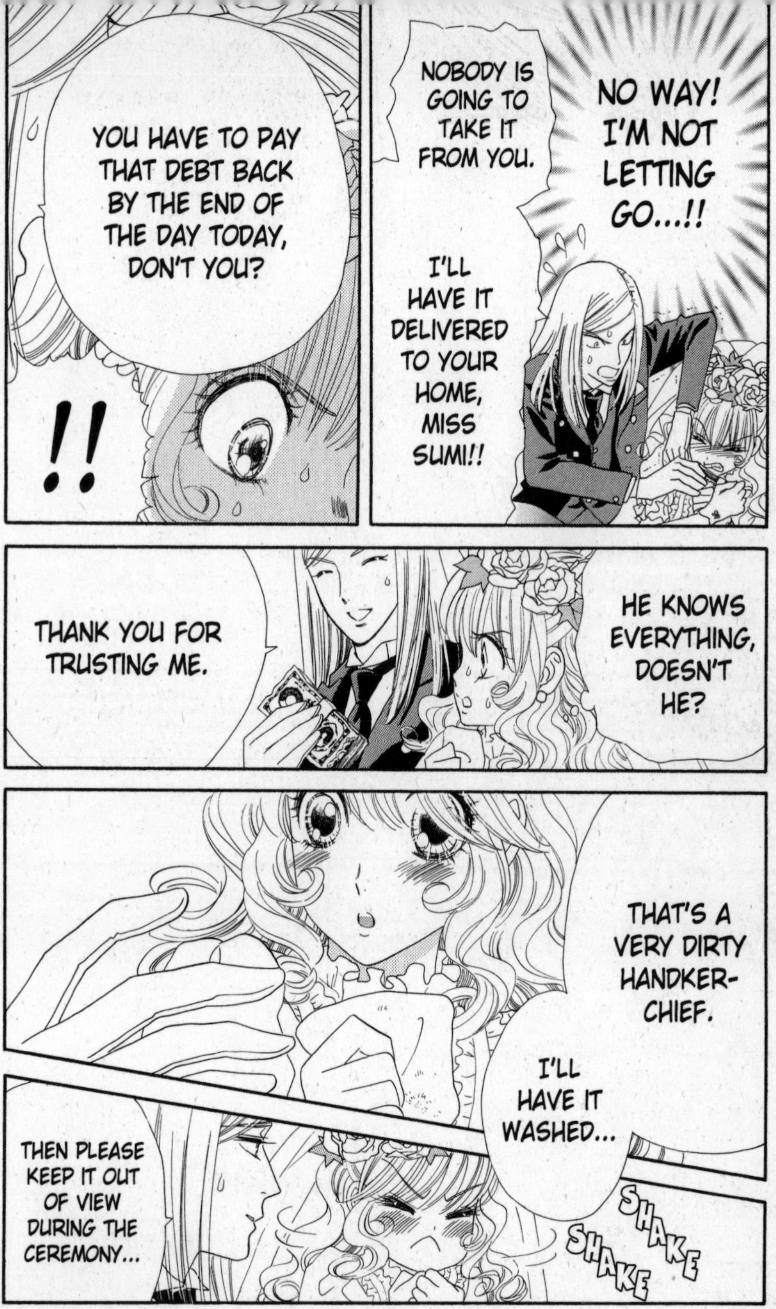
NO WAY! I'M NOT LETTING GO...!!
NOBODY IS GOING TO TAKE IT FROM YOU.
I'LL HAVE IT DELIVERED TO YOUR HOME, MISS SUMI!!
YOU HAVE TO PAY THAT DEBT BACK BY THE END OF THE DAY TODAY, DON'T YOU?
!!
HE KNOWS EVERYTHING, DOESN'T HE?
THANK YOU FOR TRUSTING ME.
THAT'S A VERY DIRTY HANDKER-CHIEF.
I'LL HAVE IT WASHED...
SHAKE
SHAKE
THEN PLEASE KEEP IT OUT OF VIEW DURING THE CEREMONY...

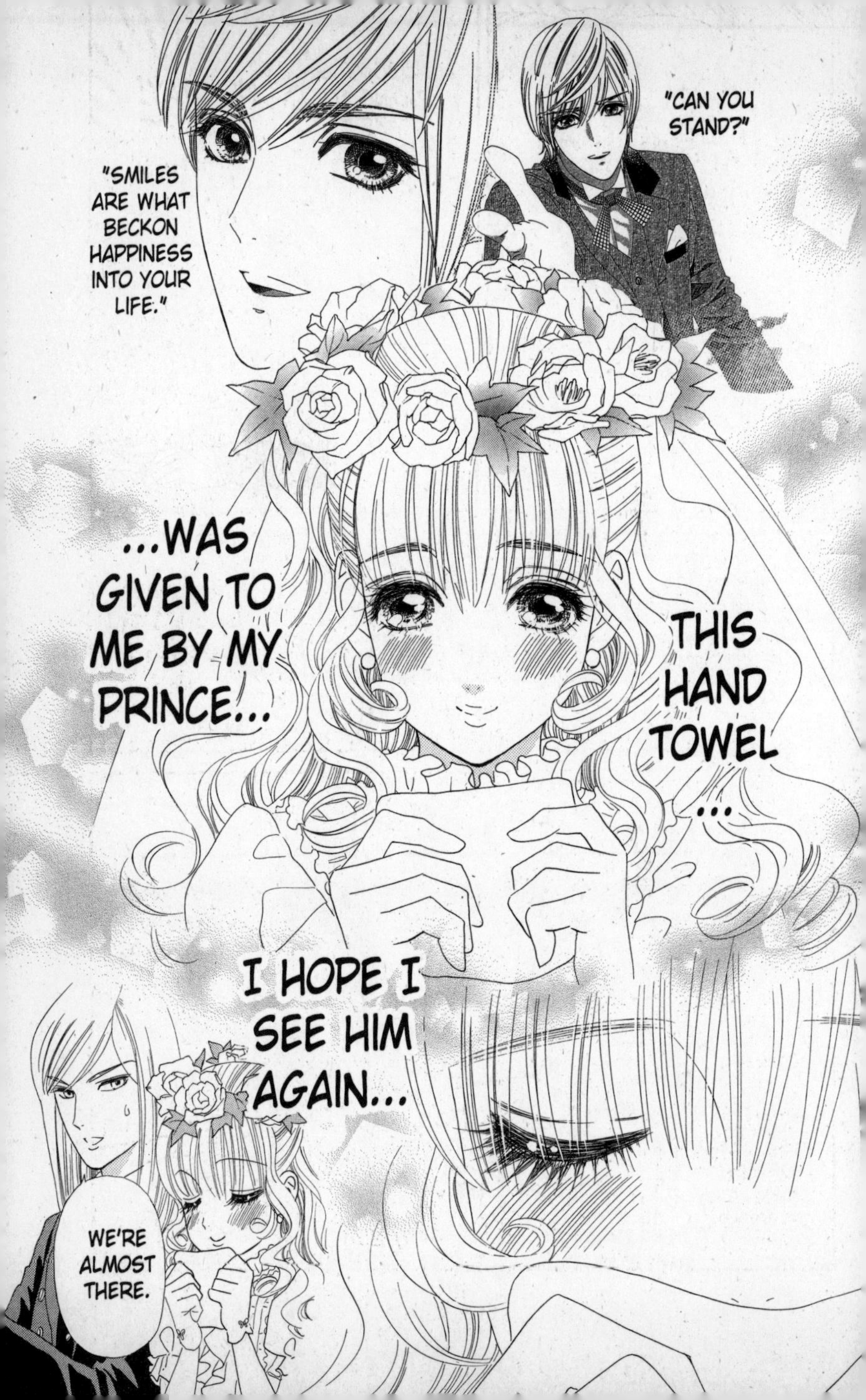
"CAN YOU STAND?"
"SMILES ARE WHAT BECKON HAPPINESS INTO YOUR LIFE."
THIS HAND TOWEL...
...WAS GIVEN TO ME BY MY PRINCE...
I HOPE I SEE HIM AGAIN...
WE'RE ALMOST THERE.

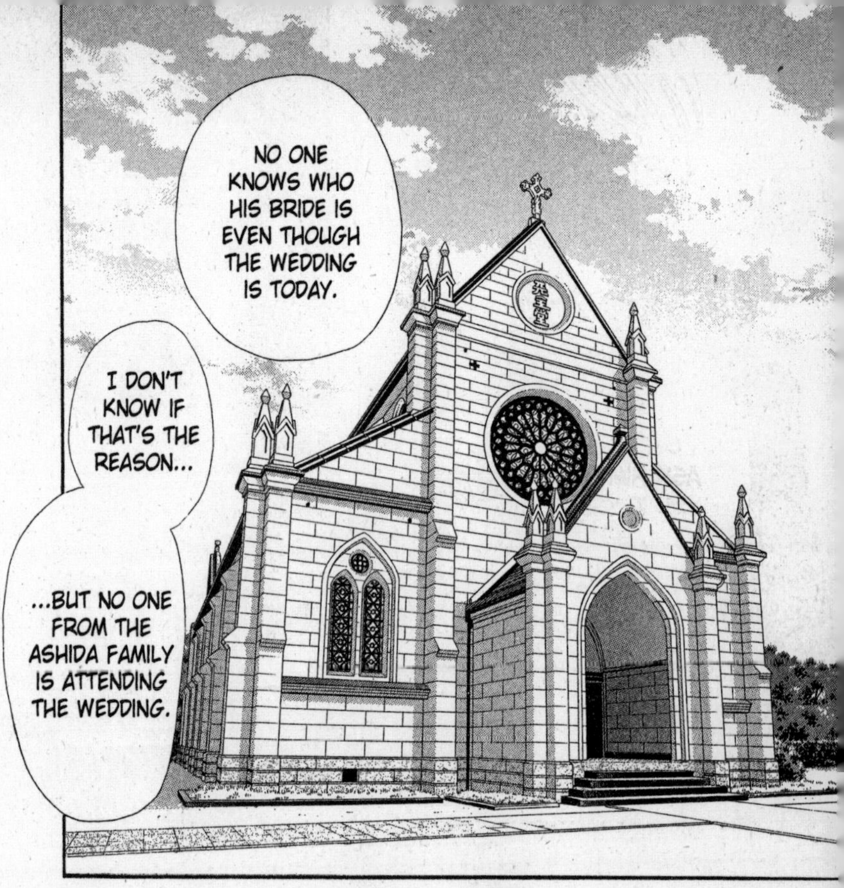
NO ONE KNOWS WHO HIS BRIDE IS EVEN THOUGH THE WEDDING IS TODAY.
I DON'T KNOW IF THAT'S THE REASON...
...BUT NO ONE FROM THE ASHIDA FAMILY IS ATTENDING THE WEDDING.
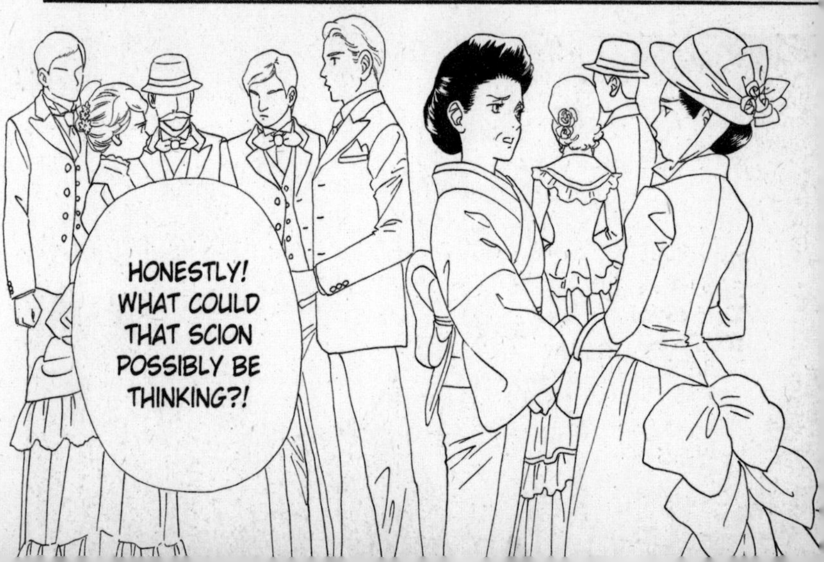
HONESTLY! WHAT COULD THAT SCION POSSIBLY BE THINKING?!

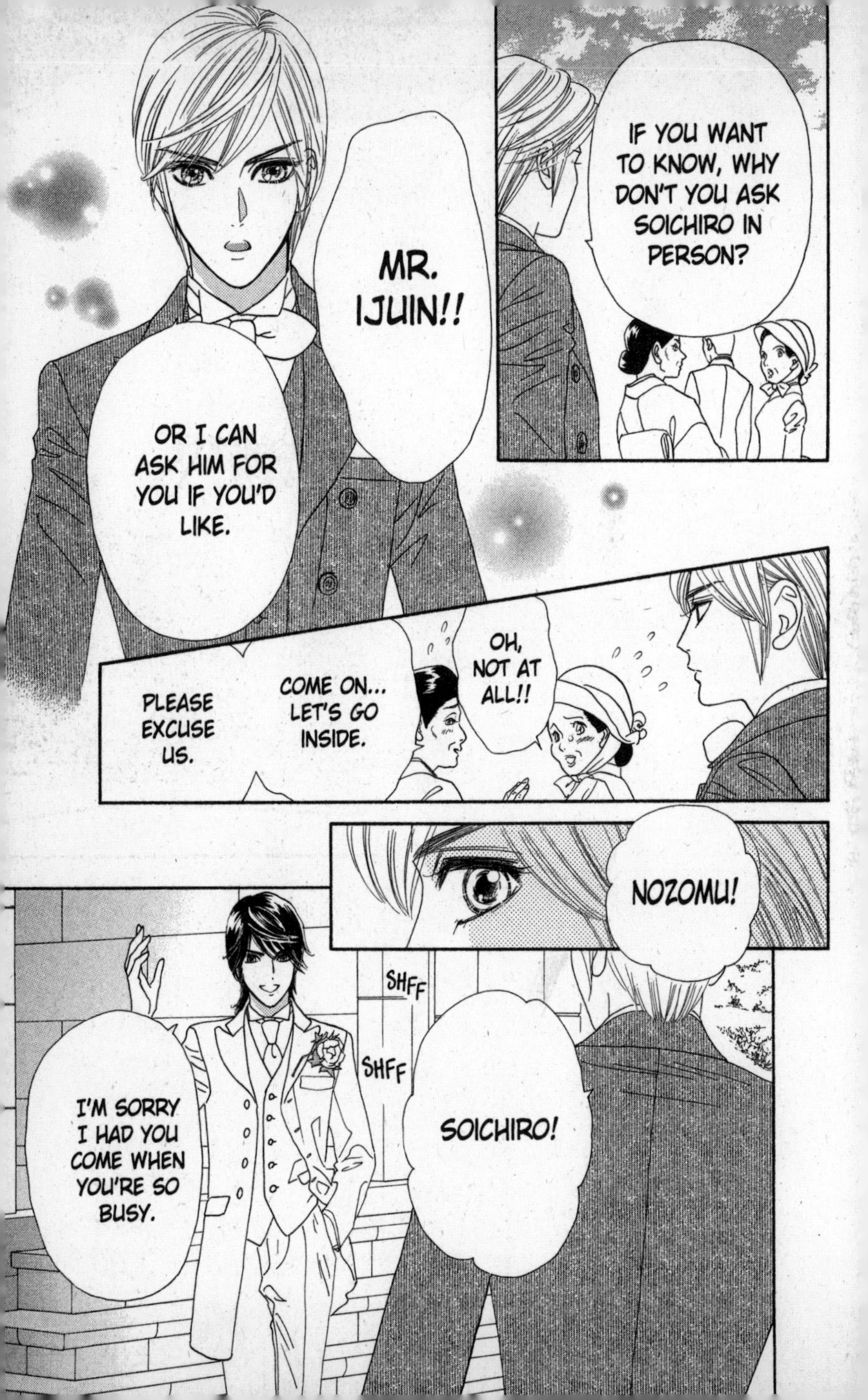
IF YOU WANT TO KNOW, WHY DON'T YOU ASK SOICHIRO IN PERSON?
MR. IJUIN!!
OR I CAN ASK HIM FOR YOU IF YOU'D LIKE.
OH, NOT AT ALL!!
COME ON... LET'S GO INSIDE.
PLEASE EXCUSE US.
NOZOMU!
SOICHIRO!
SHFF
SHFF
I'M SORRY I HAD YOU COME WHEN YOU'RE SO BUSY.

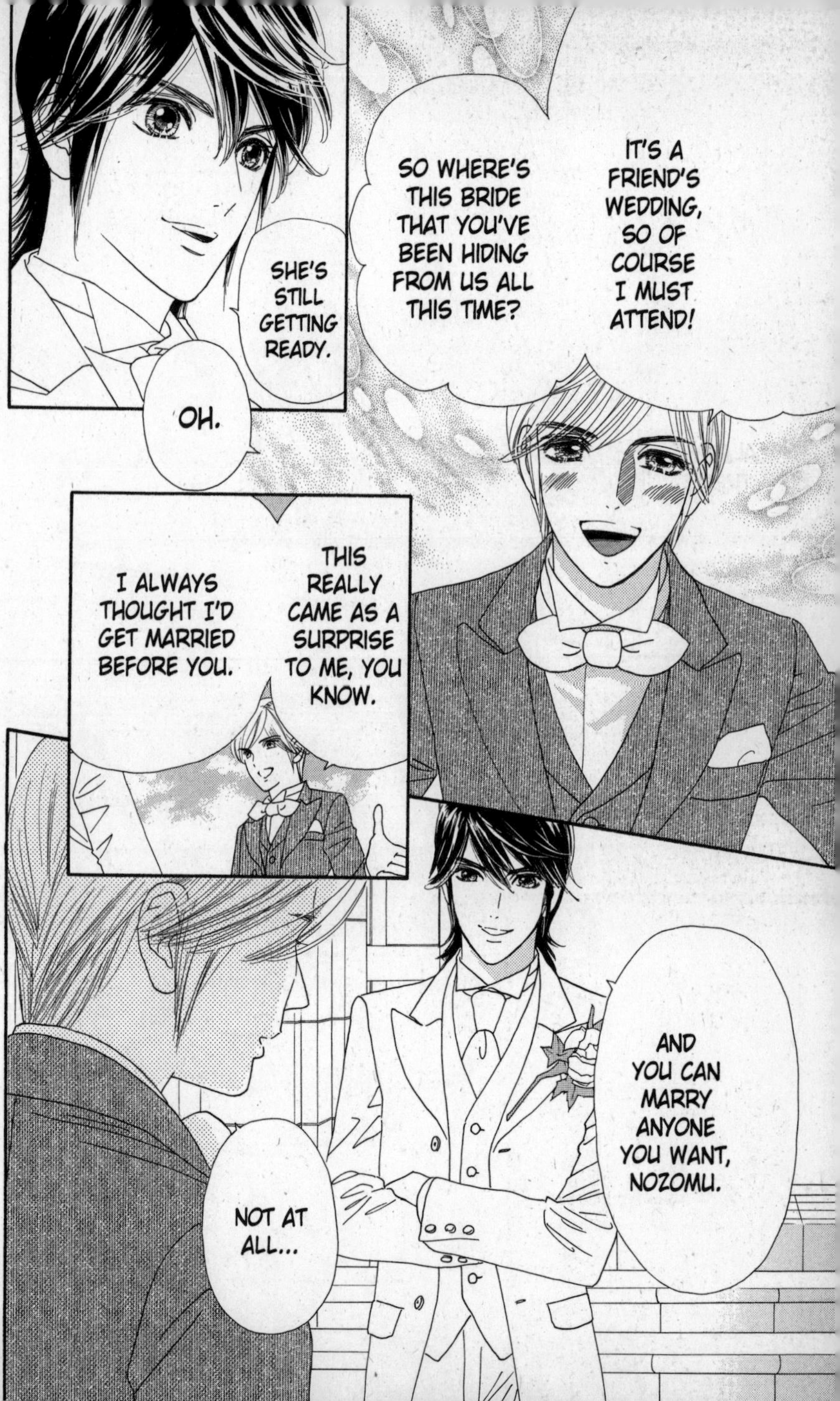
IT'S A FRIEND'S WEDDING, SO OF COURSE I MUST ATTEND!
SO WHERE'S THIS BRIDE THAT YOU'VE BEEN HIDING FROM US ALL THIS TIME?
SHE'S STILL GETTING READY.
OH.
THIS REALLY CAME AS A SURPRISE TO ME, YOU KNOW.
I ALWAYS THOUGHT I'D GET MARRIED BEFORE YOU.
AND YOU CAN MARRY ANYONE YOU WANT, NOZOMU.
NOT AT ALL...

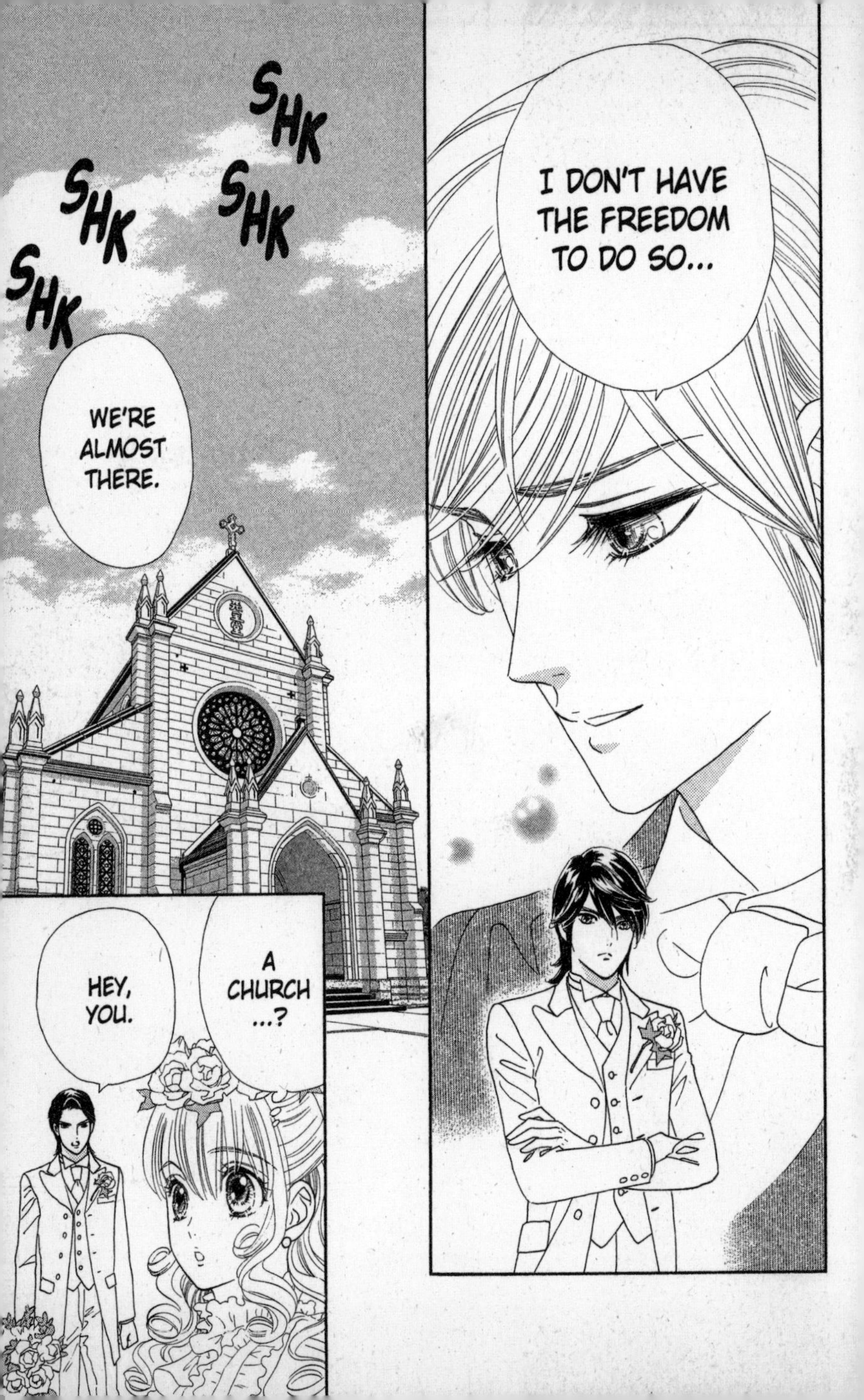
I DON'T HAVE THE FREEDOM TO DO SO...
SHK
SHK
SHK
SHK
WE'RE ALMOST THERE.
A CHURCH ...?
HEY, YOU.

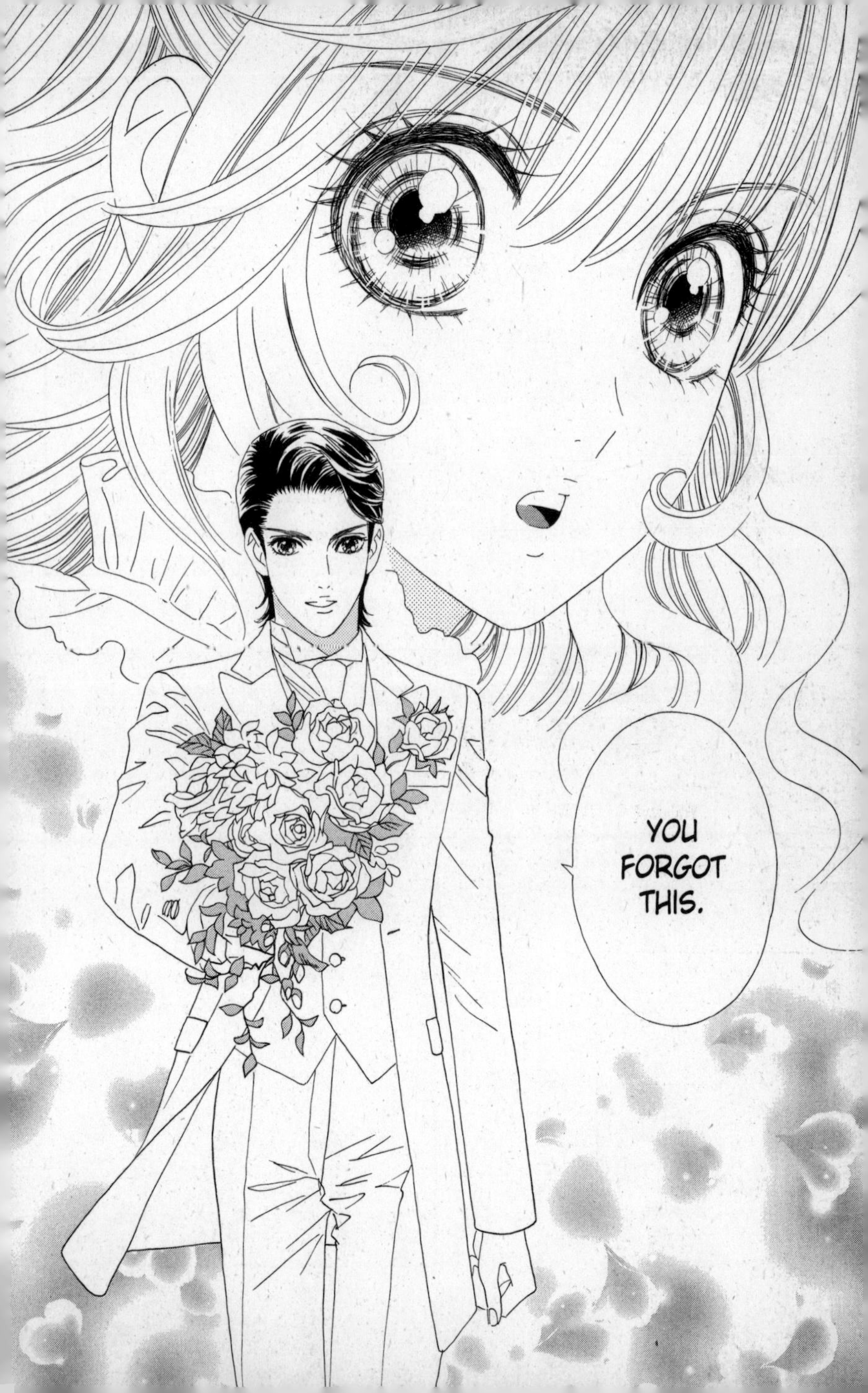
YOU FORGOT THIS.

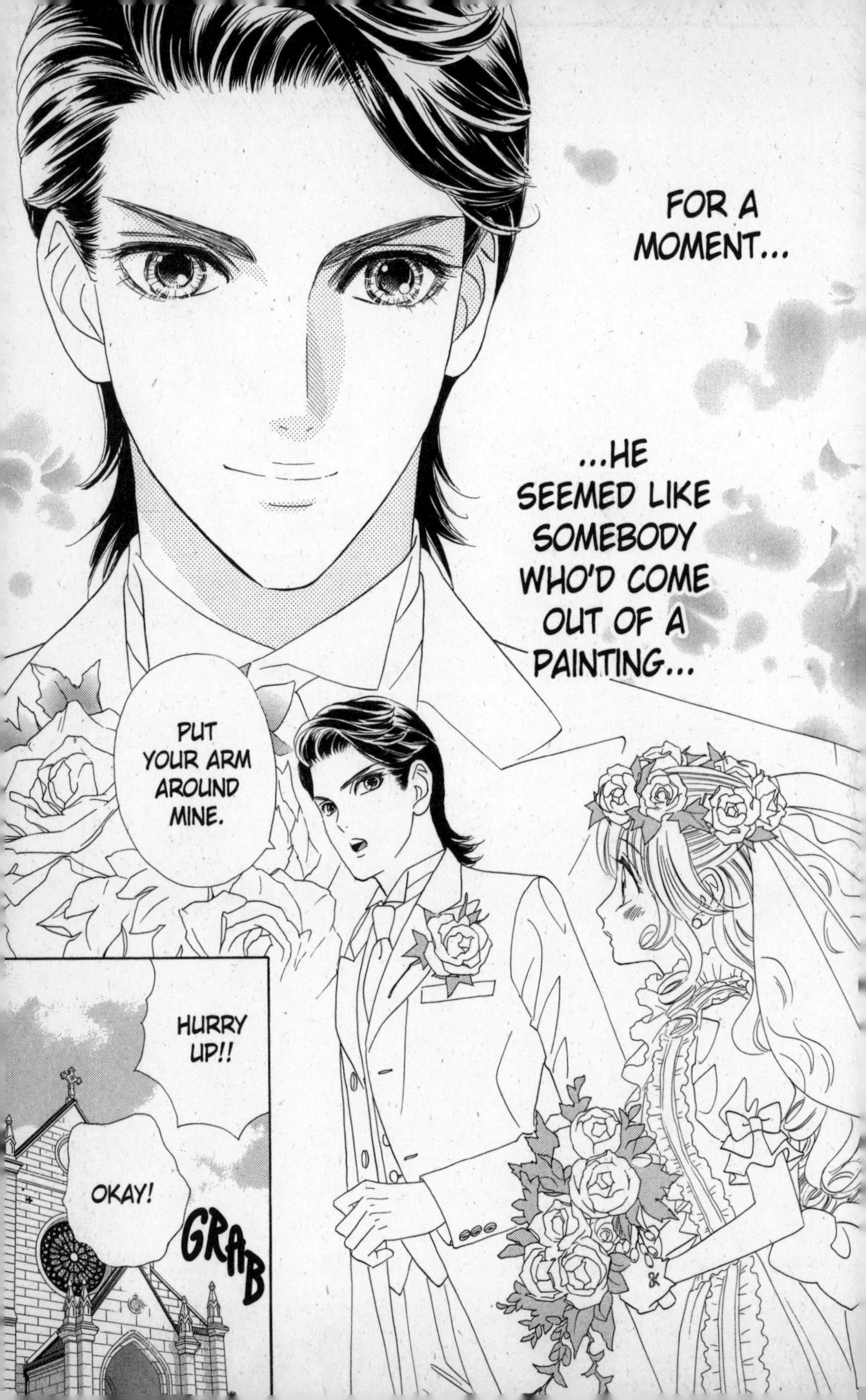
FOR A MOMENT...
...HE SEEMED LIKE SOMEBODY WHO'D COME OUT OF A PAINTING...
PUT YOUR ARM AROUND MINE.
HURRY UP!!
OKAY!
GRAB

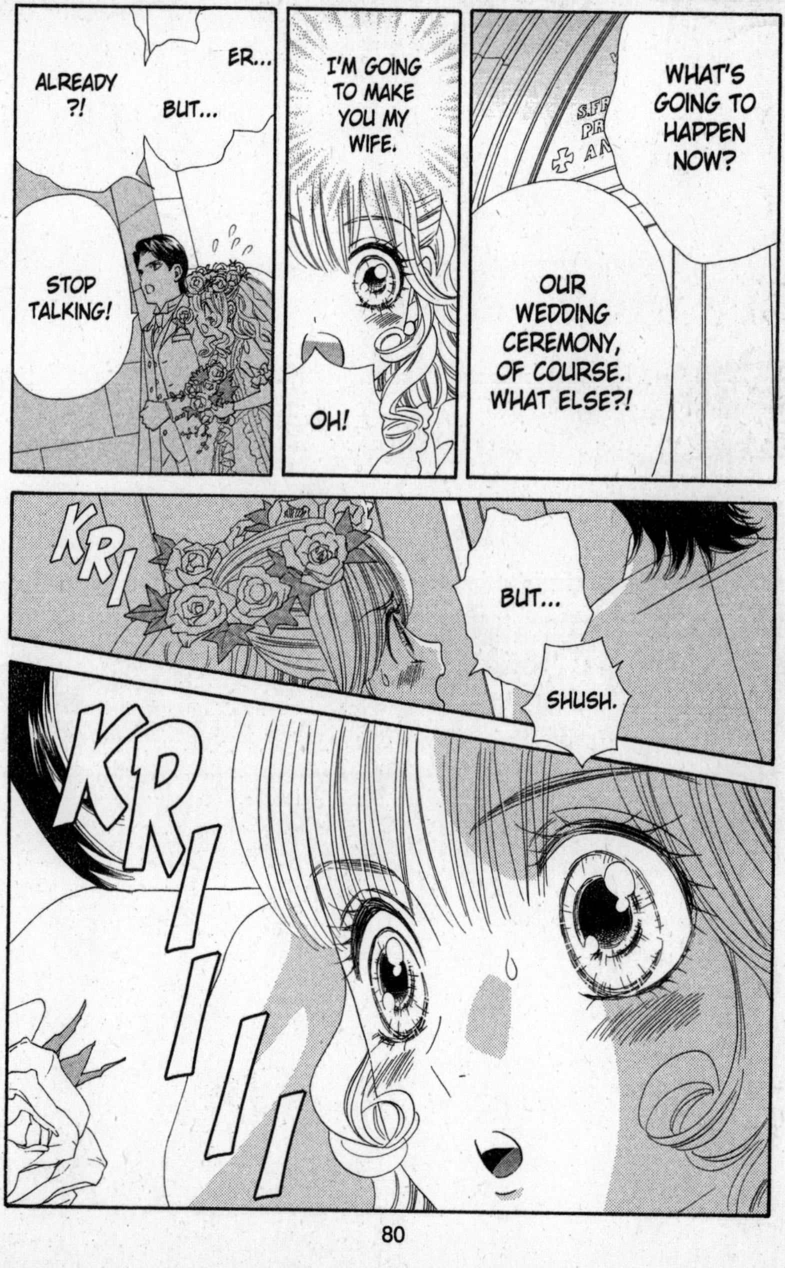
WHAT'S GOING TO HAPPEN NOW?
OUR WEDDING CEREMONY, OF COURSE. WHAT ELSE?!
I'M GOING TO MAKE YOU MY WIFE.
OH!
ER...
BUT...
ALREADY ?!
STOP TALKING!
BUT...
KRI
SHUSH.
KRIIII

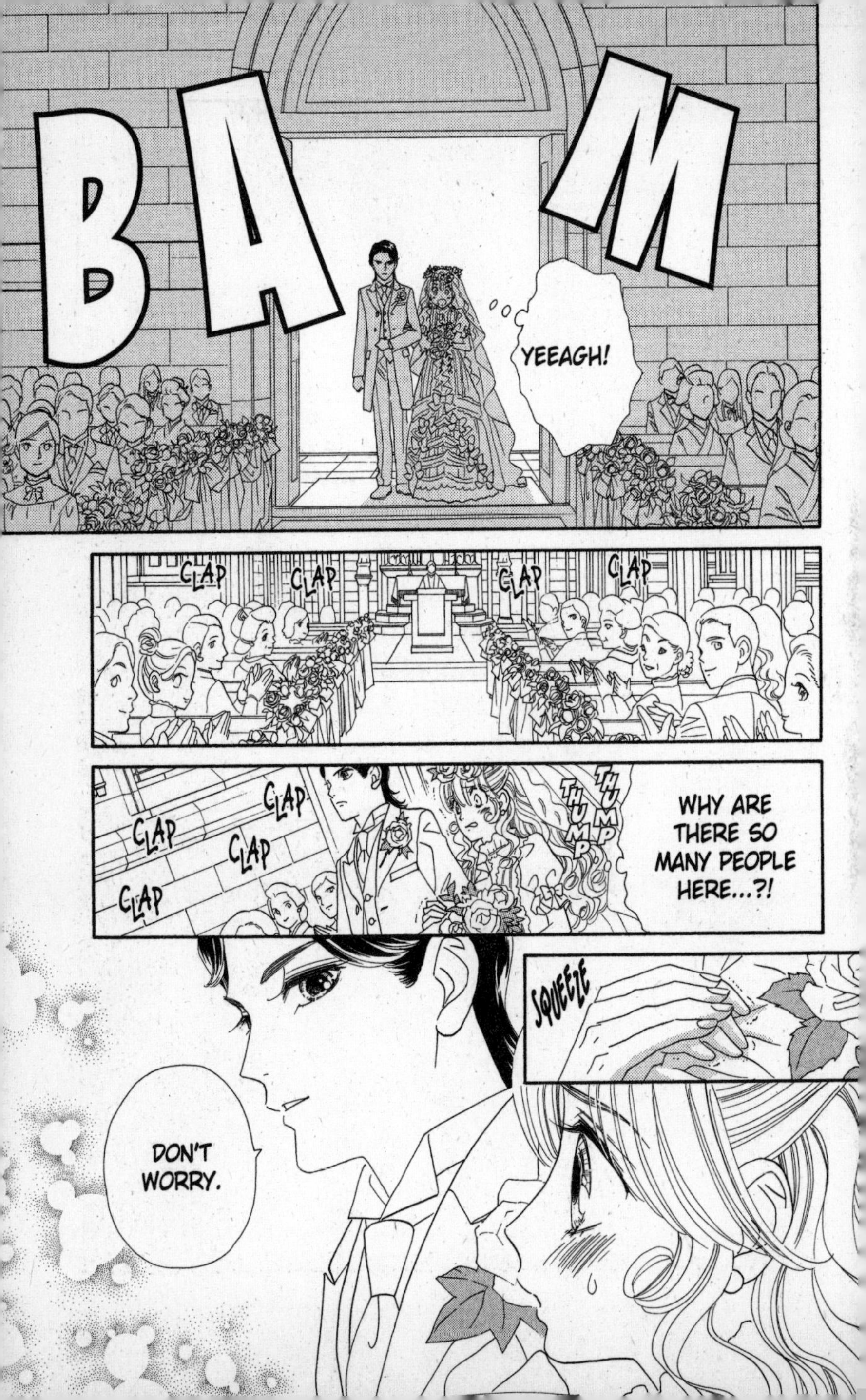
BAM
YEEAGH!
CLAP
CLAP
CLAP
CLAP
WHY ARE THERE SO MANY PEOPLE HERE...?!
THUMP
THUMP
CLAP
CLAP
CLAP
CLAP
SQUEEZE
DON'T WORRY.

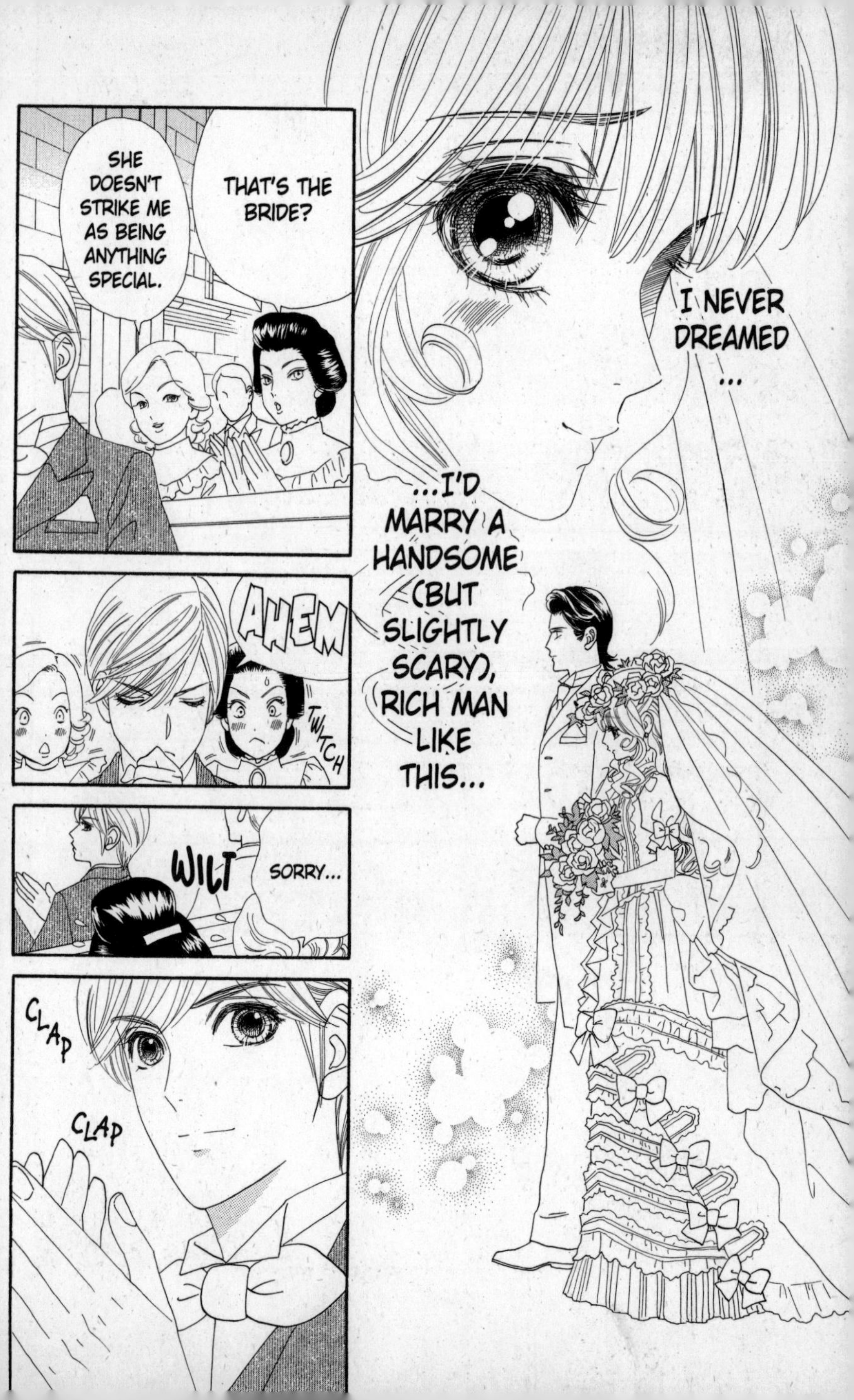
I NEVER DREAMED ...
...I'D MARRY A HANDSOME (BUT SLIGHTLY SCARY), RICH MAN LIKE THIS...
THAT'S THE BRIDE?
SHE DOESN'T STRIKE ME AS BEING ANYTHING SPECIAL.
AHEM
TWITCH
SORRY...
WILT
CLAP
CLAP

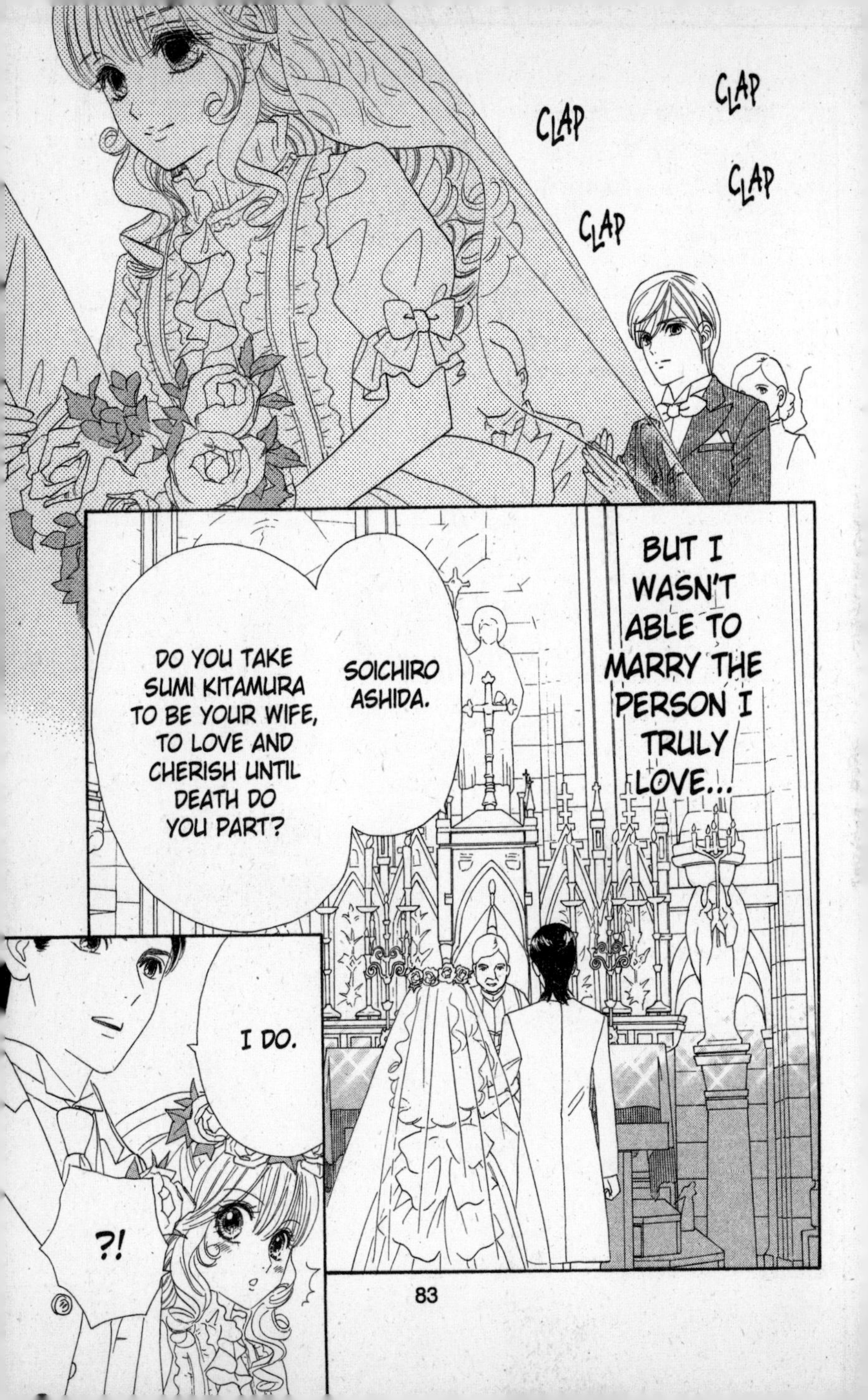
CLAP
CLAP
CLAP
CLAP
BUT I WASN'T ABLE TO MARRY THE PERSON I TRULY LOVE...
SOICHIRO ASHIDA. DO YOU TAKE SUMI KITAMURA TO BE YOUR WIFE, TO LOVE AND CHERISH UNTIL DEATH DO YOU PART?
I DO.
?!

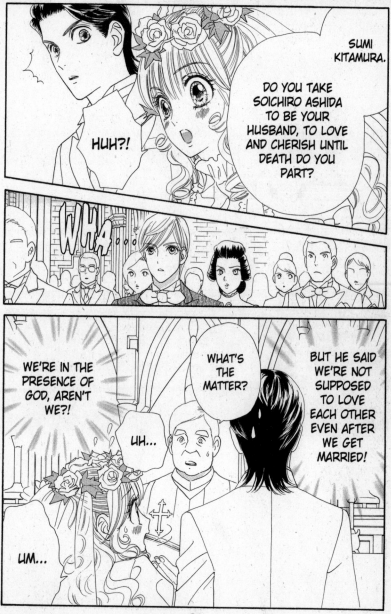

SUMI KITAMURA.
DO YOU TAKE SOICHIRO ASHIDA TO BE YOUR HUSBAND, TO LOVE AND CHERISH UNTIL DEATH DO YOU PART?
HUH?!
WHA...
BUT HE SAID WE'RE NOT SUPPOSED TO LOVE EACH OTHER EVEN AFTER WE GET MARRIED!
WHAT'S THE MATTER?
WE'RE IN THE PRESENCE OF GOD, AREN'T WE?!
UH...
UM...

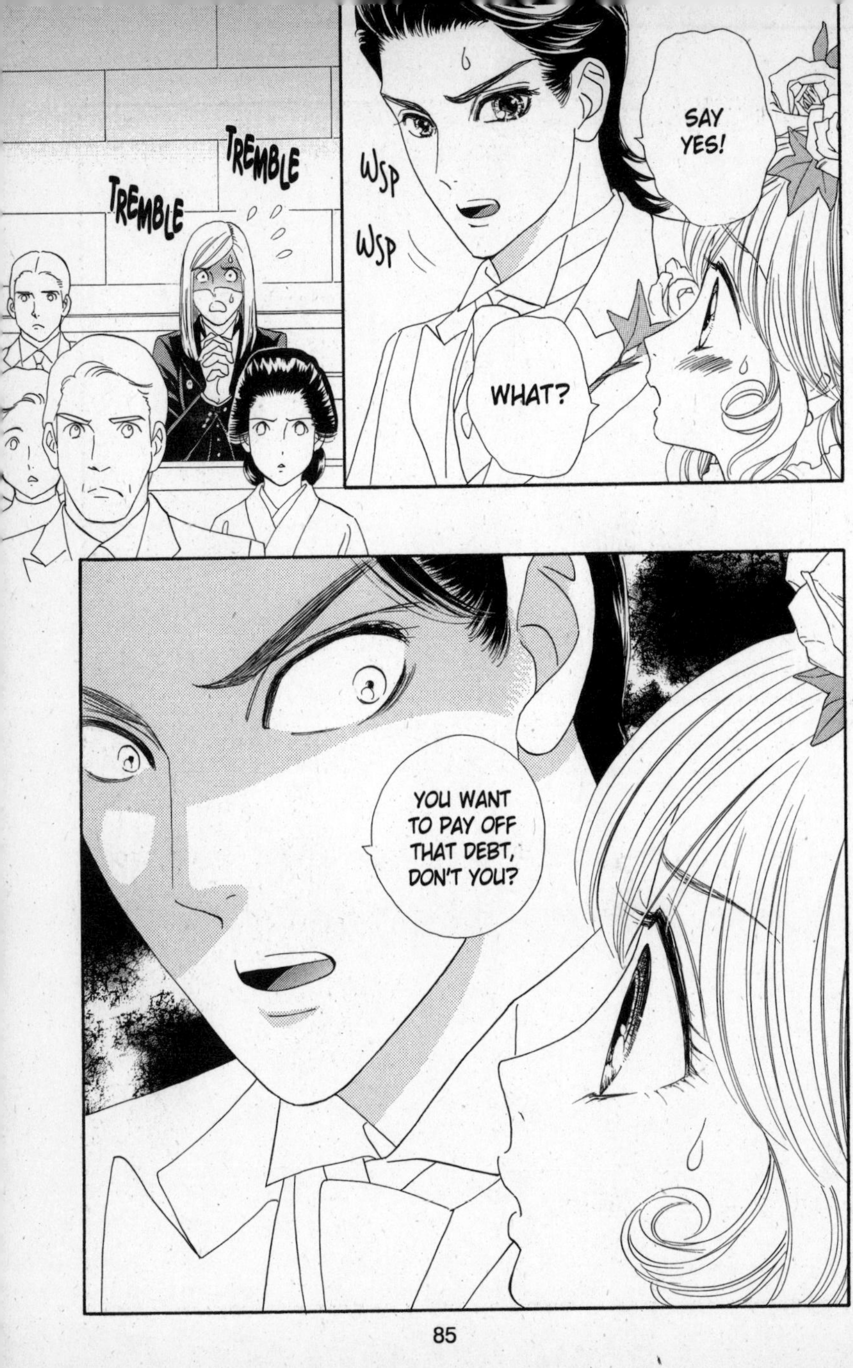
SAY YES!
WSP
WSP
WHAT?
TREMBLE
TREMBLE
YOU WANT TO PAY OFF THAT DEBT, DON'T YOU?

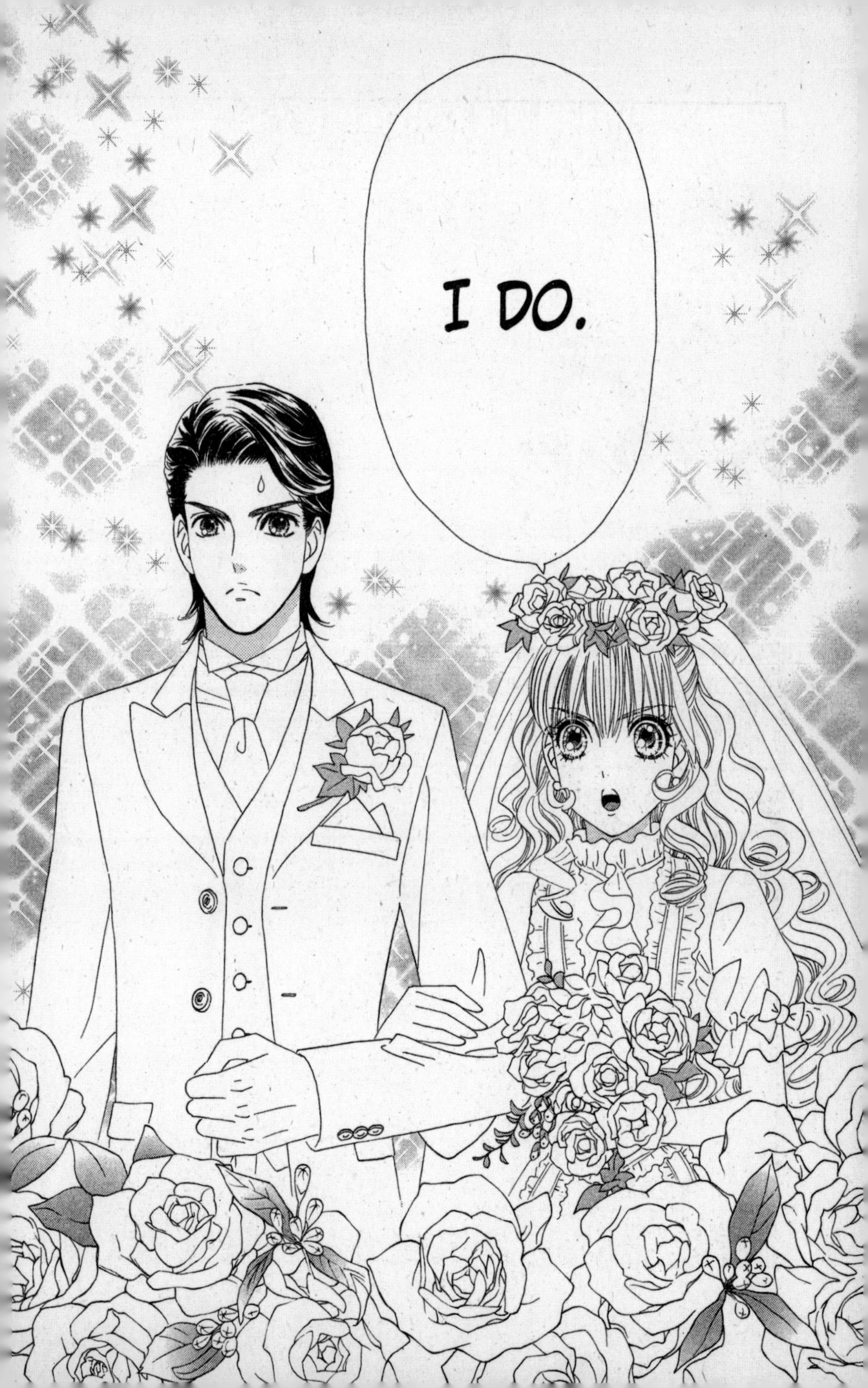
I DO.

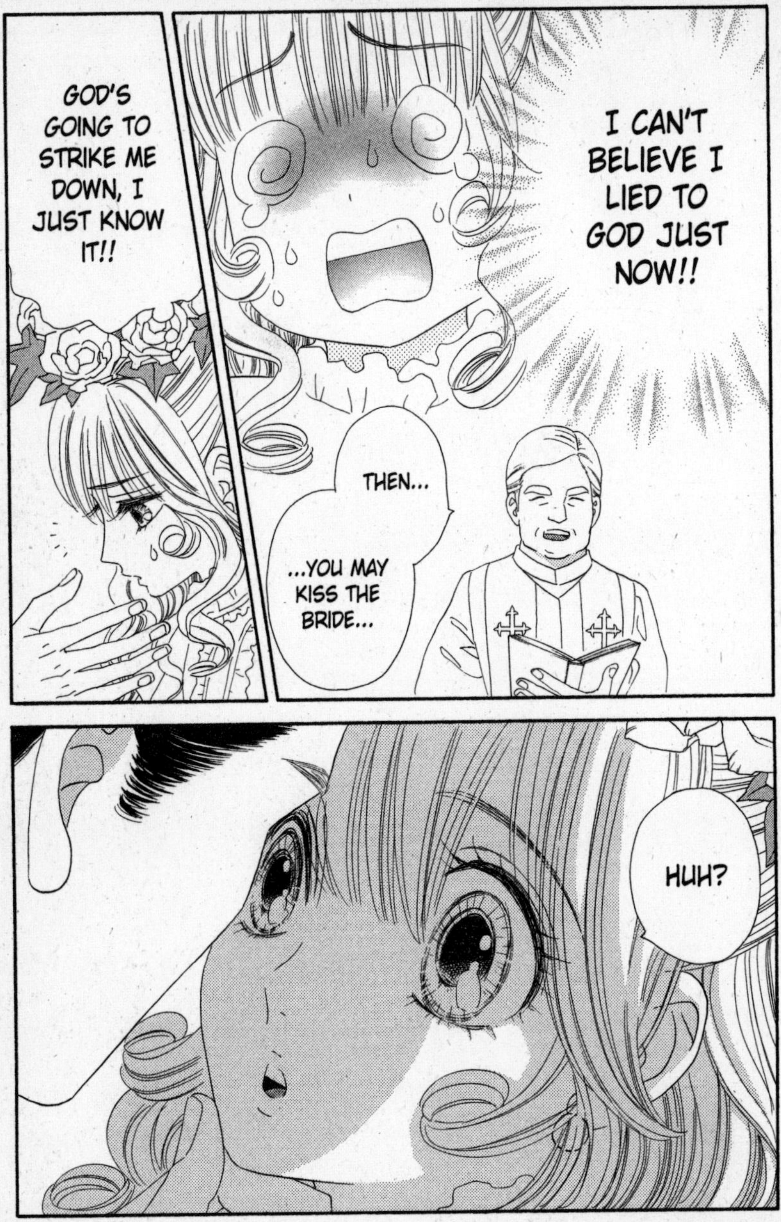
I CAN'T BELIEVE I LIED TO GOD JUST NOW!!
THEN...
...YOU MAY KISS THE BRIDE...
GOD'S GOING TO STRIKE ME DOWN, I JUST KNOW IT!!
HUH?

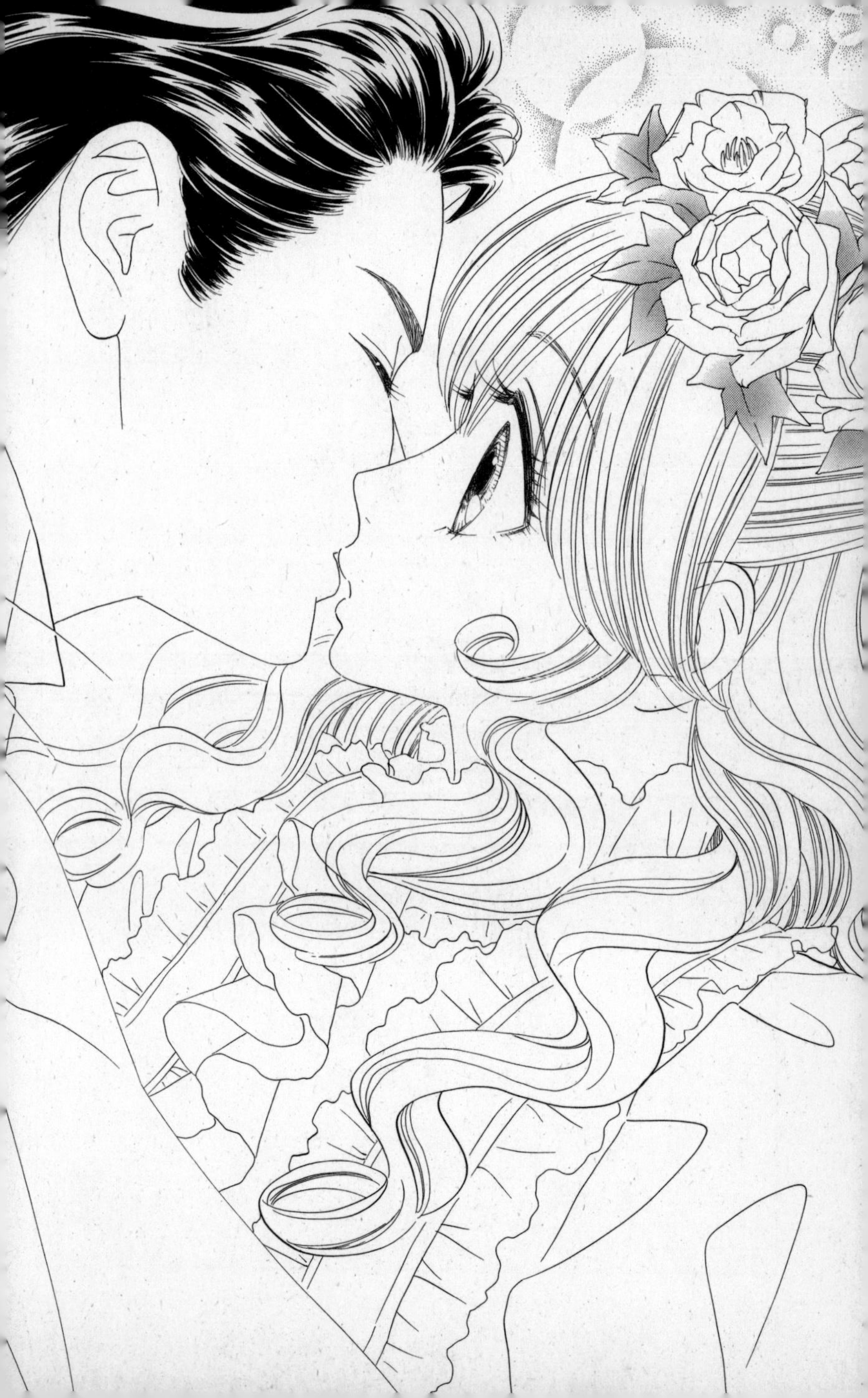

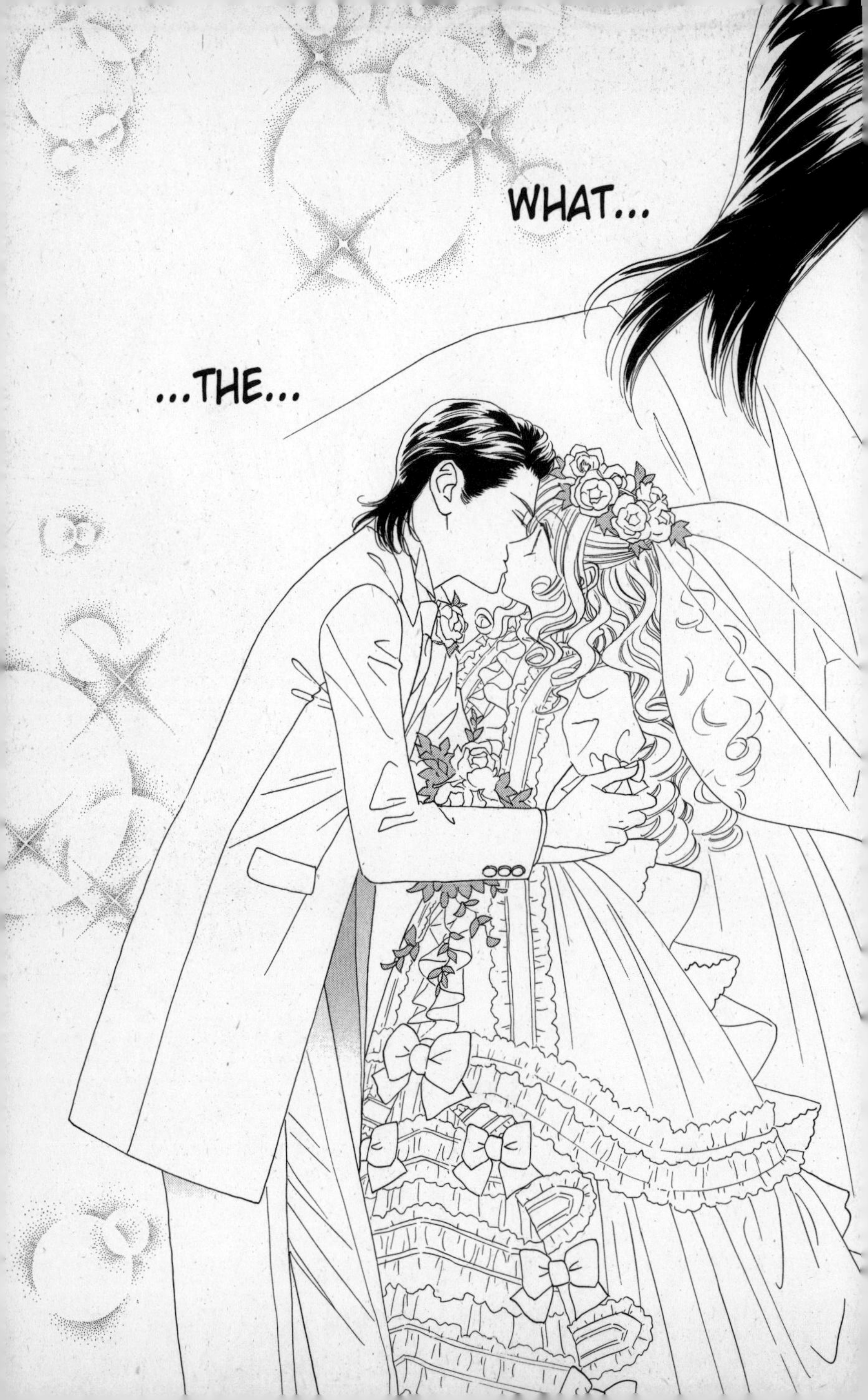
WHAT...
...THE...

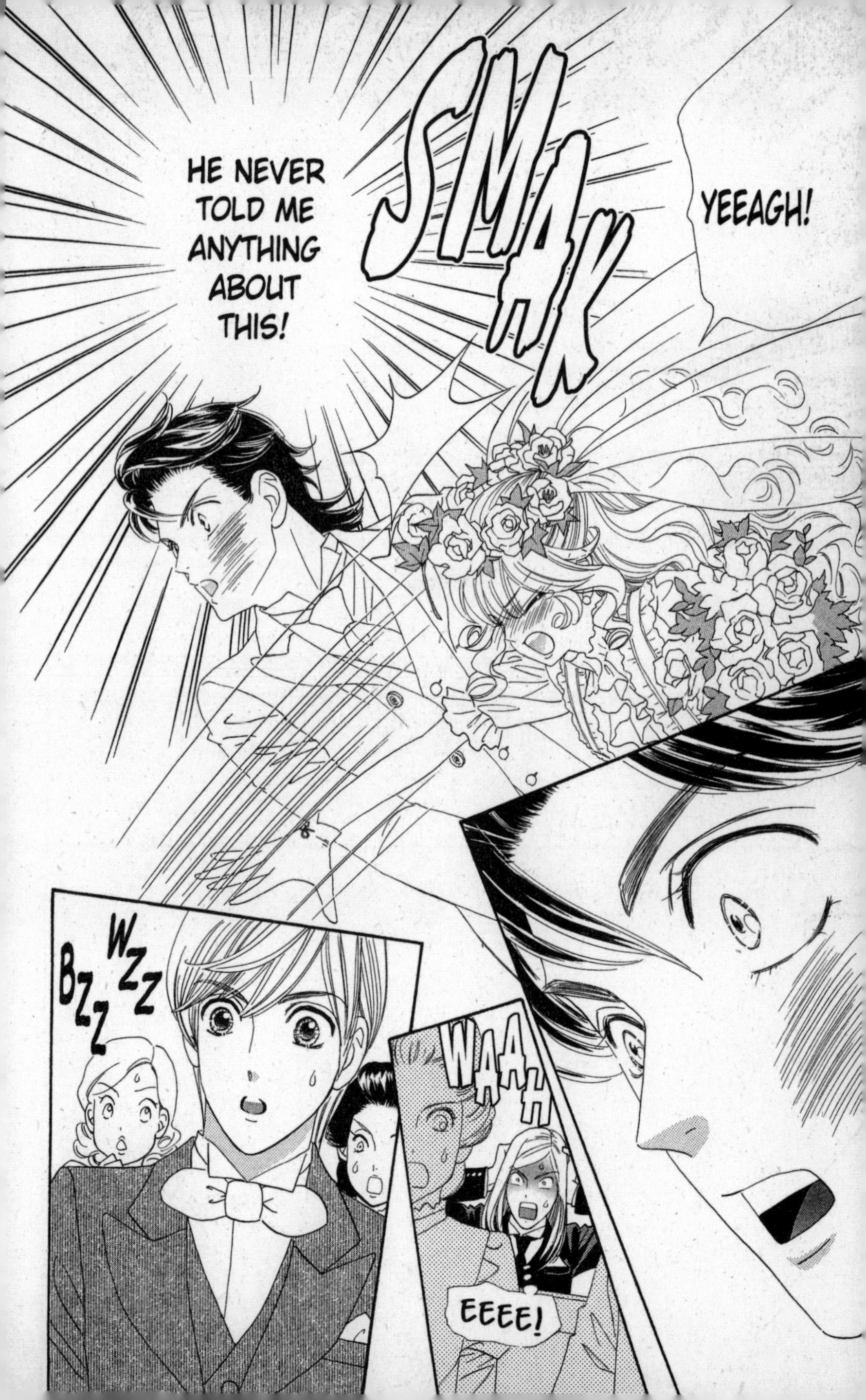
YEEAGH!
SMAK
HE NEVER TOLD ME ANYTHING ABOUT THIS!
WAAH
EEEE!
BZZZ WZZZ

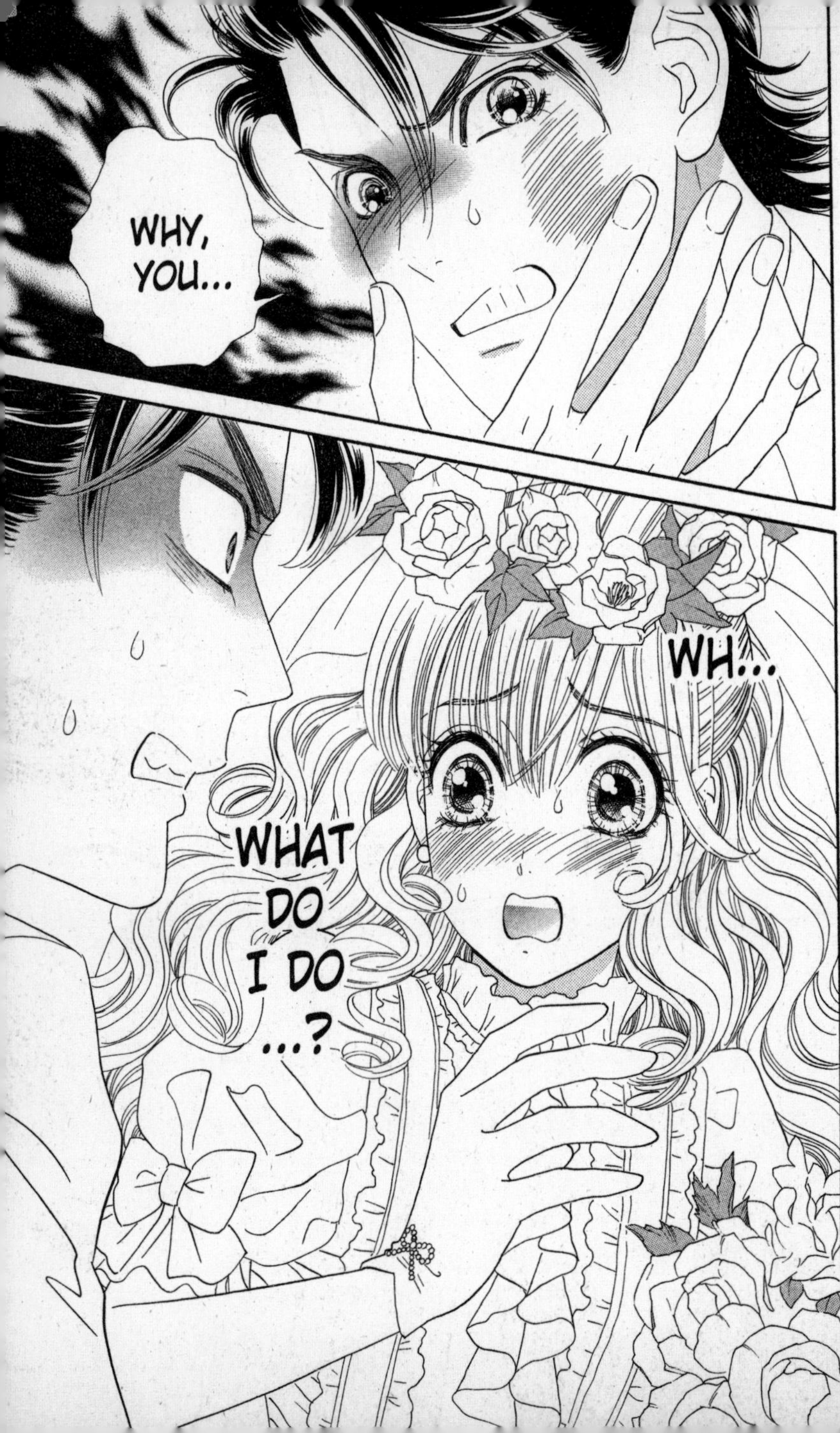
WHY, YOU...
WH...
WHAT DO I DO ...?

I HADN'T COME UP WITH A TITLE YET!! THERE WERE SOME WORDS I KNEW I WANTED TO INCLUDE THOUGH — "ROSE", "YOKOHAMA", "RED" OR "CRIMSON." THESE WORDS ARE ASSOCIATED WITH THE STORY, SO MY FIRST IDEA FOR A TITLE WAS "GREEN ROSE"!

"GREEN ROSE"... A GREEN-COLORED ROSE THAT MUST BE VERY RARE (OR DOESN'T EVEN EXIST) HAD A NICE RING TO IT! ♪ BUT WHEN I TOLD THAT TITLE TO MY EDITOR, THE REPLY I GOT WAS, "THERE'S A KOREAN TV DRAMA BY THAT TITLE." WHAAAT...?! I LOOKED IT UP AND FOUND OUT IT WAS TRUE.

THEN HOW ABOUT "ROSE GREEN"?!

IT DIDN'T SOUND RIGHT... MY FIRST IDEA OF "GREEN ROSE" SOUNDED SO MUCH BETTER, SO IT JUST DIDN'T CLICK...
SO THEN I HELD AN EMERGENCY MEETING ABOUT THE TITLE WITH THE EDITOR IN CHIEF, DEPUTY CHIEF EDITOR AND MY EDITOR. IN A KARAOKE ROOM!
EVEN THOUGH WE WERE AT A KARAOKE PLACE, NONE OF US SANG. WE JUST KEPT FLIPPING THROUGH THE PAGES OF THE SONG CATALOG FOR TWO HOURS, HOPING THAT THE NAMES OF FAMOUS SONGS WOULD INSPIRE US.

WE TRIED USING THE WORD "ROSE" INSTEAD OF "BARA" [THE WORD FOR "ROSE" IN JAPANESE]. WE ALSO TRIED USING WORDS LIKE "SEA" AND "THORN."
THEN SOMEONE SAID IN AN AGONIZED VOICE, "AMAZING..."

"AMAZING"? AS IN "A-MEIJI-NG STORY," A PUN USING THE WORD "MEIJI"?

WHOA! NO WAY! NEVER!! THAT'S WHAT I THOUGHT FOR A MOMENT, BUT I WAS SO TIRED THAT THE WORDS "ACTUALLY, THAT MIGHT WORK" CAME OUT OF MY MOUTH. THE PERSON WHO SAID "A-MEIJI-NG STORY" SAID IT WAS MEANT AS A JOKE, BUT IT HAD SUCH AN UNFORGETTABLE IMPACT THAT IT SOUNDED OKAY TO ME AT THE TIME.   TO BE CONTINUED...

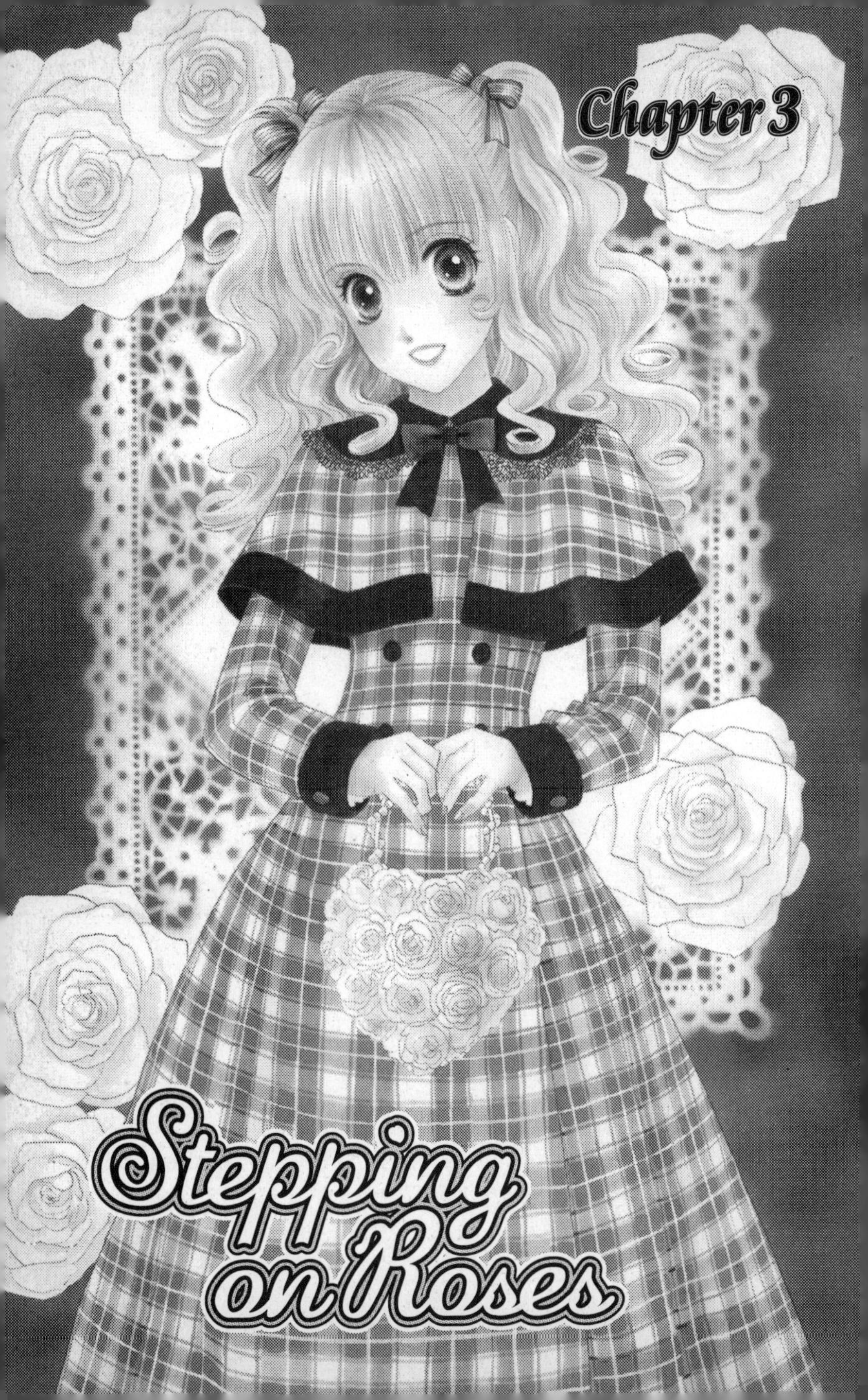
Chapter 3
Stepping on Roses

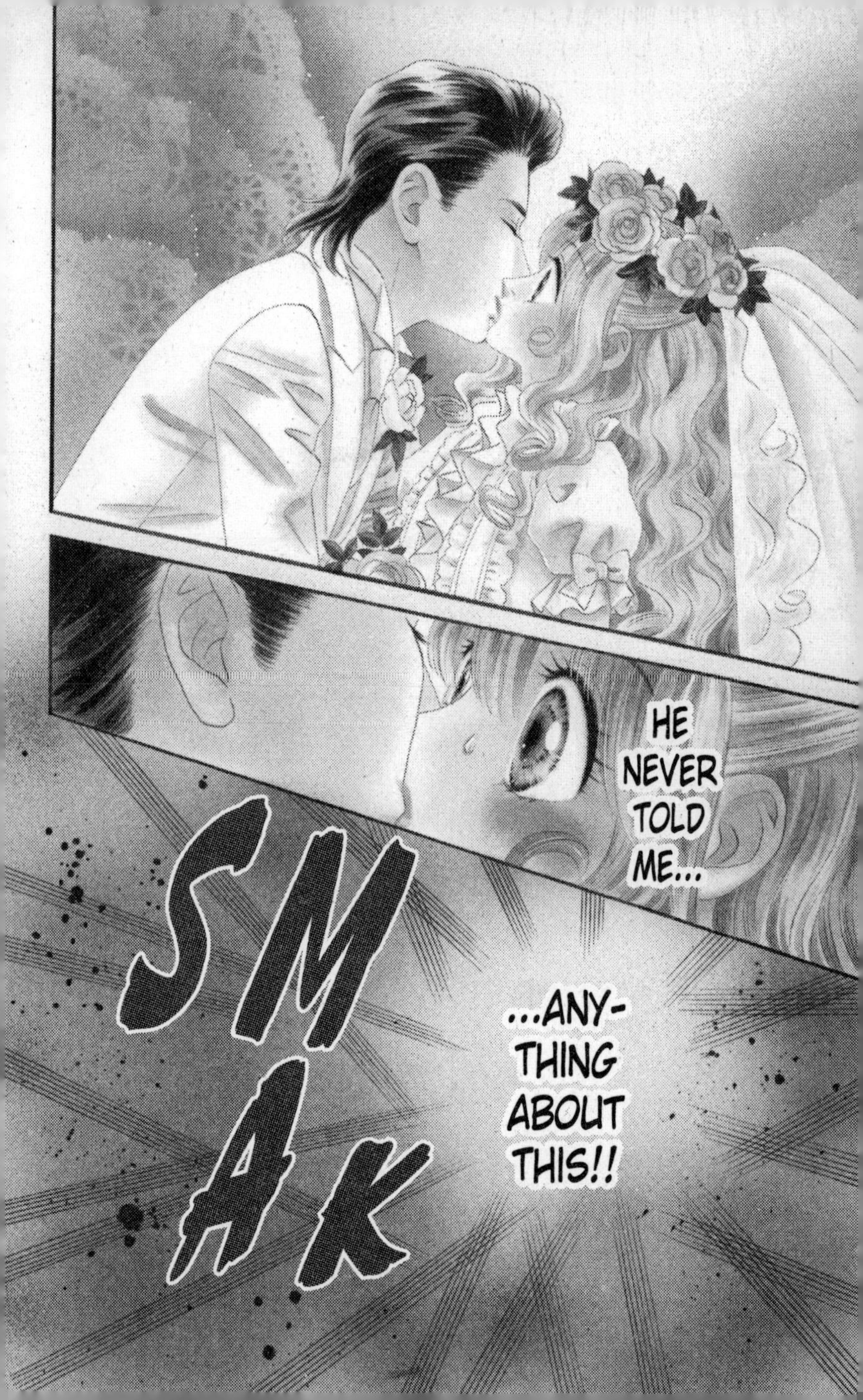
HE NEVER TOLD ME...
SMAK
...ANY-THING ABOUT THIS!!

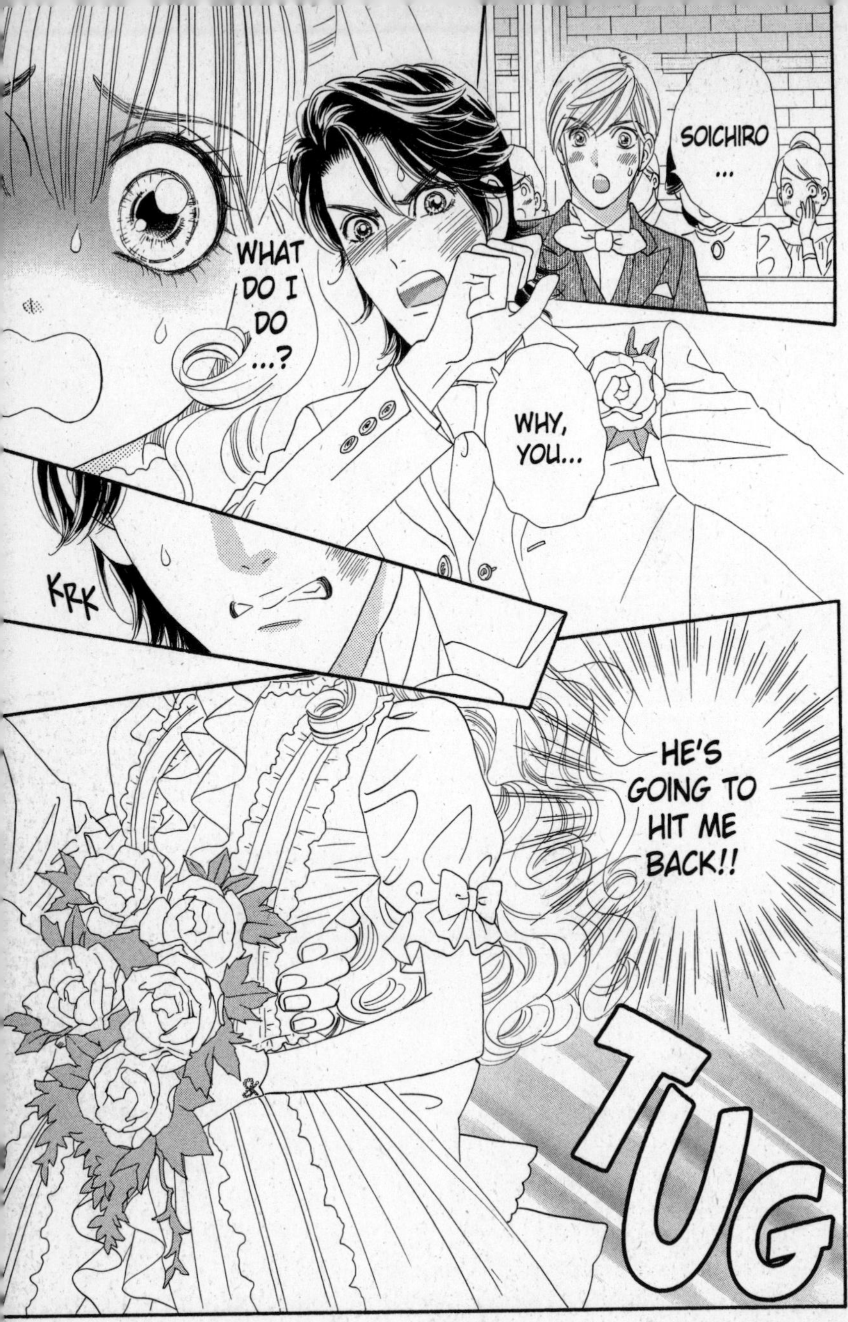
SOICHIRO ...
WHAT DO I DO ...?
WHY, YOU...
KRK
HE'S GOING TO HIT ME BACK!!
TUG

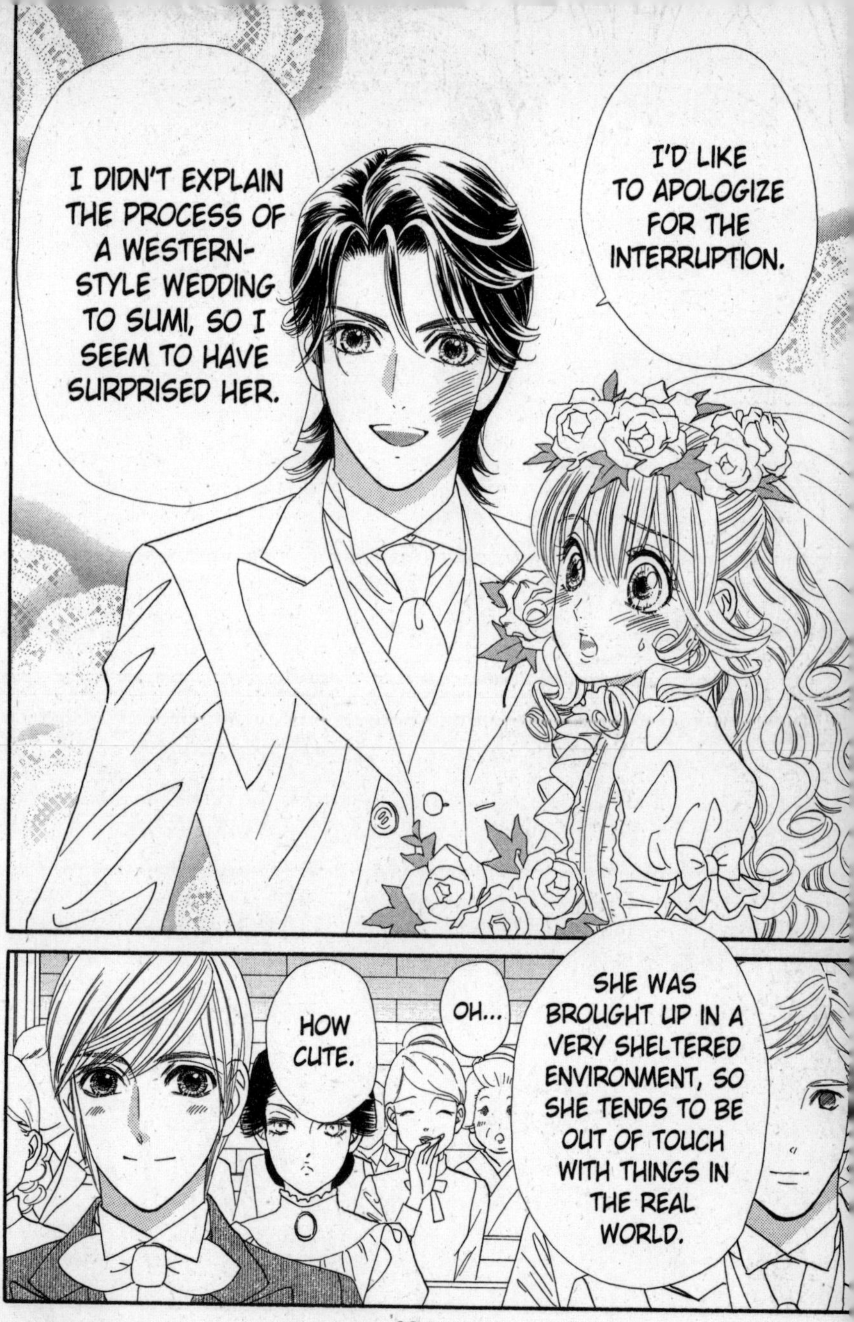
I'D LIKE TO APOLOGIZE FOR THE INTERRUPTION.
I DIDN'T EXPLAIN THE PROCESS OF A WESTERN-STYLE WEDDING TO SUMI, SO I SEEM TO HAVE SURPRISED HER.
SHE WAS BROUGHT UP IN A VERY SHELTERED ENVIRONMENT, SO SHE TENDS TO BE OUT OF TOUCH WITH THINGS IN THE REAL WORLD.
OH...
HOW CUTE.

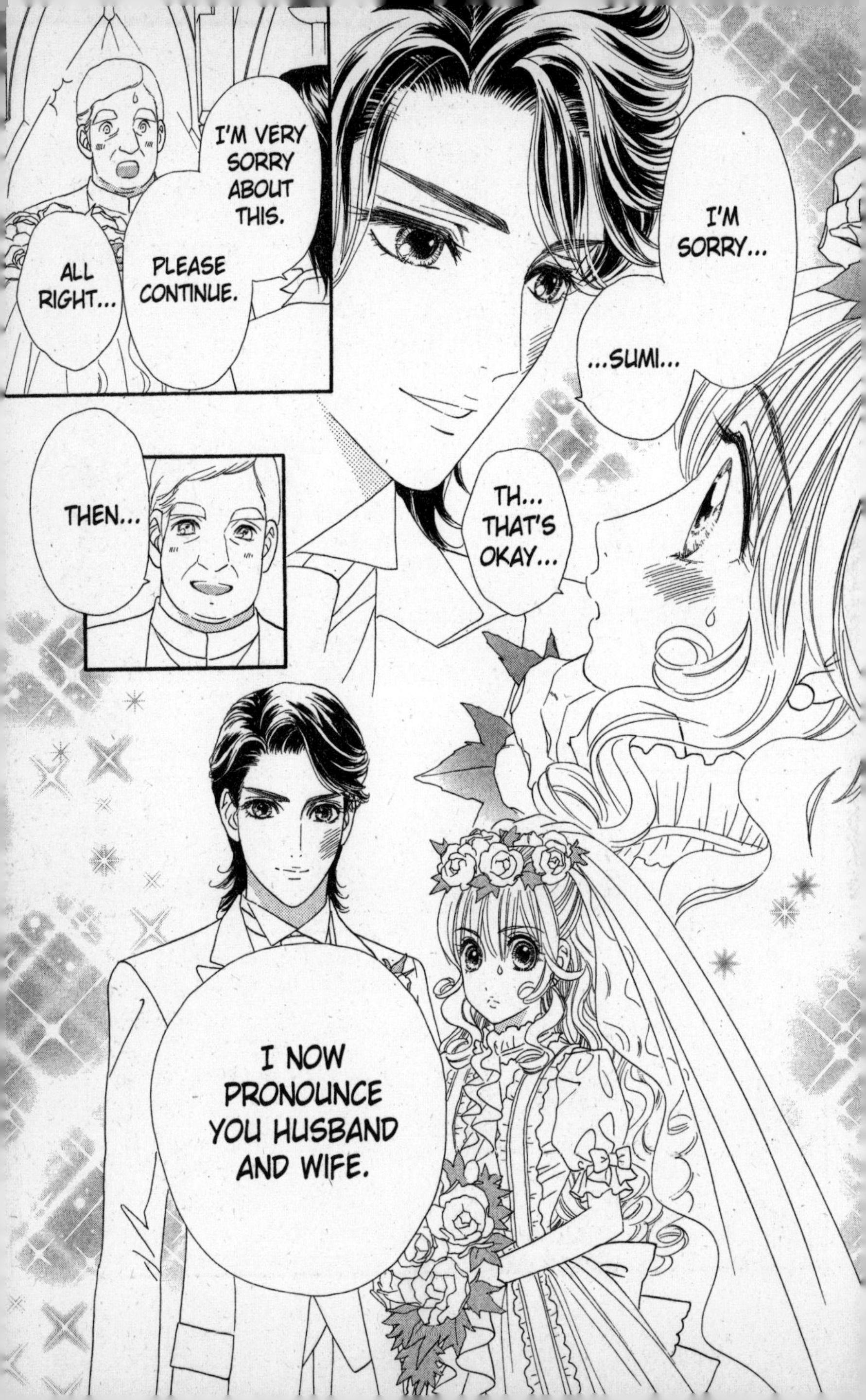
I'M SORRY...
...SUMI...
TH... THAT'S OKAY...
I'M VERY SORRY ABOUT THIS.
PLEASE CONTINUE.
ALL RIGHT...
THEN...
I NOW PRONOUNCE YOU HUSBAND AND WIFE.

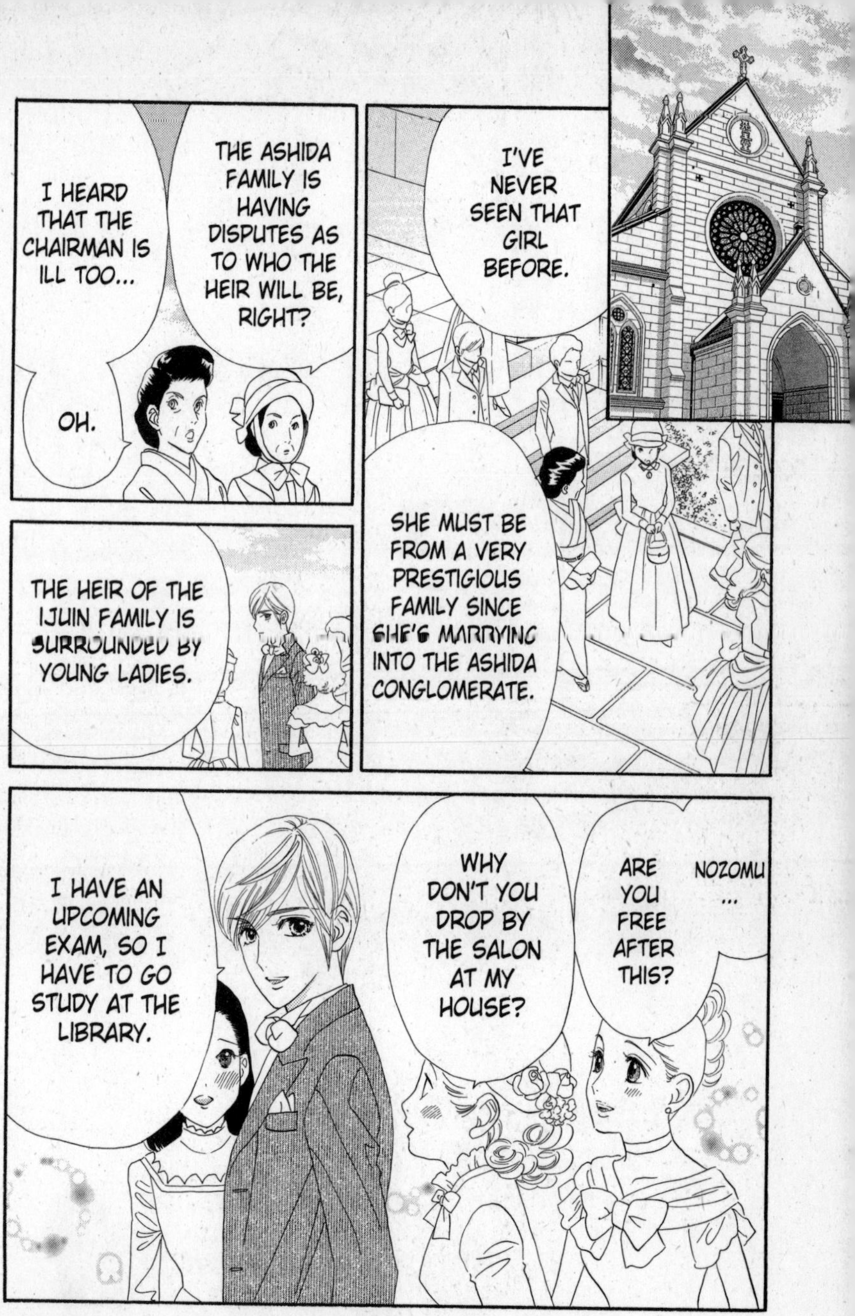
I'VE NEVER SEEN THAT GIRL BEFORE.
SHE MUST BE FROM A VERY PRESTIGIOUS FAMILY SINCE SHE'S MARRYING INTO THE ASHIDA CONGLOMERATE.
THE ASHIDA FAMILY IS HAVING DISPUTES AS TO WHO THE HEIR WILL BE, RIGHT?
I HEARD THAT THE CHAIRMAN IS ILL TOO...
OH.
THE HEIR OF THE IJUIN FAMILY IS SURROUNDED BY YOUNG LADIES.
NOZOMU...
ARE YOU FREE AFTER THIS?
WHY DON'T YOU DROP BY THE SALON AT MY HOUSE?
I HAVE AN UPCOMING EXAM, SO I HAVE TO GO STUDY AT THE LIBRARY.

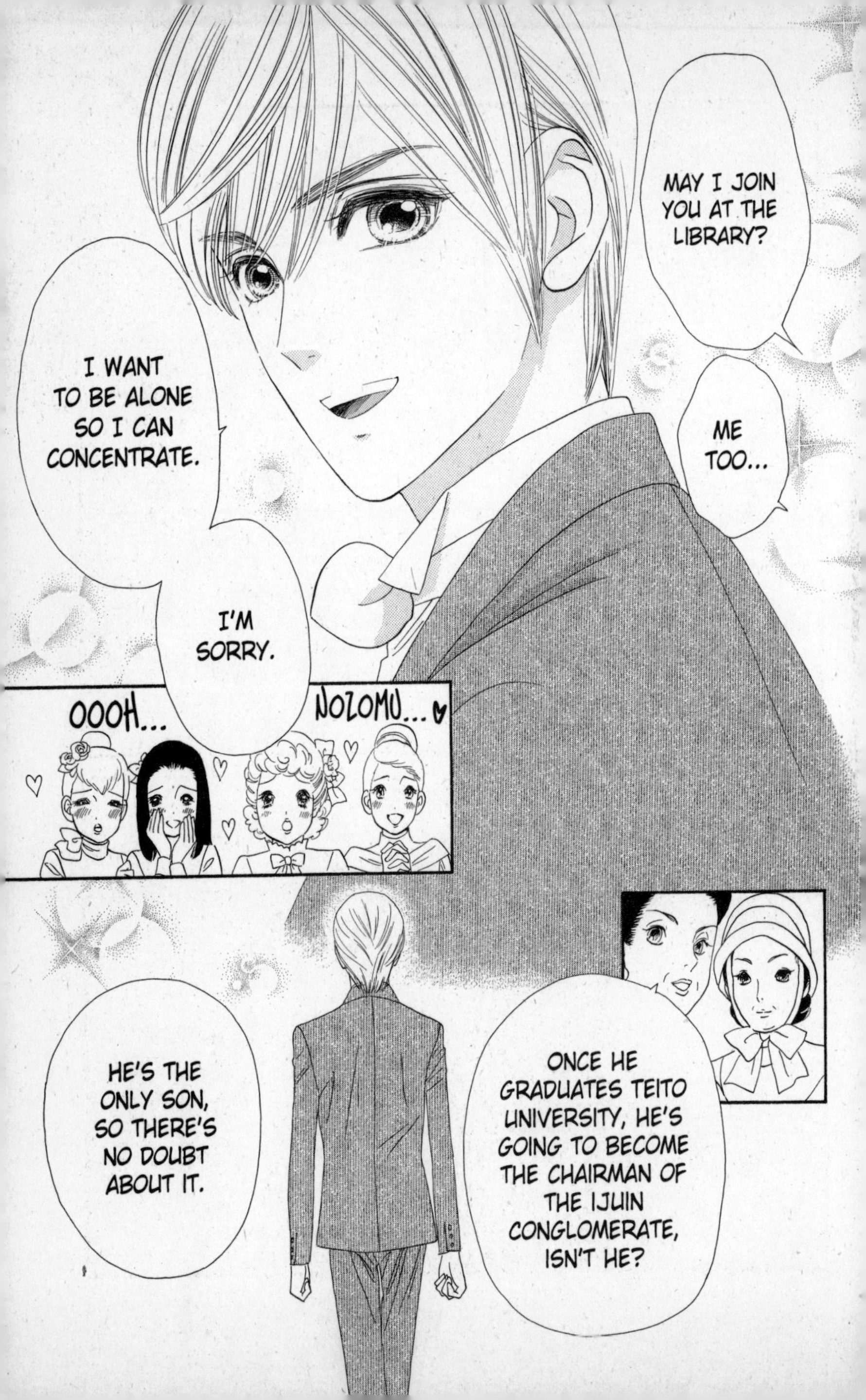
MAY I JOIN YOU AT THE LIBRARY?
ME TOO...
I WANT TO BE ALONE SO I CAN CONCENTRATE.
I'M SORRY.
NOZOMU...♥
OOOH...
ONCE HE GRADUATES TEITO UNIVERSITY, HE'S GOING TO BECOME THE CHAIRMAN OF THE IJUIN CONGLOMERATE, ISN'T HE?
HE'S THE ONLY SON, SO THERE'S NO DOUBT ABOUT IT.

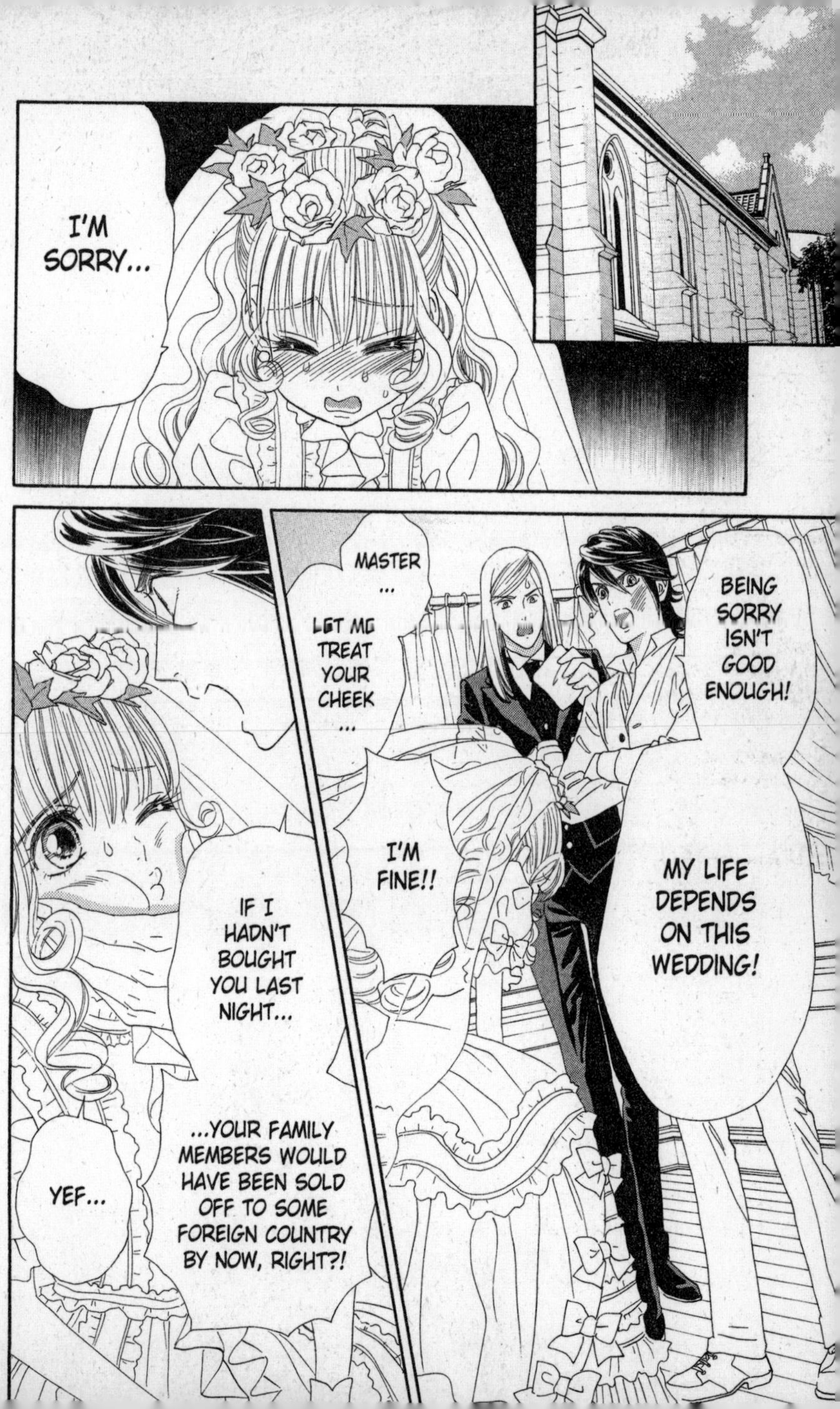
I'M SORRY...
BEING SORRY ISN'T GOOD ENOUGH!
MASTER... LET ME TREAT YOUR CHEEK...
MY LIFE DEPENDS ON THIS WEDDING!
I'M FINE!!
IF I HADN'T BOUGHT YOU LAST NIGHT...
...YOUR FAMILY MEMBERS WOULD HAVE BEEN SOLD OFF TO SOME FOREIGN COUNTRY BY NOW, RIGHT?!
YEF...

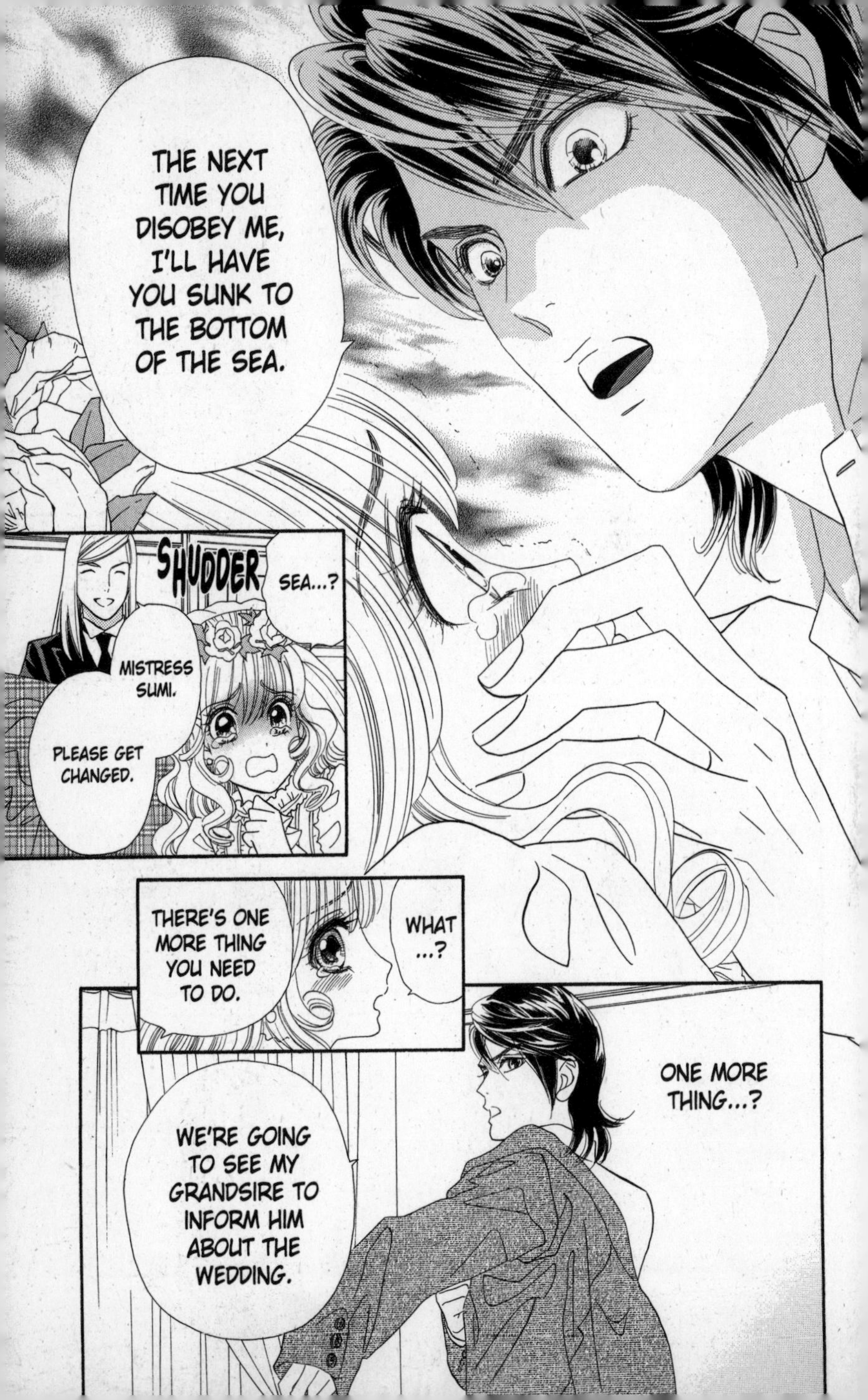
THE NEXT TIME YOU DISOBEY ME, I'LL HAVE YOU SUNK TO THE BOTTOM OF THE SEA.
SEA...?
SHUDDER
MISTRESS SUMI.
PLEASE GET CHANGED.
WHAT ...?
THERE'S ONE MORE THING YOU NEED TO DO.
ONE MORE THING...?
WE'RE GOING TO SEE MY GRANDSIRE TO INFORM HIM ABOUT THE WEDDING.

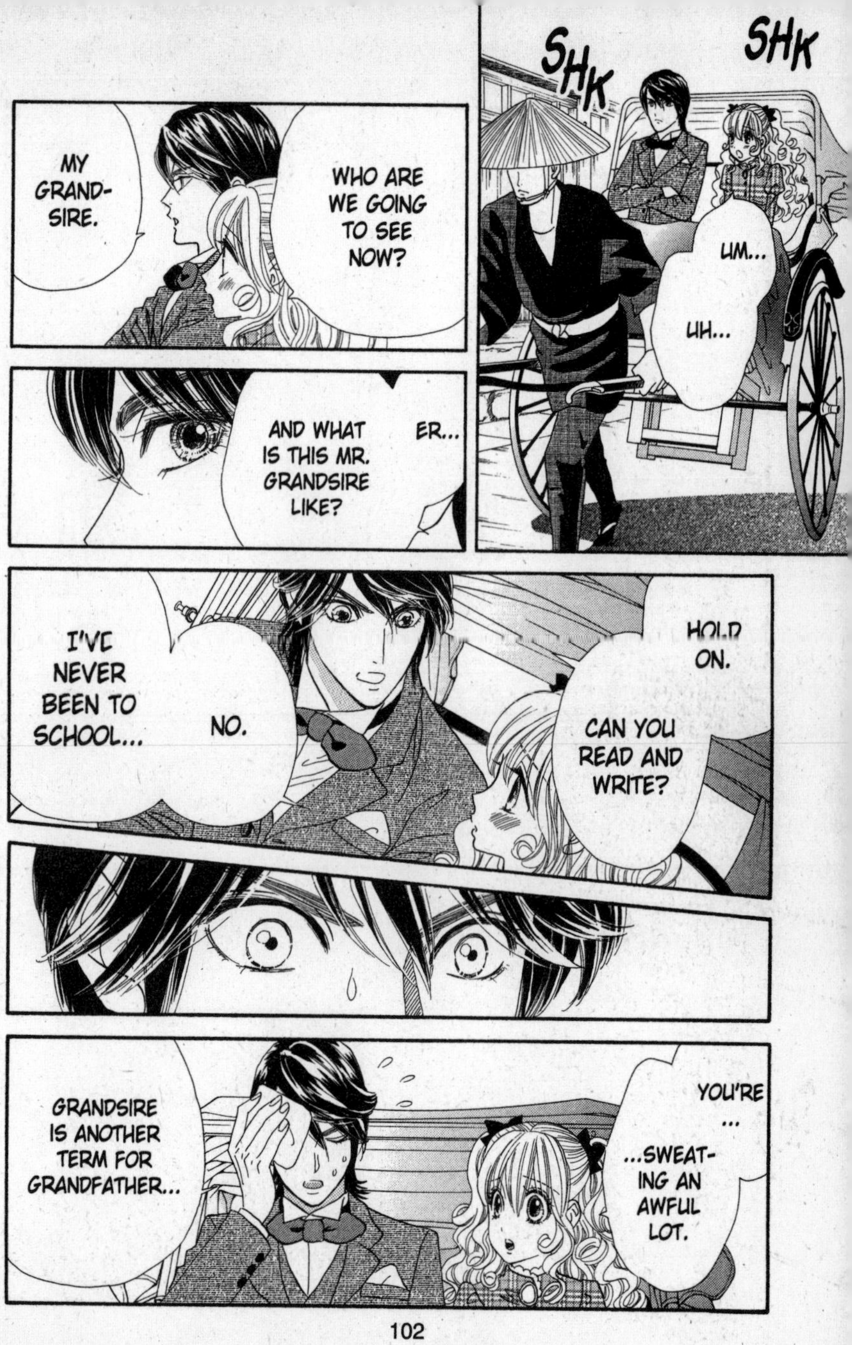
SHK
SHK
UM...
UH...
WHO ARE WE GOING TO SEE NOW?
MY GRAND-SIRE.
ER...
AND WHAT IS THIS MR. GRANDSIRE LIKE?
HOLD ON.
CAN YOU READ AND WRITE?
NO.
I'VE NEVER BEEN TO SCHOOL...
YOU'RE ...
...SWEAT-ING AN AWFUL LOT.
GRANDSIRE IS ANOTHER TERM FOR GRANDFATHER...

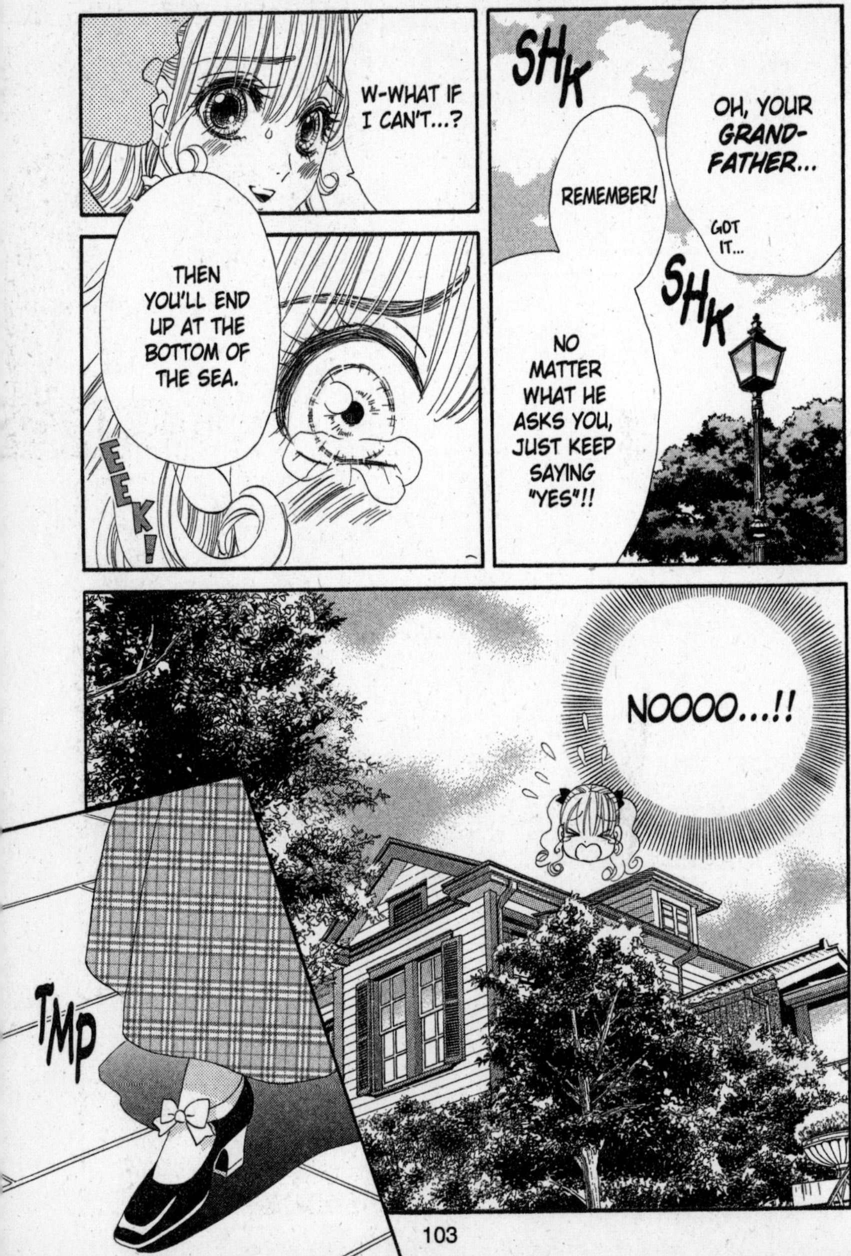
OH, YOUR GRAND-FATHER...
GOT IT...
SHK
REMEMBER!
SHK
NO MATTER WHAT HE ASKS YOU, JUST KEEP SAYING "YES"!!
W-WHAT IF I CAN'T...?
THEN YOU'LL END UP AT THE BOTTOM OF THE SEA.
EEEK!
NOOOO...!!
TMP

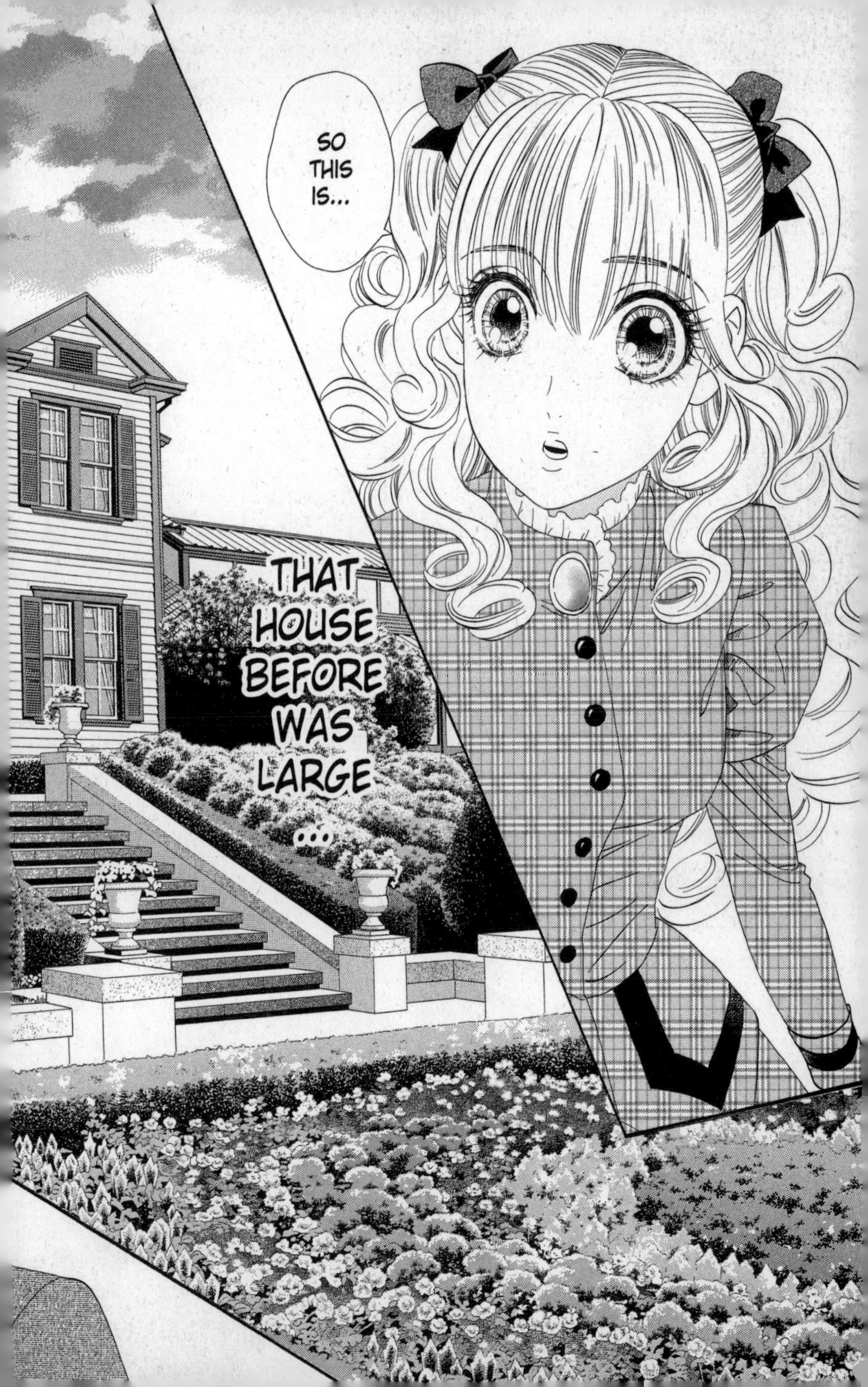
SO THIS IS...
THAT HOUSE BEFORE WAS LARGE...

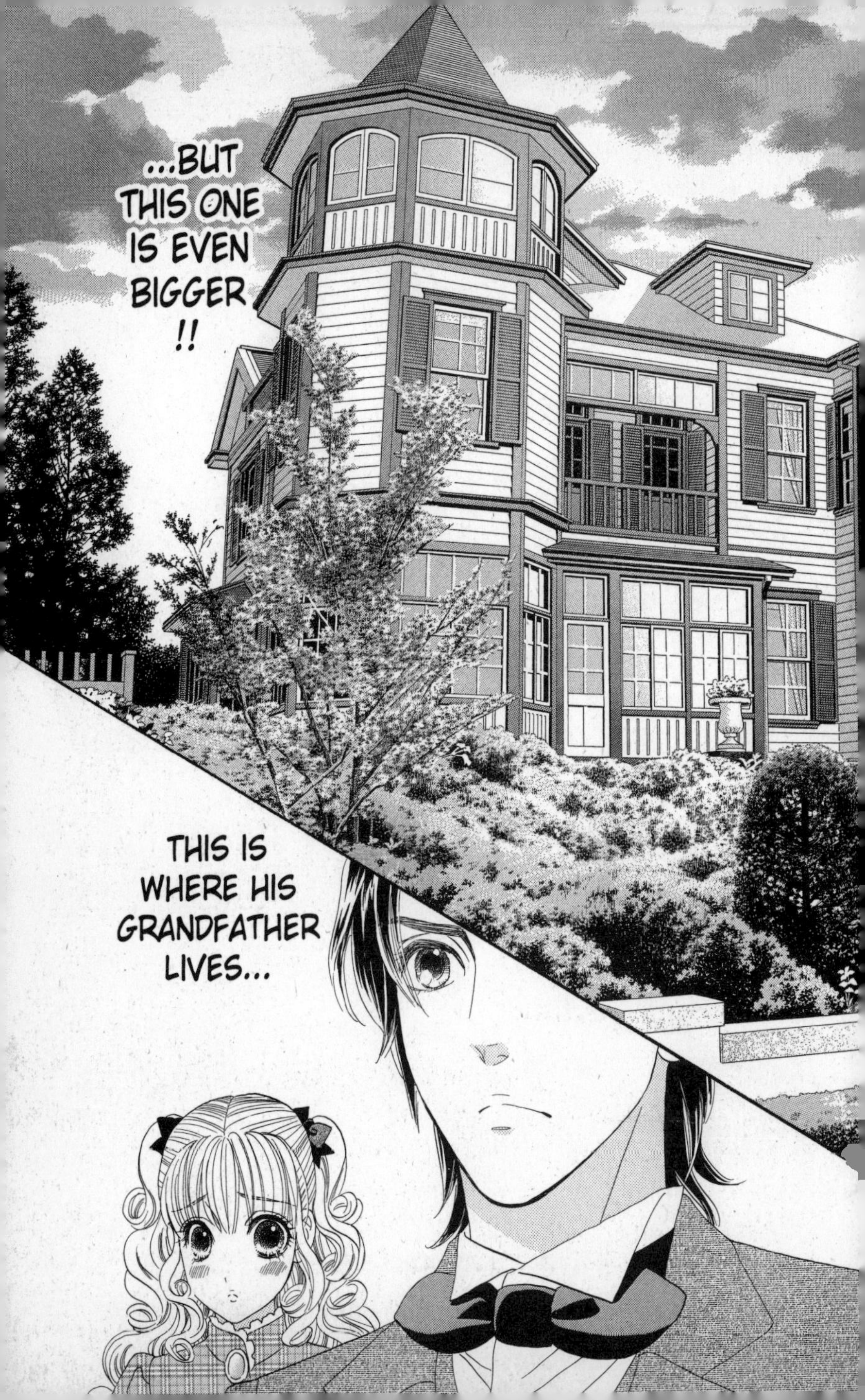
...BUT THIS ONE IS EVEN BIGGER !!
THIS IS WHERE HIS GRANDFATHER LIVES...

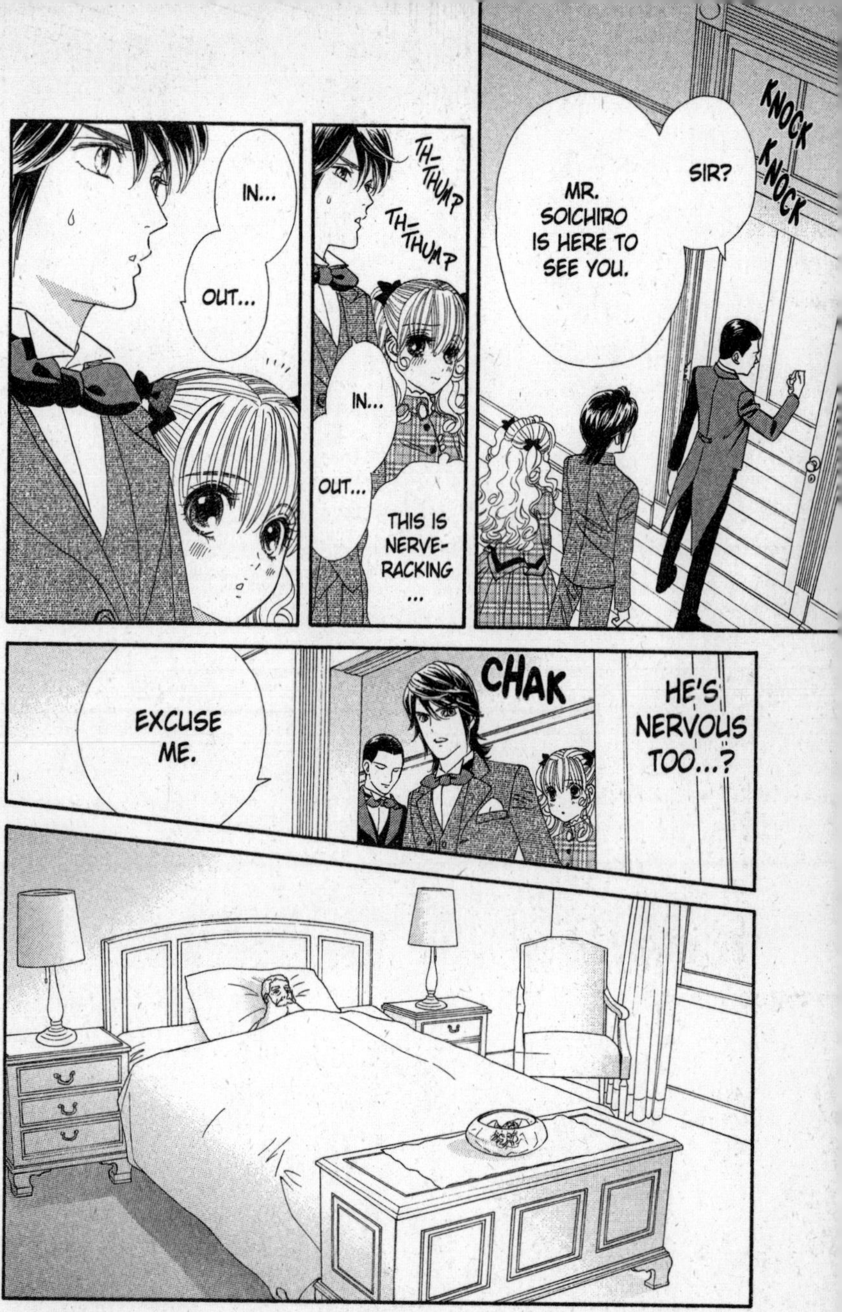
KNOCK KNOCK
SIR?
MR. SOICHIRO IS HERE TO SEE YOU.
TH-THUMP TH-THUMP
IN...
OUT...
THIS IS NERVE-RACKING...
IN...
OUT...
HE'S NERVOUS TOO...?
CHAK
EXCUSE ME.

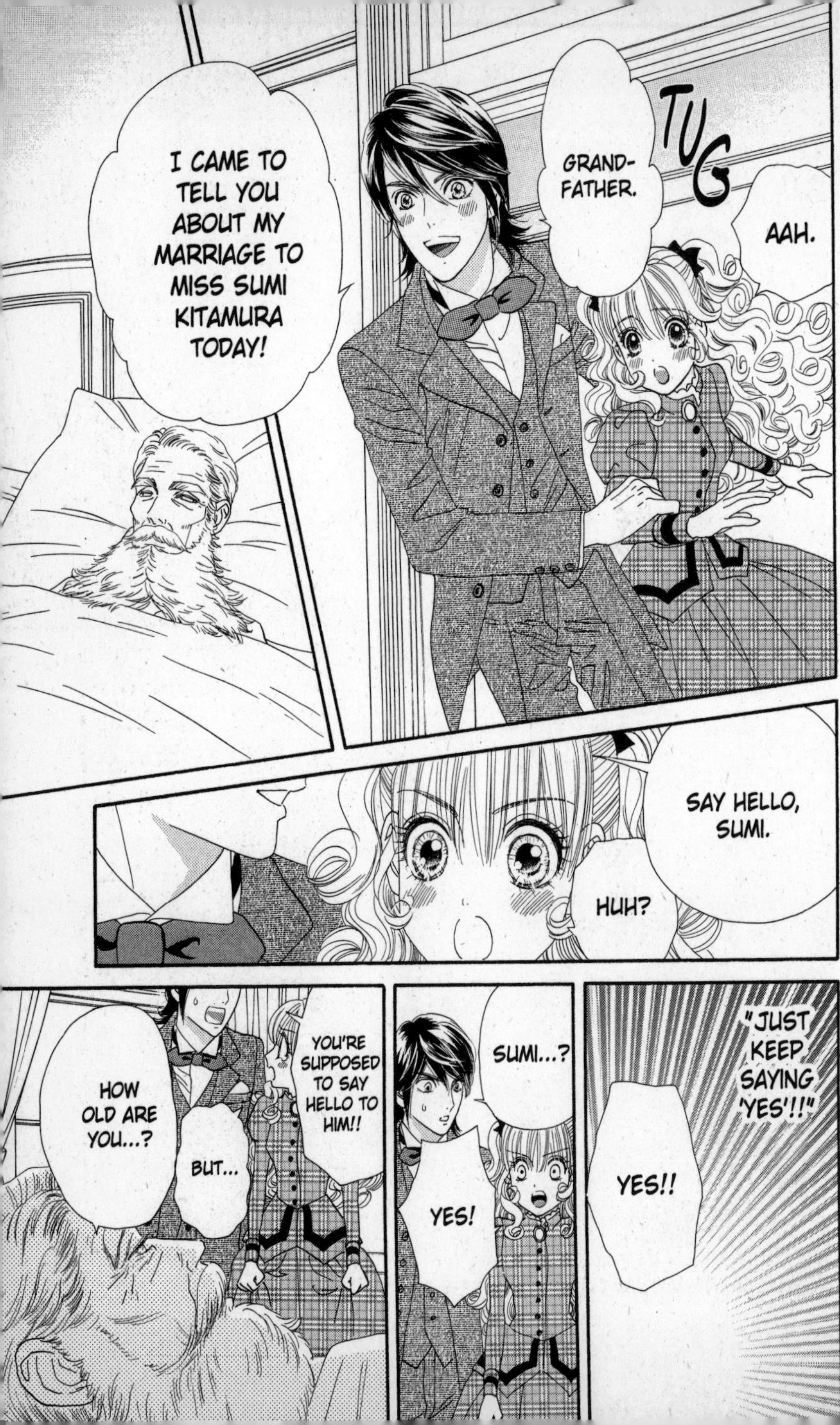
GRAND-FATHER.
TUG
AAH.
I CAME TO TELL YOU ABOUT MY MARRIAGE TO MISS SUMI KITAMURA TODAY!
SAY HELLO, SUMI.
HUH?
"JUST KEEP SAYING 'YES'!!"
YES!!
SUMI...?
YES!
YOU'RE SUPPOSED TO SAY HELLO TO HIM!!
BUT...
HOW OLD ARE YOU...?

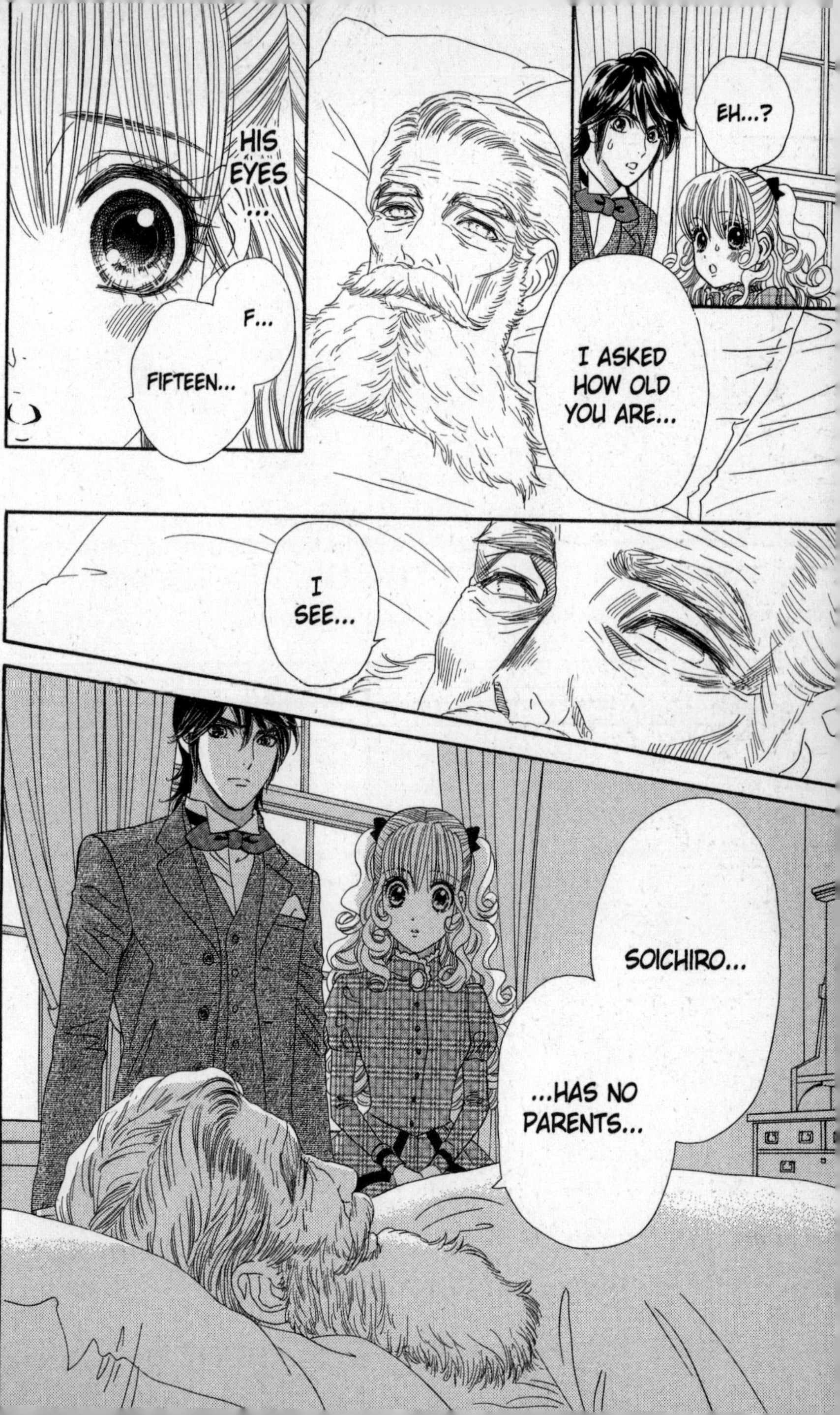
EH...?
I ASKED HOW OLD YOU ARE...
HIS EYES...
F...
FIFTEEN...
I SEE...
SOICHIRO...
...HAS NO PARENTS...

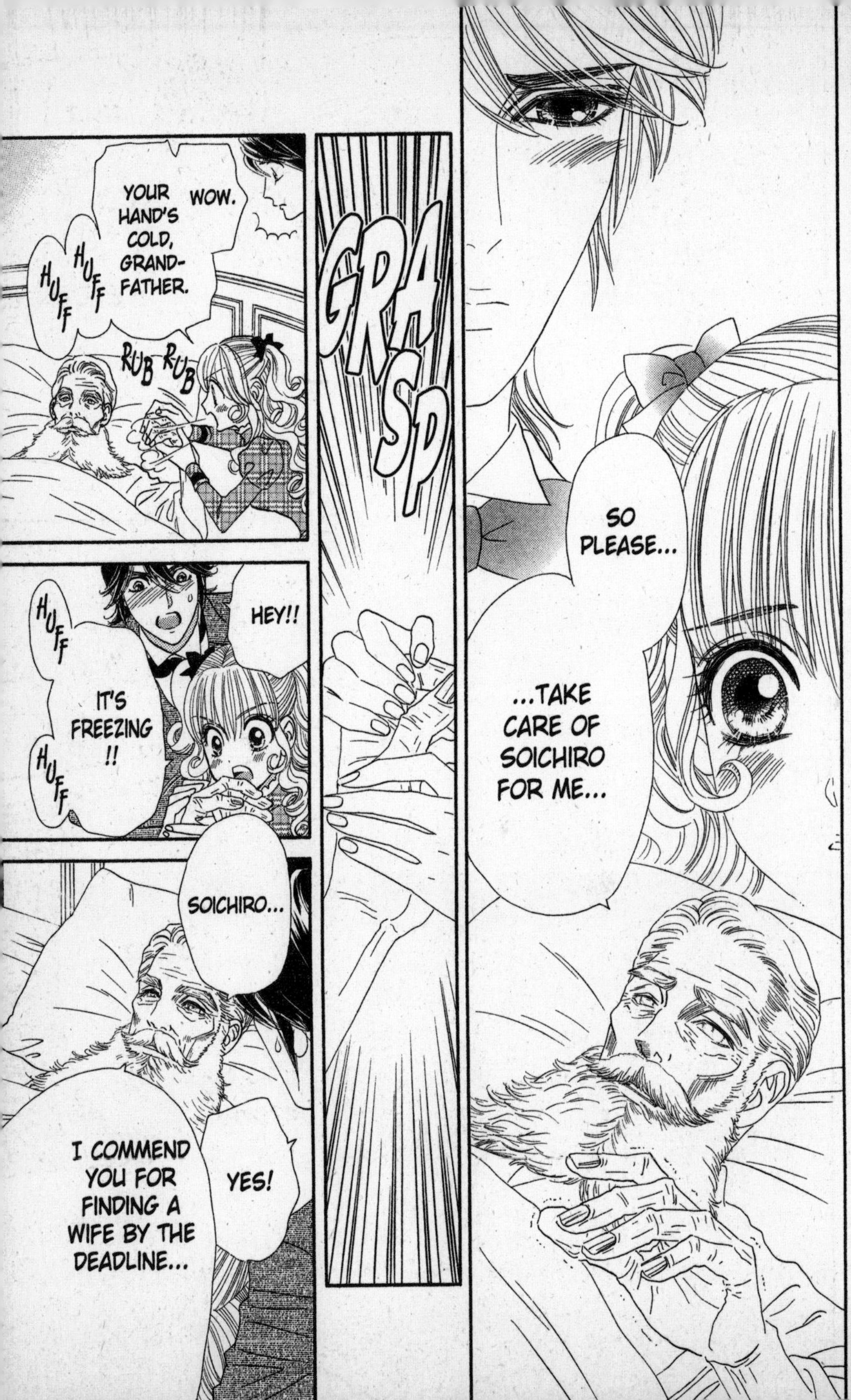
WOW.
YOUR HAND'S COLD, GRANDFATHER.
HUFF HUFF
RUB RUB
HEY!!
IT'S FREEZING!!
HUFF HUFF
SOICHIRO...
I COMMEND YOU FOR FINDING A WIFE BY THE DEADLINE...
YES!
GRASP
SO PLEASE...
...TAKE CARE OF SOICHIRO FOR ME...

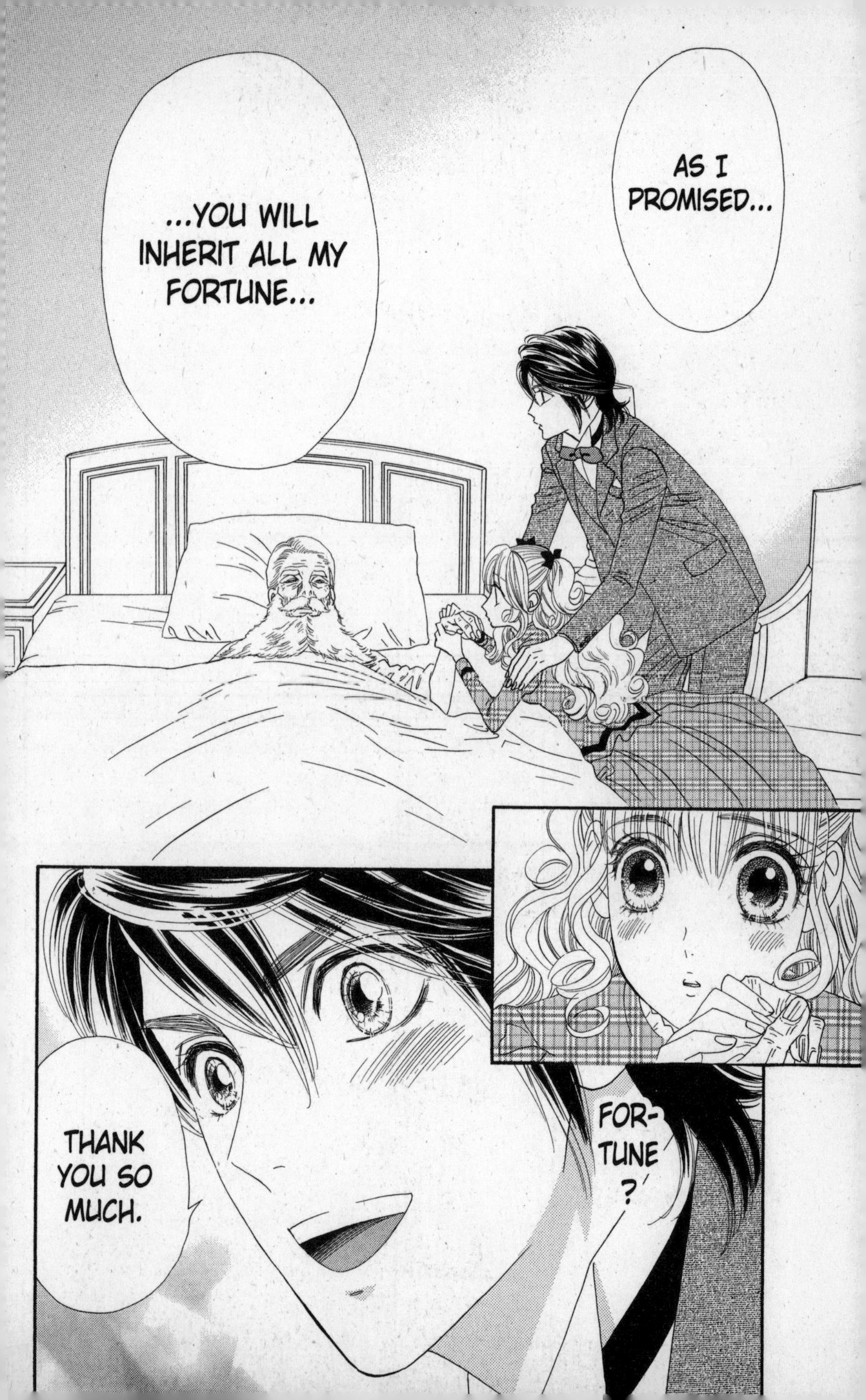
AS I PROMISED...
...YOU WILL INHERIT ALL MY FORTUNE...
FOR-TUNE?
THANK YOU SO MUCH.

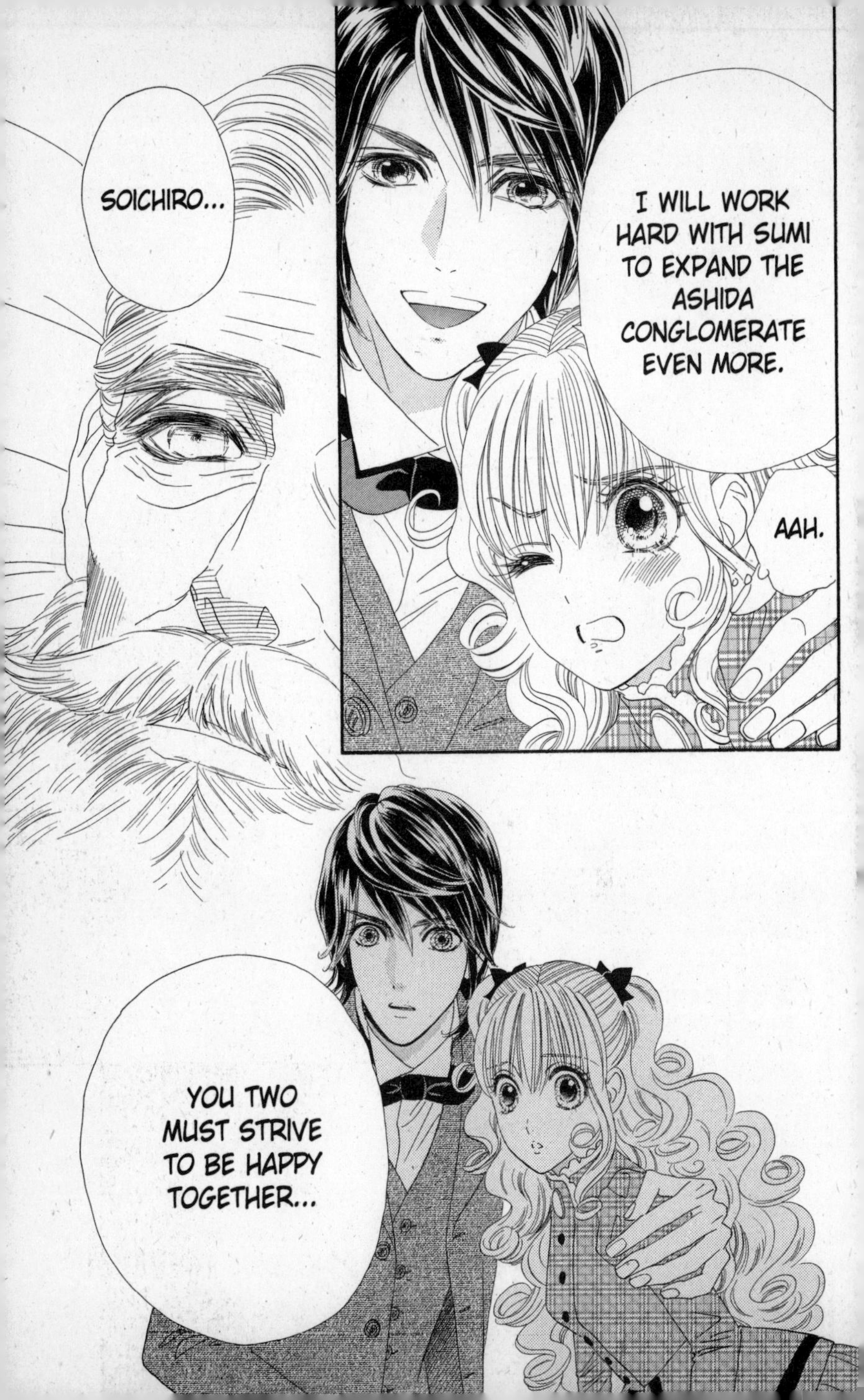
I WILL WORK HARD WITH SUMI TO EXPAND THE ASHIDA CONGLOMERATE EVEN MORE.
AAH.
SOICHIRO...
YOU TWO MUST STRIVE TO BE HAPPY TOGETHER...

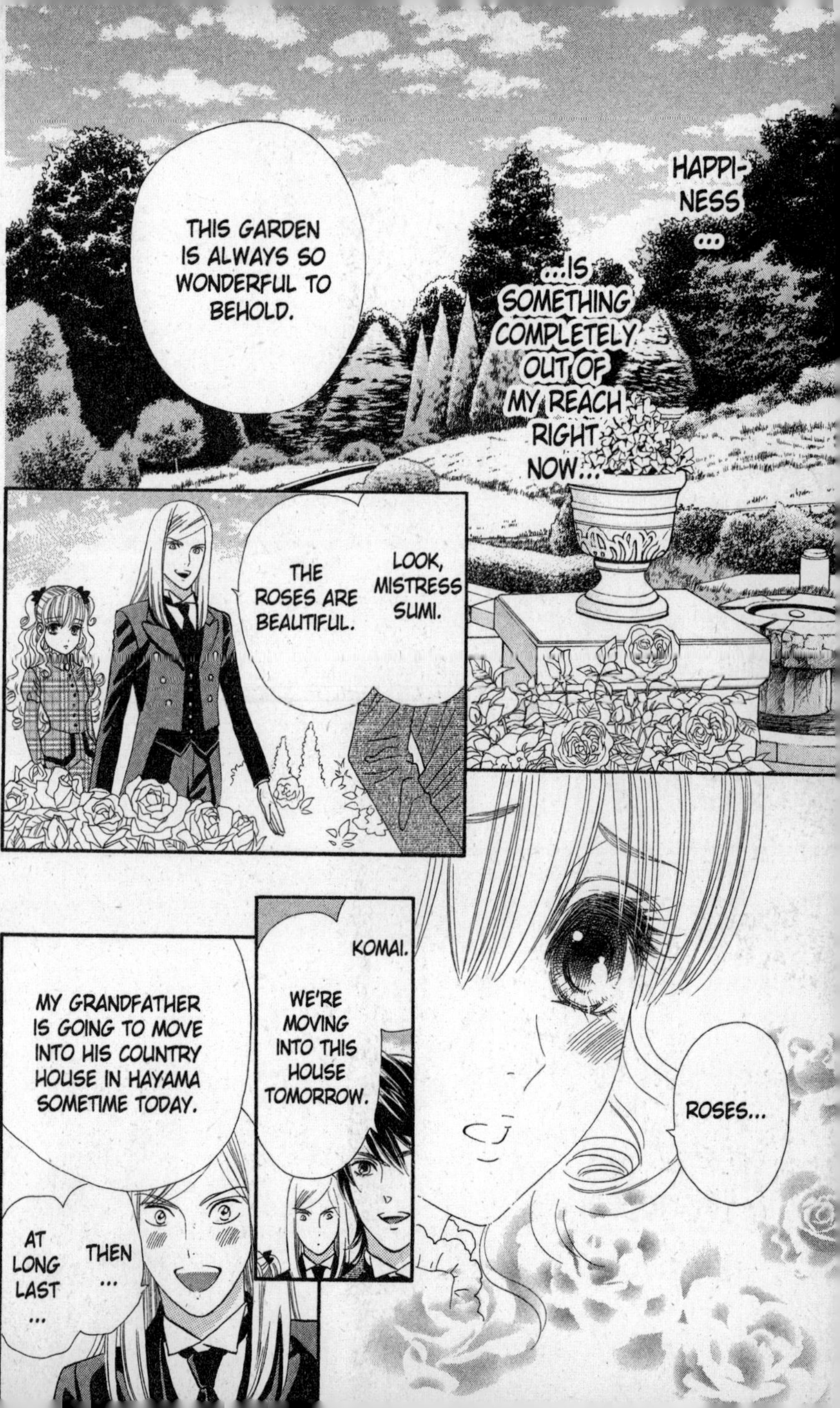
HAPPINESS...
...IS SOMETHING COMPLETELY OUT OF MY REACH RIGHT NOW...
THIS GARDEN IS ALWAYS SO WONDERFUL TO BEHOLD.
LOOK, MISTRESS SUMI.
THE ROSES ARE BEAUTIFUL.
ROSES...
KOMAI.
WE'RE MOVING INTO THIS HOUSE TOMORROW.
MY GRANDFATHER IS GOING TO MOVE INTO HIS COUNTRY HOUSE IN HAYAMA SOMETIME TODAY.
THEN...
AT LONG LAST...

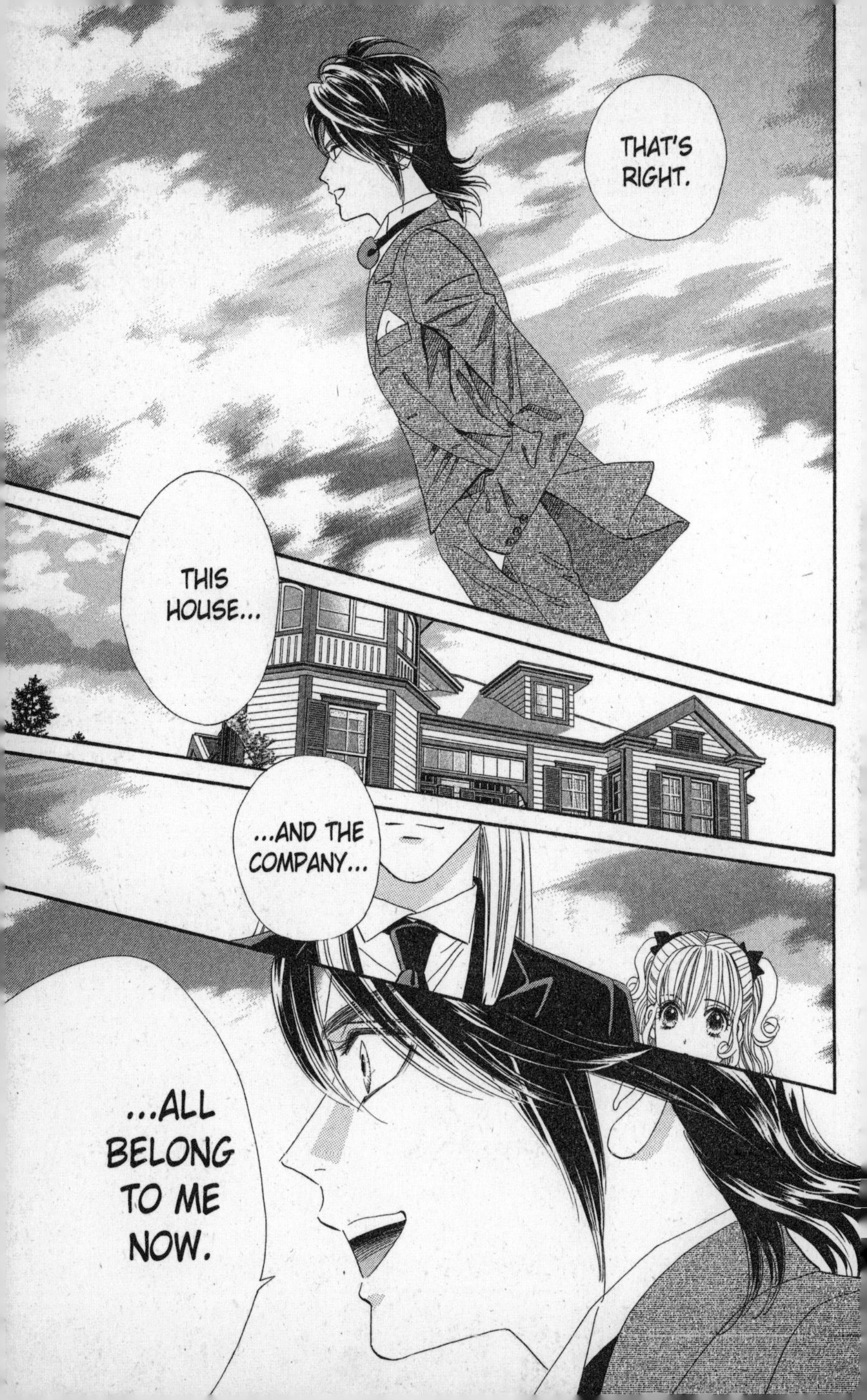
THAT'S RIGHT.
THIS HOUSE...
...AND THE COMPANY...
...ALL BELONG TO ME NOW.

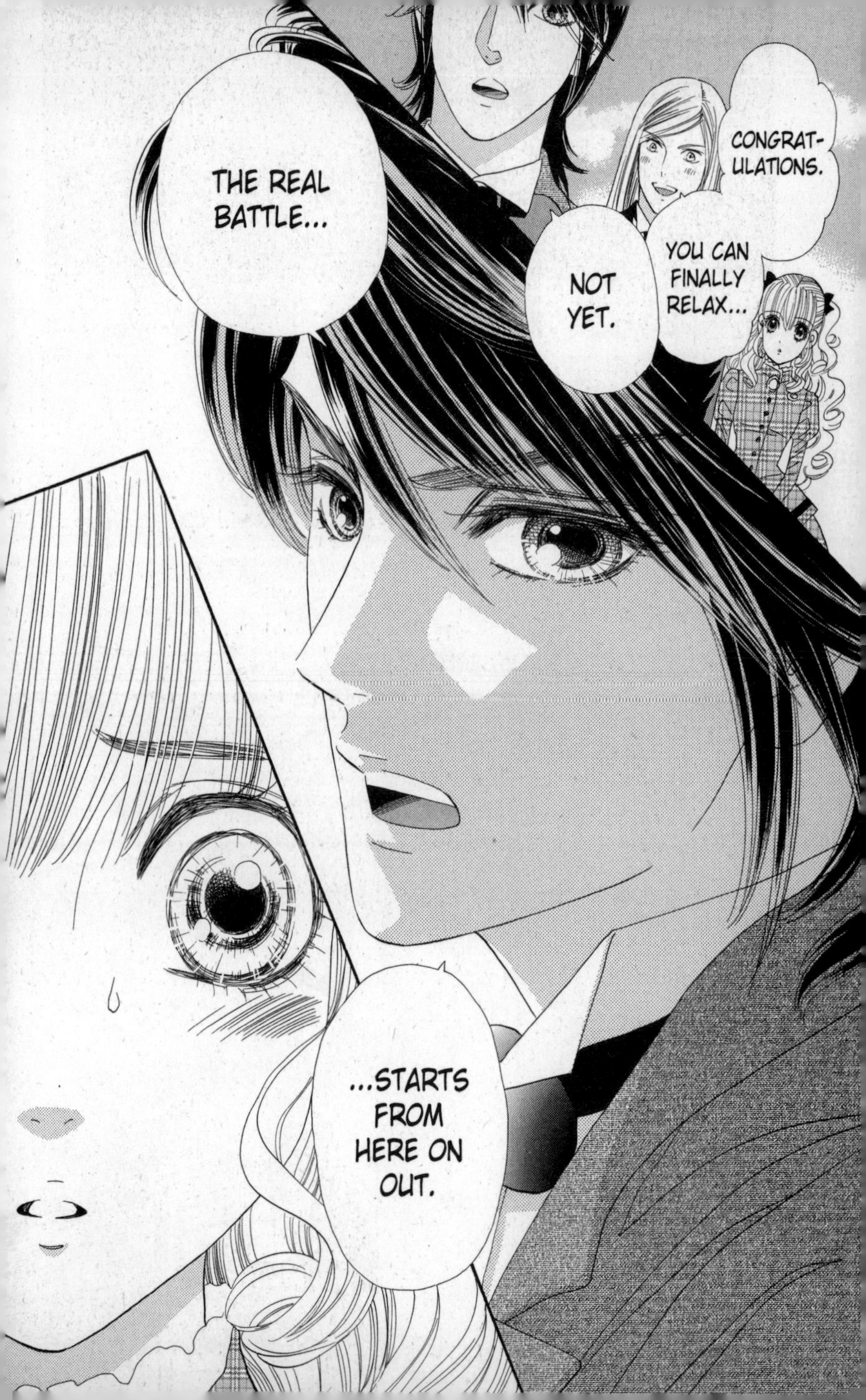
CONGRAT-ULATIONS.
YOU CAN FINALLY RELAX...
NOT YET.
THE REAL BATTLE...
...STARTS FROM HERE ON OUT.

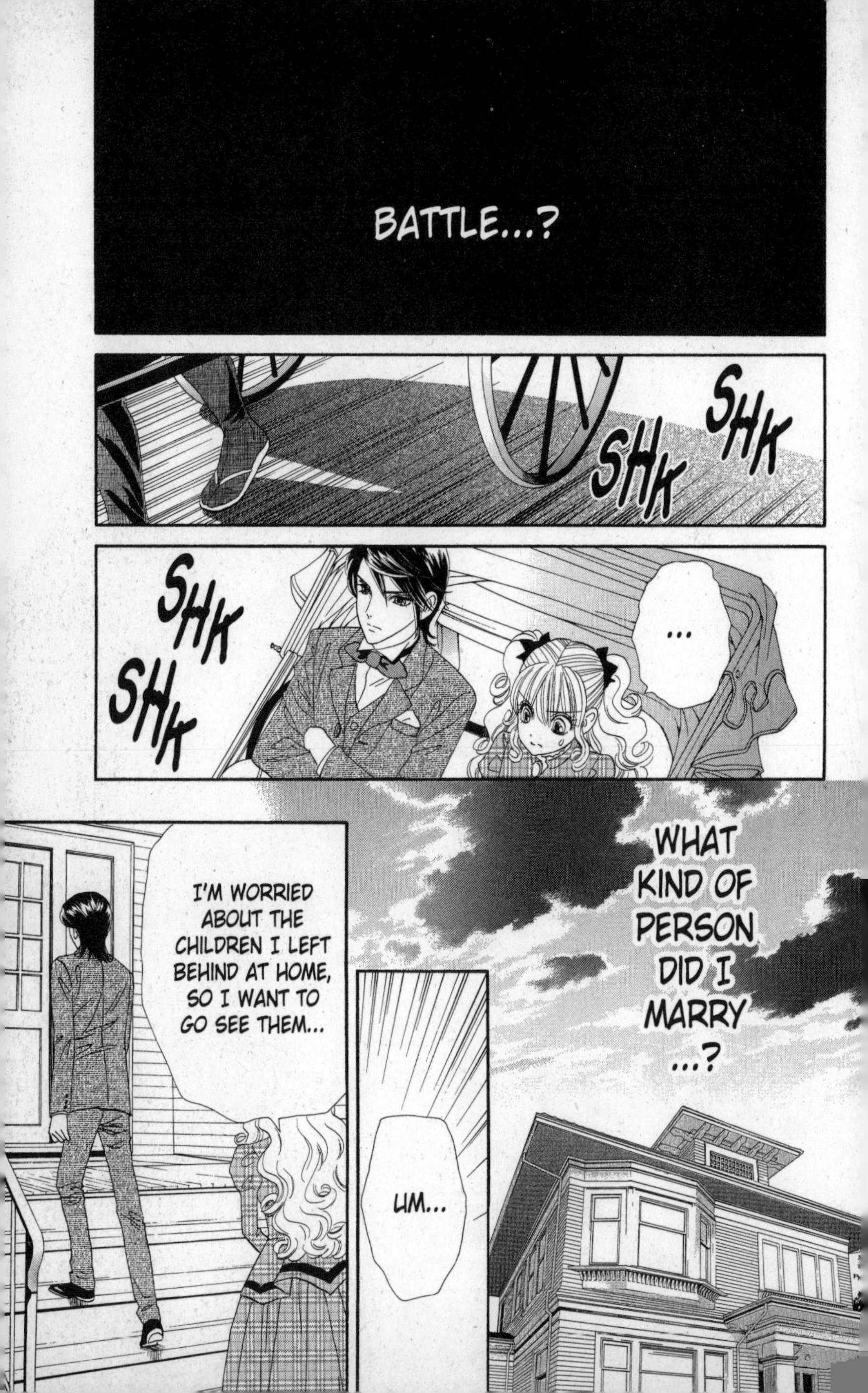
BATTLE...?
SHK
SHK
...
SHK
SHK
WHAT KIND OF PERSON DID I MARRY ...?
UM...
I'M WORRIED ABOUT THE CHILDREN I LEFT BEHIND AT HOME, SO I WANT TO GO SEE THEM...

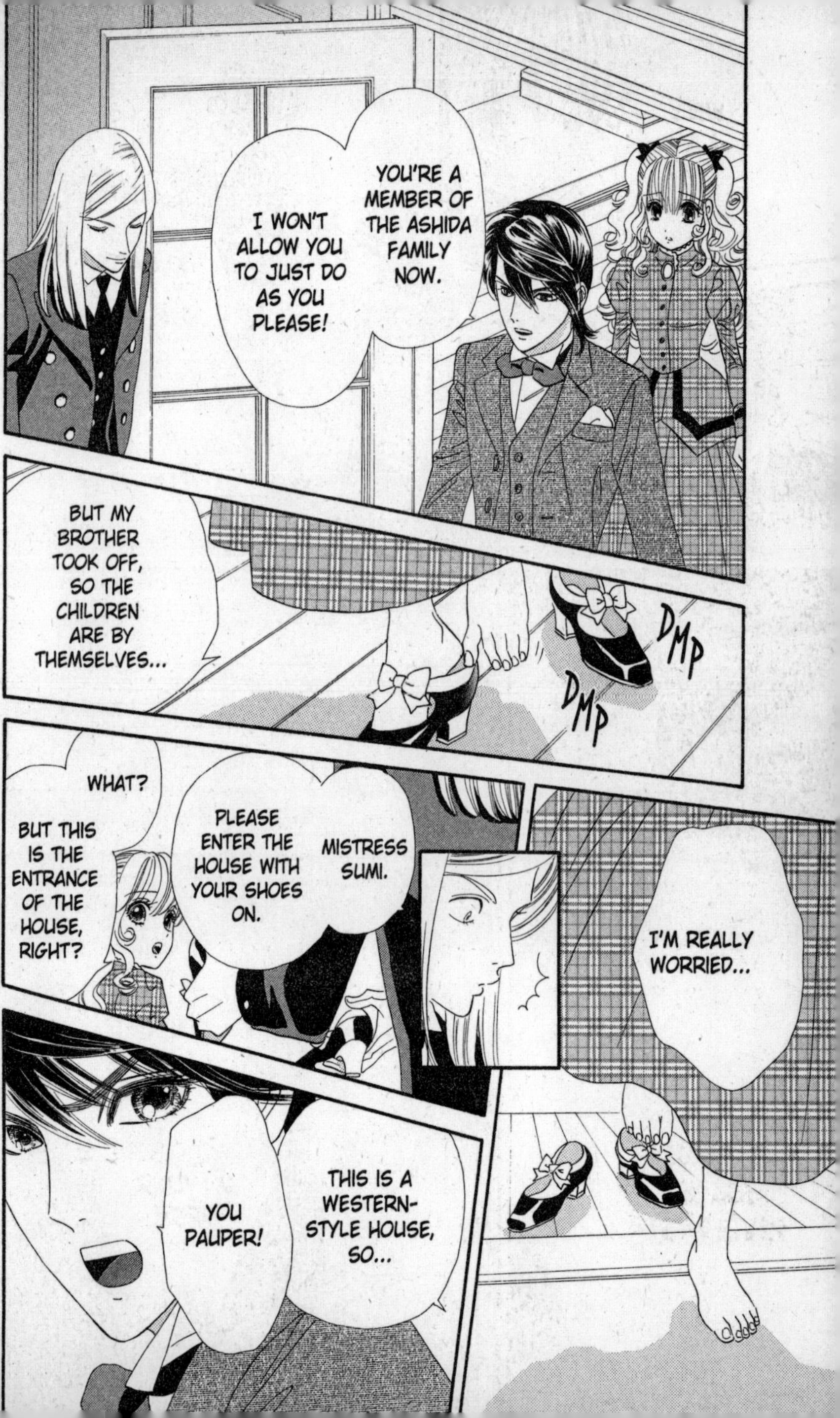
YOU'RE A MEMBER OF THE ASHIDA FAMILY NOW.
I WON'T ALLOW YOU TO JUST DO AS YOU PLEASE!
DMP
DMP
BUT MY BROTHER TOOK OFF, SO THE CHILDREN ARE BY THEMSELVES...
I'M REALLY WORRIED...
MISTRESS SUMI.
PLEASE ENTER THE HOUSE WITH YOUR SHOES ON.
WHAT?
BUT THIS IS THE ENTRANCE OF THE HOUSE, RIGHT?
THIS IS A WESTERN-STYLE HOUSE, SO...
YOU PAUPER!

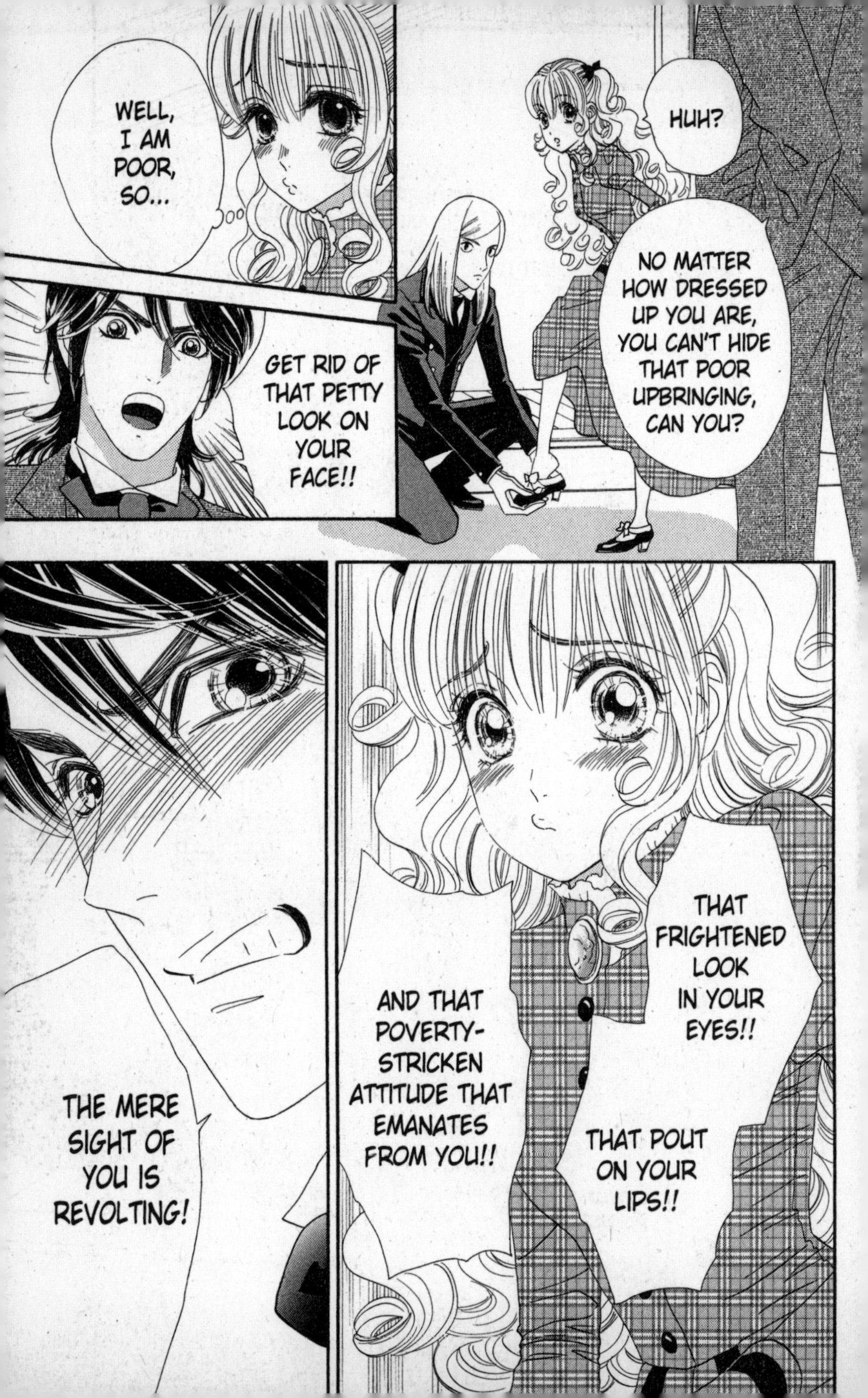
HUH?
NO MATTER HOW DRESSED UP YOU ARE, YOU CAN'T HIDE THAT POOR UPBRINGING, CAN YOU?
WELL, I AM POOR, SO...
GET RID OF THAT PETTY LOOK ON YOUR FACE!!
THAT FRIGHTENED LOOK IN YOUR EYES!!
THAT POUT ON YOUR LIPS!!
AND THAT POVERTY-STRICKEN ATTITUDE THAT EMANATES FROM YOU!!
THE MERE SIGHT OF YOU IS REVOLTING!

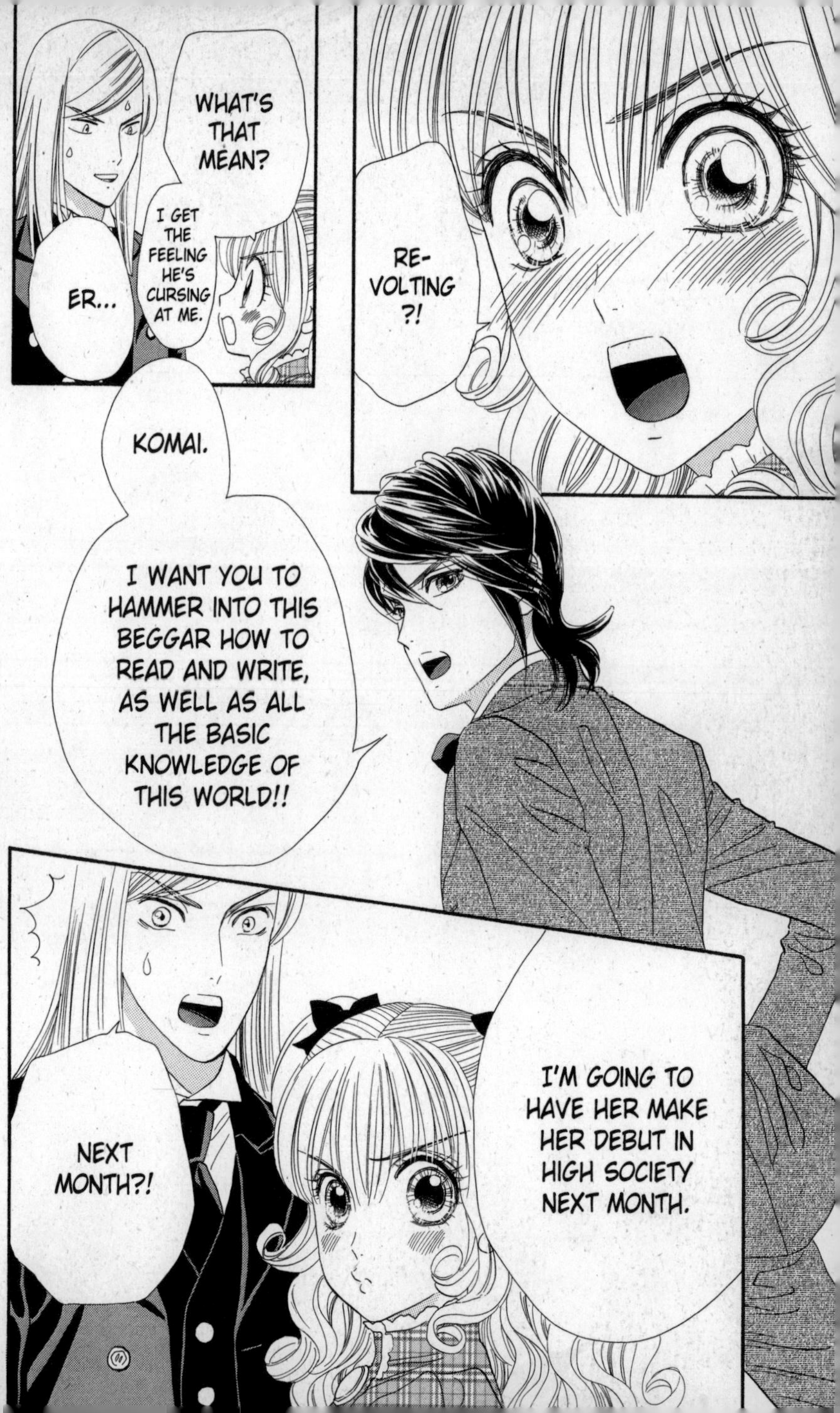
RE-VOLTING?!
WHAT'S THAT MEAN?
I GET THE FEELING HE'S CURSING AT ME.
ER...
KOMAI.
I WANT YOU TO HAMMER INTO THIS BEGGAR HOW TO READ AND WRITE, AS WELL AS ALL THE BASIC KNOWLEDGE OF THIS WORLD!!
I'M GOING TO HAVE HER MAKE HER DEBUT IN HIGH SOCIETY NEXT MONTH.
NEXT MONTH?!

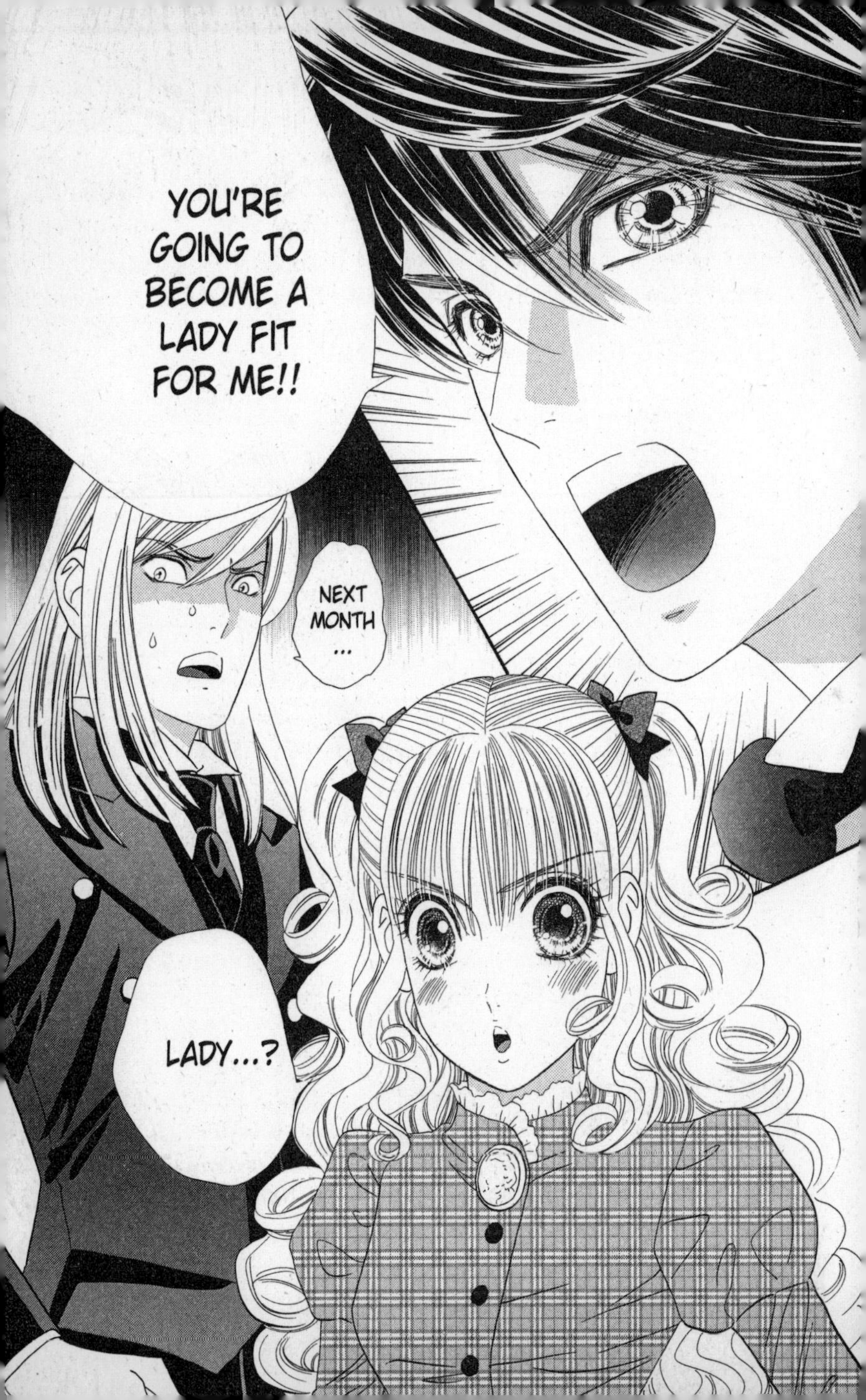
YOU'RE GOING TO BECOME A LADY FIT FOR ME!!
NEXT MONTH ...
LADY...?

No.

Date

FOR A MOMENT I THOUGHT, "WE'LL GO WITH 'A-MEIJI-NG STORY'!" BUT I SOON CAME TO MY SENSES AND TURNED THAT TITLE DOWN. I THEN GAVE THE TITLE MORE SERIOUS THOUGHT. I TEND TO BE SLIGHTLY MASOCHISTIC, AND I LIKE LINES WHERE PEOPLE ARE GIVING ORDERS TO OTHER PEOPLE, SO I WANTED THE TITLE TO SOUND LIKE A COMMAND. I ADDED THE WORD "BARA" ("ROSE") AND CAME UP WITH THE TITLE.

HOW'S "HADASHI DE BARA WO FUME" SOUND? [THIS JAPANESE TITLE LITERALLY TRANSLATES TO "STEP ON THE ROSES BAREFOOT."] EVERYBODY WAS SO TIRED THAT THEY WERE LIKE, "SURE, WHY NOT?" AND "OKAY, LET'S GO HOME..."

LOOK! THIS IS THE ACTUAL NOTE I WROTE WHEN I WAS TRYING TO FIGURE OUT THE TITLE!!

BUT FIRST I HAD TO WRITE OUT ALL THE TITLE CHOICES TO DECIDE WHETHER WE'D HAVE "HADASHI" ("BAREFOOT") IN KANJI CHARACTERS, HIRAGANA OR KATAKANA.

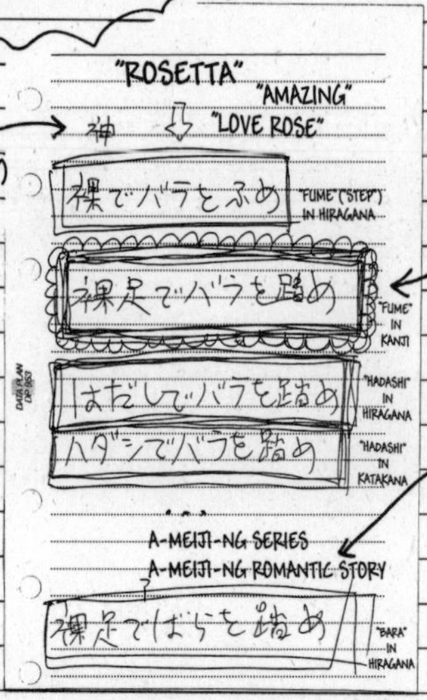
"ROSETTA"
"AMAZING"
"LOVE ROSE"
神
裸でバラとふめ
"FUME" ("STEP") IN HIRAGANA
裸足でバラを踏め
"FUME" IN KANJI
はだしでバラを踏め
"HADASHI" IN HIRAGANA
ハダシでバラを踏め
"HADASHI" IN KATAKANA
A-MEIJI-NG SERIES
A-MEIJI-NG ROMANTIC STORY
裸足でばらを踏め
"BARA" IN HIRAGANA

I TRIED TO WRITE 裸 ("BARE") AND MADE A MISTAKE.

A SILLY LOOKING FRAME AROUND THE CHOSEN TITLE... IT BRINGS TEARS TO MY EYES.

IT TAKES ME A WHILE TO REMEMBER THE KANJI FOR "FUME." BUT WE DON'T REALLY WRITE 踏 THAT OFTEN, DO WE? DO WE?

THE SKETCHY TITLE THAT MADE ITS WAY INTO THE LIST OF LAST CHOICES.

OH NO! I'VE BEEN DOING SO MUCH SMALL TALK THAT I DON'T HAVE ANY SPACE LEFT TO WRITE ABOUT HOW I DECIDED THE NAMES OF THE CHARACTERS. CHECK OUT THE NEXT VOLUME!

Rinko Ueda

SEE YOU!

PLEASE SEND YOUR REMARKS AND REQUESTS TO THE FOLLOWING ADDRESS:

RINKO UEDA
C/O STEPPING ON ROSES EDITOR
VIZ MEDIA
P.O. BOX 77010
SAN FRANCISCO, CA 94107

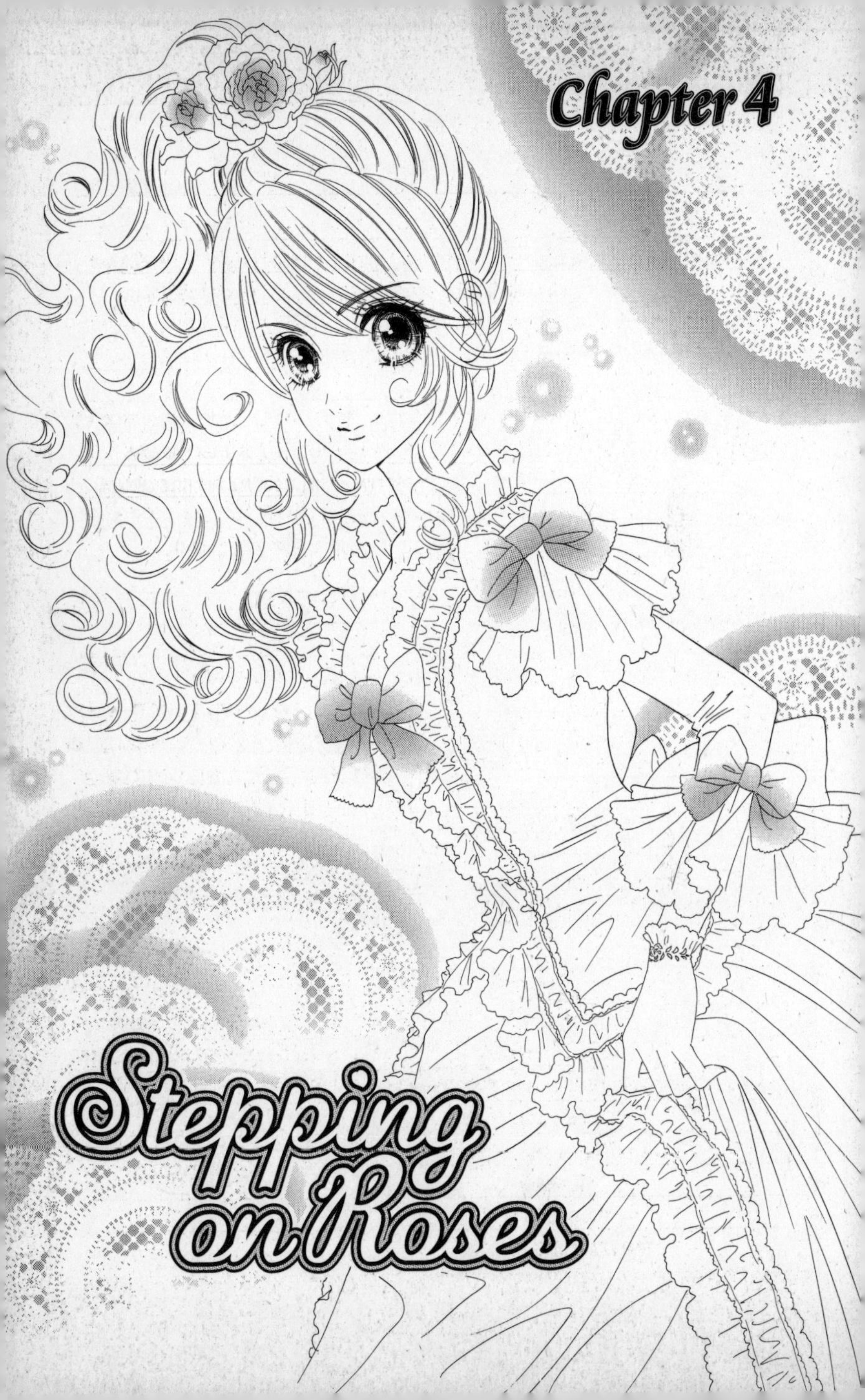
Chapter 4
Stepping on Roses

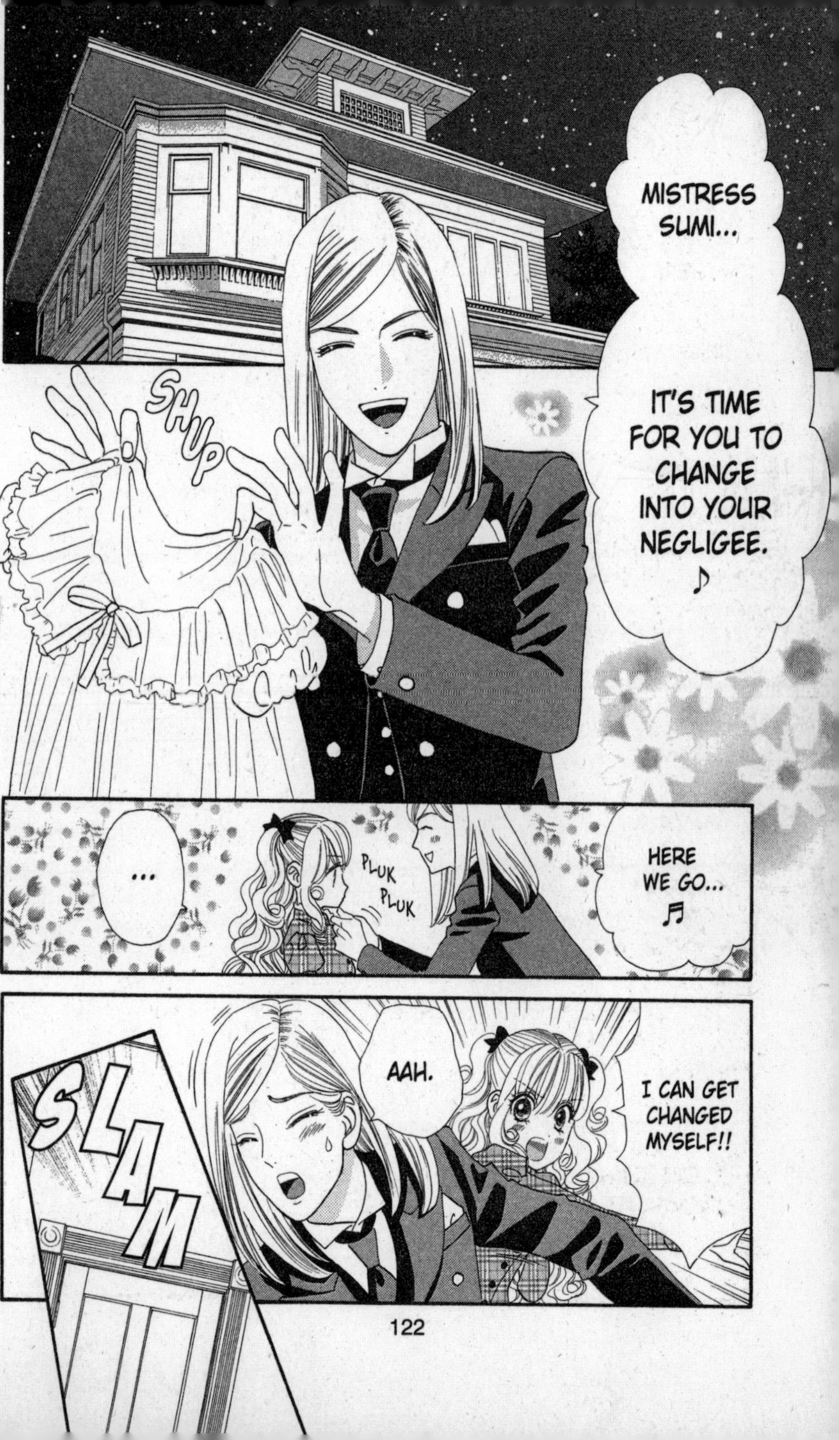
MISTRESS SUMI...
IT'S TIME FOR YOU TO CHANGE INTO YOUR NEGLIGEE. ♪
SHUP
HERE WE GO... ♬
PLUK PLUK
...
I CAN GET CHANGED MYSELF!!
AAH.
SLAM

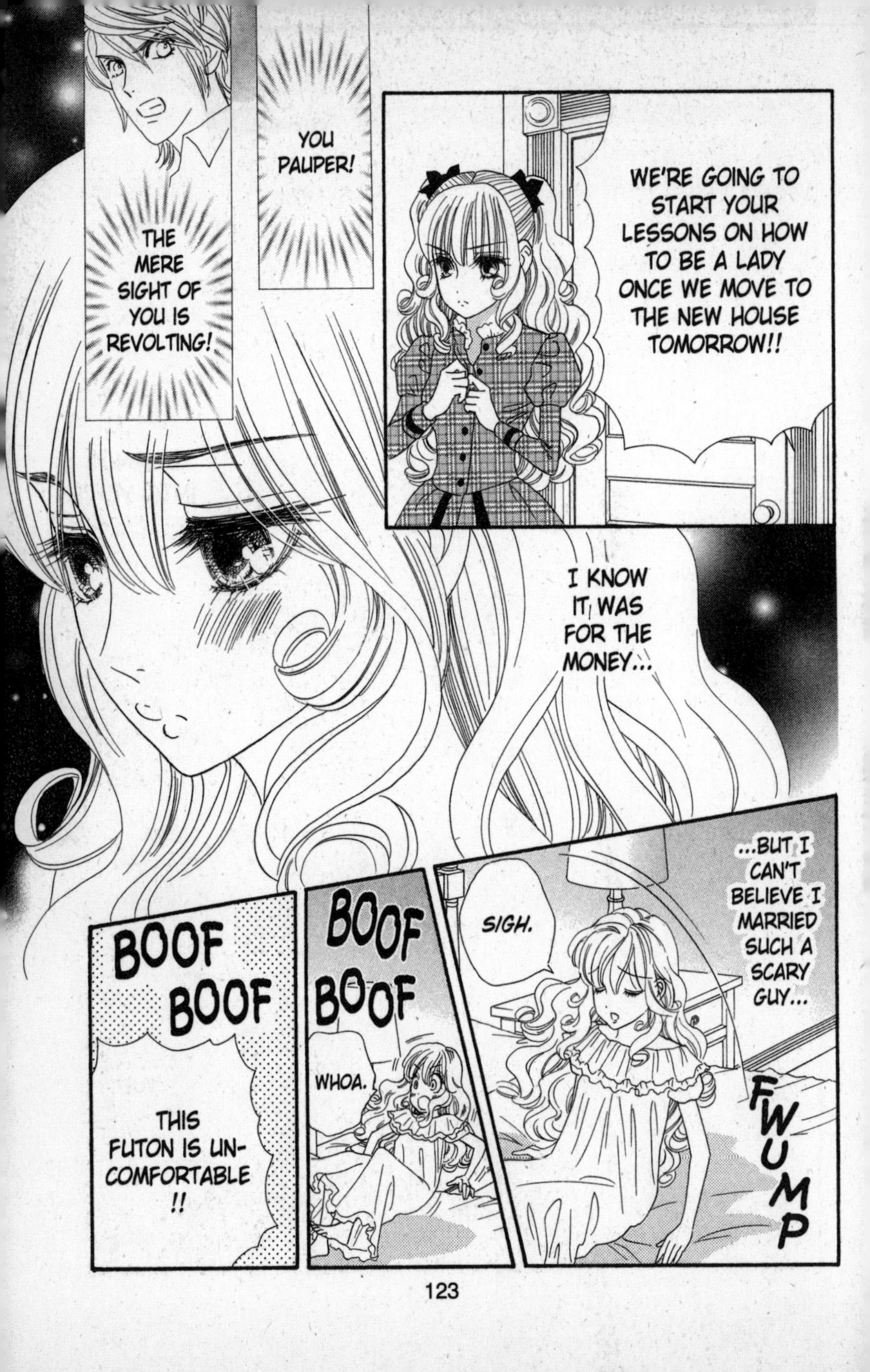
WE'RE GOING TO START YOUR LESSONS ON HOW TO BE A LADY ONCE WE MOVE TO THE NEW HOUSE TOMORROW!!
YOU PAUPER!
THE MERE SIGHT OF YOU IS REVOLTING!
I KNOW IT WAS FOR THE MONEY...
...BUT I CAN'T BELIEVE I MARRIED SUCH A SCARY GUY...
SIGH.
FWUMP
BOOF BOOF
WHOA.
BOOF BOOF
THIS FUTON IS UN-COMFORTABLE !!

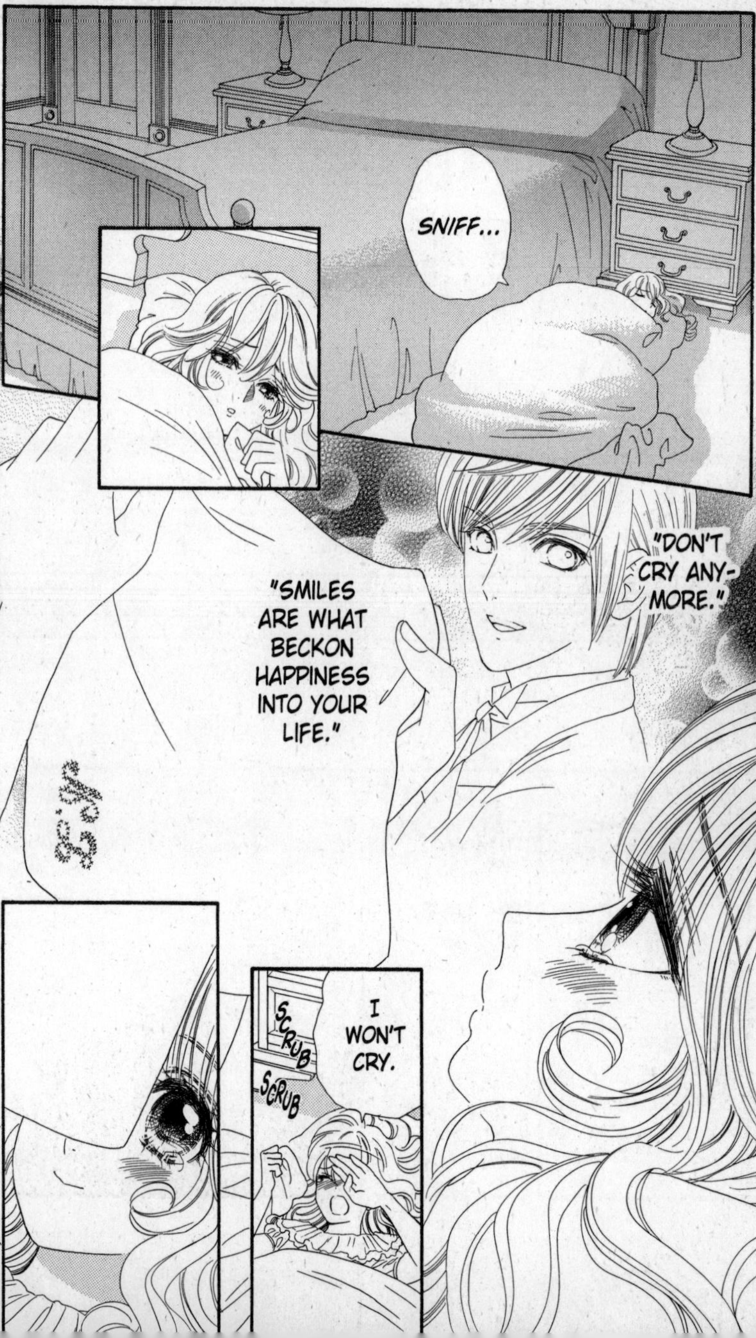
SNIFF...
"DON'T CRY ANY-MORE."
"SMILES ARE WHAT BECKON HAPPINESS INTO YOUR LIFE."
I WON'T CRY.
SCRUB
SCRUB

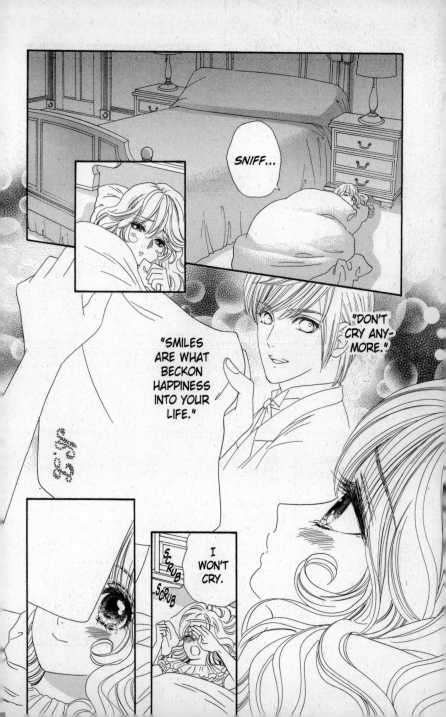

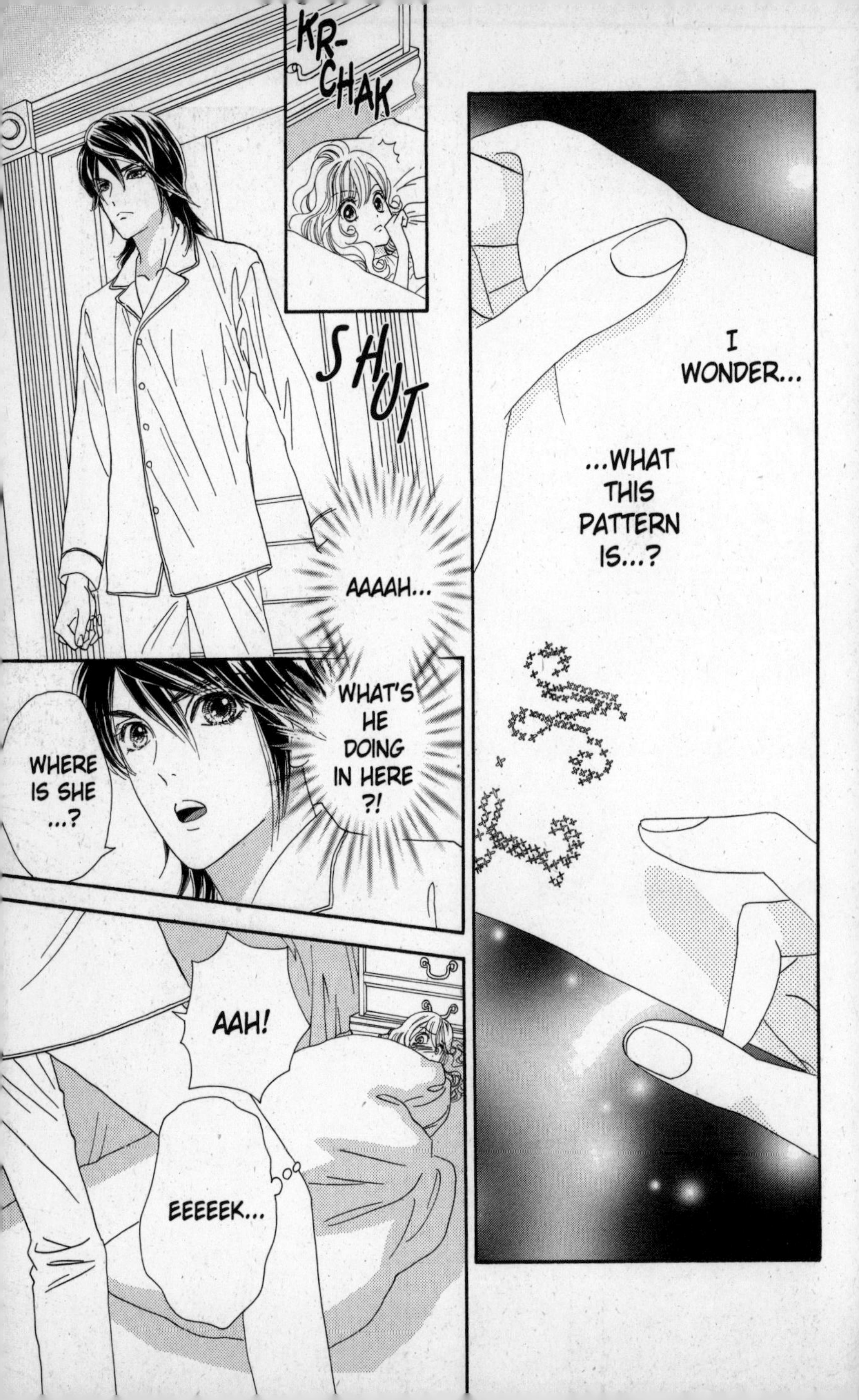
I WONDER...
...WHAT THIS PATTERN IS...?
KR-CHAK
SHUT
AAAAH...
WHAT'S HE DOING IN HERE?!
WHERE IS SHE...?
AAH!
EEEEEK...

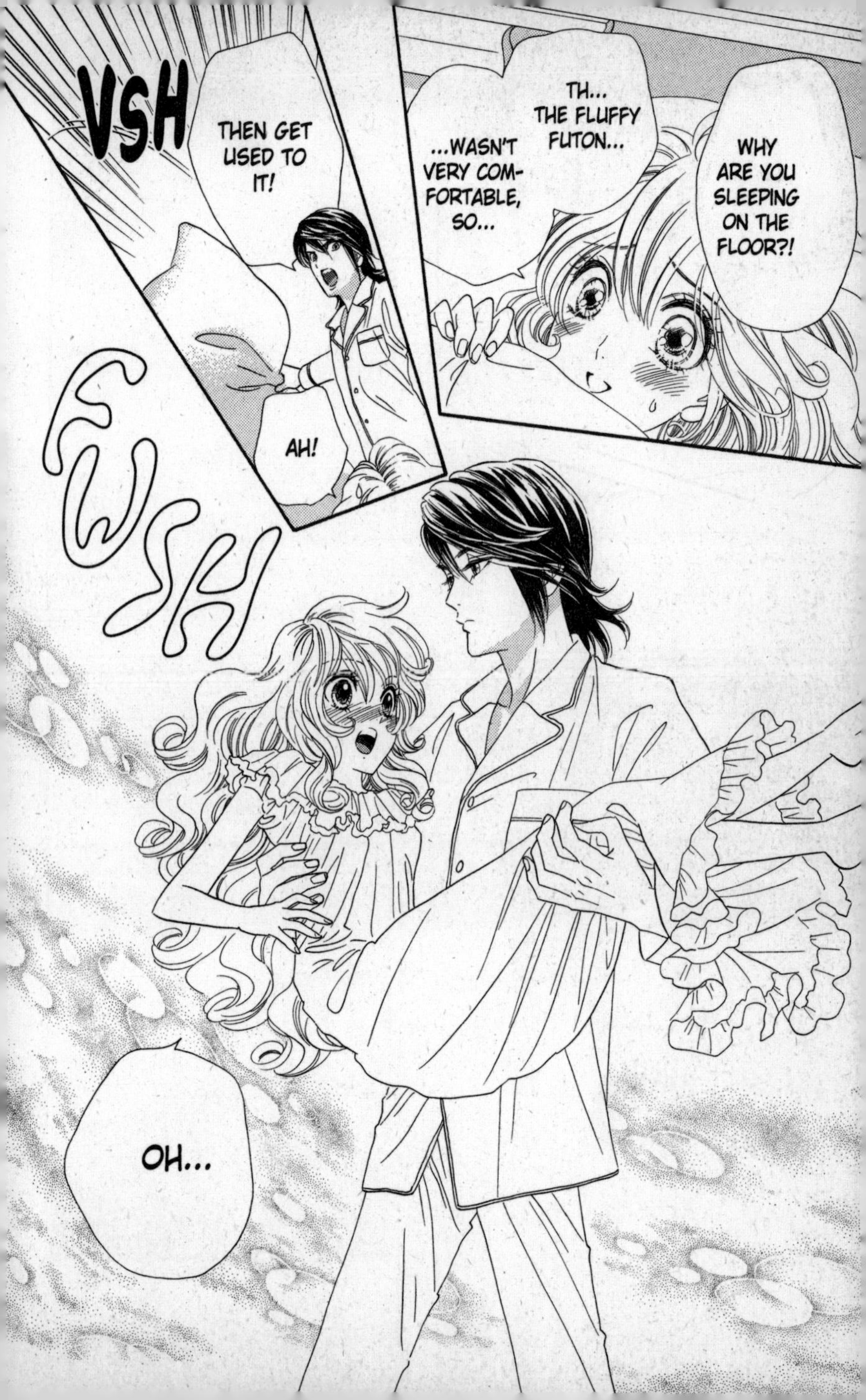
WHY ARE YOU SLEEPING ON THE FLOOR?!
TH... THE FLUFFY FUTON...
...WASN'T VERY COM-FORTABLE, SO...
VSH
THEN GET USED TO IT!
AH!
FWSH
OH...

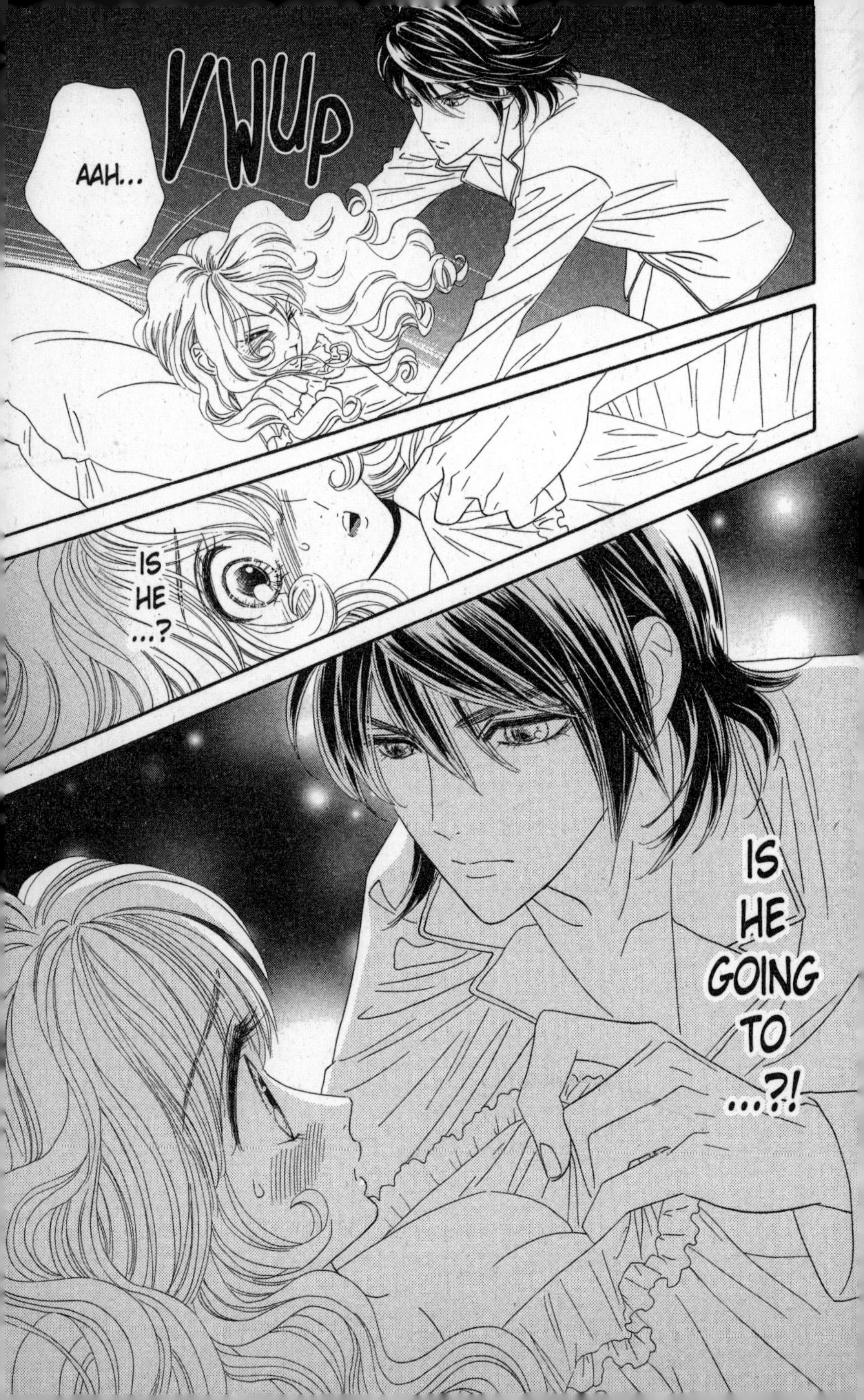
VWUP
AAH...
IS HE ...?
IS HE GOING TO ...?!

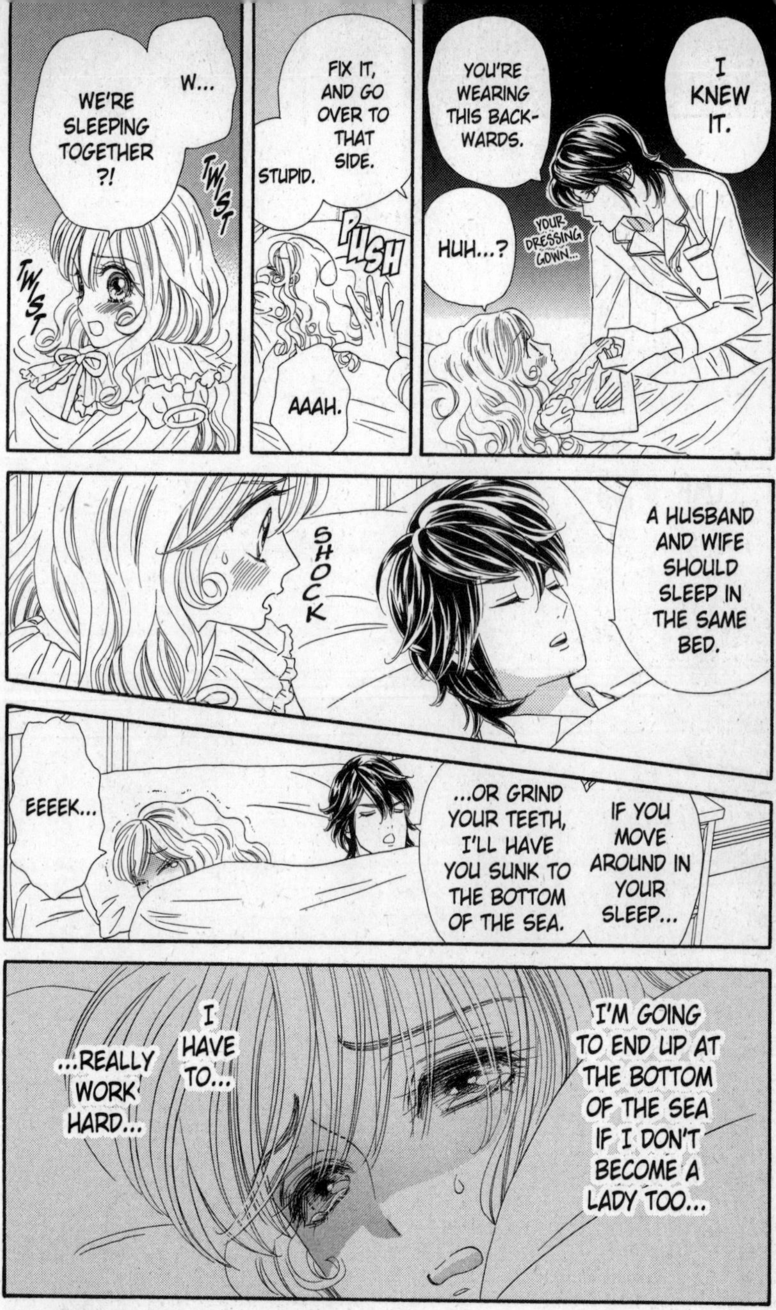
I KNEW IT.
YOU'RE WEARING THIS BACK-WARDS.
YOUR DRESSING GOWN...
HUH...?
FIX IT, AND GO OVER TO THAT SIDE.
STUPID.
PUSH
AAAH.
W...
WE'RE SLEEPING TOGETHER ?!
TWIST
TWIST
A HUSBAND AND WIFE SHOULD SLEEP IN THE SAME BED.
SHOCK
IF YOU MOVE AROUND IN YOUR SLEEP...
...OR GRIND YOUR TEETH, I'LL HAVE YOU SUNK TO THE BOTTOM OF THE SEA.
EEEEK...
I'M GOING TO END UP AT THE BOTTOM OF THE SEA IF I DON'T BECOME A LADY TOO...
I HAVE TO...
...REALLY WORK HARD...

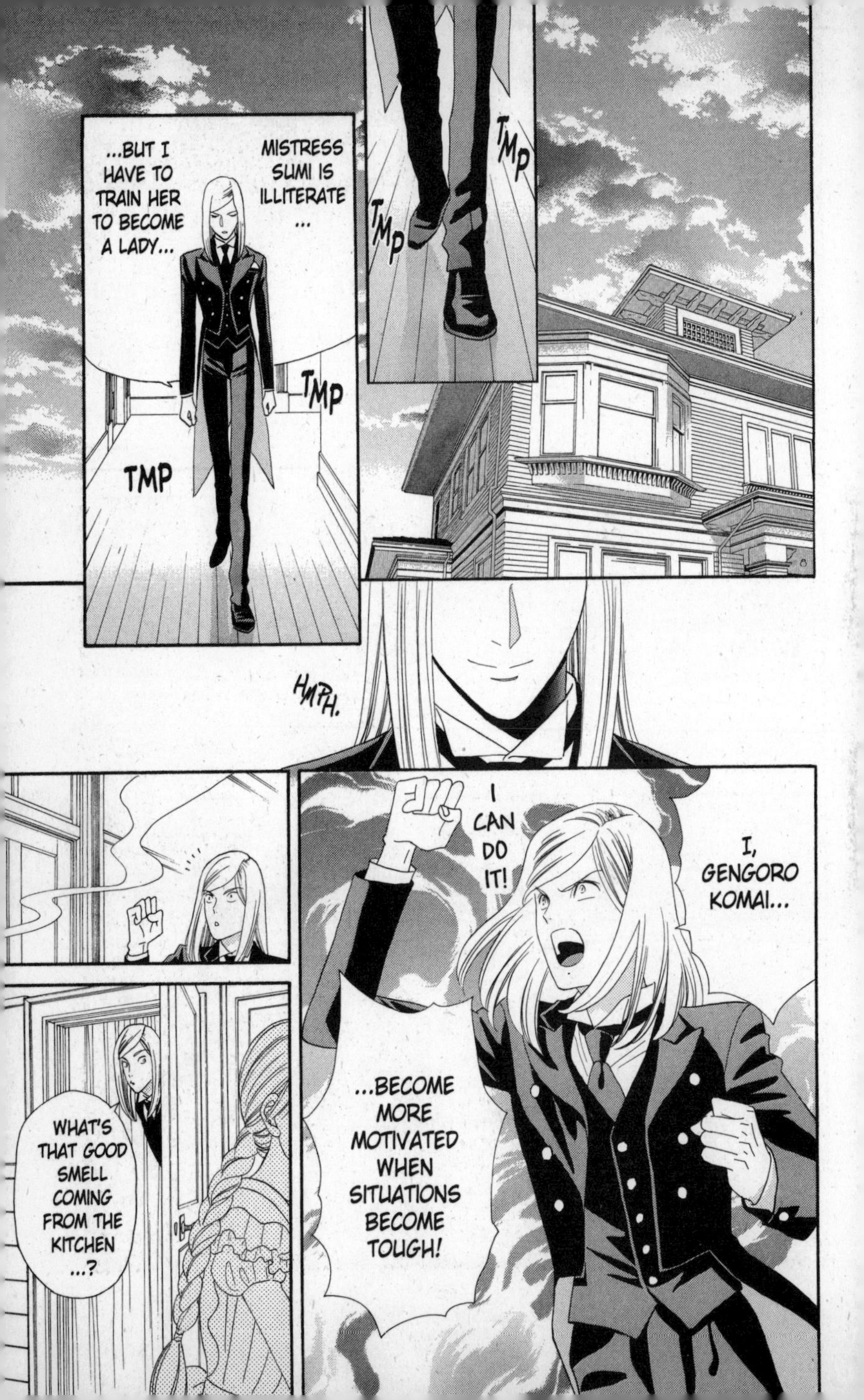
TMP
TMP
MISTRESS SUMI IS ILLITERATE ...
...BUT I HAVE TO TRAIN HER TO BECOME A LADY...
TMP
TMP
HMPH.
I, GENGORO KOMAI...
...BECOME MORE MOTIVATED WHEN SITUATIONS BECOME TOUGH!
I CAN DO IT!
WHAT'S THAT GOOD SMELL COMING FROM THE KITCHEN ...?

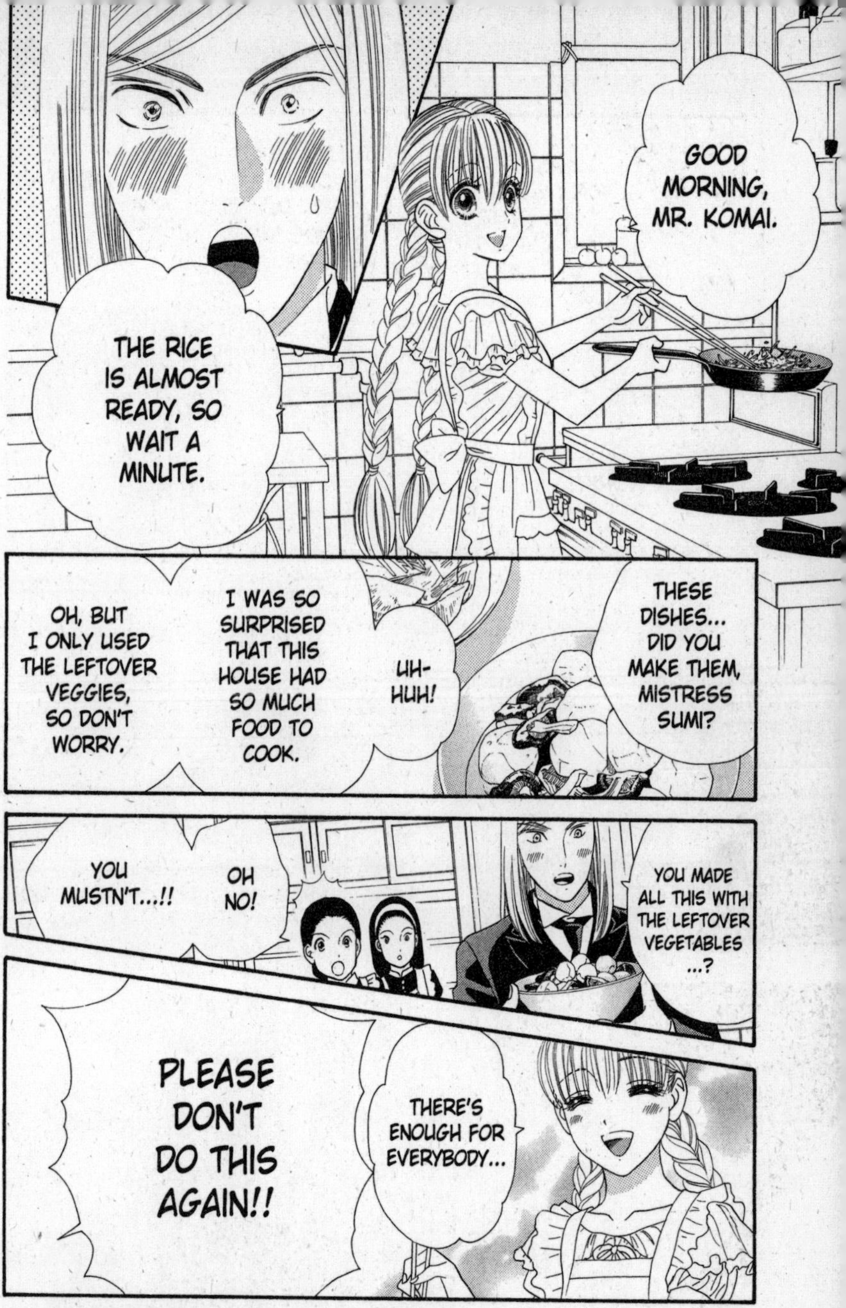
GOOD MORNING, MR. KOMAI.
THE RICE IS ALMOST READY, SO WAIT A MINUTE.
THESE DISHES... DID YOU MAKE THEM, MISTRESS SUMI?
UH-HUH!
I WAS SO SURPRISED THAT THIS HOUSE HAD SO MUCH FOOD TO COOK.
OH, BUT I ONLY USED THE LEFTOVER VEGGIES, SO DON'T WORRY.
YOU MADE ALL THIS WITH THE LEFTOVER VEGETABLES ...?
OH NO!
YOU MUSTN'T...!!
THERE'S ENOUGH FOR EVERYBODY...
PLEASE DON'T DO THIS AGAIN!!

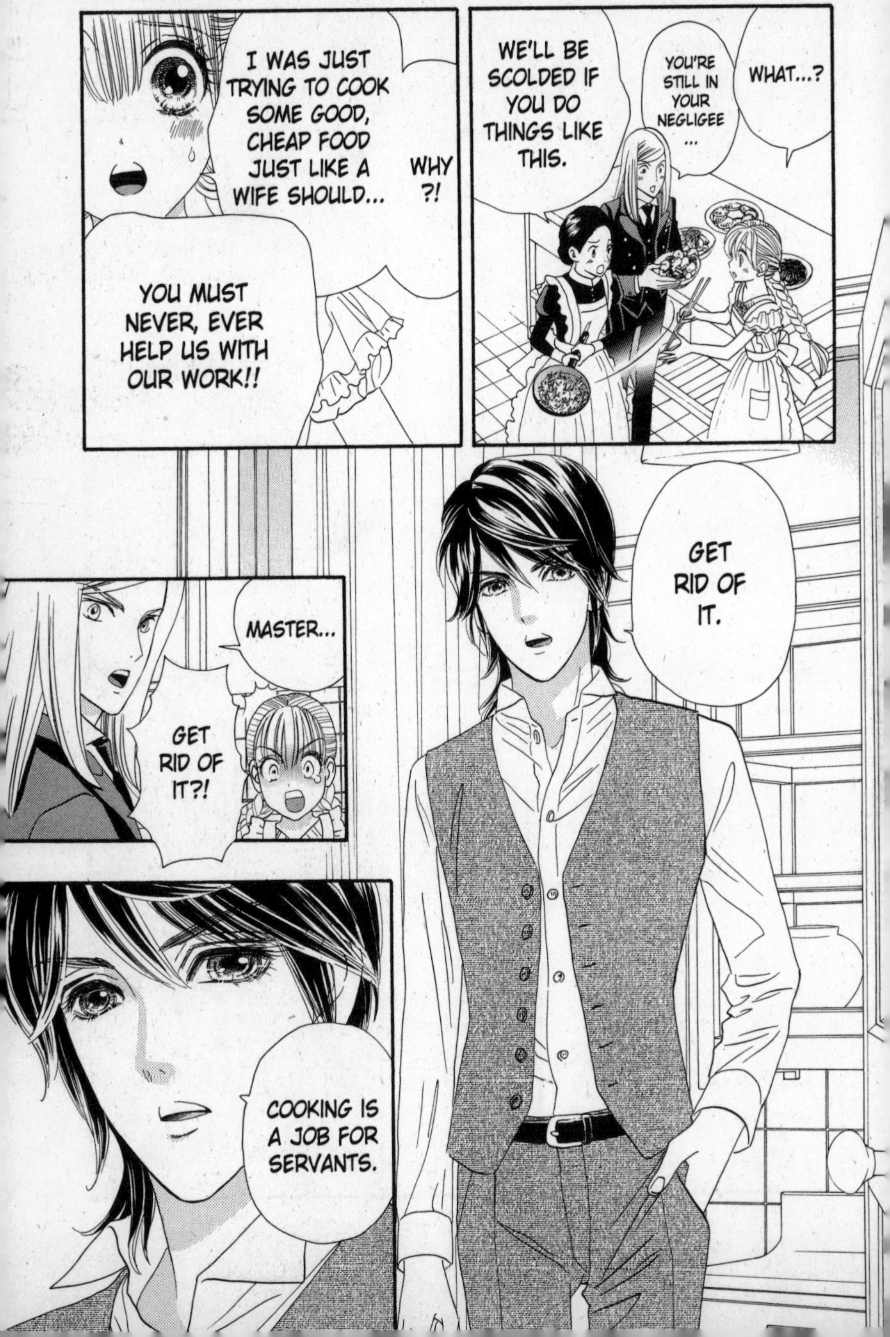
WHAT...?
YOU'RE STILL IN YOUR NEGLIGEE ...
WE'LL BE SCOLDED IF YOU DO THINGS LIKE THIS.
WHY ?!
I WAS JUST TRYING TO COOK SOME GOOD, CHEAP FOOD JUST LIKE A WIFE SHOULD...
YOU MUST NEVER, EVER HELP US WITH OUR WORK!!
GET RID OF IT.
MASTER...
GET RID OF IT?!
COOKING IS A JOB FOR SERVANTS.

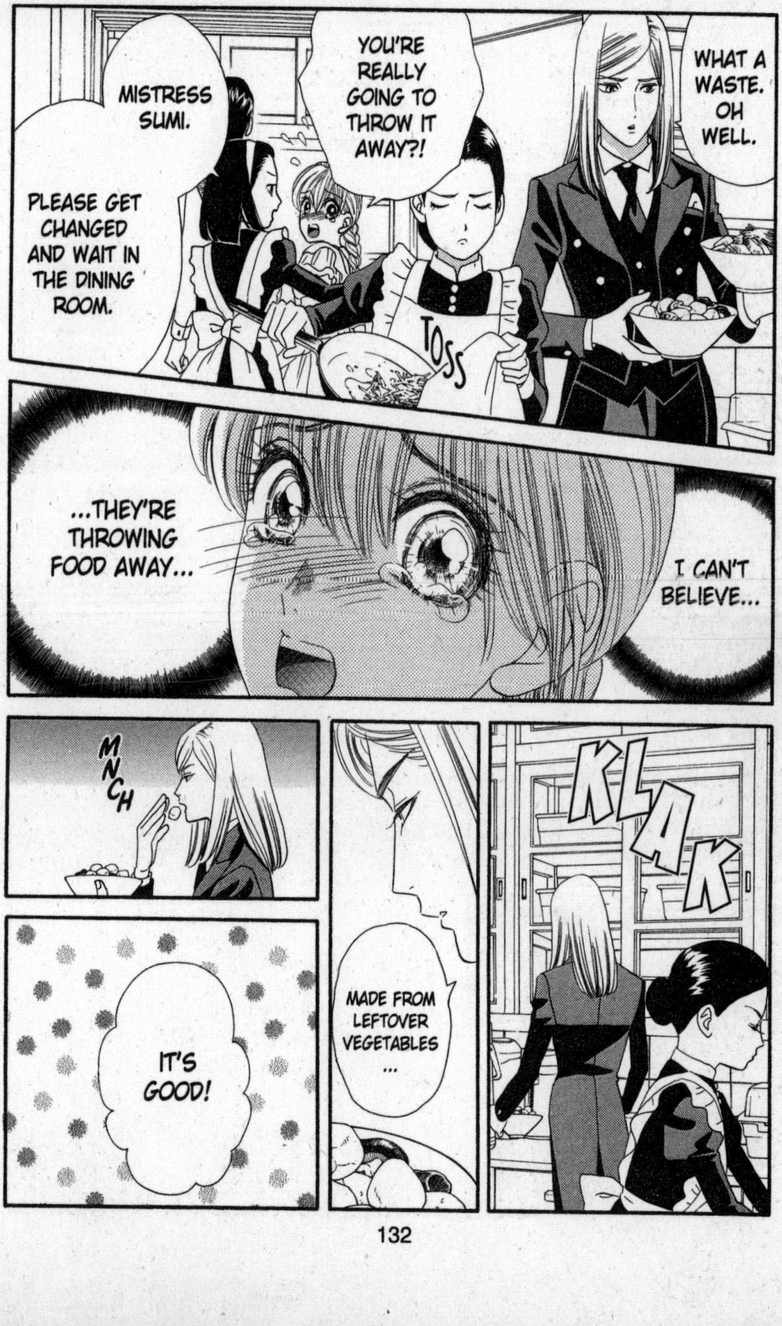
WHAT A WASTE. OH WELL.
YOU'RE REALLY GOING TO THROW IT AWAY?!
TOSS
MISTRESS SUMI.
PLEASE GET CHANGED AND WAIT IN THE DINING ROOM.
I CAN'T BELIEVE...
...THEY'RE THROWING FOOD AWAY...
KLAK
MADE FROM LEFTOVER VEGETABLES ...
MNCH
IT'S GOOD!

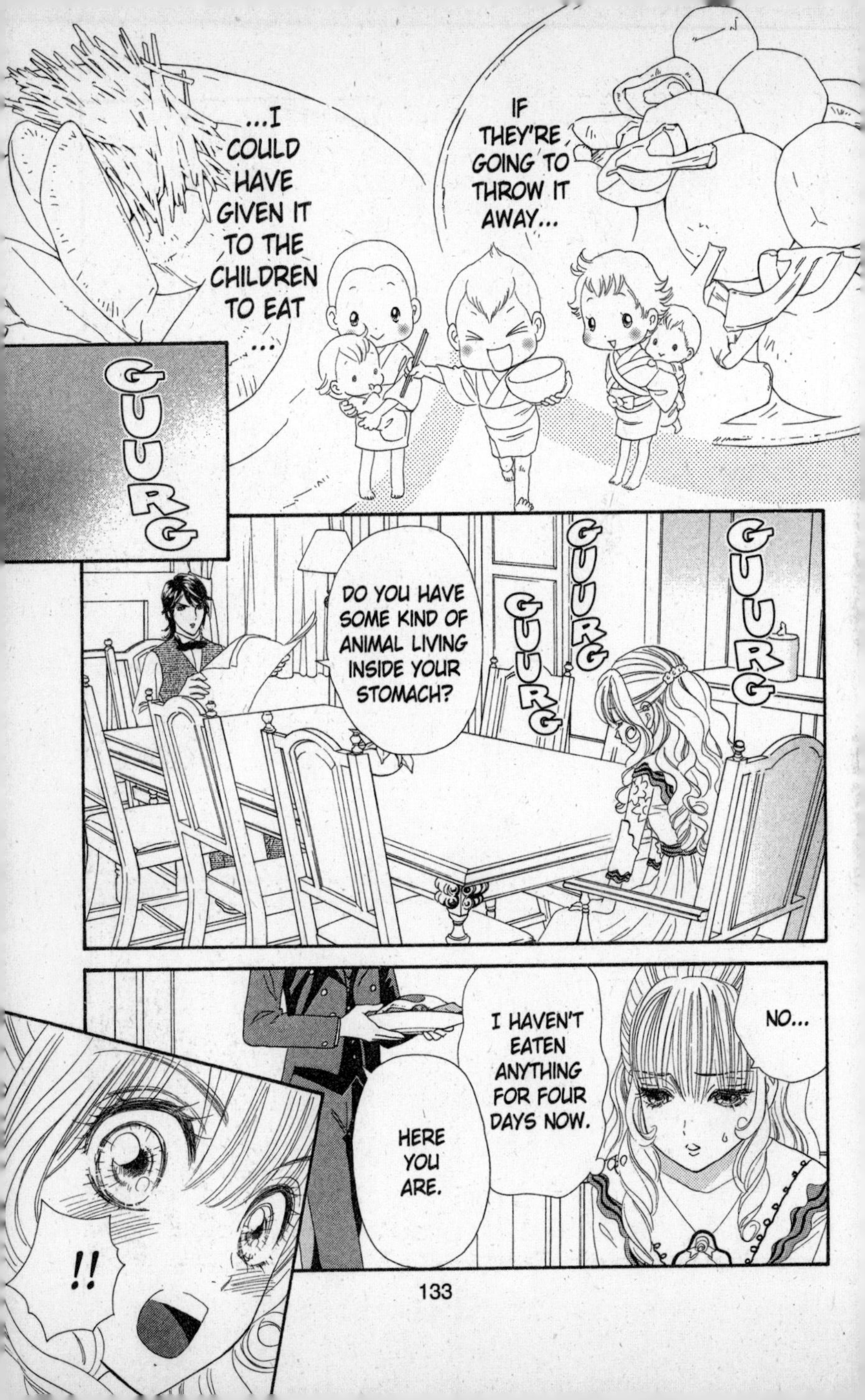
IF THEY'RE GOING TO THROW IT AWAY...
...I COULD HAVE GIVEN IT TO THE CHILDREN TO EAT ...
GUURG
GUURG
GUURG
GUURG
DO YOU HAVE SOME KIND OF ANIMAL LIVING INSIDE YOUR STOMACH?
NO...
I HAVEN'T EATEN ANYTHING FOR FOUR DAYS NOW.
HERE YOU ARE.
!!

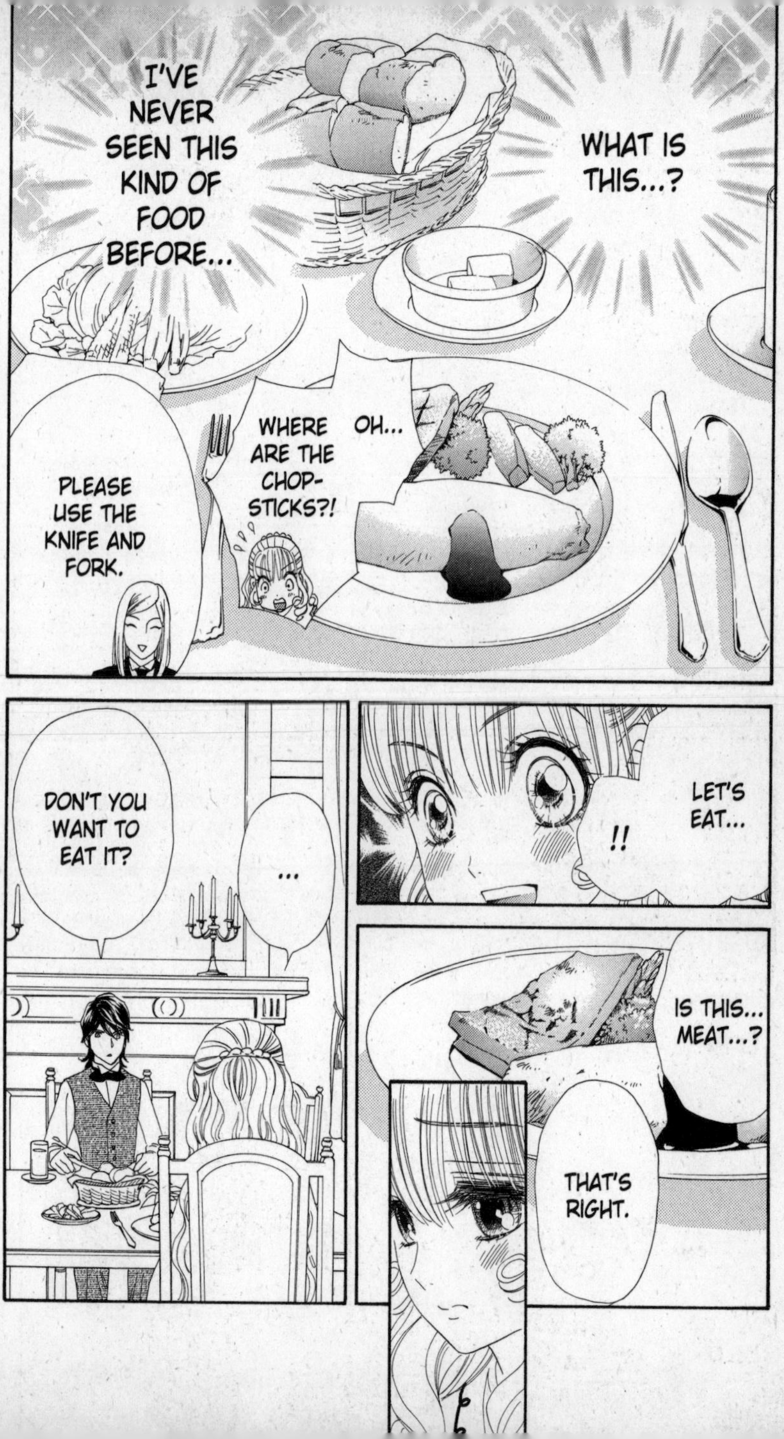
WHAT IS THIS...?
I'VE NEVER SEEN THIS KIND OF FOOD BEFORE...
OH...
WHERE ARE THE CHOP-STICKS?!
PLEASE USE THE KNIFE AND FORK.
LET'S EAT...
!!
IS THIS... MEAT...?
THAT'S RIGHT.
...
DON'T YOU WANT TO EAT IT?

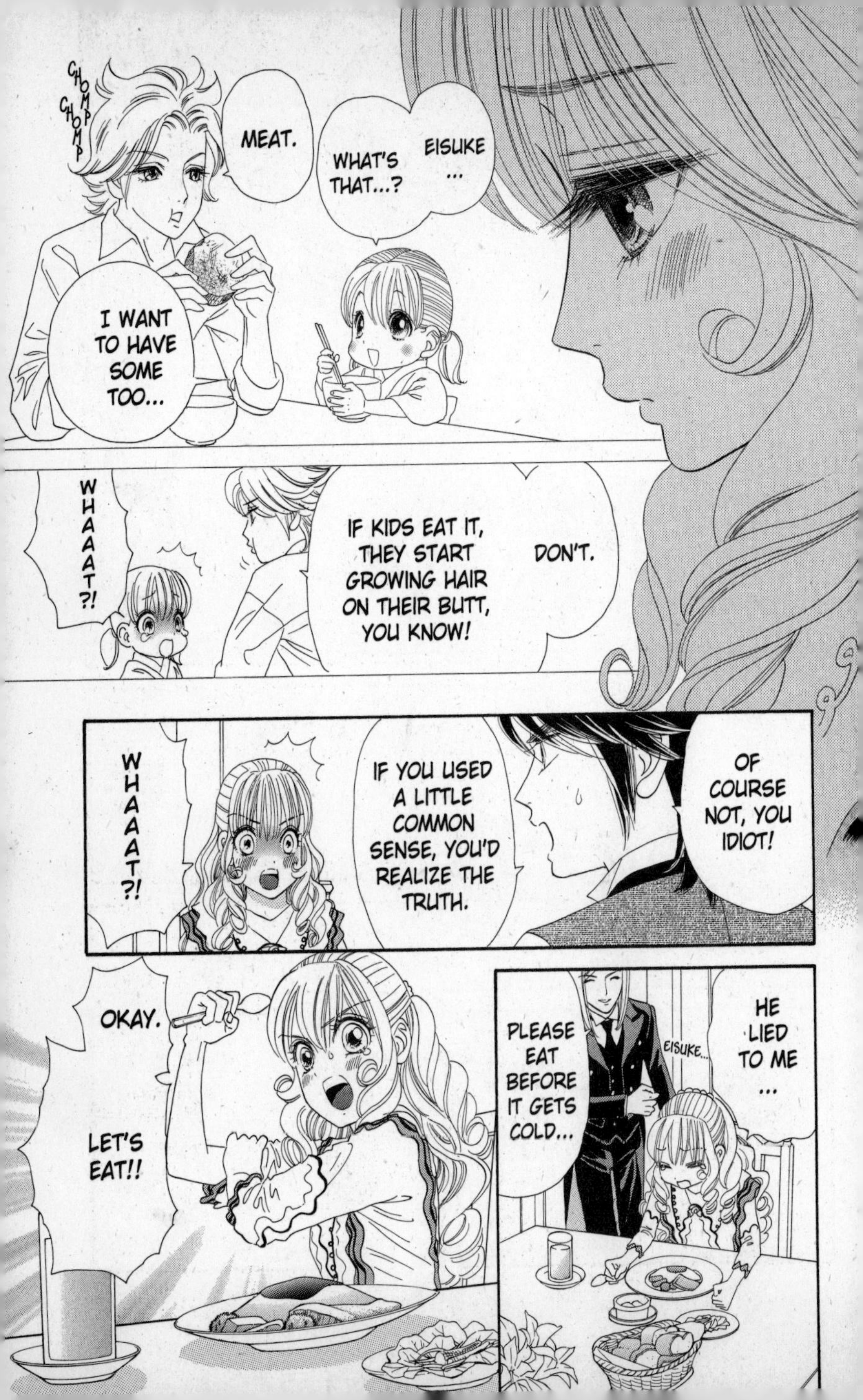
EISUKE...
WHAT'S THAT...?
MEAT.
CHOMP CHOMP
I WANT TO HAVE SOME TOO...
DON'T.
IF KIDS EAT IT, THEY START GROWING HAIR ON THEIR BUTT, YOU KNOW!
WHAAAAT?!
OF COURSE NOT, YOU IDIOT!
IF YOU USED A LITTLE COMMON SENSE, YOU'D REALIZE THE TRUTH.
WHAAAAT?!
HE LIED TO ME...
EISUKE...
PLEASE EAT BEFORE IT GETS COLD...
OKAY.
LET'S EAT!!

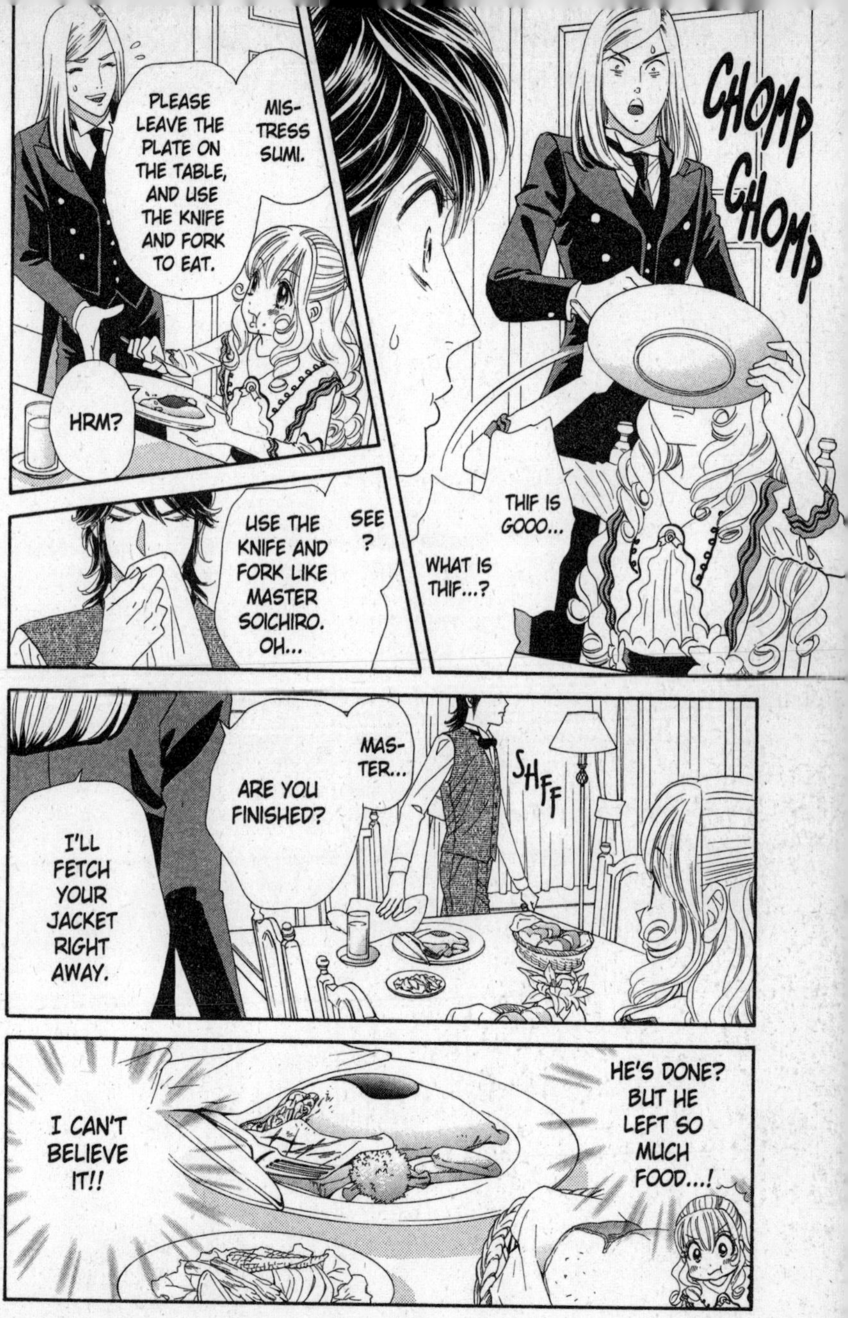
CHOMP CHOMP
THIF IS GOOO...
WHAT IS THIF...?
MIS-TRESS SUMI.
PLEASE LEAVE THE PLATE ON THE TABLE, AND USE THE KNIFE AND FORK TO EAT.
HRM?
SEE?
USE THE KNIFE AND FORK LIKE MASTER SOICHIRO. OH...
MAS-TER...
ARE YOU FINISHED?
SHFF
I'LL FETCH YOUR JACKET RIGHT AWAY.
HE'S DONE? BUT HE LEFT SO MUCH FOOD...!
I CAN'T BELIEVE IT!!

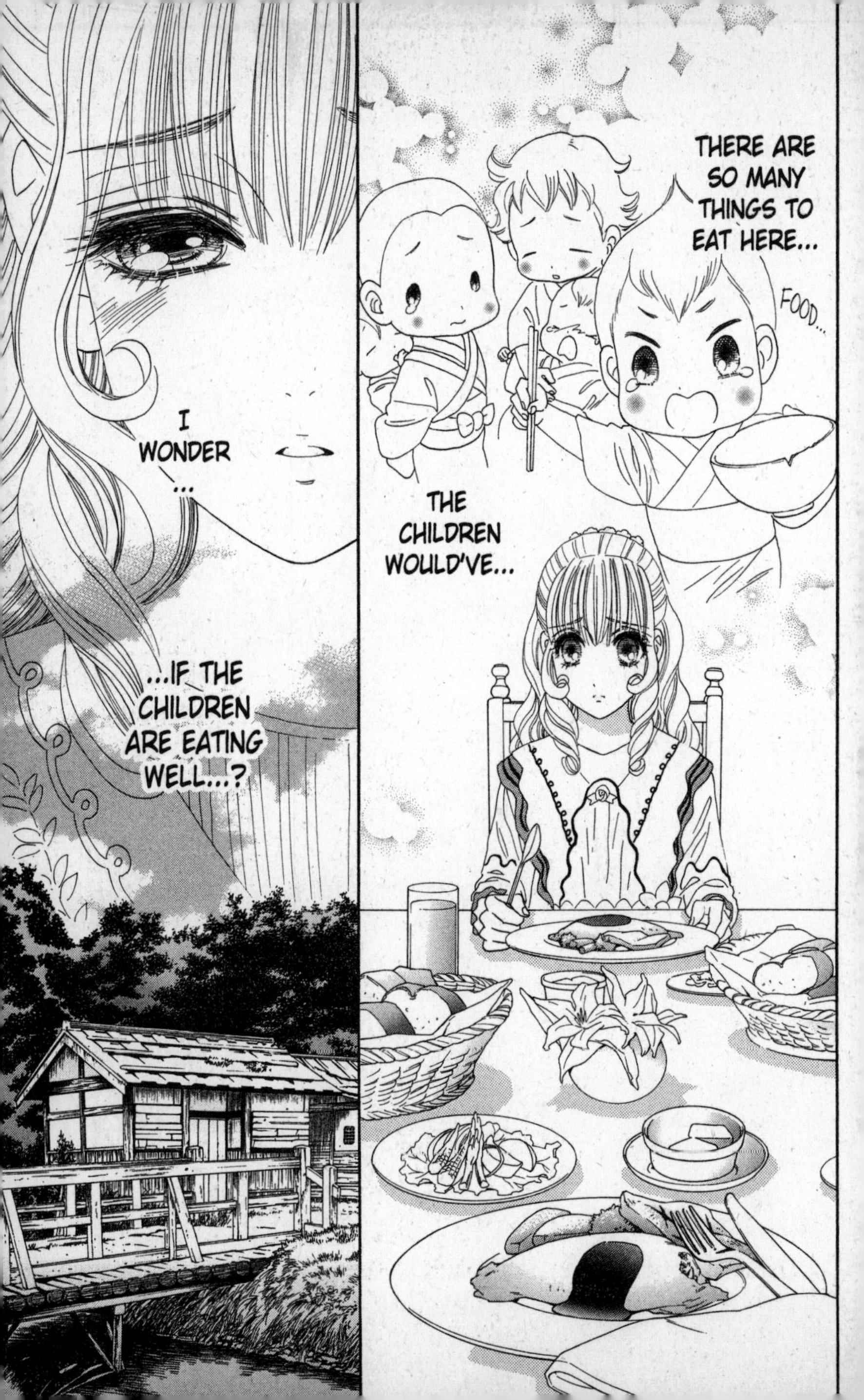
THERE ARE SO MANY THINGS TO EAT HERE...
FOOD...
THE CHILDREN WOULD'VE...
I WONDER ...
...IF THE CHILDREN ARE EATING WELL...?

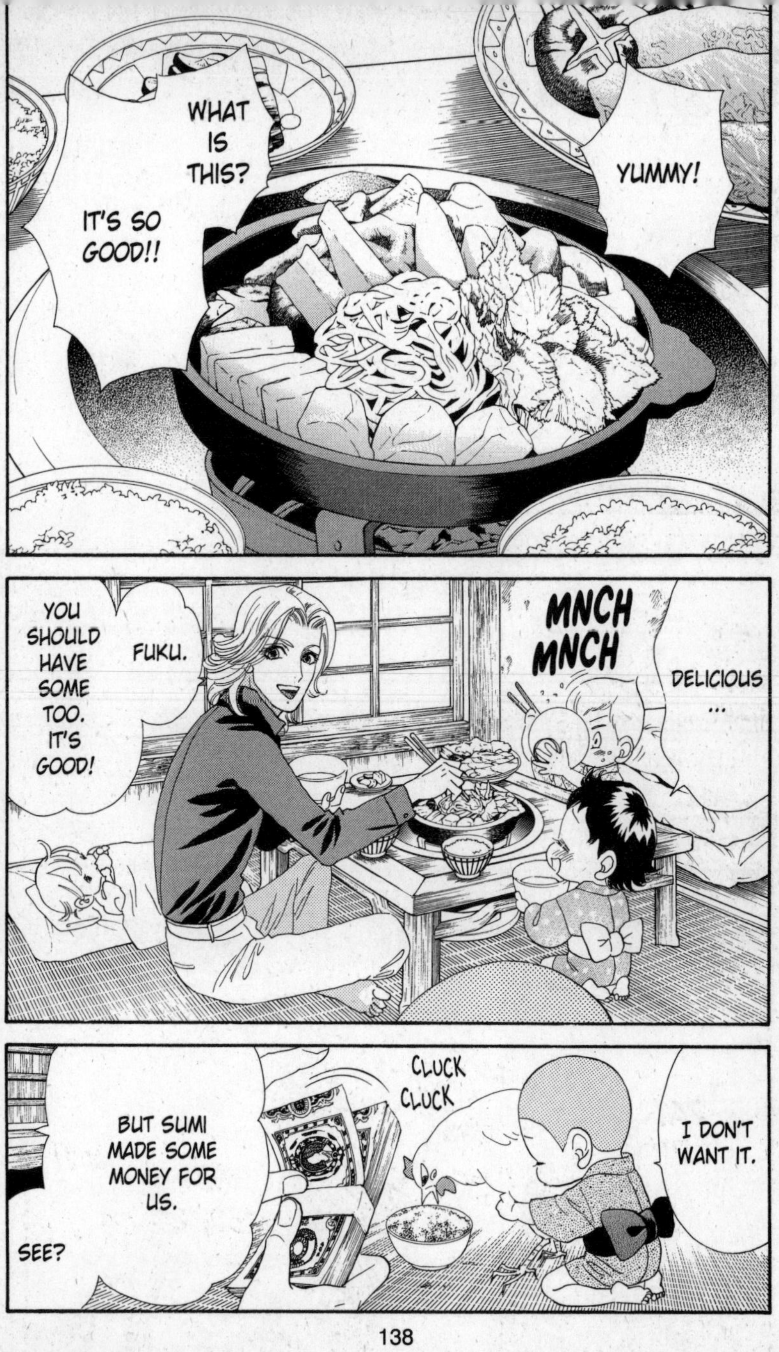
YUMMY!
WHAT IS THIS?
IT'S SO GOOD!!
DELICIOUS ...
MNCH MNCH
FUKU.
YOU SHOULD HAVE SOME TOO. IT'S GOOD!
I DON'T WANT IT.
CLUCK CLUCK
BUT SUMI MADE SOME MONEY FOR US.
SEE?

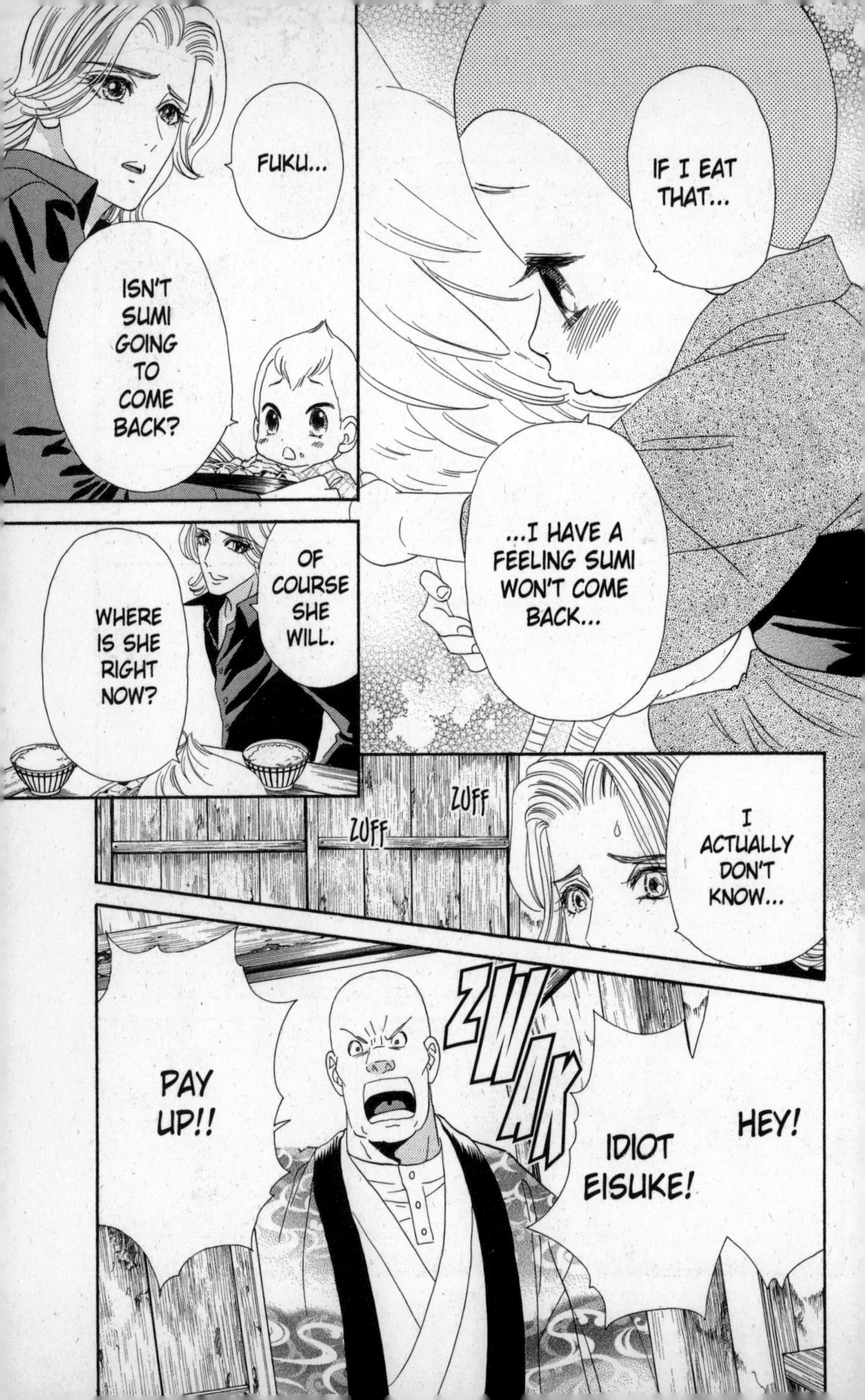
IF I EAT THAT...
...I HAVE A FEELING SUMI WON'T COME BACK...
FUKU...
ISN'T SUMI GOING TO COME BACK?
OF COURSE SHE WILL.
WHERE IS SHE RIGHT NOW?
I ACTUALLY DON'T KNOW...
ZUFF
ZUFF
HEY!
IDIOT EISUKE!
ZWAK
PAY UP!!

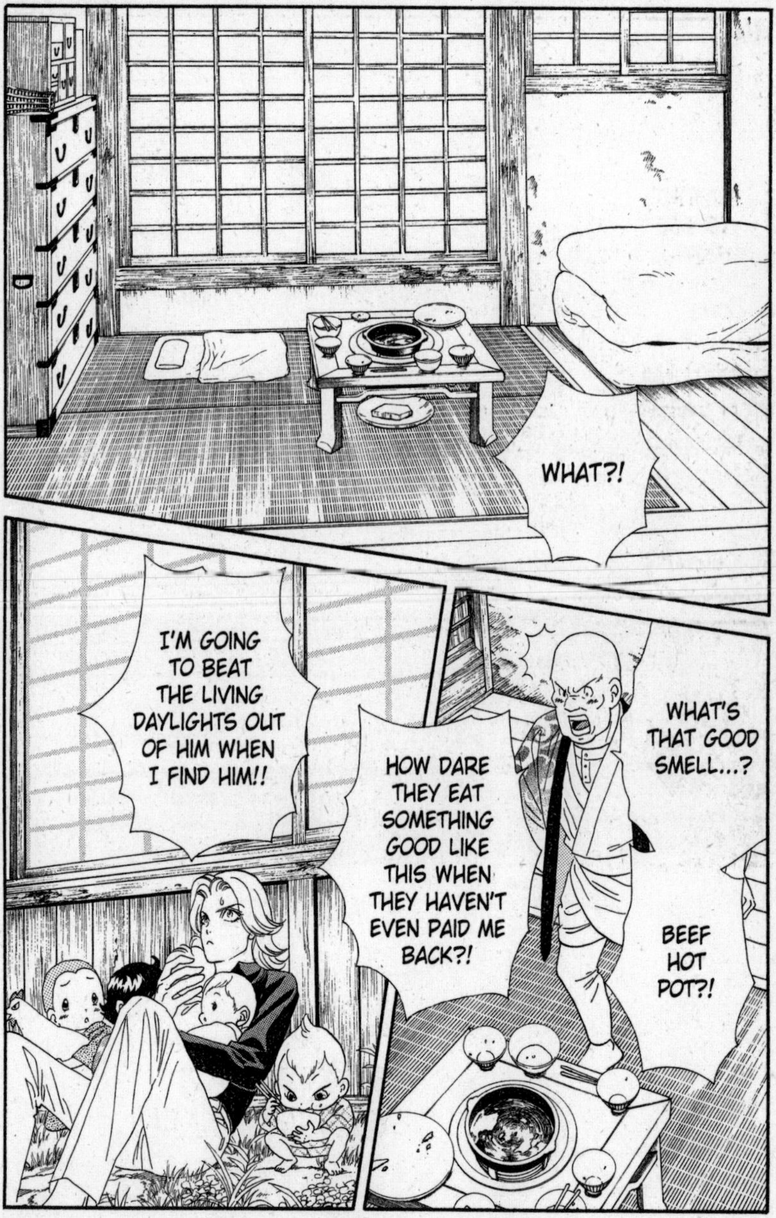
WHAT?!
WHAT'S THAT GOOD SMELL...?
BEEF HOT POT?!
HOW DARE THEY EAT SOMETHING GOOD LIKE THIS WHEN THEY HAVEN'T EVEN PAID ME BACK?!
I'M GOING TO BEAT THE LIVING DAYLIGHTS OUT OF HIM WHEN I FIND HIM!!

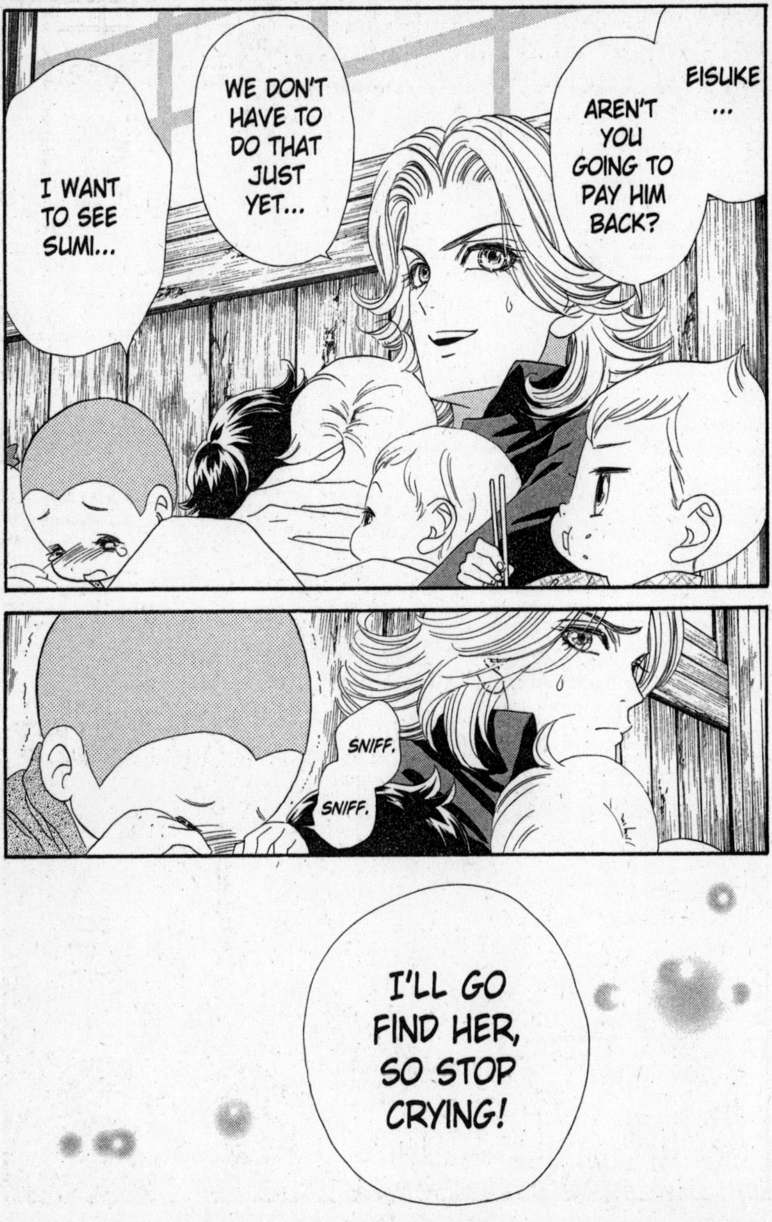
EISUKE...
AREN'T YOU GOING TO PAY HIM BACK?
WE DON'T HAVE TO DO THAT JUST YET...
I WANT TO SEE SUMI...
SNIFF.
SNIFF.
I'LL GO FIND HER, SO STOP CRYING!

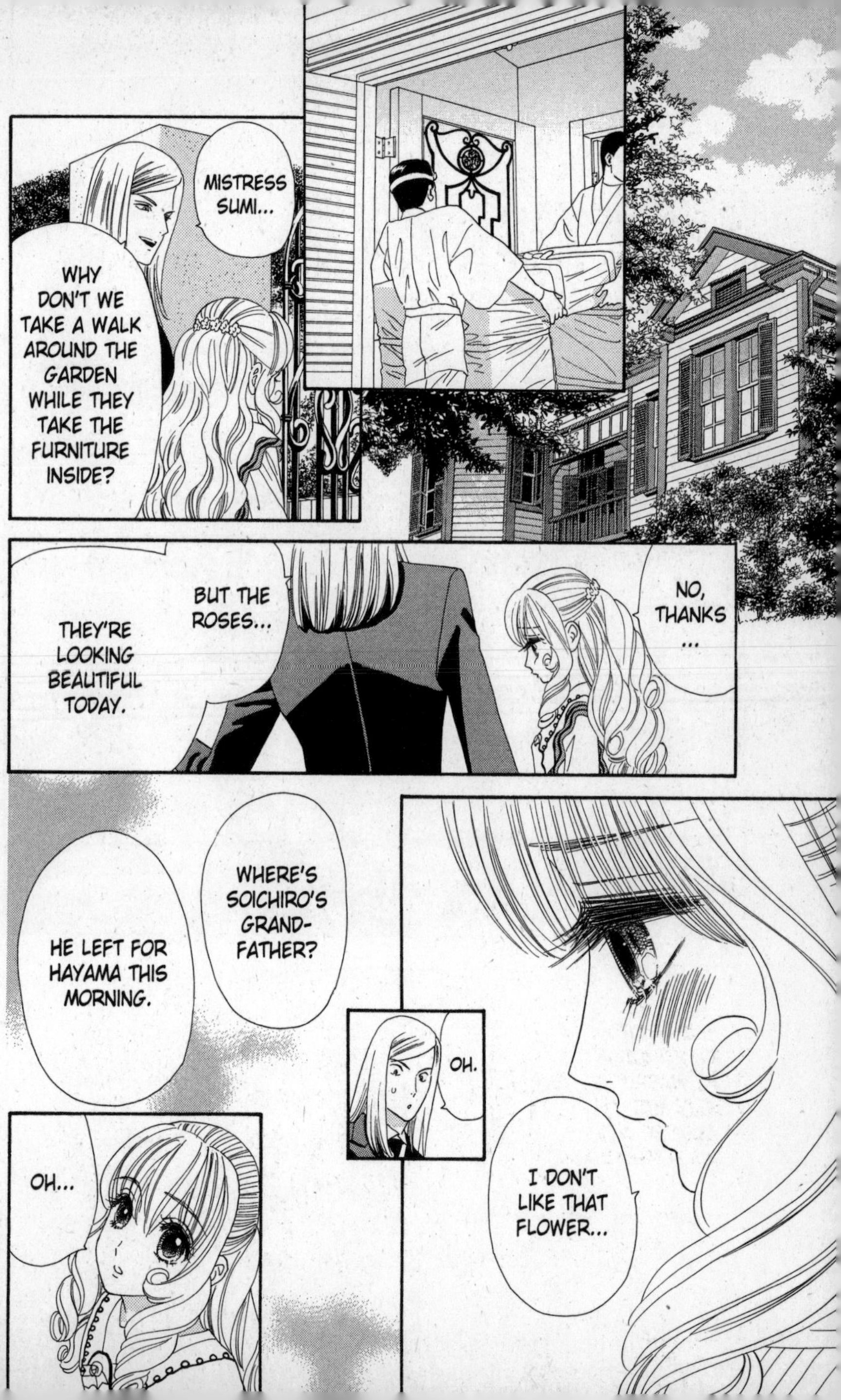
MISTRESS SUMI...
WHY DON'T WE TAKE A WALK AROUND THE GARDEN WHILE THEY TAKE THE FURNITURE INSIDE?
NO, THANKS ...
BUT THE ROSES...
THEY'RE LOOKING BEAUTIFUL TODAY.
I DON'T LIKE THAT FLOWER...
OH.
WHERE'S SOICHIRO'S GRAND-FATHER?
HE LEFT FOR HAYAMA THIS MORNING.
OH...

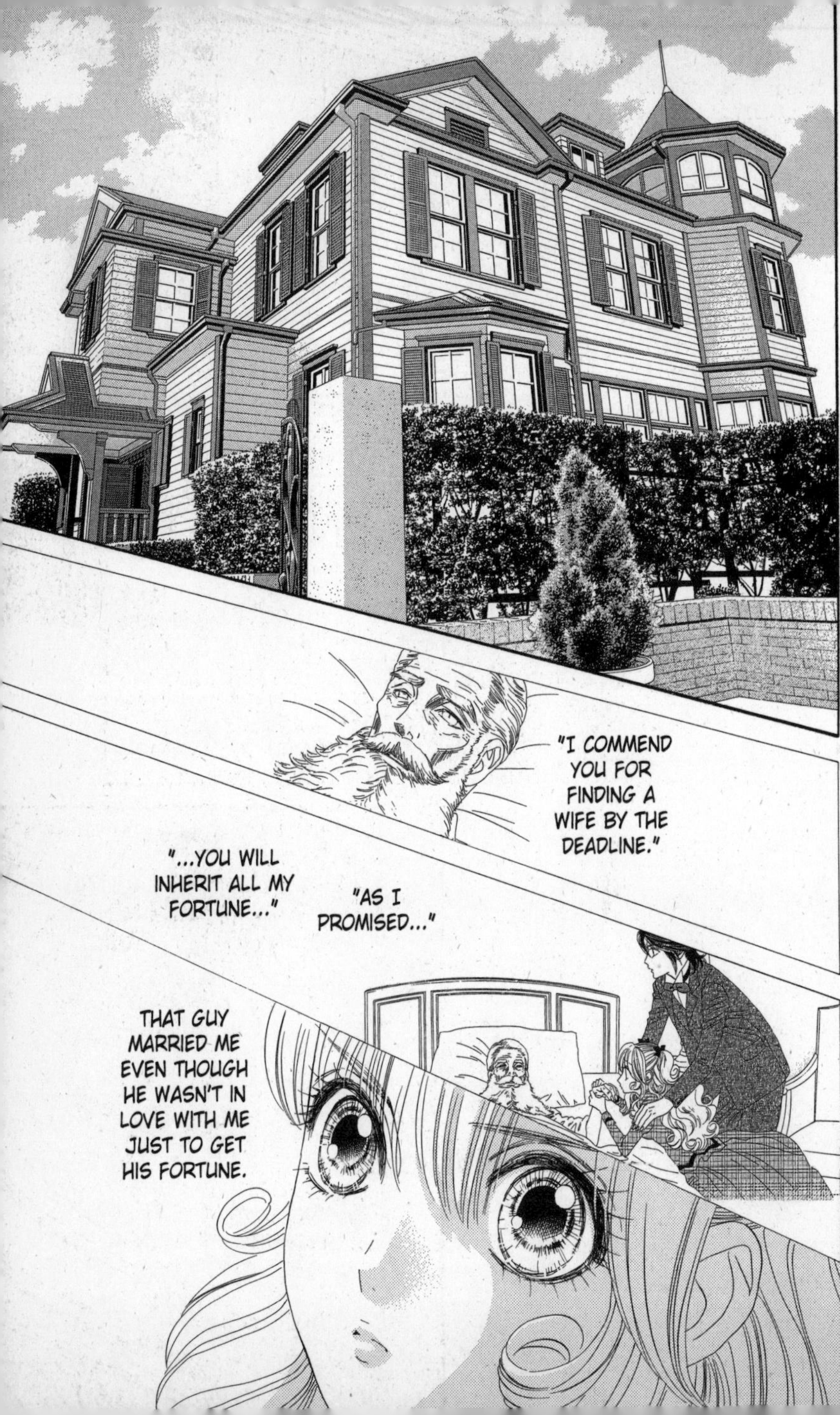
"I COMMEND YOU FOR FINDING A WIFE BY THE DEADLINE."
"AS I PROMISED..."
"...YOU WILL INHERIT ALL MY FORTUNE..."
THAT GUY MARRIED ME EVEN THOUGH HE WASN'T IN LOVE WITH ME JUST TO GET HIS FORTUNE.

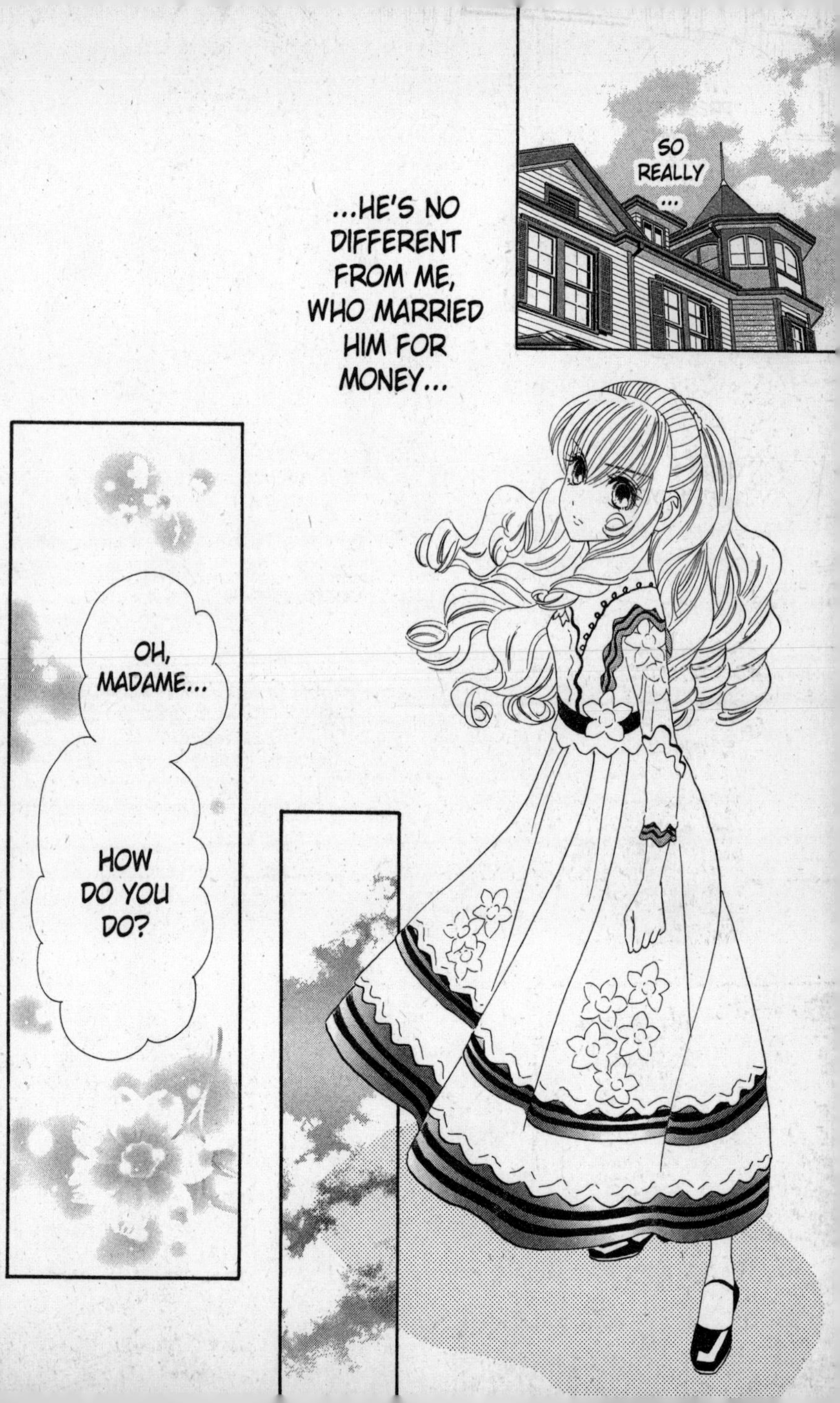
SO REALLY ...
...HE'S NO DIFFERENT FROM ME, WHO MARRIED HIM FOR MONEY...
OH, MADAME...
HOW DO YOU DO?

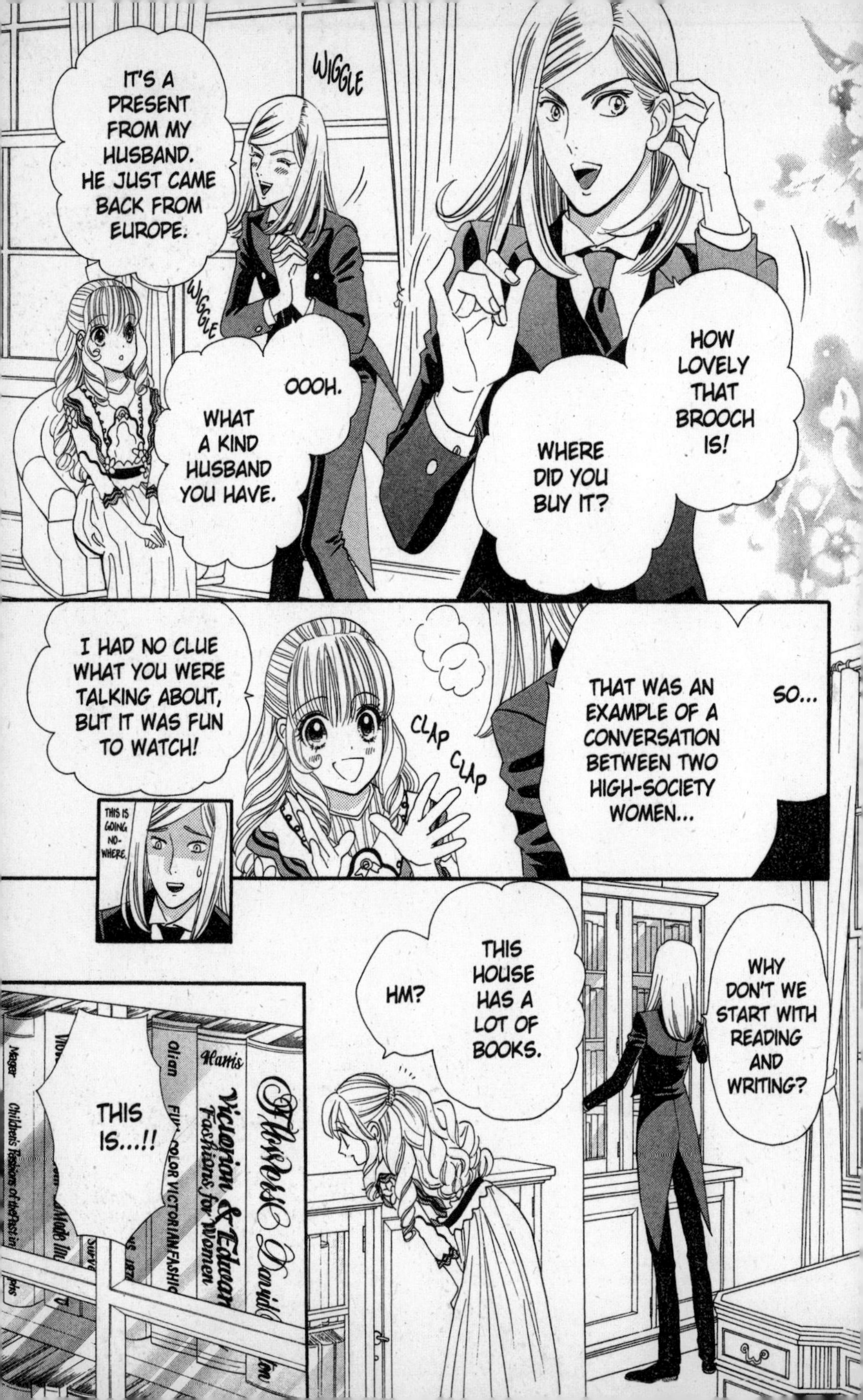
HOW LOVELY THAT BROOCH IS!
WHERE DID YOU BUY IT?
IT'S A PRESENT FROM MY HUSBAND. HE JUST CAME BACK FROM EUROPE.
WIGGLE
WIGGLE
OOOH.
WHAT A KIND HUSBAND YOU HAVE.
SO...
THAT WAS AN EXAMPLE OF A CONVERSATION BETWEEN TWO HIGH-SOCIETY WOMEN...
CLAP CLAP
I HAD NO CLUE WHAT YOU WERE TALKING ABOUT, BUT IT WAS FUN TO WATCH!
THIS IS GOING NOWHERE.
WHY DON'T WE START WITH READING AND WRITING?
THIS HOUSE HAS A LOT OF BOOKS.
HM?
THIS IS...!!

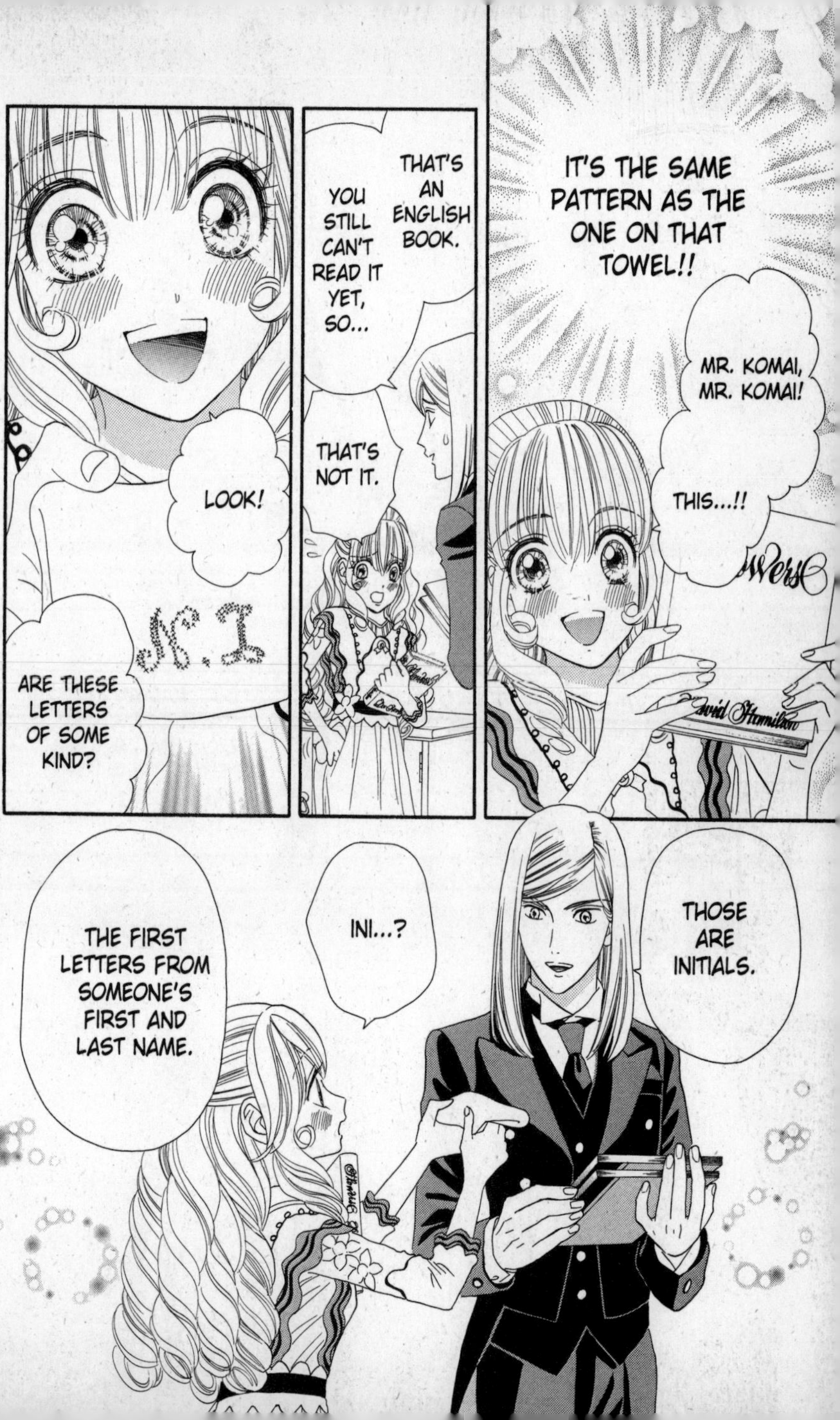
IT'S THE SAME PATTERN AS THE ONE ON THAT TOWEL!!
MR. KOMAI, MR. KOMAI!
THIS...!!
THAT'S AN ENGLISH BOOK.
YOU STILL CAN'T READ IT YET, SO...
THAT'S NOT IT.
LOOK!
ARE THESE LETTERS OF SOME KIND?
THOSE ARE INITIALS.
INI...?
THE FIRST LETTERS FROM SOMEONE'S FIRST AND LAST NAME.

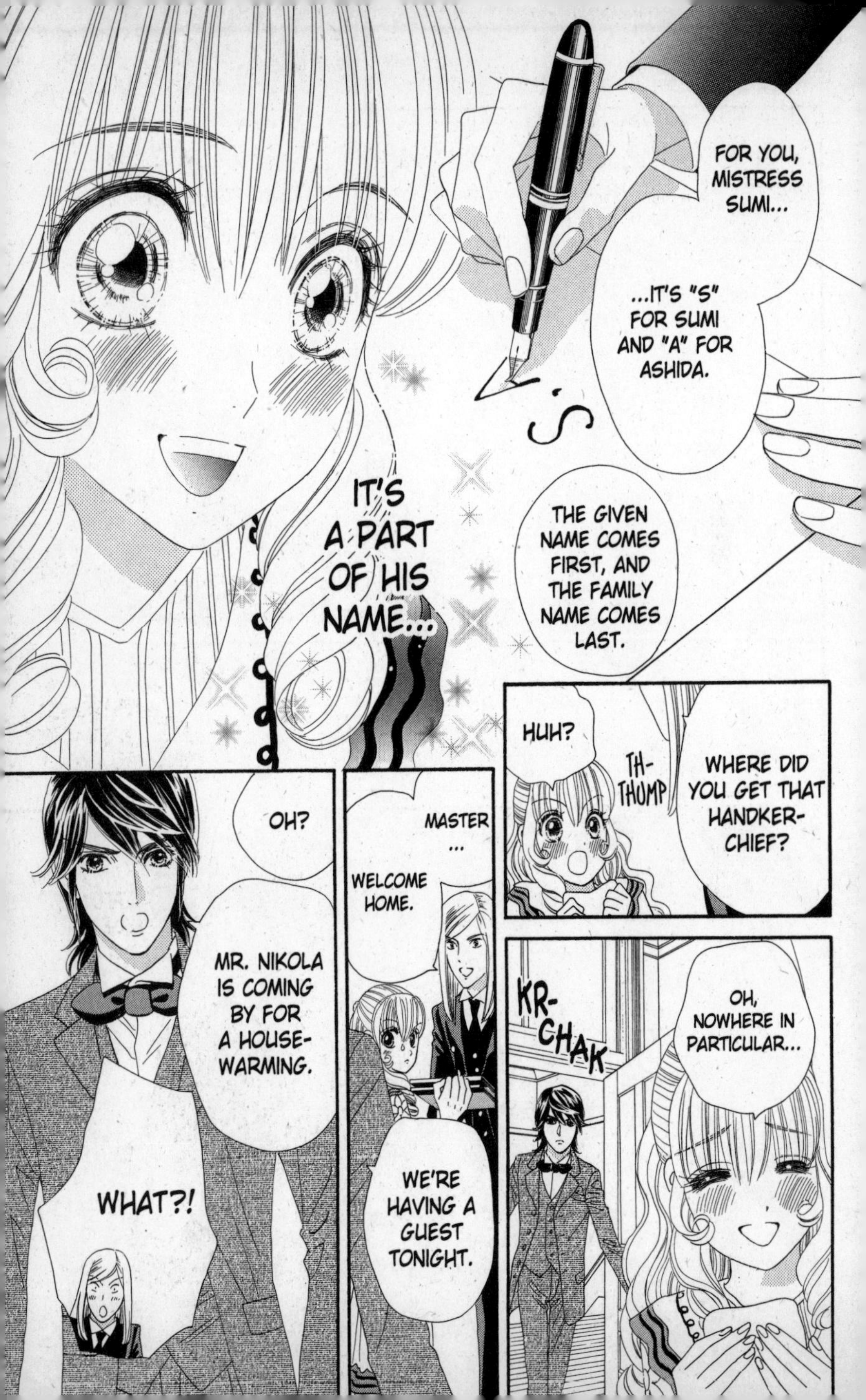
FOR YOU, MISTRESS SUMI...
...IT'S "S" FOR SUMI AND "A" FOR ASHIDA.
THE GIVEN NAME COMES FIRST, AND THE FAMILY NAME COMES LAST.
IT'S A PART OF HIS NAME...
HUH?
TH-THUMP
WHERE DID YOU GET THAT HANDKER-CHIEF?
KR-CHAK
OH, NOWHERE IN PARTICULAR...
MASTER ...
WELCOME HOME.
WE'RE HAVING A GUEST TONIGHT.
OH?
MR. NIKOLA IS COMING BY FOR A HOUSE-WARMING.
WHAT?!

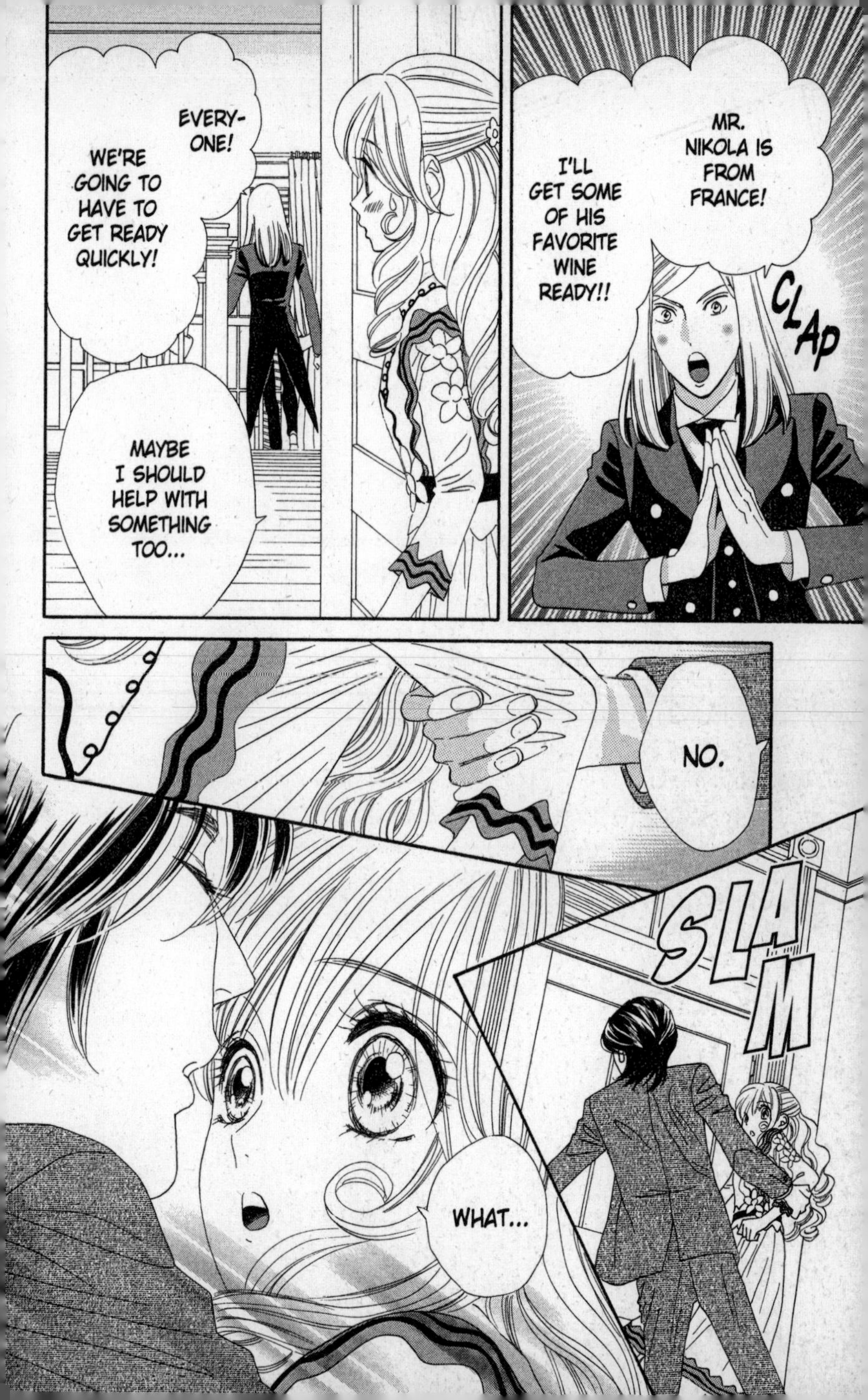
MR. NIKOLA IS FROM FRANCE!
I'LL GET SOME OF HIS FAVORITE WINE READY!!
CLAP
EVERY-ONE!
WE'RE GOING TO HAVE TO GET READY QUICKLY!
MAYBE I SHOULD HELP WITH SOMETHING TOO...
NO.
SLAM
WHAT...

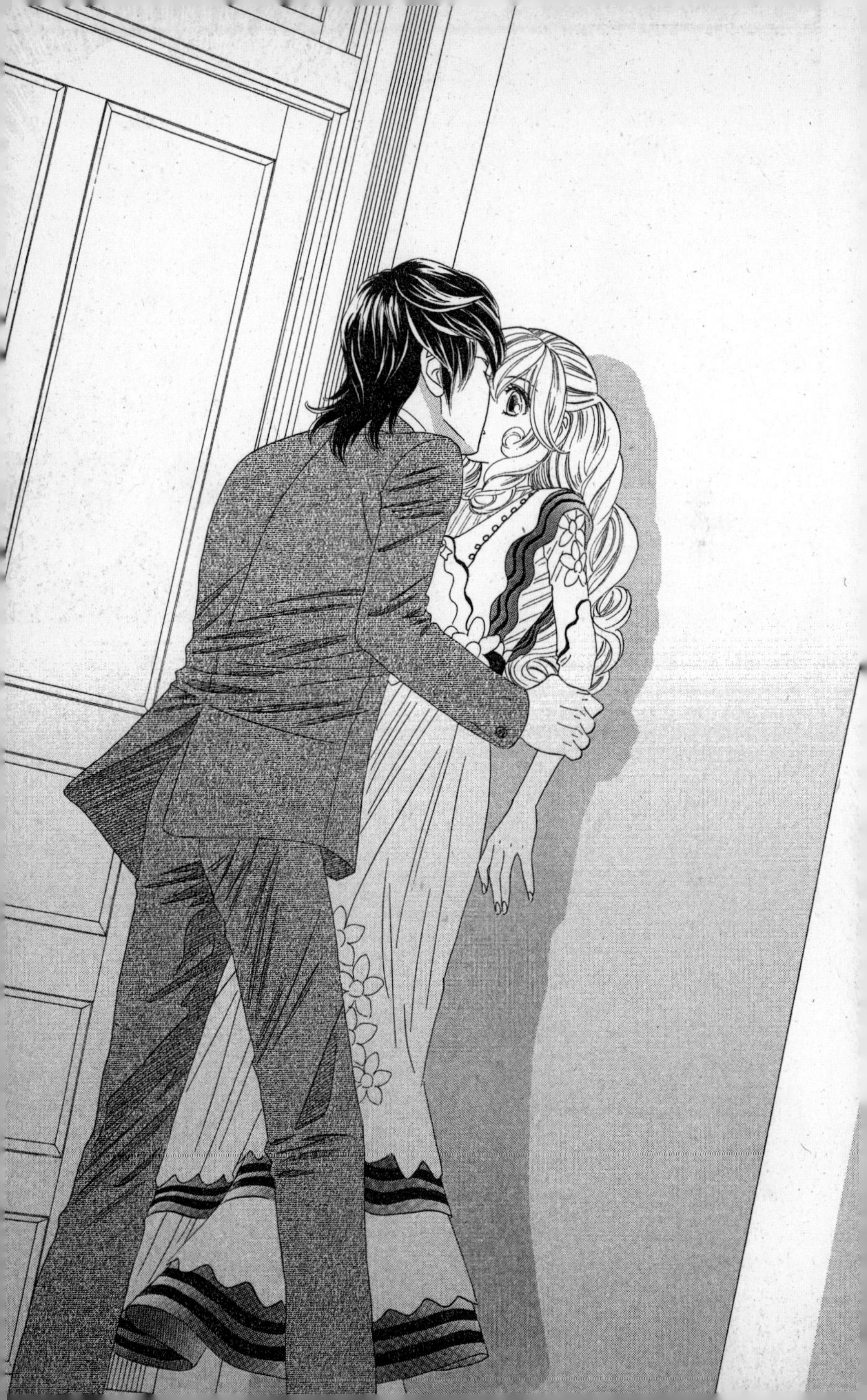

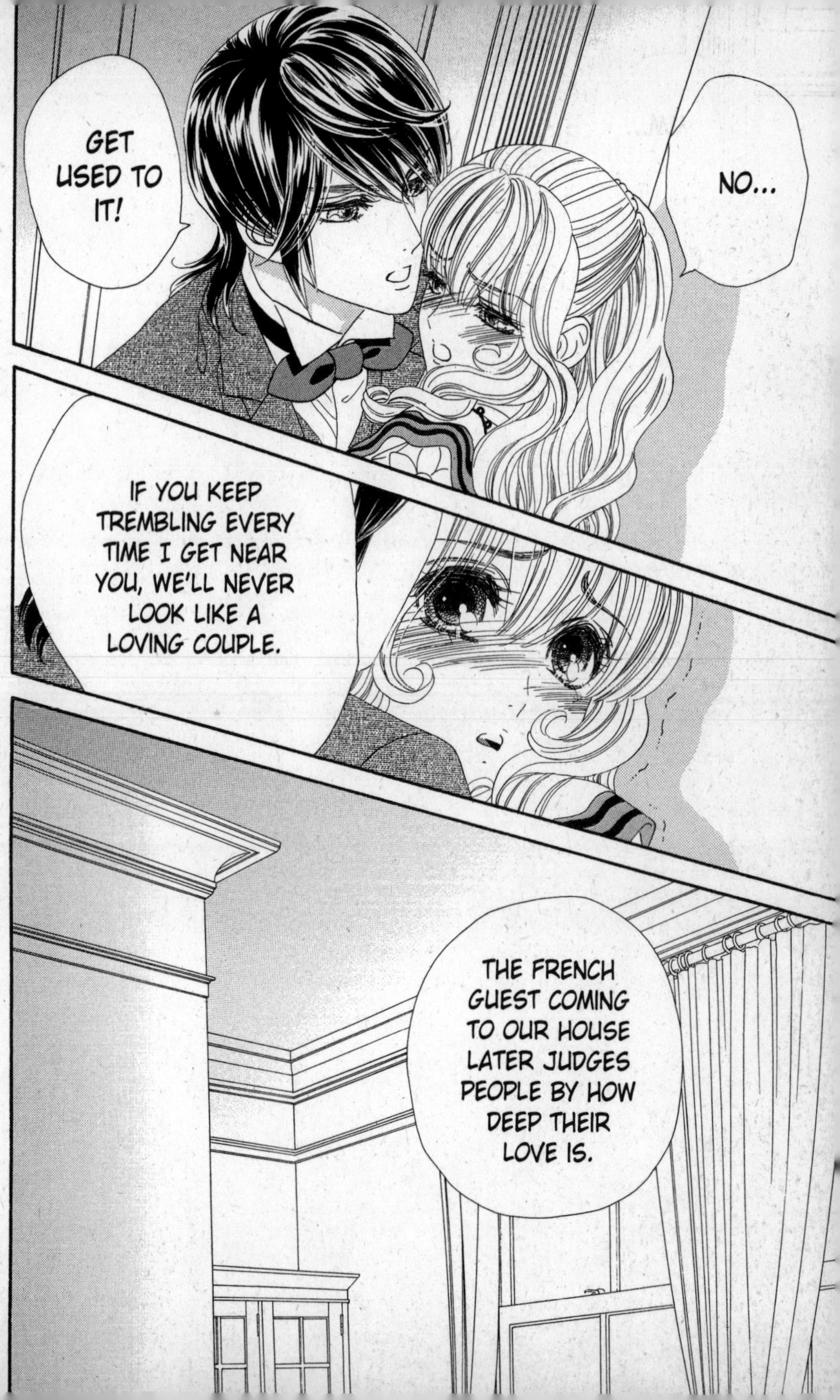
NO...
GET USED TO IT!
IF YOU KEEP TREMBLING EVERY TIME I GET NEAR YOU, WE'LL NEVER LOOK LIKE A LOVING COUPLE.
THE FRENCH GUEST COMING TO OUR HOUSE LATER JUDGES PEOPLE BY HOW DEEP THEIR LOVE IS.

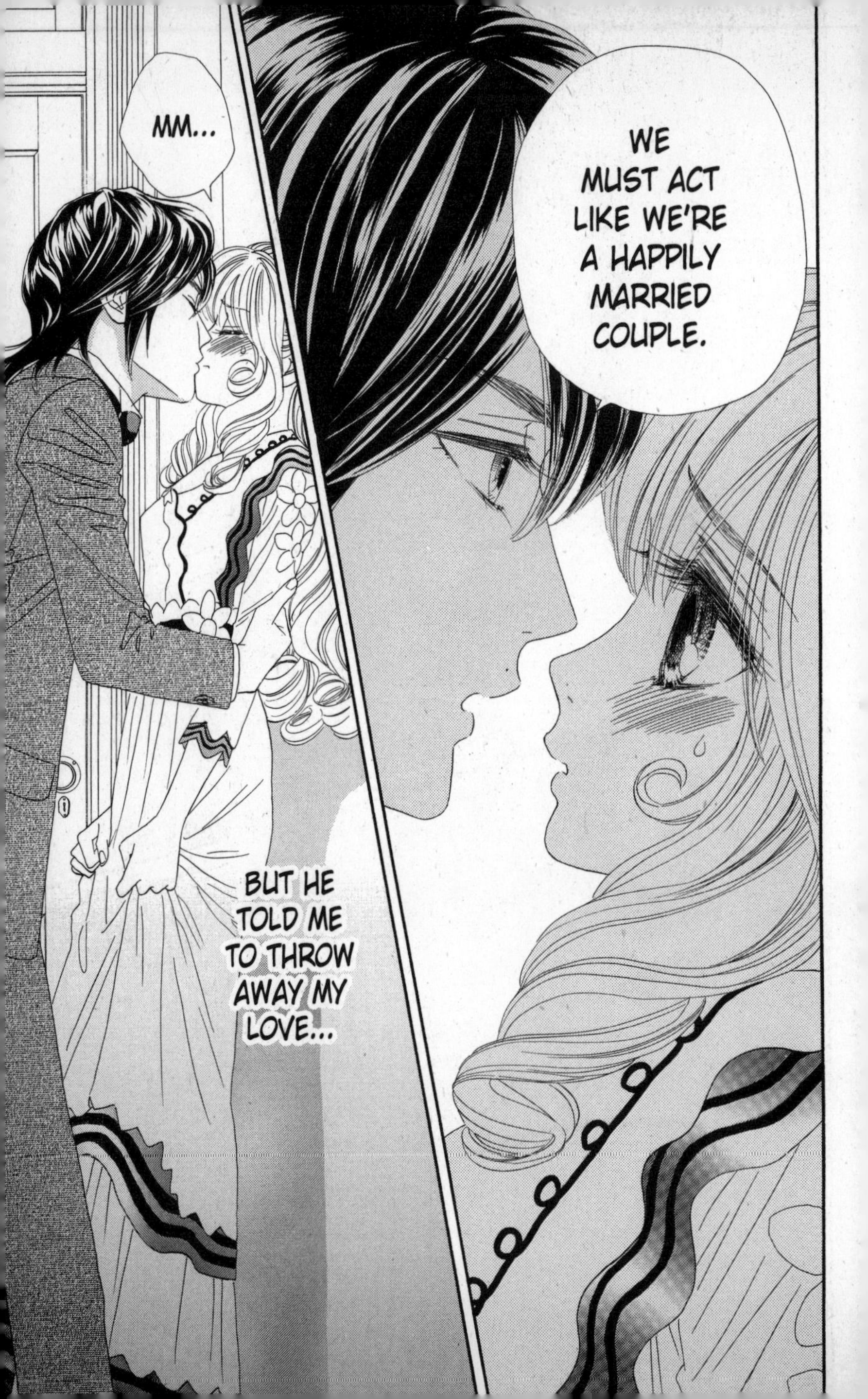
WE MUST ACT LIKE WE'RE A HAPPILY MARRIED COUPLE.
MM...
BUT HE TOLD ME TO THROW AWAY MY LOVE...

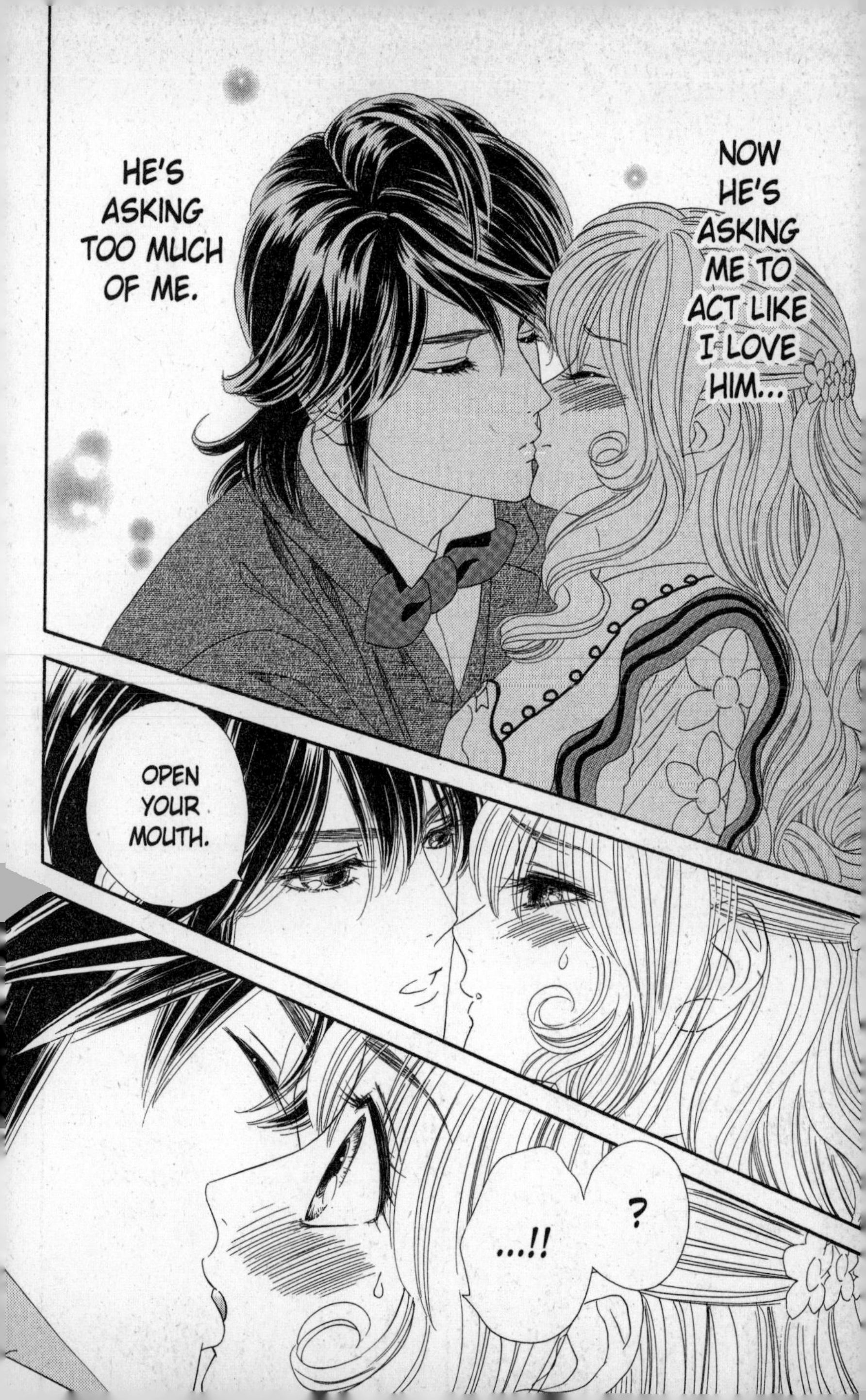
NOW HE'S ASKING ME TO ACT LIKE I LOVE HIM...
HE'S ASKING TOO MUCH OF ME.
OPEN YOUR MOUTH.
?
...!!

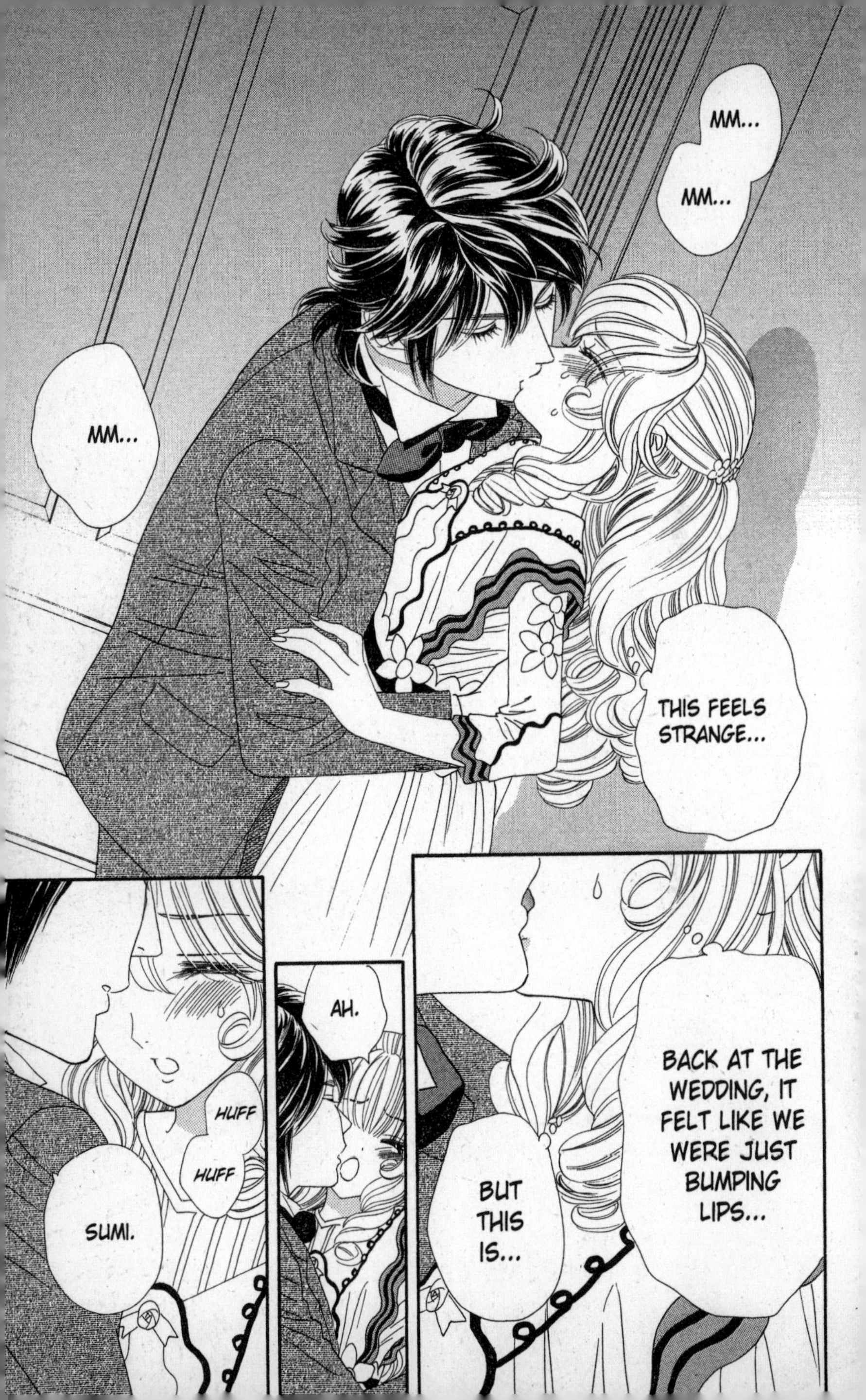
MM...
MM...
MM...
THIS FEELS STRANGE...
BACK AT THE WEDDING, IT FELT LIKE WE WERE JUST BUMPING LIPS...
BUT THIS IS...
AH.
HUFF
HUFF
SUMI.

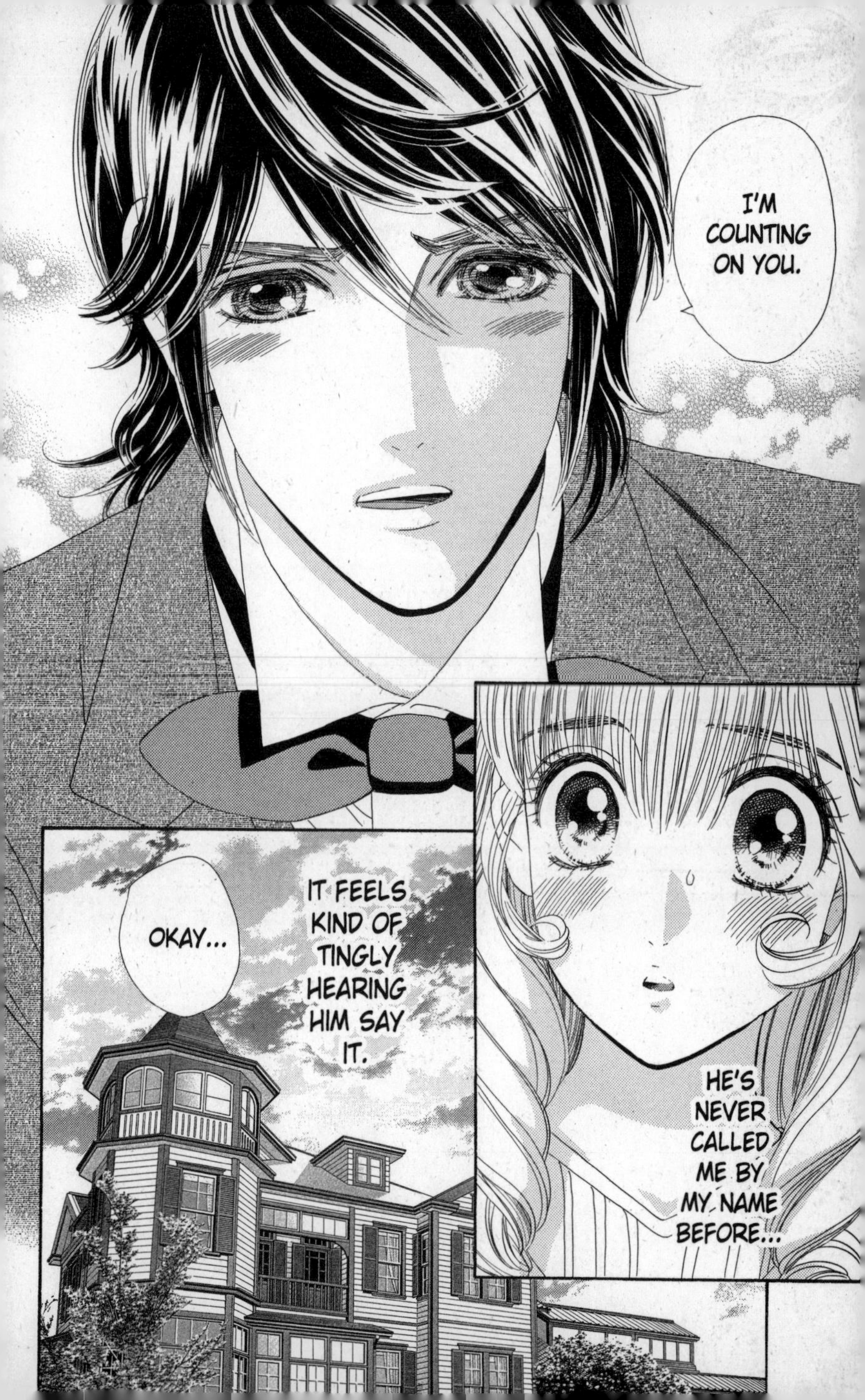
I'M COUNTING ON YOU.
HE'S NEVER CALLED ME BY MY NAME BEFORE...
IT FEELS KIND OF TINGLY HEARING HIM SAY IT.
OKAY...

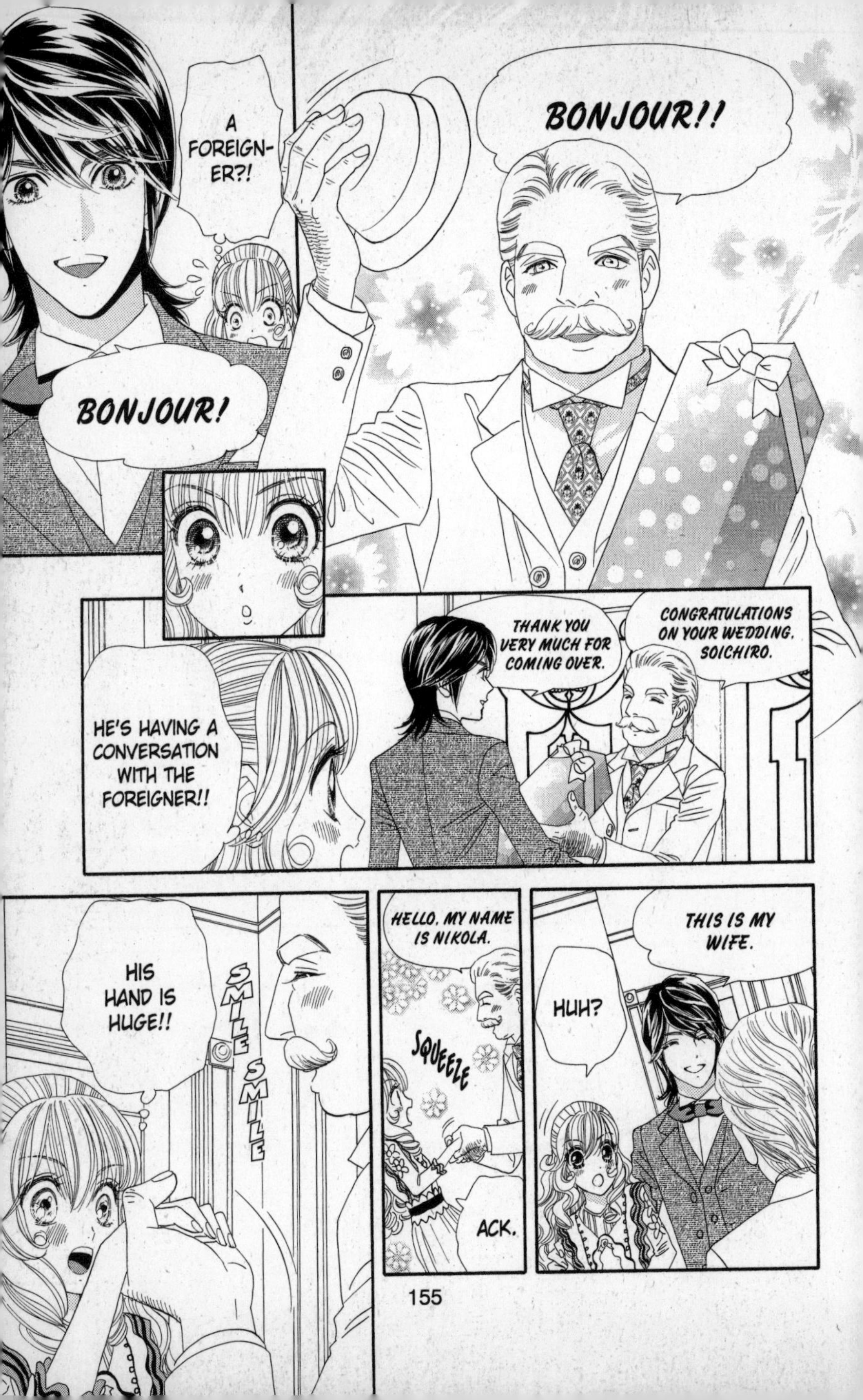
BONJOUR!!
A FOREIGNER?!
BONJOUR!
CONGRATULATIONS ON YOUR WEDDING, SOICHIRO.
THANK YOU VERY MUCH FOR COMING OVER.
HE'S HAVING A CONVERSATION WITH THE FOREIGNER!!
THIS IS MY WIFE.
HUH?
HELLO. MY NAME IS NIKOLA.
SQUEEZE
ACK.
SMILE
SMILE
HIS HAND IS HUGE!!

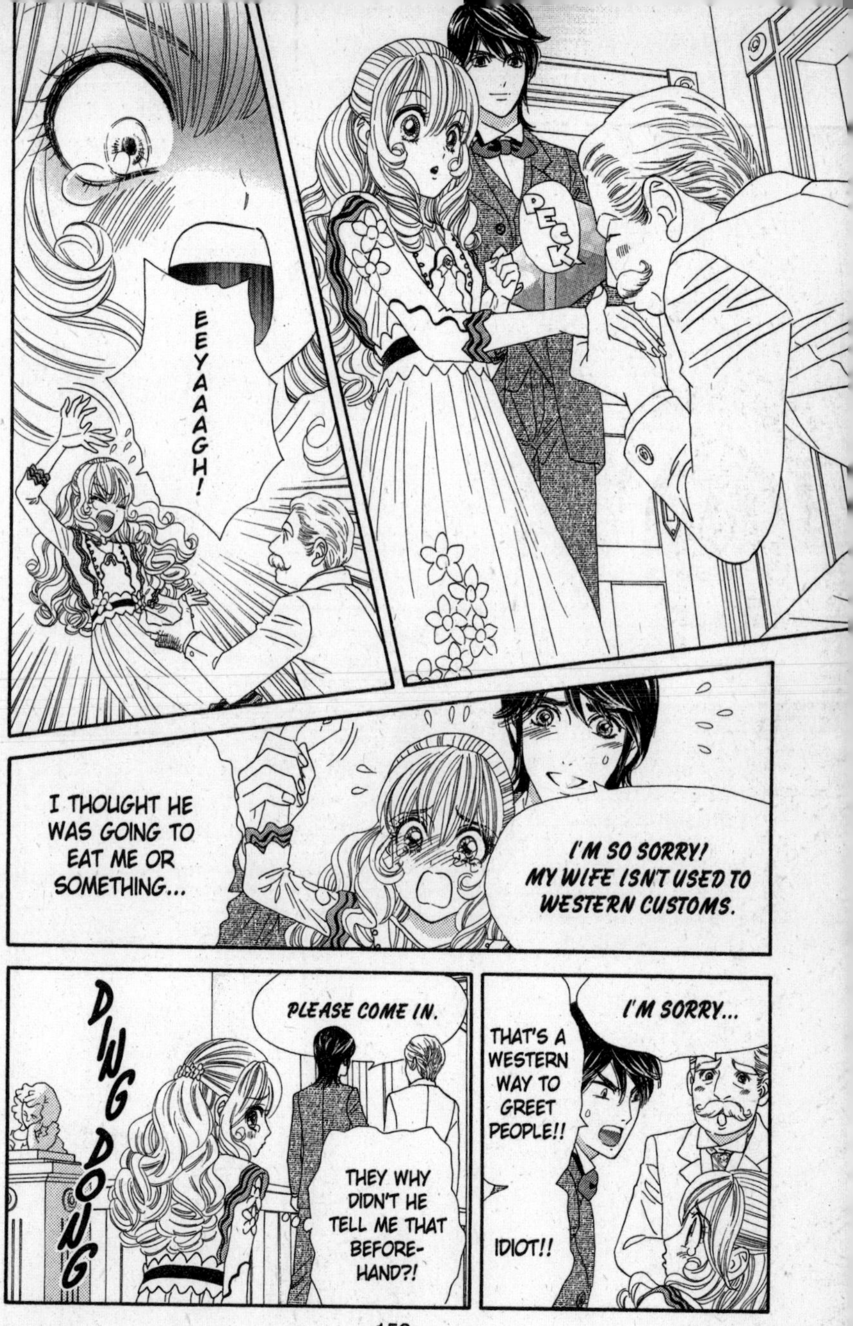
PECK
EEYAAAAGH!
I'M SO SORRY! MY WIFE ISN'T USED TO WESTERN CUSTOMS.
I THOUGHT HE WAS GOING TO EAT ME OR SOMETHING...
I'M SORRY...
THAT'S A WESTERN WAY TO GREET PEOPLE!!
IDIOT!!
PLEASE COME IN.
DING DONG
THEY WHY DIDN'T HE TELL ME THAT BEFORE-HAND?!

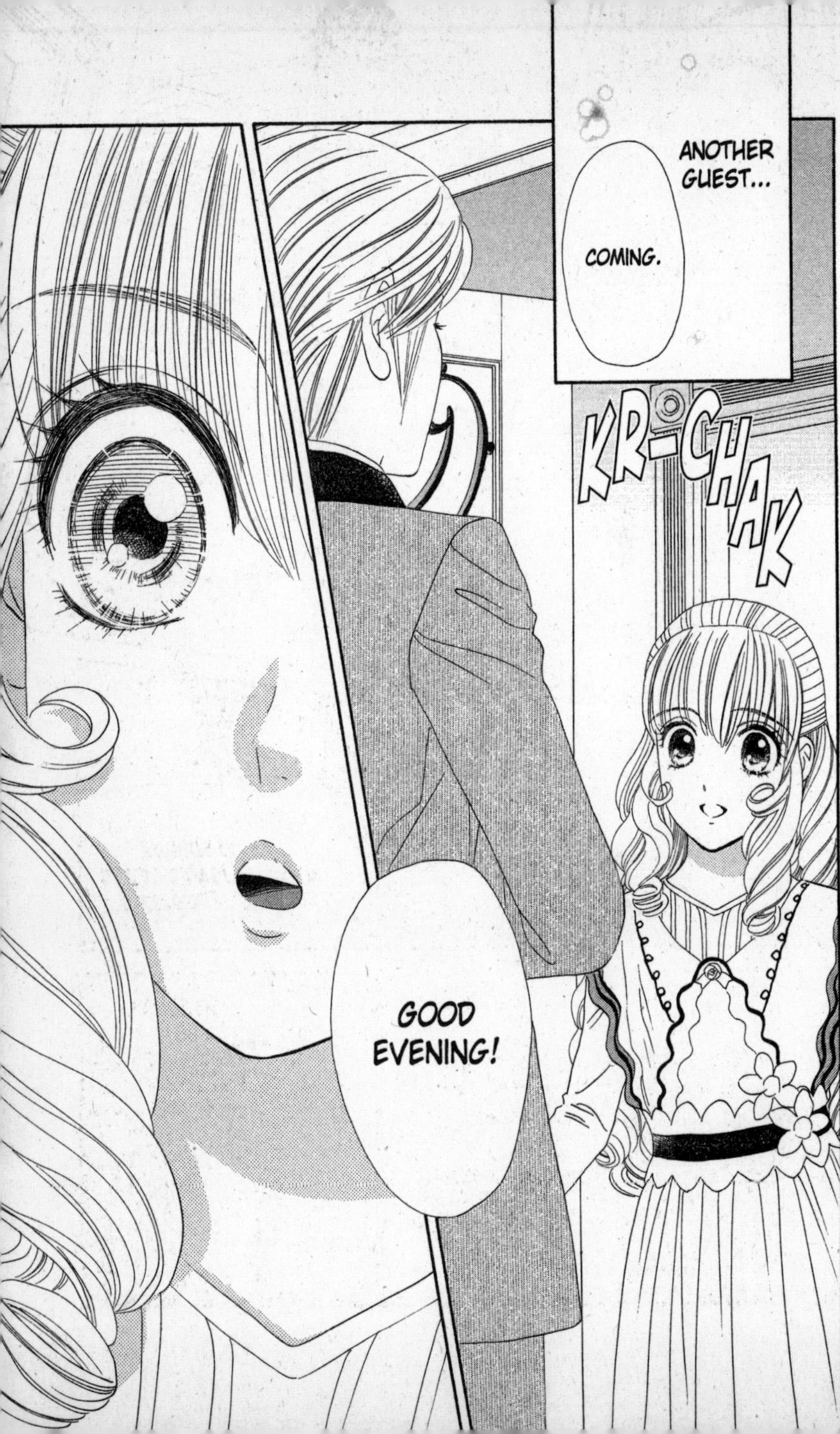
ANOTHER GUEST...
COMING.
KR-CHAK
GOOD EVENING!

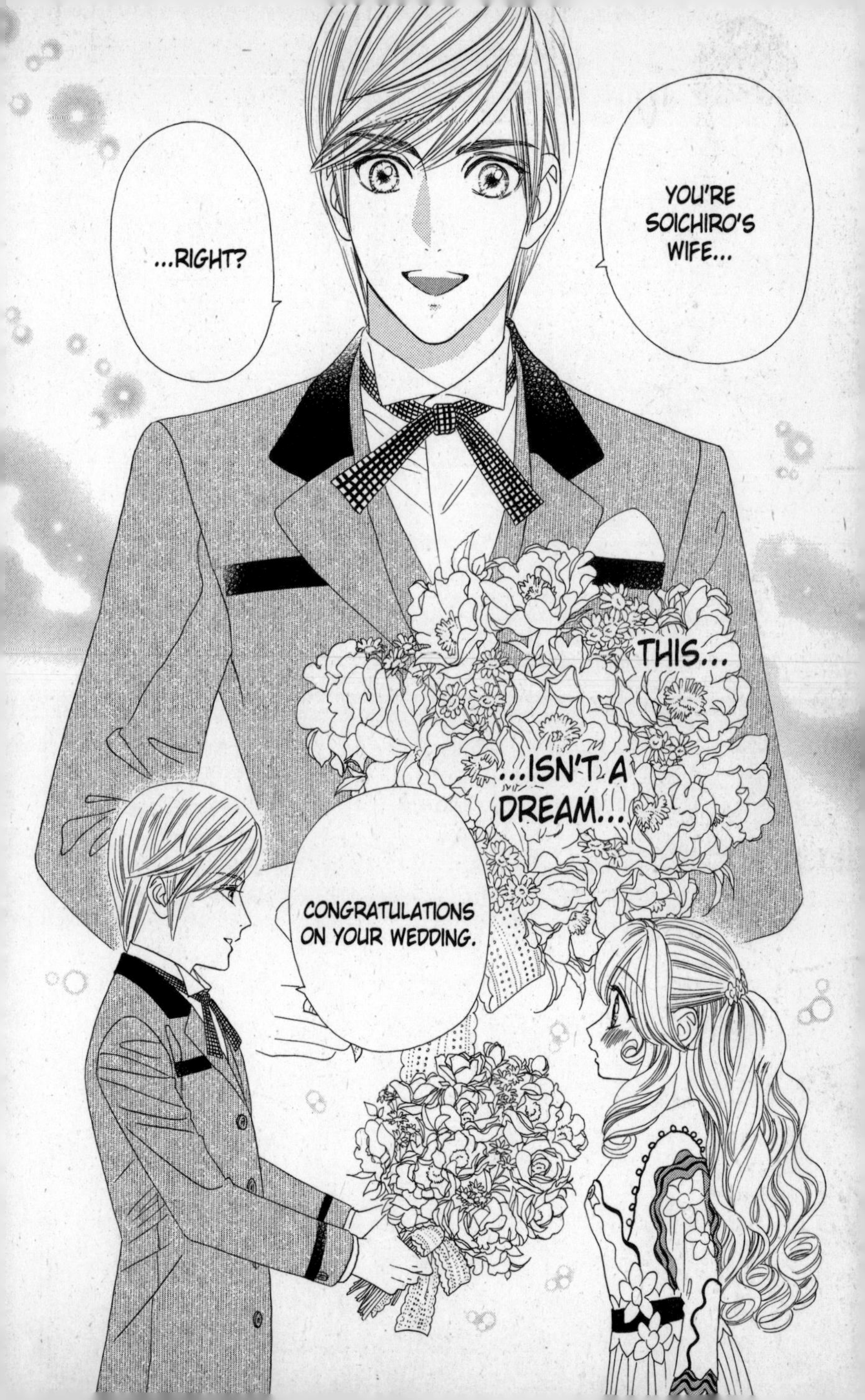
YOU'RE SOICHIRO'S WIFE...
...RIGHT?
THIS...
...ISN'T A DREAM...
CONGRATULATIONS ON YOUR WEDDING.

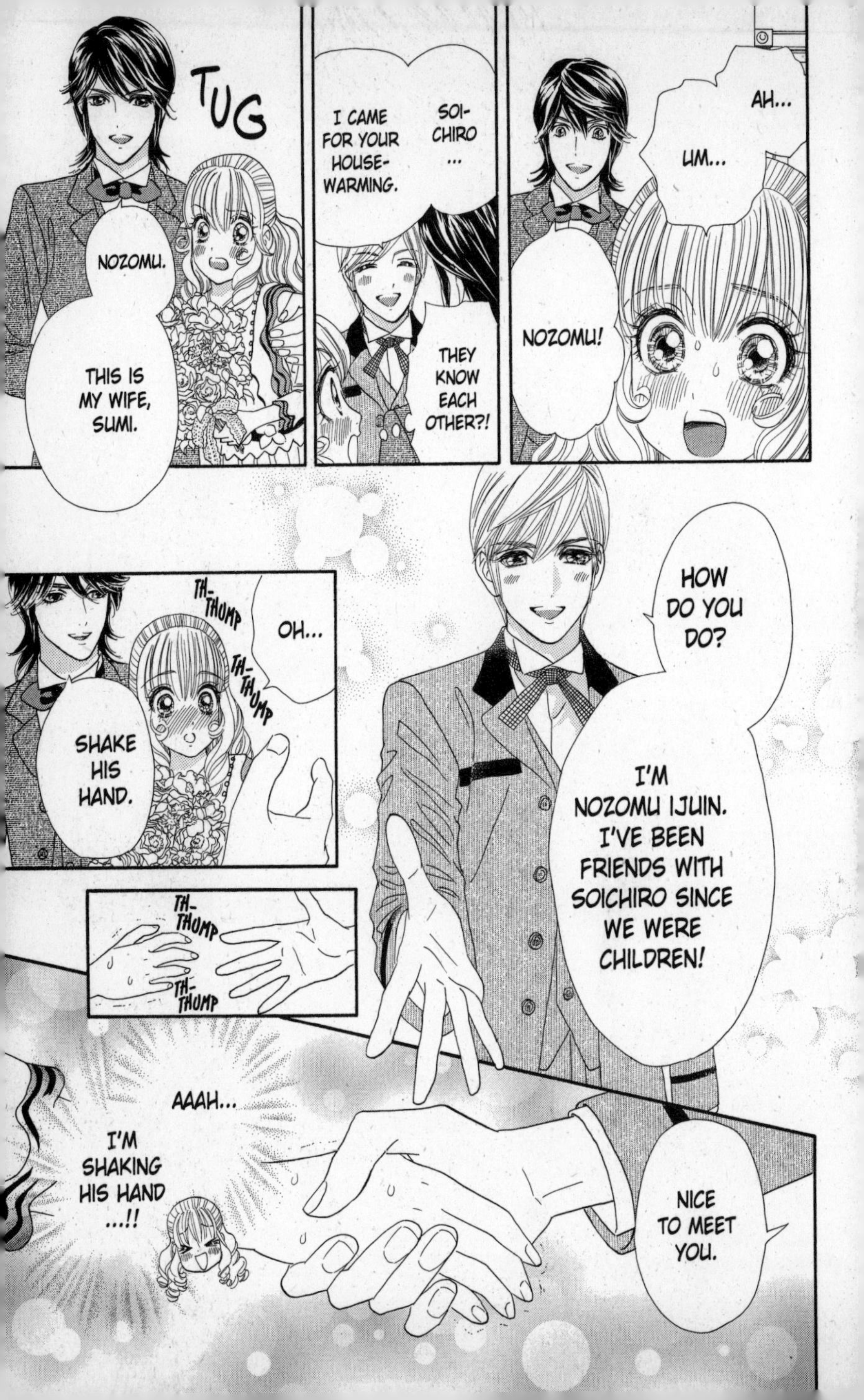
AH...
UM...
NOZOMU!
SOI-CHIRO...
I CAME FOR YOUR HOUSE-WARMING.
THEY KNOW EACH OTHER?!
TUG
NOZOMU.
THIS IS MY WIFE, SUMI.
HOW DO YOU DO?
I'M NOZOMU IJUIN. I'VE BEEN FRIENDS WITH SOICHIRO SINCE WE WERE CHILDREN!
TH-THUMP TH-THUMP
OH...
SHAKE HIS HAND.
TH-THUMP TH-THUMP
NICE TO MEET YOU.
AAAH...
I'M SHAKING HIS HAND ...!!

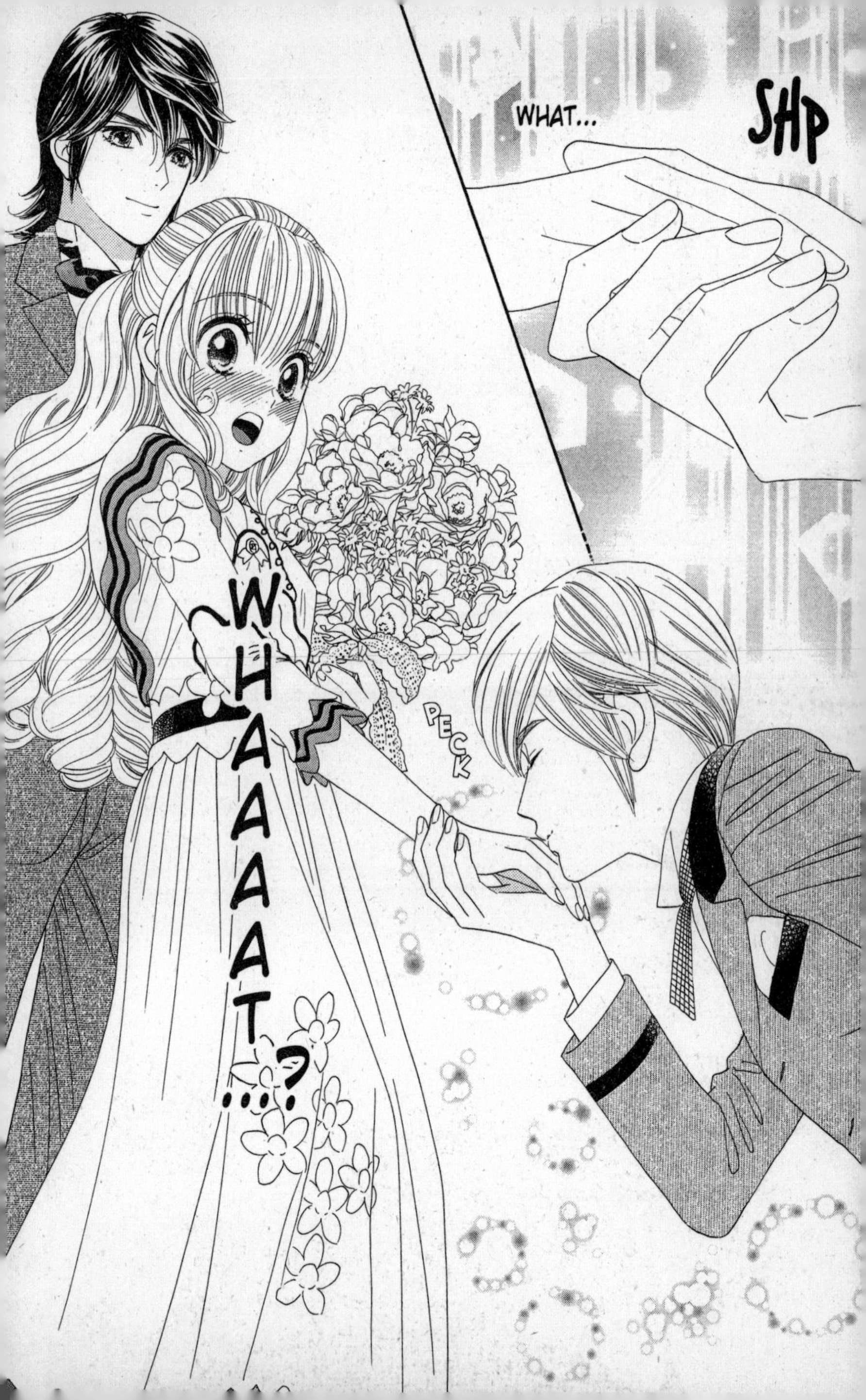
SHP
WHAT...
WHAAAT...?
PECK

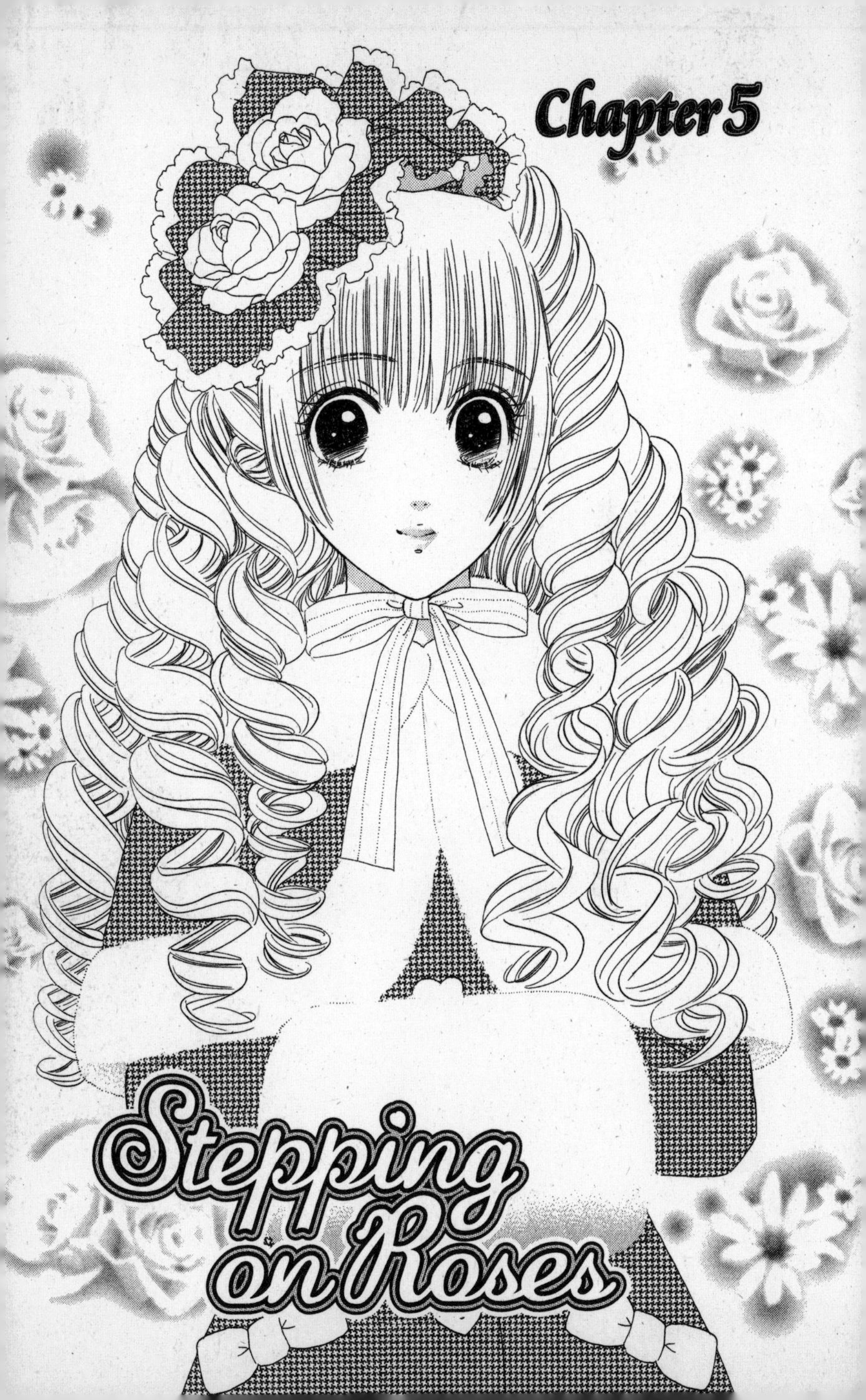
Chapter 5
Stepping on Roses

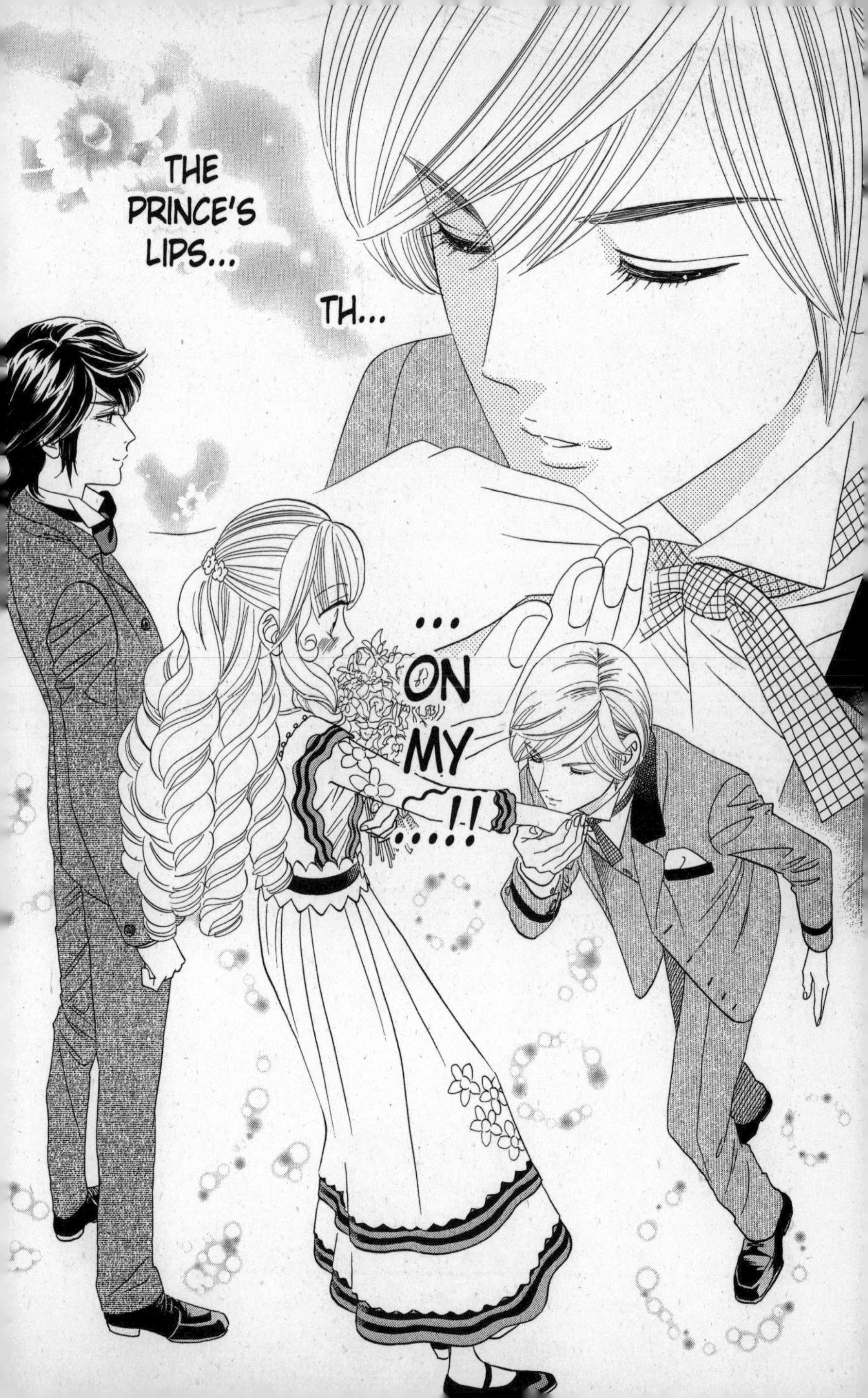
THE PRINCE'S LIPS...
TH...
...ON MY ~!!
....!!

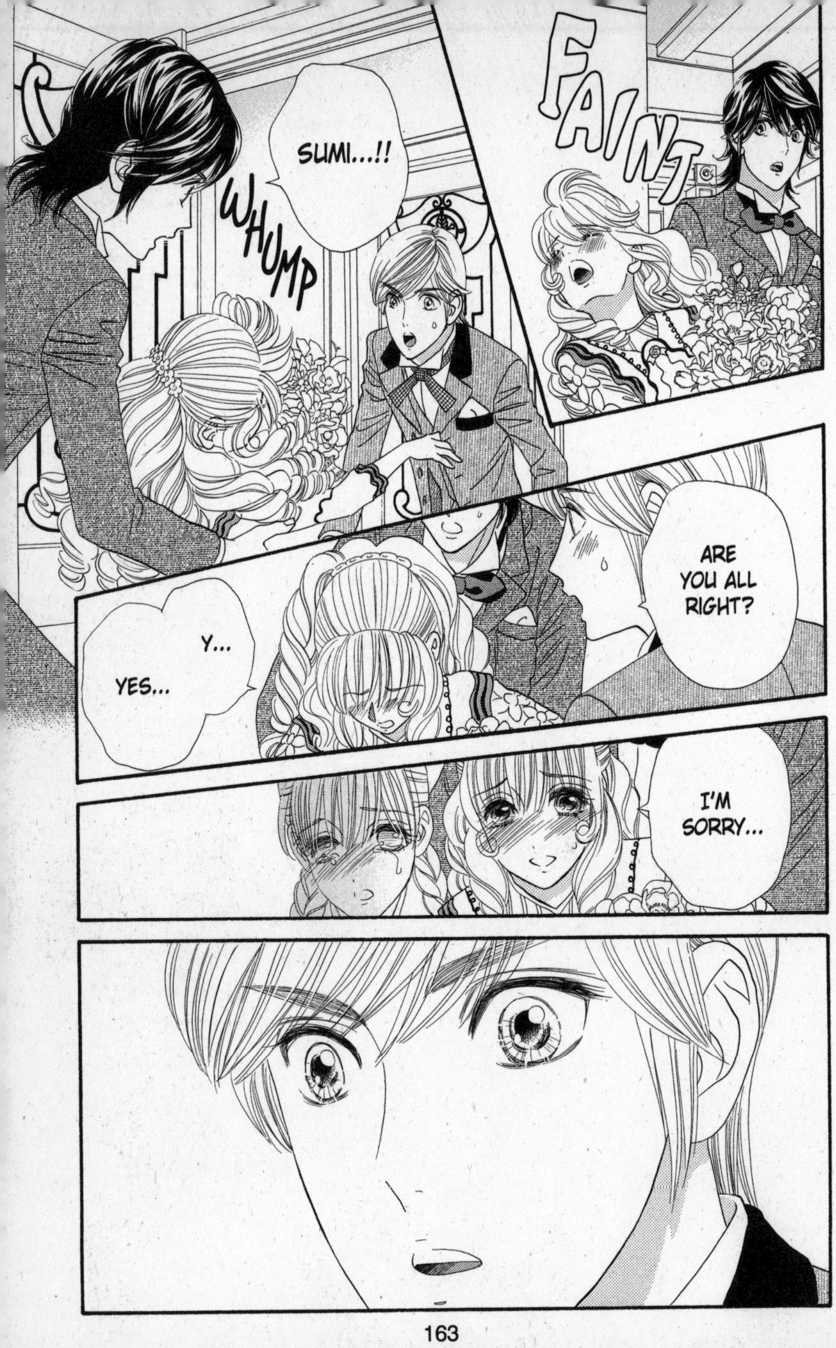
FAINT
SUMI...!!
WHUMP
ARE YOU ALL RIGHT?
Y... YES...
I'M SORRY...

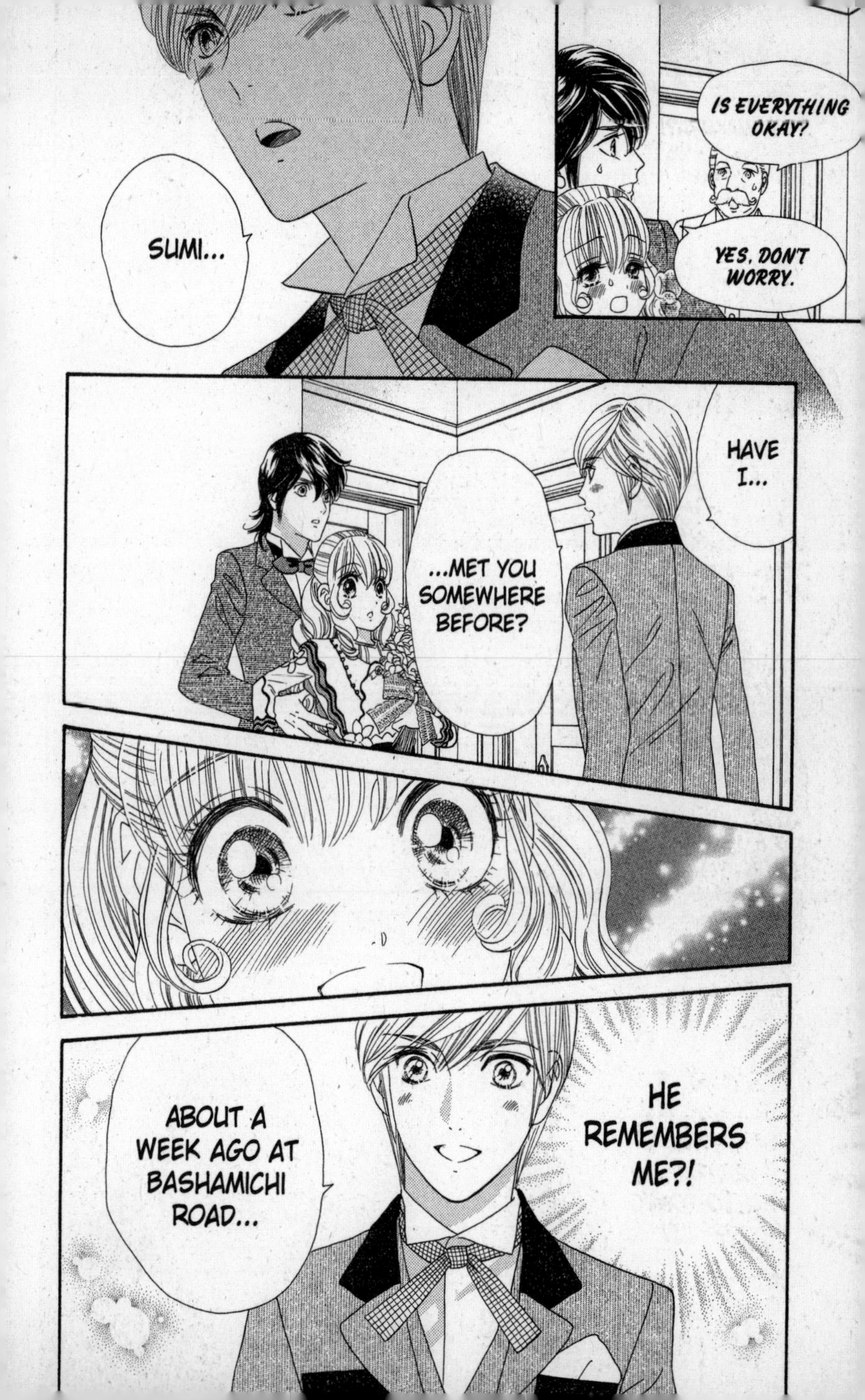
IS EVERYTHING OKAY?
YES, DON'T WORRY.
SUMI...
HAVE I...
...MET YOU SOMEWHERE BEFORE?
HE REMEMBERS ME?!
ABOUT A WEEK AGO AT BASHAMICHI ROAD...

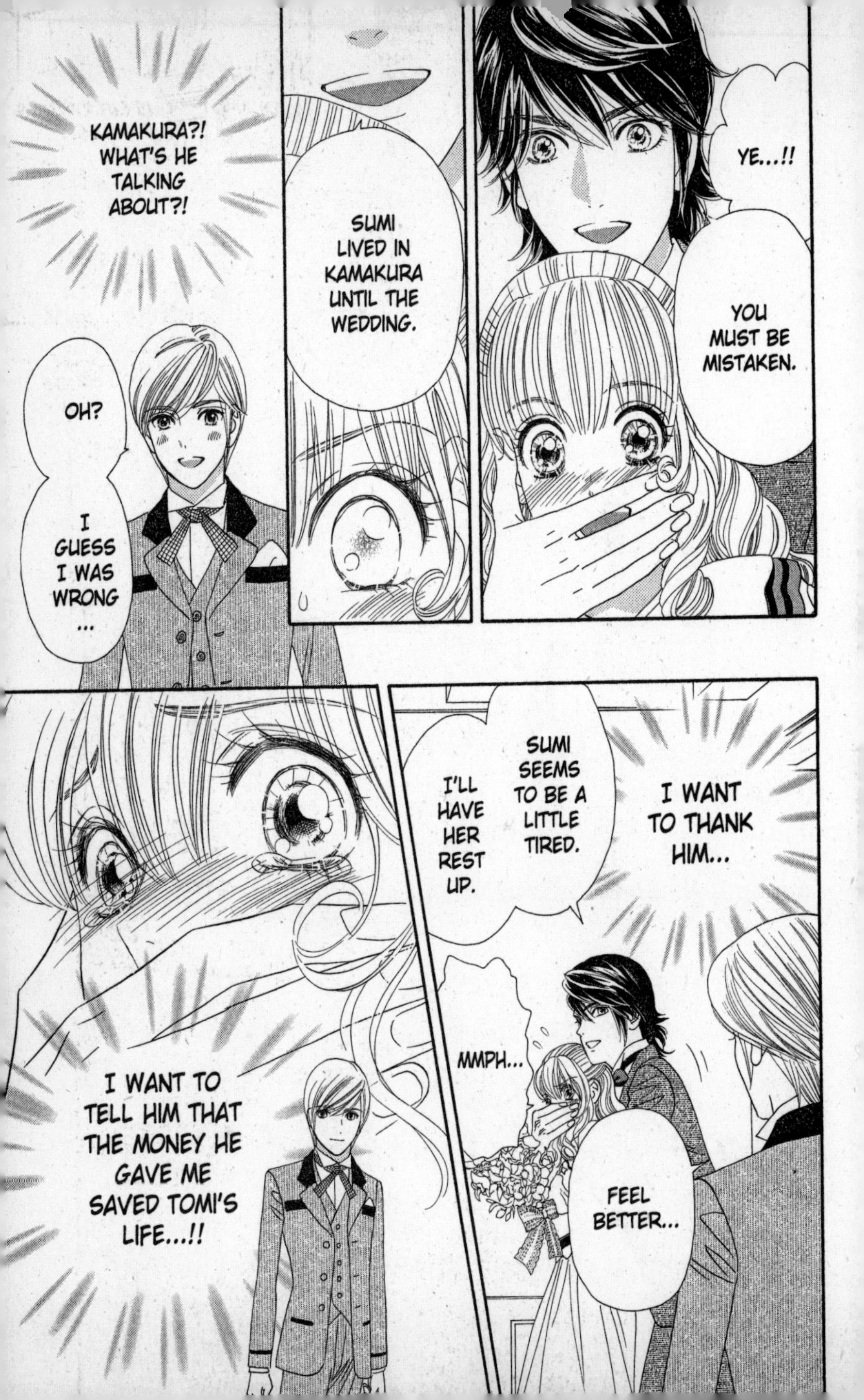
YE...!!
YOU MUST BE MISTAKEN.
SUMI LIVED IN KAMAKURA UNTIL THE WEDDING.
KAMAKURA?! WHAT'S HE TALKING ABOUT?!
OH?
I GUESS I WAS WRONG...
I WANT TO THANK HIM...
SUMI SEEMS TO BE A LITTLE TIRED.
I'LL HAVE HER REST UP.
MMPH...
FEEL BETTER...
I WANT TO TELL HIM THAT THE MONEY HE GAVE ME SAVED TOMI'S LIFE...!!

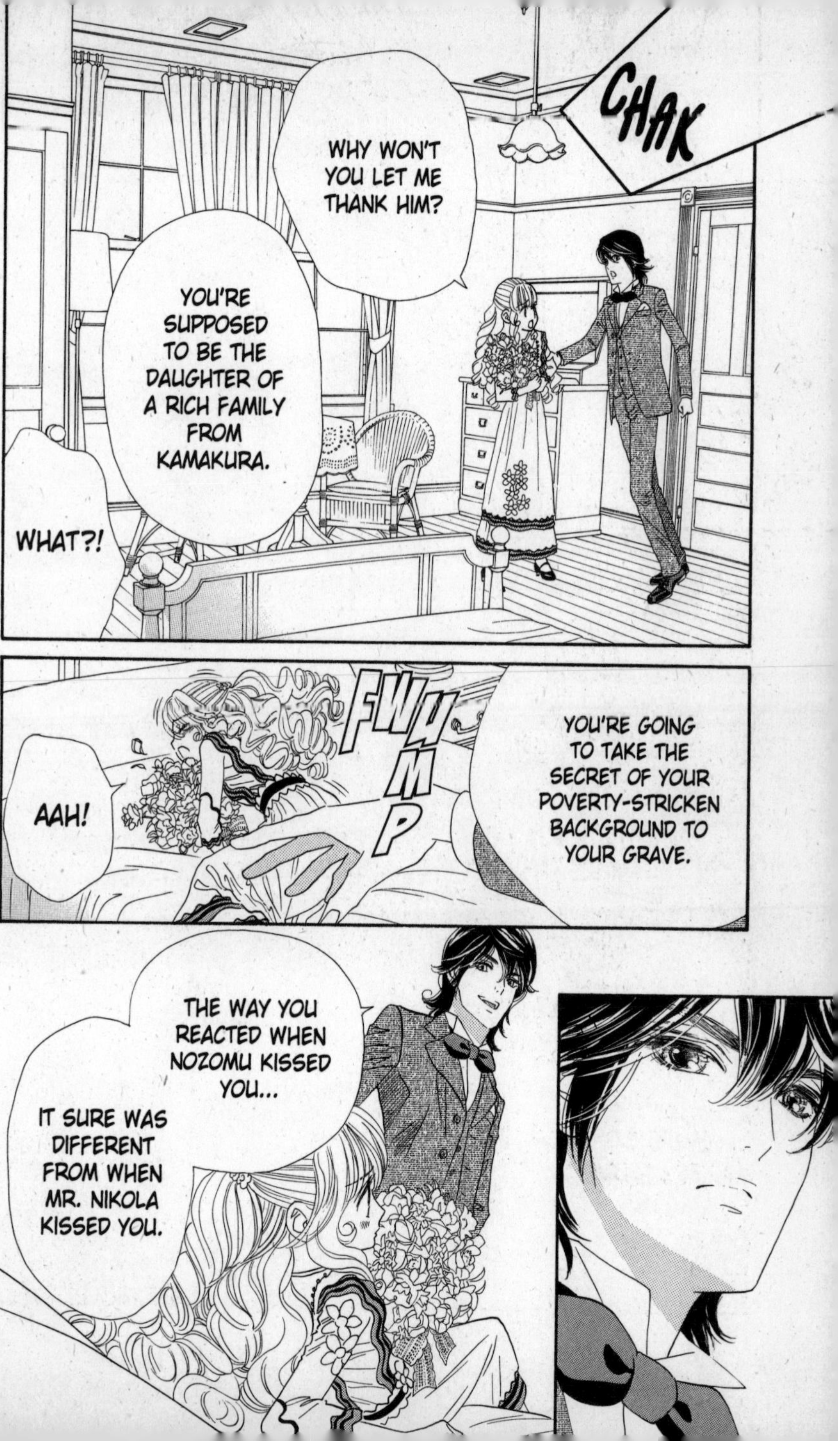
CHAK
WHY WON'T YOU LET ME THANK HIM?
YOU'RE SUPPOSED TO BE THE DAUGHTER OF A RICH FAMILY FROM KAMAKURA.
WHAT?!
YOU'RE GOING TO TAKE THE SECRET OF YOUR POVERTY-STRICKEN BACKGROUND TO YOUR GRAVE.
FWUMP
AAH!
THE WAY YOU REACTED WHEN NOZOMU KISSED YOU...
IT SURE WAS DIFFERENT FROM WHEN MR. NIKOLA KISSED YOU.

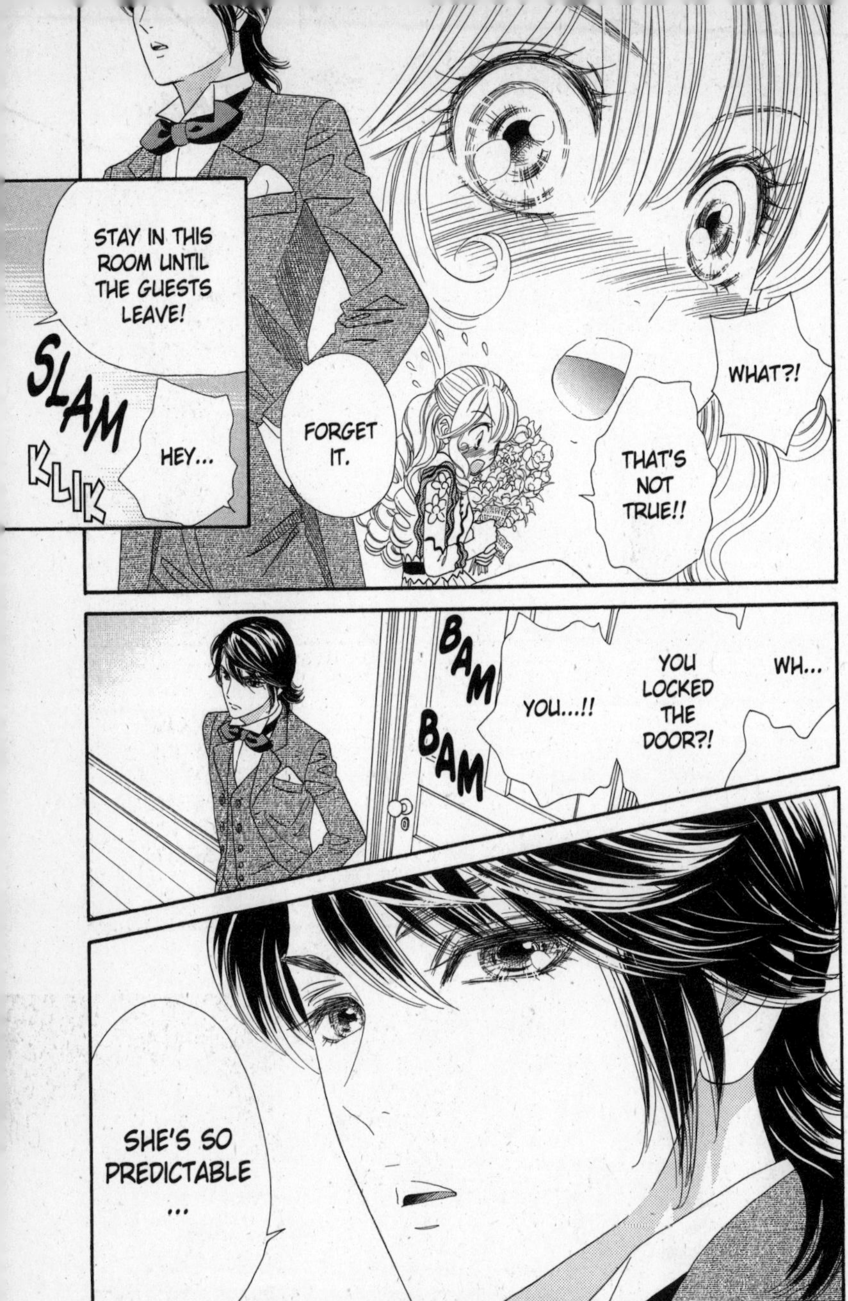
WHAT?!
THAT'S NOT TRUE!!
FORGET IT.
STAY IN THIS ROOM UNTIL THE GUESTS LEAVE!
HEY...
SLAM
KLIK
WH...
YOU LOCKED THE DOOR?!
YOU...!!
BAM BAM
SHE'S SO PREDICTABLE ...

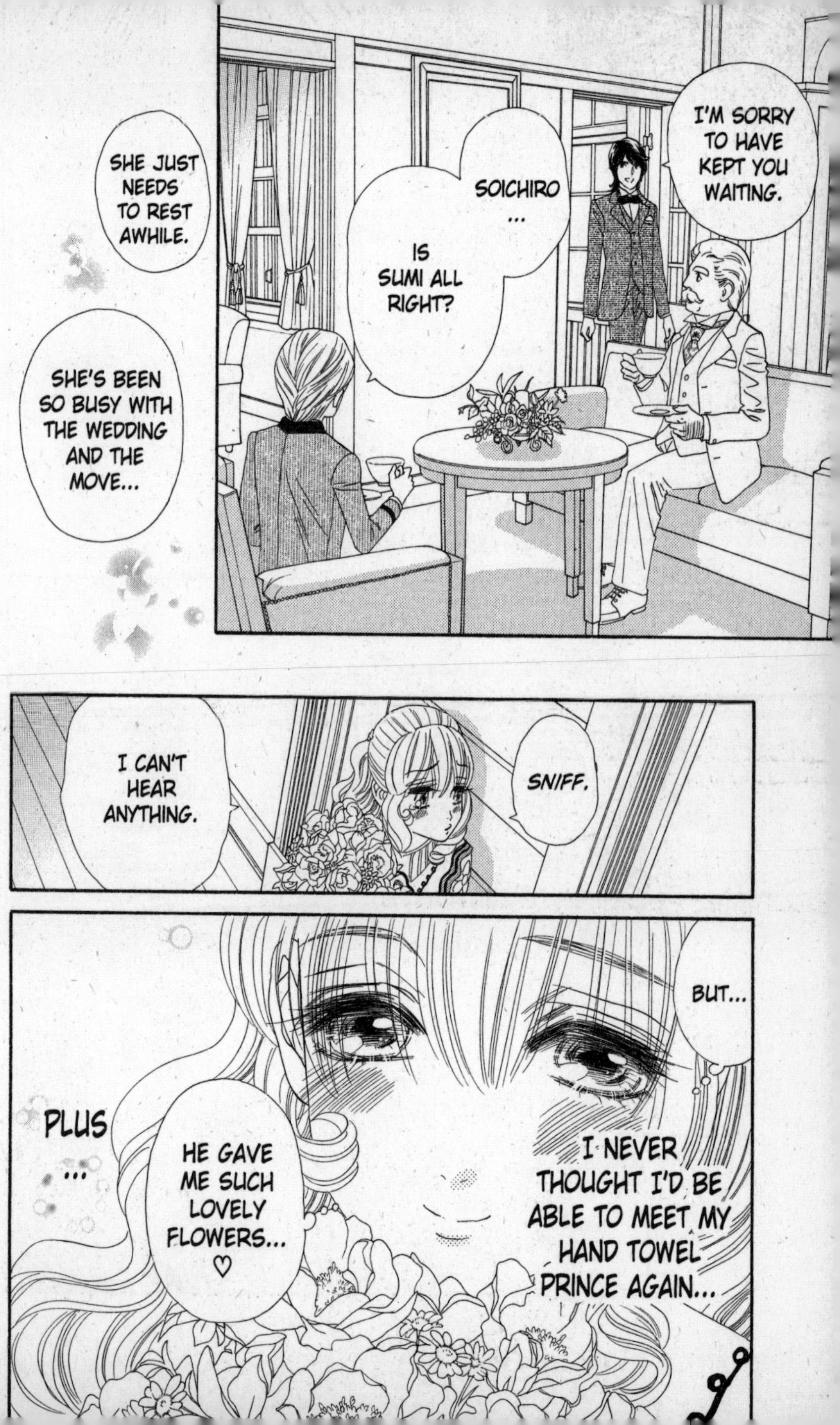
I'M SORRY TO HAVE KEPT YOU WAITING.
SOICHIRO...
IS SUMI ALL RIGHT?
SHE JUST NEEDS TO REST AWHILE.
SHE'S BEEN SO BUSY WITH THE WEDDING AND THE MOVE...
SNIFF.
I CAN'T HEAR ANYTHING.
BUT...
I NEVER THOUGHT I'D BE ABLE TO MEET MY HAND TOWEL PRINCE AGAIN...
HE GAVE ME SUCH LOVELY FLOWERS... ♡
PLUS...

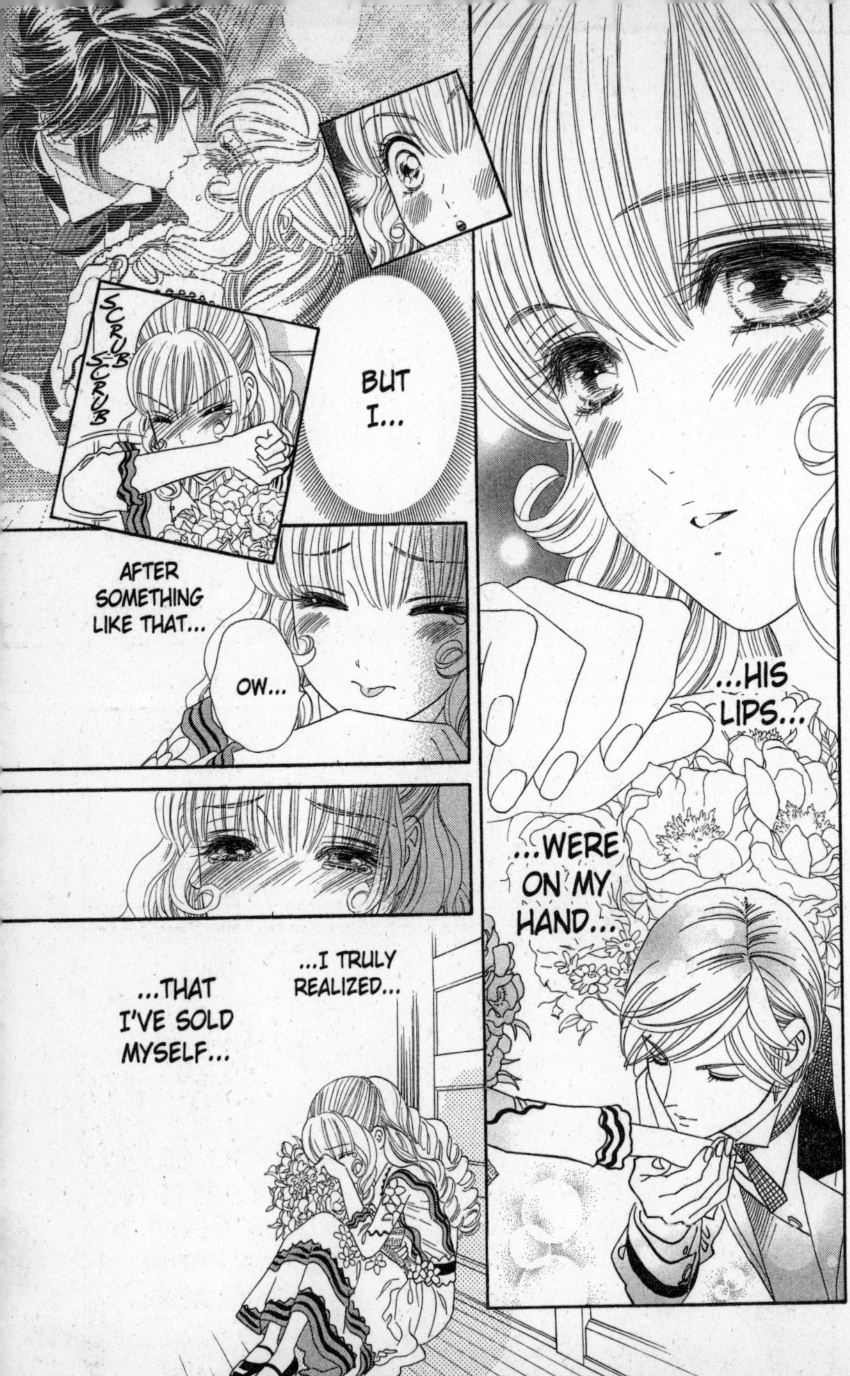
...HIS LIPS...
...WERE ON MY HAND...
BUT I...
SCRUB SCRUB
AFTER SOMETHING LIKE THAT...
OW...
...I TRULY REALIZED...
...THAT I'VE SOLD MYSELF...

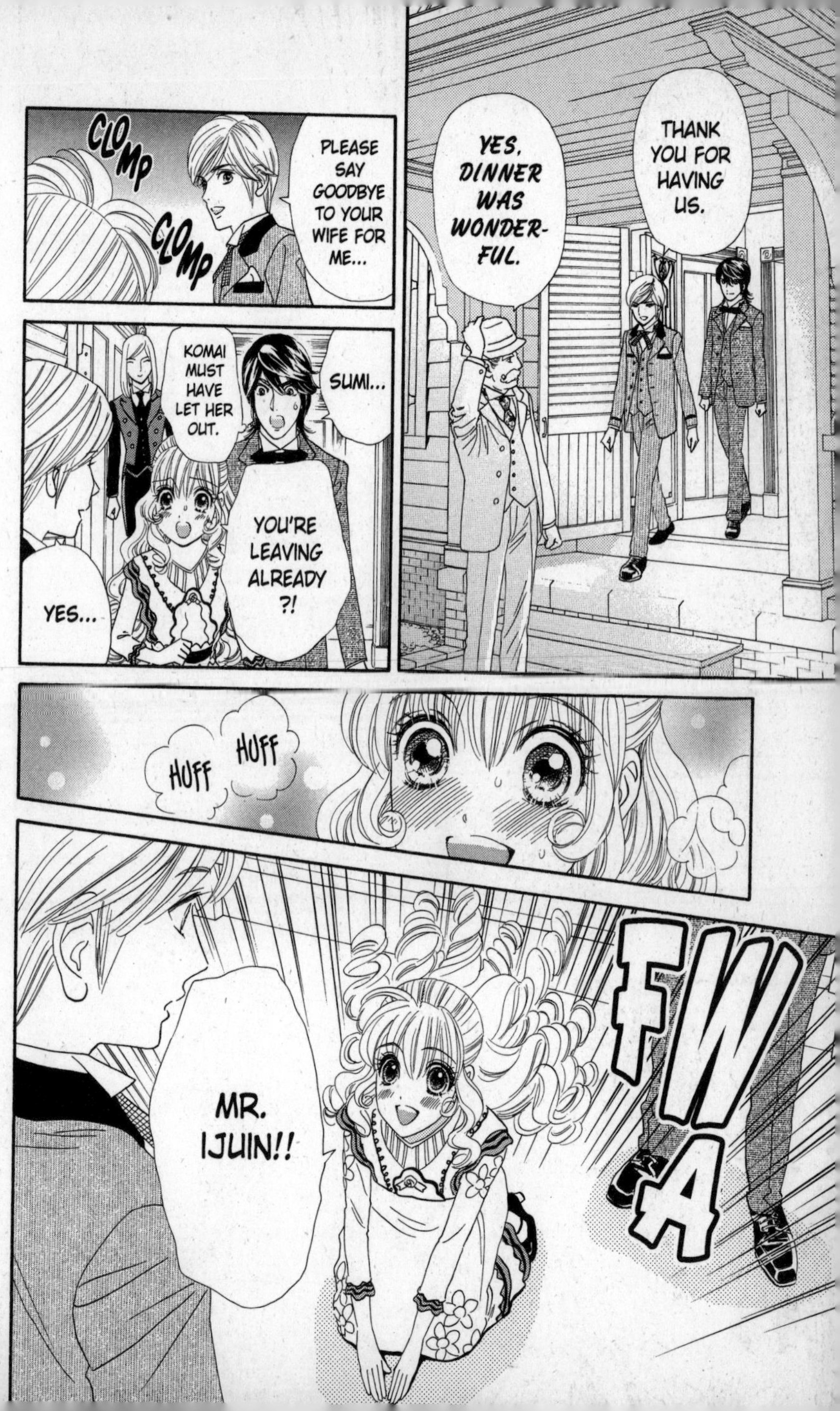
THANK YOU FOR HAVING US.
YES, DINNER WAS WONDERFUL.
PLEASE SAY GOODBYE TO YOUR WIFE FOR ME...
CLOMP
CLOMP
SUMI...
KOMAI MUST HAVE LET HER OUT.
YOU'RE LEAVING ALREADY ?!
YES...
HUFF
HUFF
FWA
MR. IJUIN!!

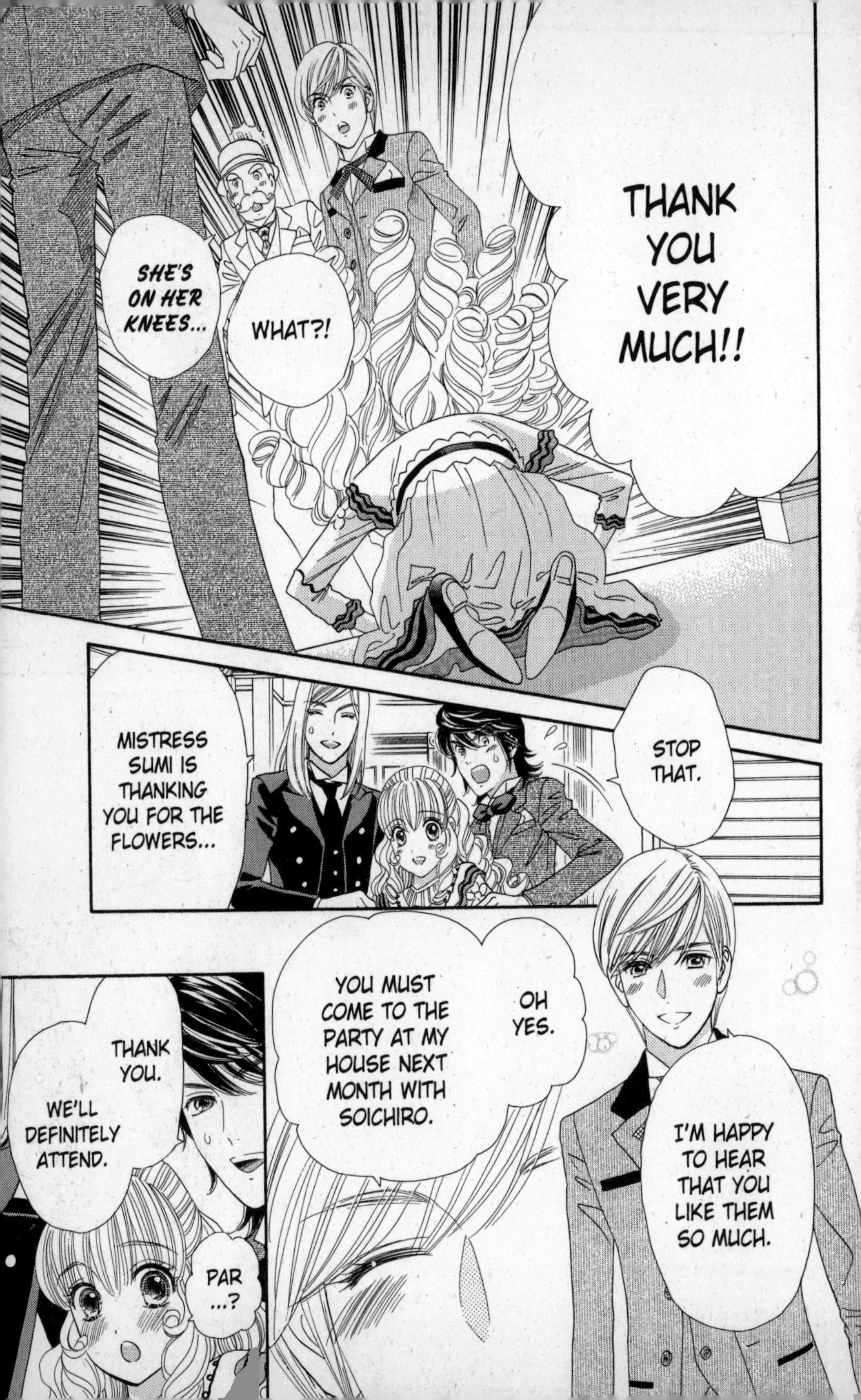
THANK YOU VERY MUCH!!
WHAT?!
SHE'S ON HER KNEES...
STOP THAT.
MISTRESS SUMI IS THANKING YOU FOR THE FLOWERS...
I'M HAPPY TO HEAR THAT YOU LIKE THEM SO MUCH.
OH YES.
YOU MUST COME TO THE PARTY AT MY HOUSE NEXT MONTH WITH SOICHIRO.
THANK YOU.
WE'LL DEFINITELY ATTEND.
PAR ...?

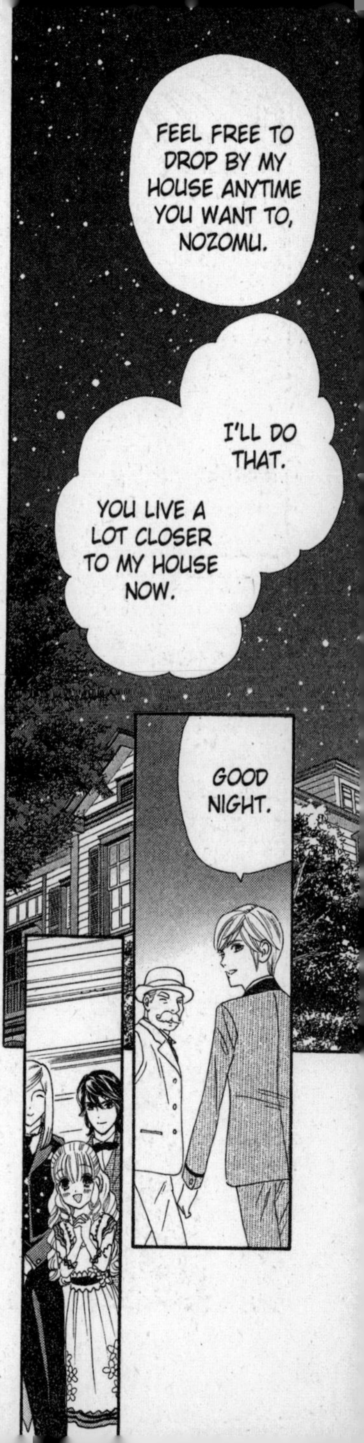
FEEL FREE TO DROP BY MY HOUSE ANYTIME YOU WANT TO, NOZOMU.
I'LL DO THAT.
YOU LIVE A LOT CLOSER TO MY HOUSE NOW.
GOOD NIGHT.

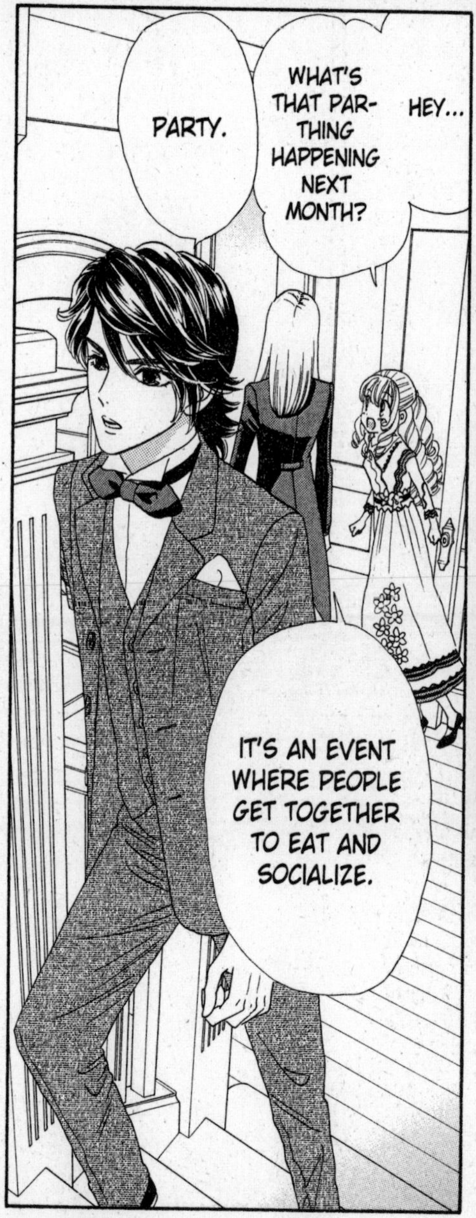
HEY...
WHAT'S THAT PAR-THING HAPPENING NEXT MONTH?
PARTY.
IT'S AN EVENT WHERE PEOPLE GET TOGETHER TO EAT AND SOCIALIZE.

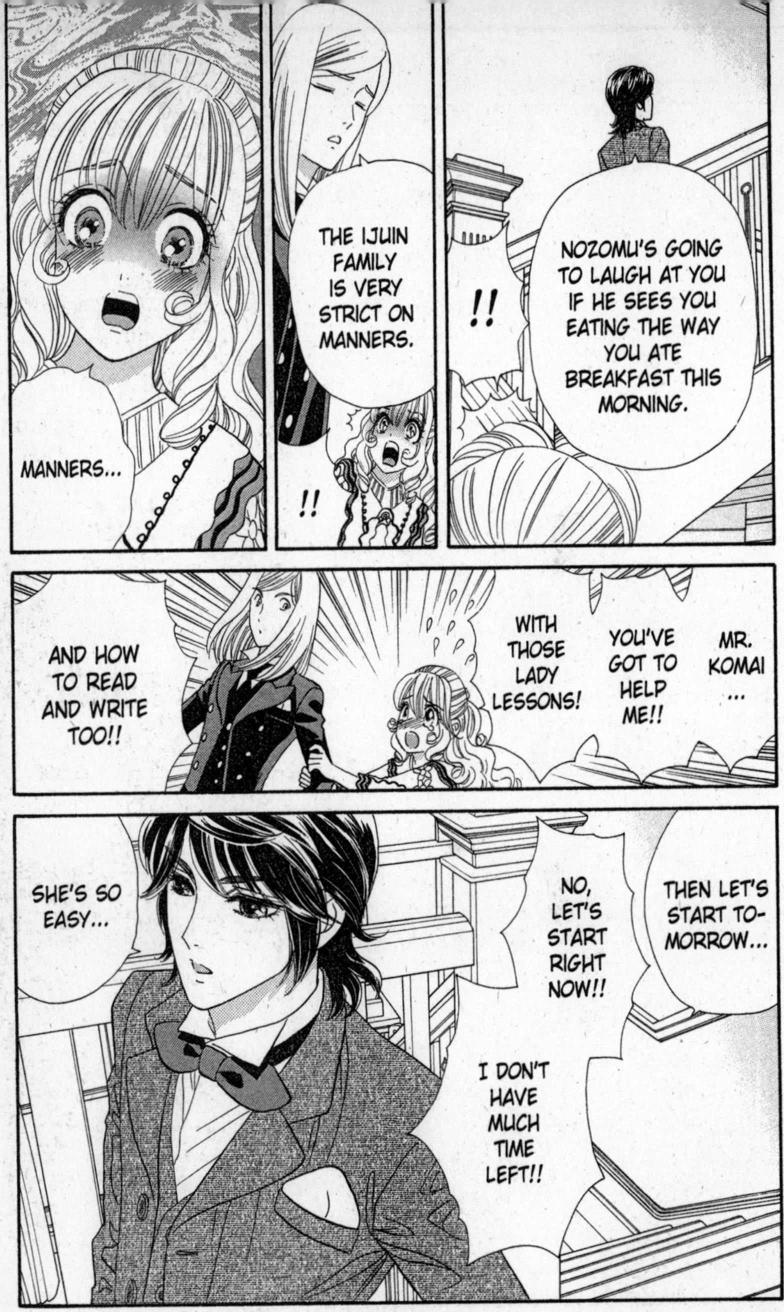
NOZOMU'S GOING TO LAUGH AT YOU IF HE SEES YOU EATING THE WAY YOU ATE BREAKFAST THIS MORNING.
!!
THE IJUIN FAMILY IS VERY STRICT ON MANNERS.
!!
MANNERS...
MR. KOMAI ...
YOU'VE GOT TO HELP ME!!
WITH THOSE LADY LESSONS!
AND HOW TO READ AND WRITE TOO!!
THEN LET'S START TO-MORROW...
NO, LET'S START RIGHT NOW!!
I DON'T HAVE MUCH TIME LEFT!!
SHE'S SO EASY...

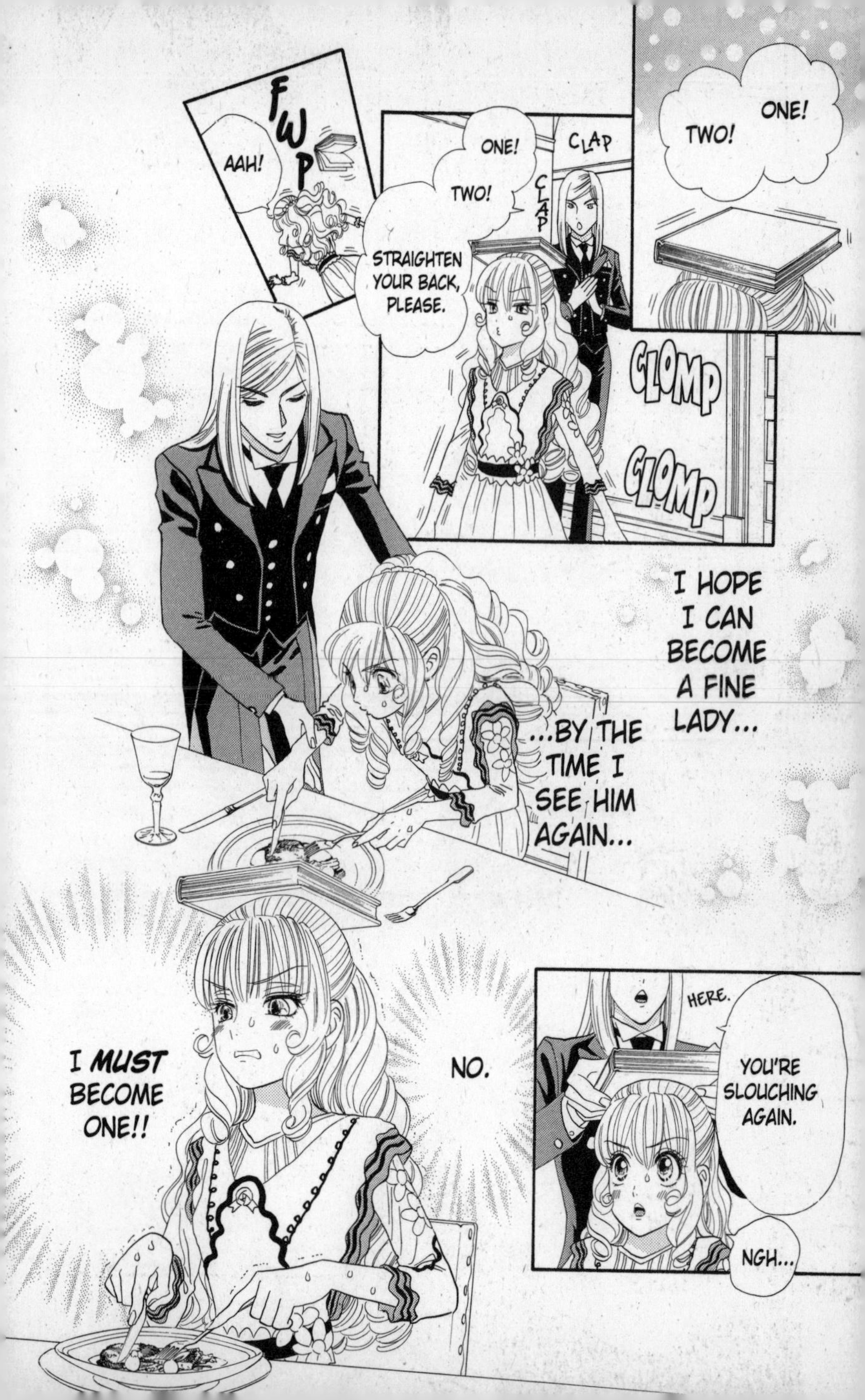
ONE!
TWO!
CLAP
ONE!
TWO!
CLAP
STRAIGHTEN YOUR BACK, PLEASE.
FWP
AAH!
CLOMP
CLOMP
I HOPE I CAN BECOME A FINE LADY...
...BY THE TIME I SEE HIM AGAIN...
HERE.
YOU'RE SLOUCHING AGAIN.
NGH...
NO.
I *MUST* BECOME ONE!!

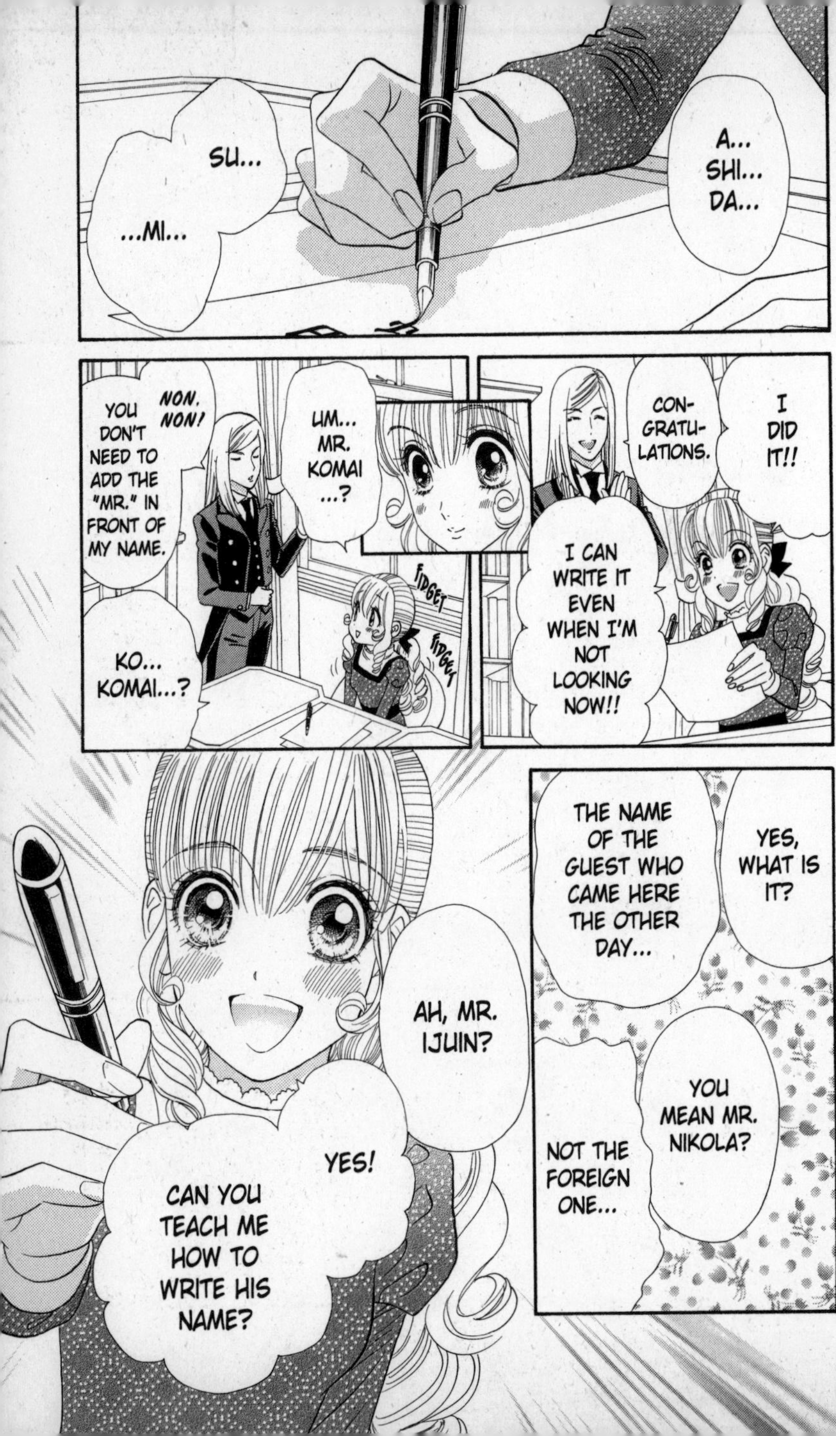
A... SHI... DA...
SU...
...MI...
I DID IT!!
CON-GRATU-LATIONS.
I CAN WRITE IT EVEN WHEN I'M NOT LOOKING NOW!!
UM... MR. KOMAI ...?
NON, NON!
YOU DON'T NEED TO ADD THE "MR." IN FRONT OF MY NAME.
FIDGET
FIDGET
KO... KOMAI...?
YES, WHAT IS IT?
THE NAME OF THE GUEST WHO CAME HERE THE OTHER DAY...
YOU MEAN MR. NIKOLA?
NOT THE FOREIGN ONE...
AH, MR. IJUIN?
YES!
CAN YOU TEACH ME HOW TO WRITE HIS NAME?

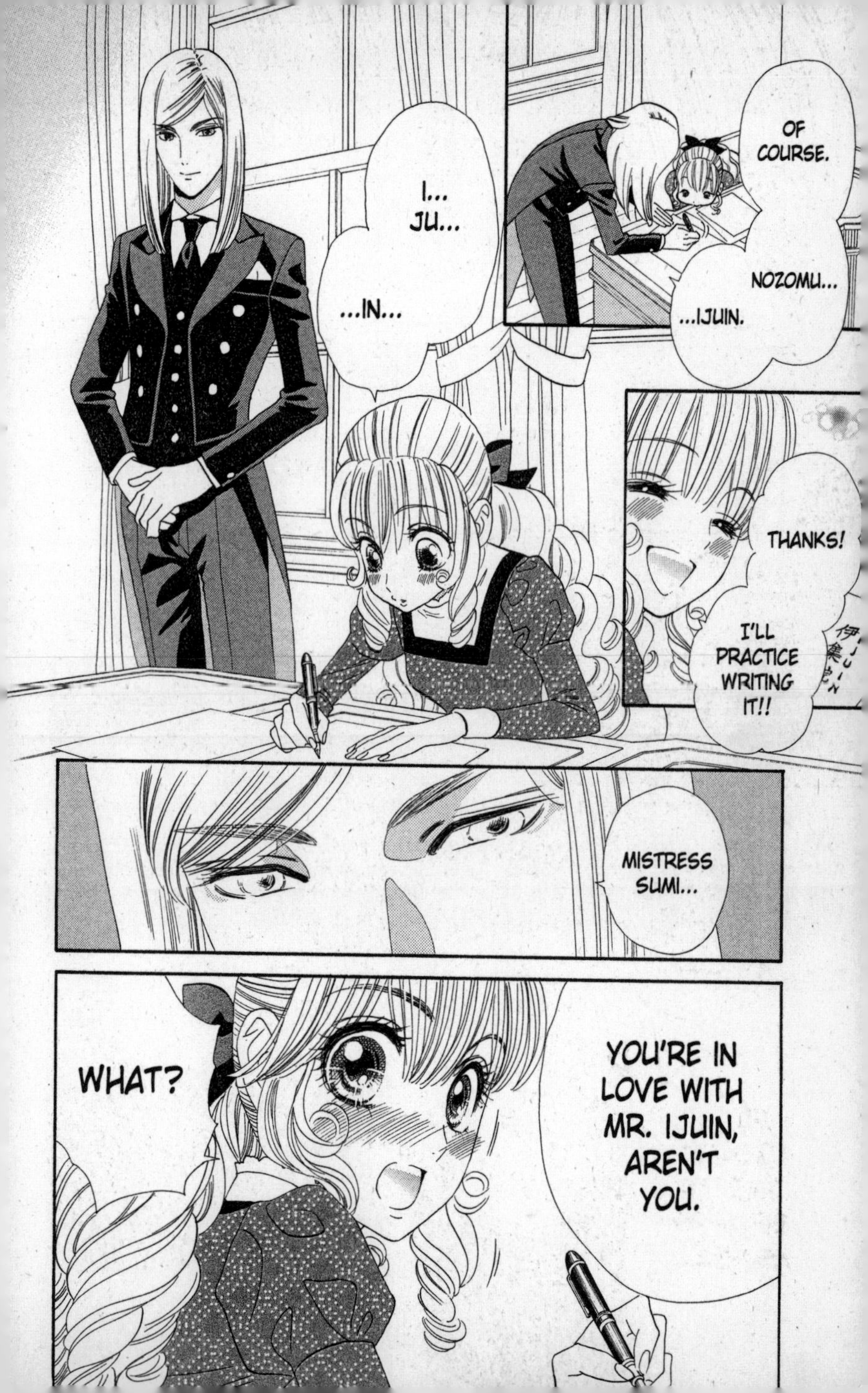

OF COURSE.
NOZOMU...
...IJUIN.
THANKS!
I'LL PRACTICE WRITING IT!!
伊集院
I... JU...
...IN...
MISTRESS SUMI...
YOU'RE IN LOVE WITH MR. IJUIN, AREN'T YOU.
WHAT?

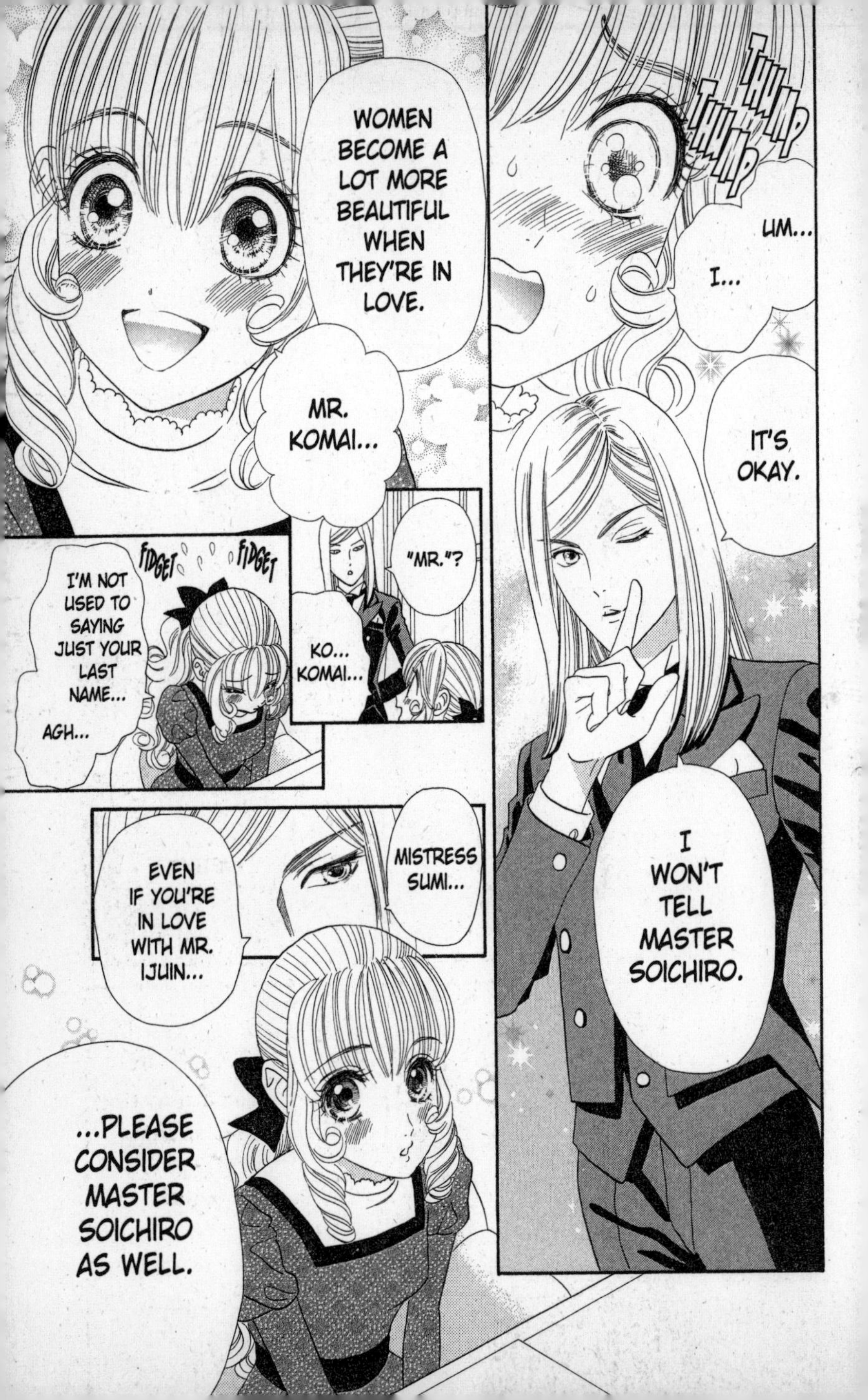
THUMP THUMP
UM...
I...
IT'S OKAY.
I WON'T TELL MASTER SOICHIRO.
WOMEN BECOME A LOT MORE BEAUTIFUL WHEN THEY'RE IN LOVE.
MR. KOMAI...
"MR."?
KO... KOMAI...
FIDGET FIDGET
I'M NOT USED TO SAYING JUST YOUR LAST NAME...
AGH...
MISTRESS SUMI...
EVEN IF YOU'RE IN LOVE WITH MR. IJUIN...
...PLEASE CONSIDER MASTER SOICHIRO AS WELL.

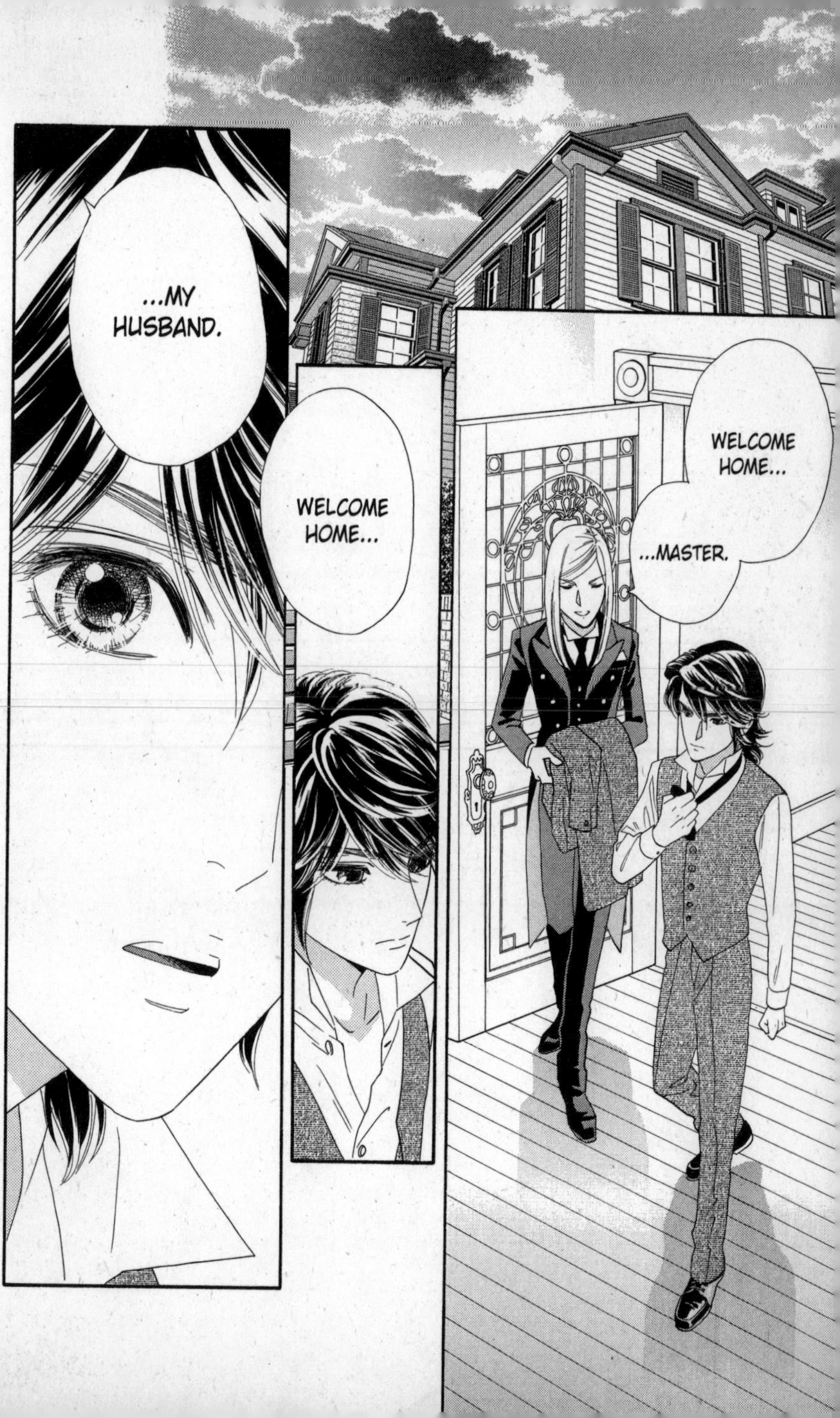
WELCOME HOME...
...MASTER.
WELCOME HOME...
...MY HUSBAND.

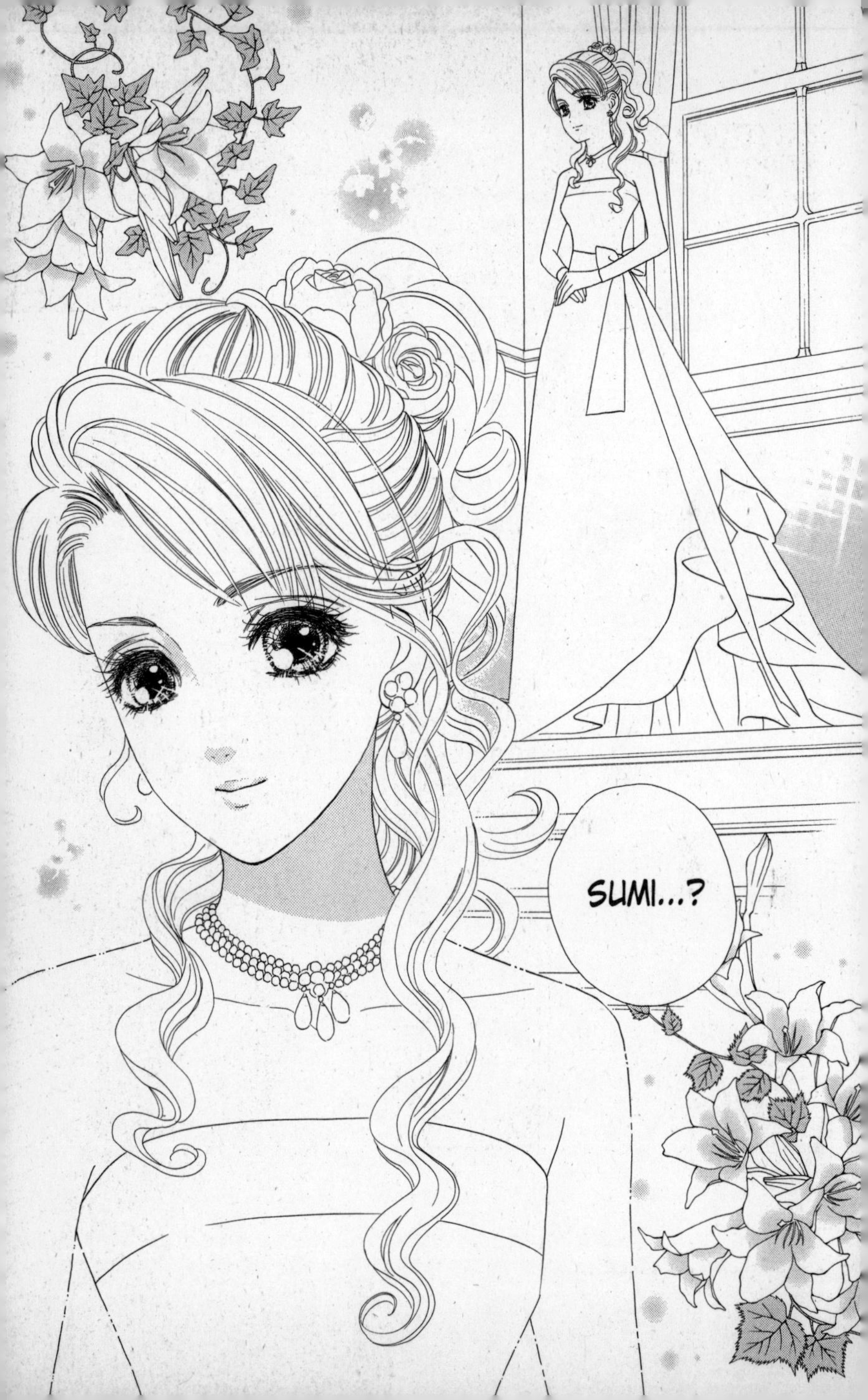
SUMI...?

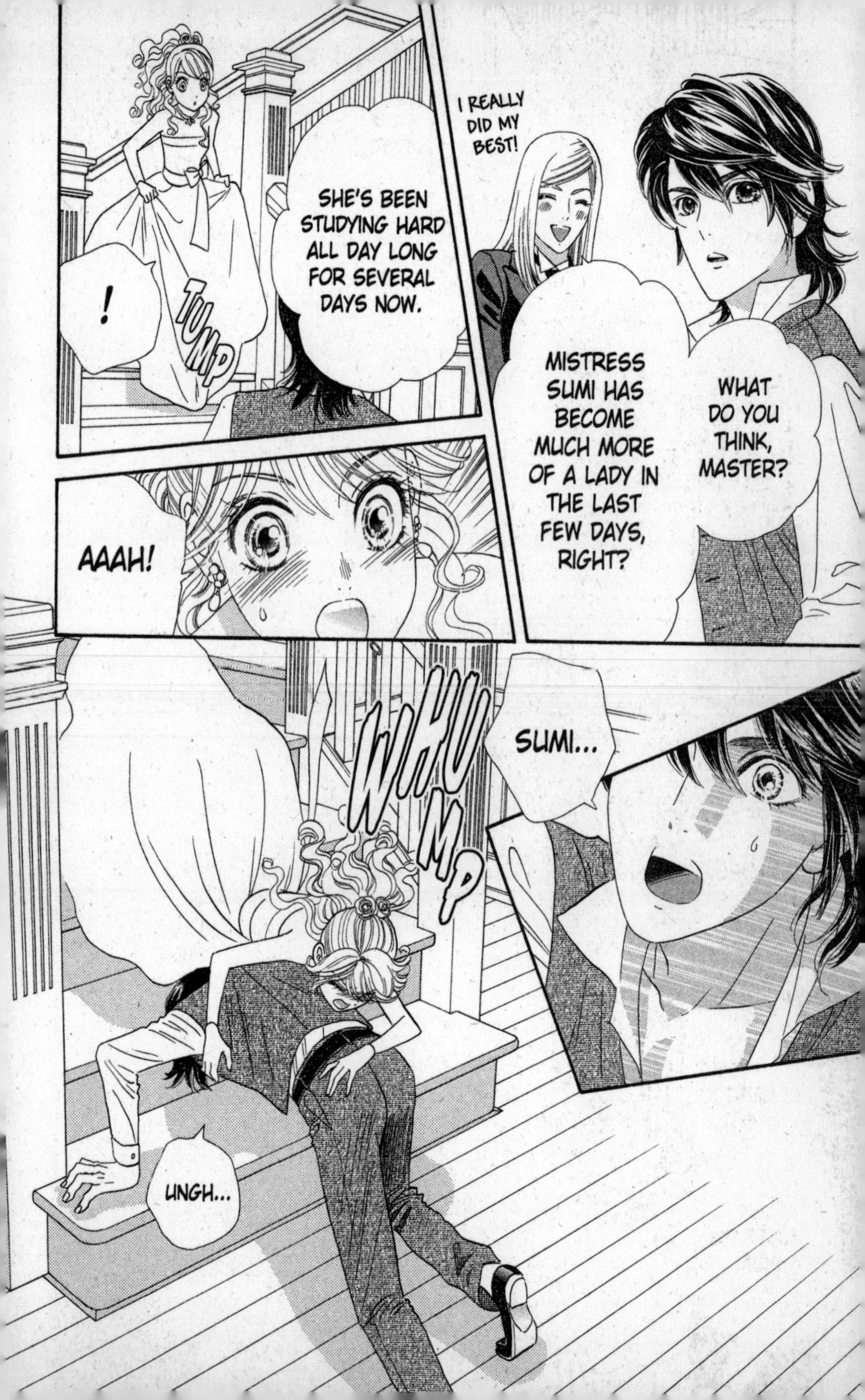
I REALLY DID MY BEST!
SHE'S BEEN STUDYING HARD ALL DAY LONG FOR SEVERAL DAYS NOW.
MISTRESS SUMI HAS BECOME MUCH MORE OF A LADY IN THE LAST FEW DAYS, RIGHT?
WHAT DO YOU THINK, MASTER?
!
TUMP
AAAH!
SUMI...
WHUMP
UNGH...

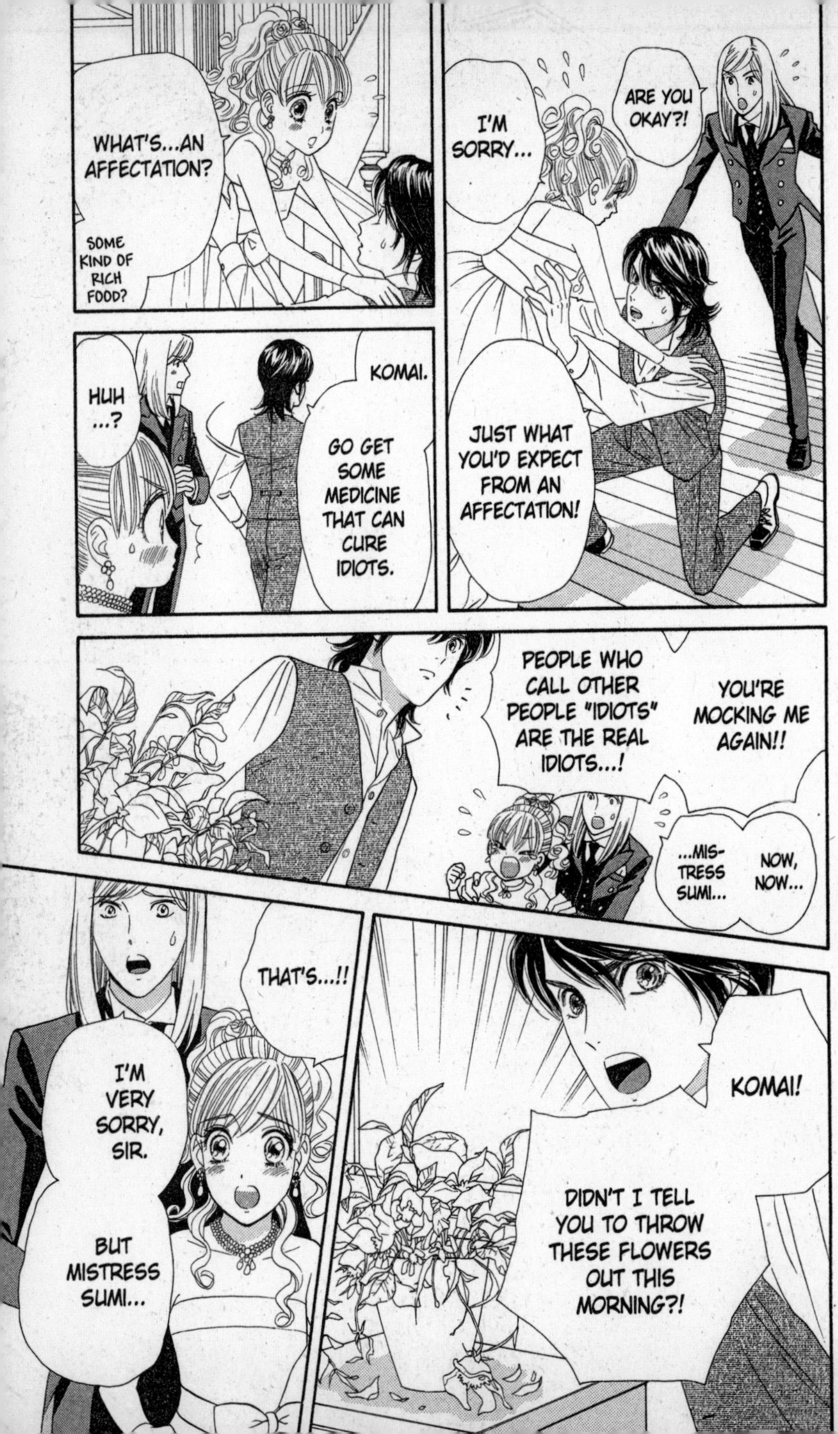
ARE YOU OKAY?!
I'M SORRY...
JUST WHAT YOU'D EXPECT FROM AN AFFECTATION!
WHAT'S...AN AFFECTATION?
SOME KIND OF RICH FOOD?
KOMAI.
GO GET SOME MEDICINE THAT CAN CURE IDIOTS.
HUH ...?
YOU'RE MOCKING ME AGAIN!!
PEOPLE WHO CALL OTHER PEOPLE "IDIOTS" ARE THE REAL IDIOTS...!
NOW, NOW...
...MIS-TRESS SUMI...
KOMAI!
DIDN'T I TELL YOU TO THROW THESE FLOWERS OUT THIS MORNING?!
THAT'S...!!
I'M VERY SORRY, SIR.
BUT MISTRESS SUMI...

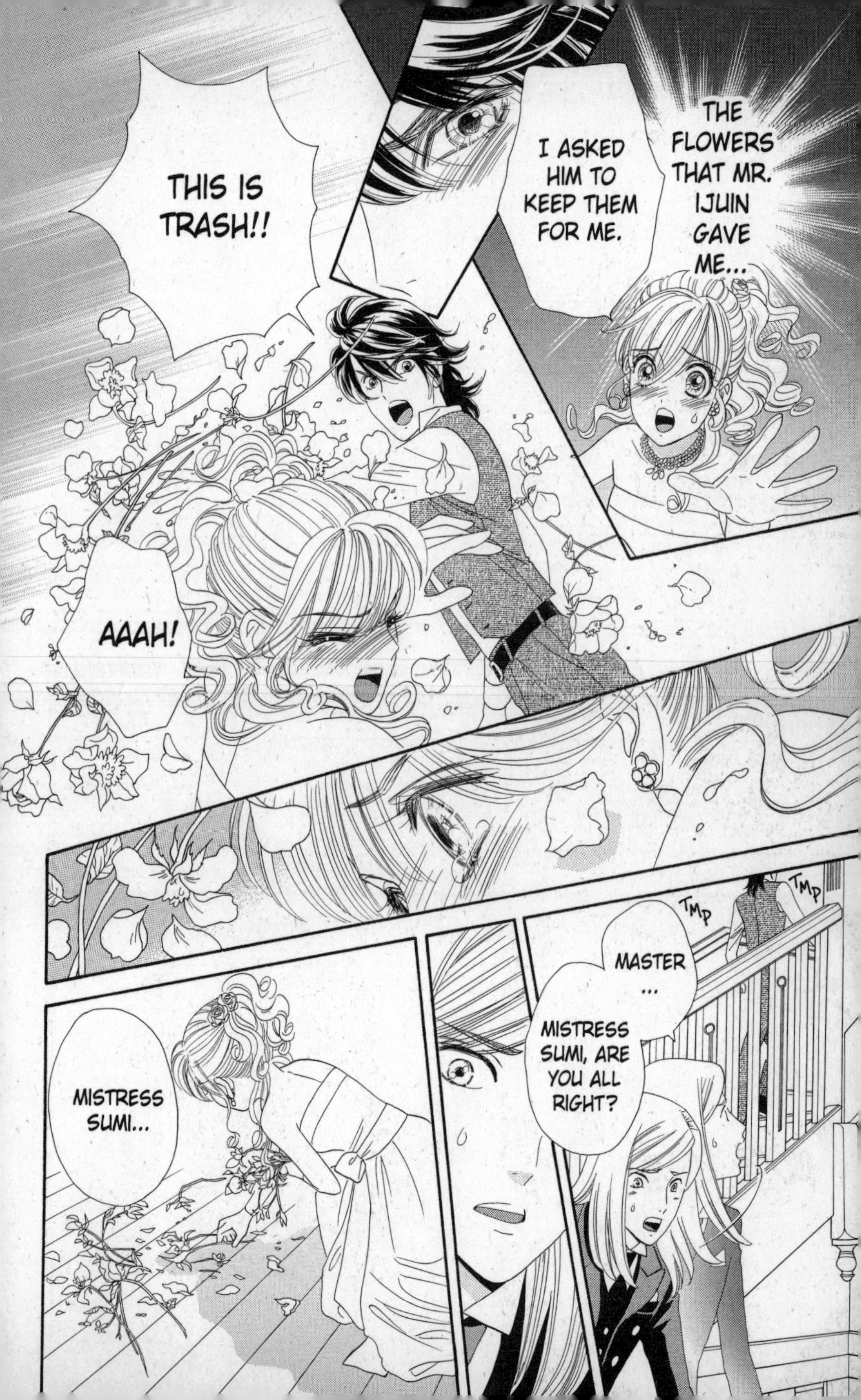
THE FLOWERS THAT MR. IJUIN GAVE ME...
I ASKED HIM TO KEEP THEM FOR ME.
THIS IS TRASH!!
AAAH!
TMP
TMP
MASTER ...
MISTRESS SUMI, ARE YOU ALL RIGHT?
MISTRESS SUMI...

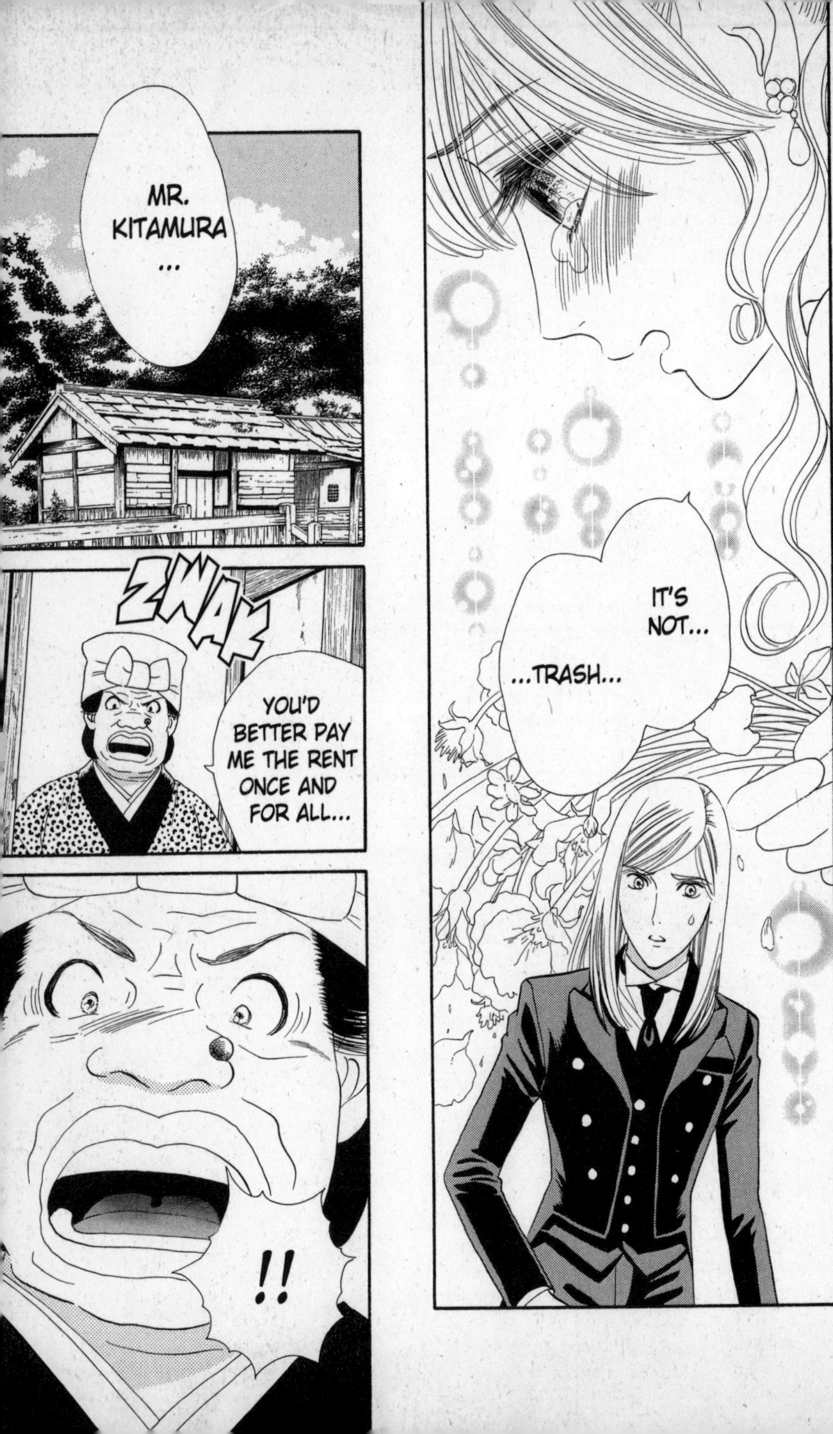
IT'S NOT...
...TRASH...
MR. KITAMURA ...
ZWAK
YOU'D BETTER PAY ME THE RENT ONCE AND FOR ALL...
!!

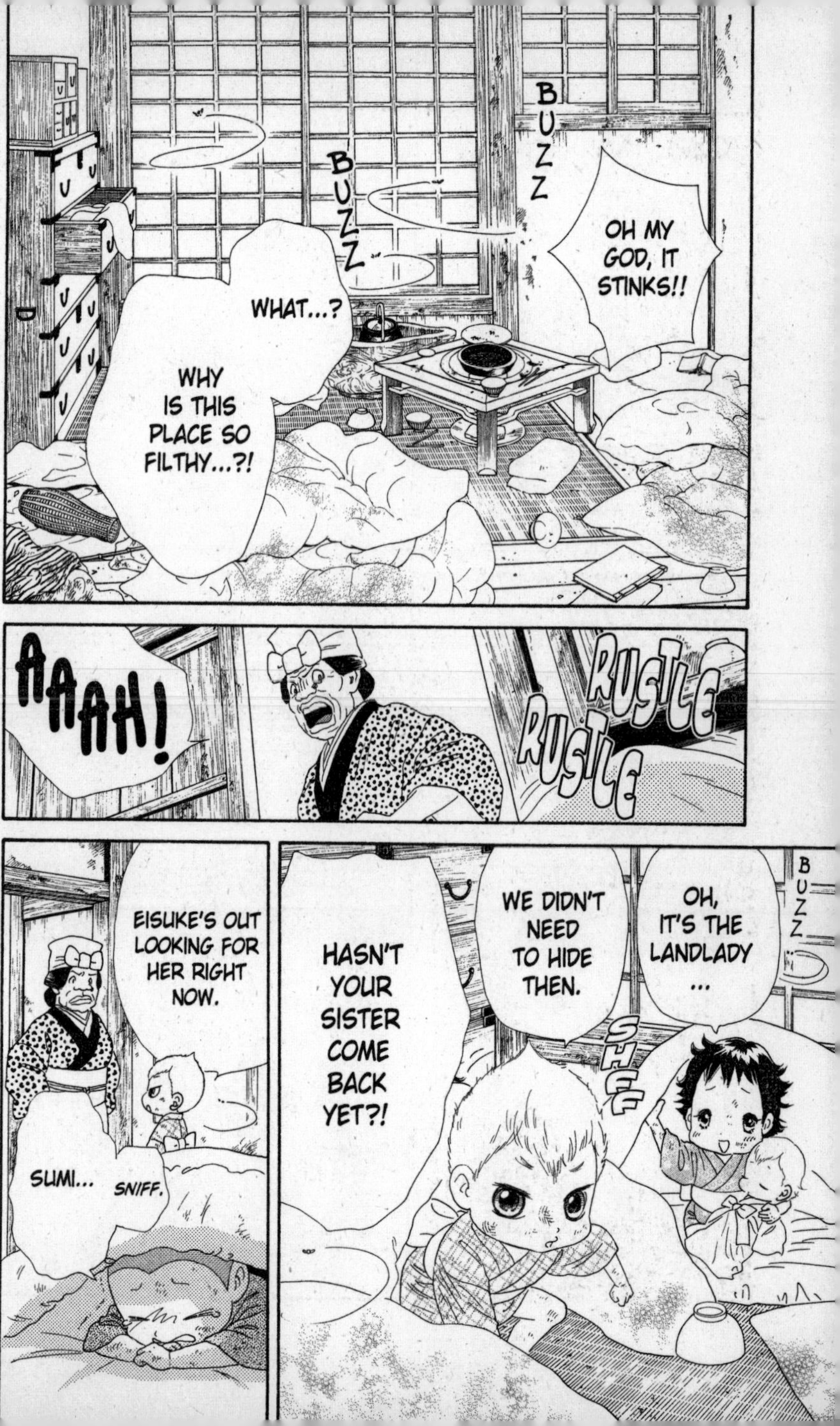
BUZZ
OH MY GOD, IT STINKS!!
BUZZ
WHAT...?
WHY IS THIS PLACE SO FILTHY...?!
RUSTLE RUSTLE
AAAH!
BUZZ
OH, IT'S THE LANDLADY...
SHEF
WE DIDN'T NEED TO HIDE THEN.
HASN'T YOUR SISTER COME BACK YET?!
EISUKE'S OUT LOOKING FOR HER RIGHT NOW.
SUMI...
SNIFF.

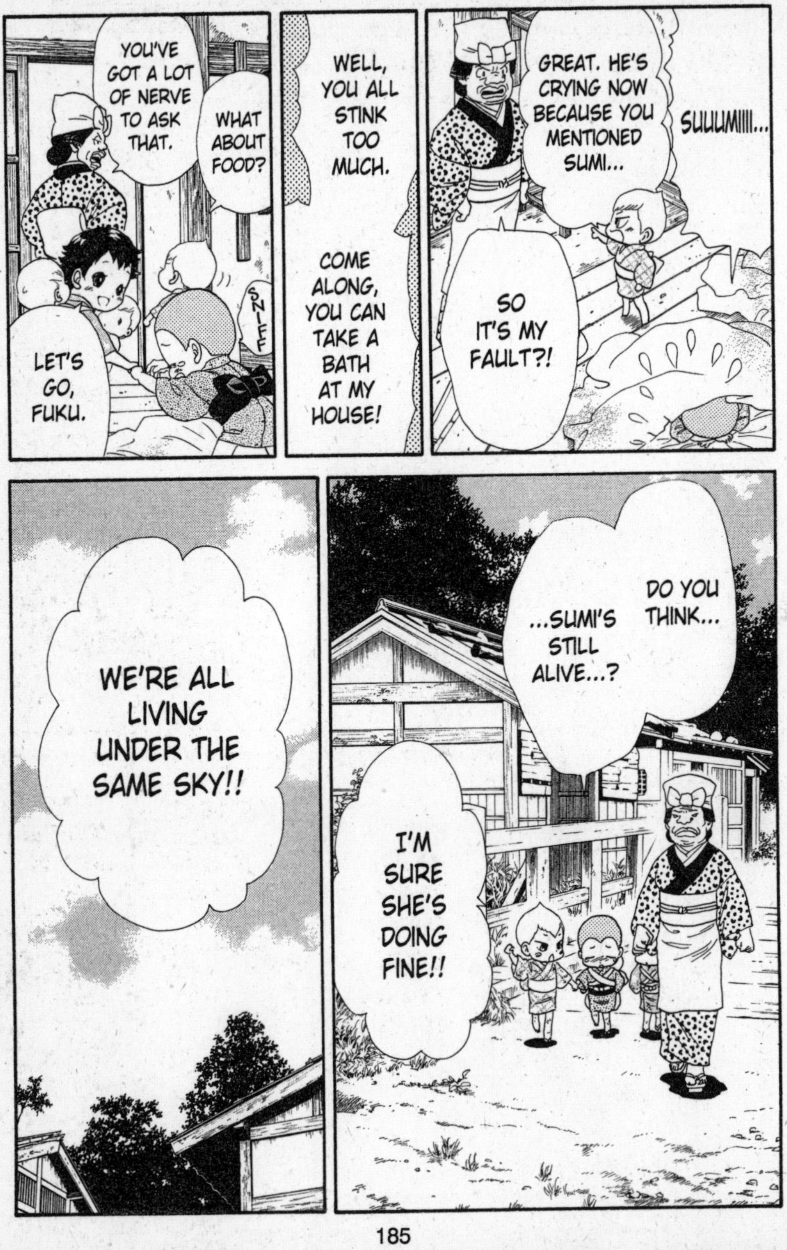
SUUUMIIII...
GREAT. HE'S CRYING NOW BECAUSE YOU MENTIONED SUMI...
SO IT'S MY FAULT?!
WELL, YOU ALL STINK TOO MUCH.
COME ALONG, YOU CAN TAKE A BATH AT MY HOUSE!
WHAT ABOUT FOOD?
YOU'VE GOT A LOT OF NERVE TO ASK THAT.
SNIFF
LET'S GO, FUKU.
DO YOU THINK...
...SUMI'S STILL ALIVE...?
I'M SURE SHE'S DOING FINE!!
WE'RE ALL LIVING UNDER THE SAME SKY!!

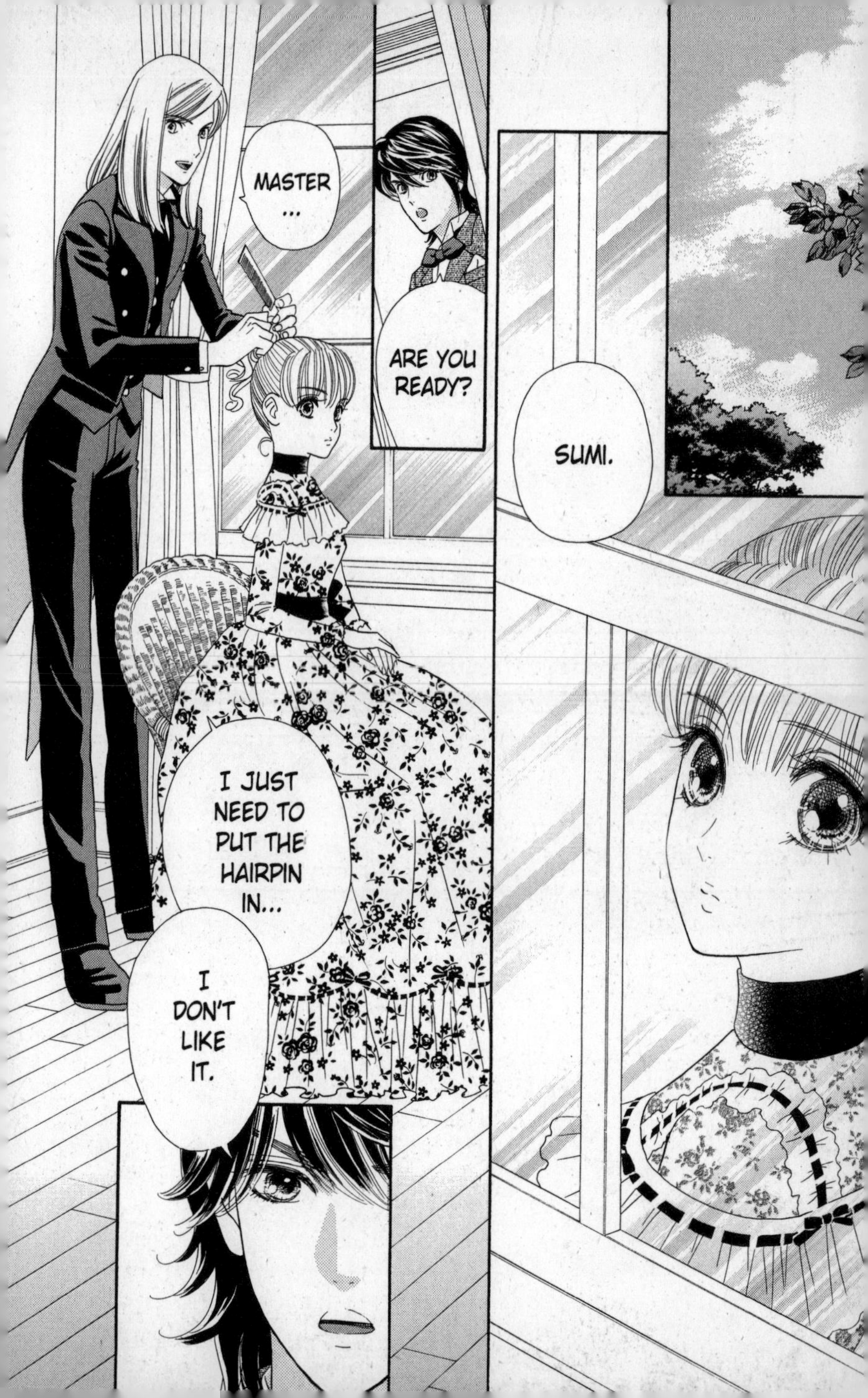
SUMI.
MASTER...
ARE YOU READY?
I JUST NEED TO PUT THE HAIRPIN IN...
I DON'T LIKE IT.

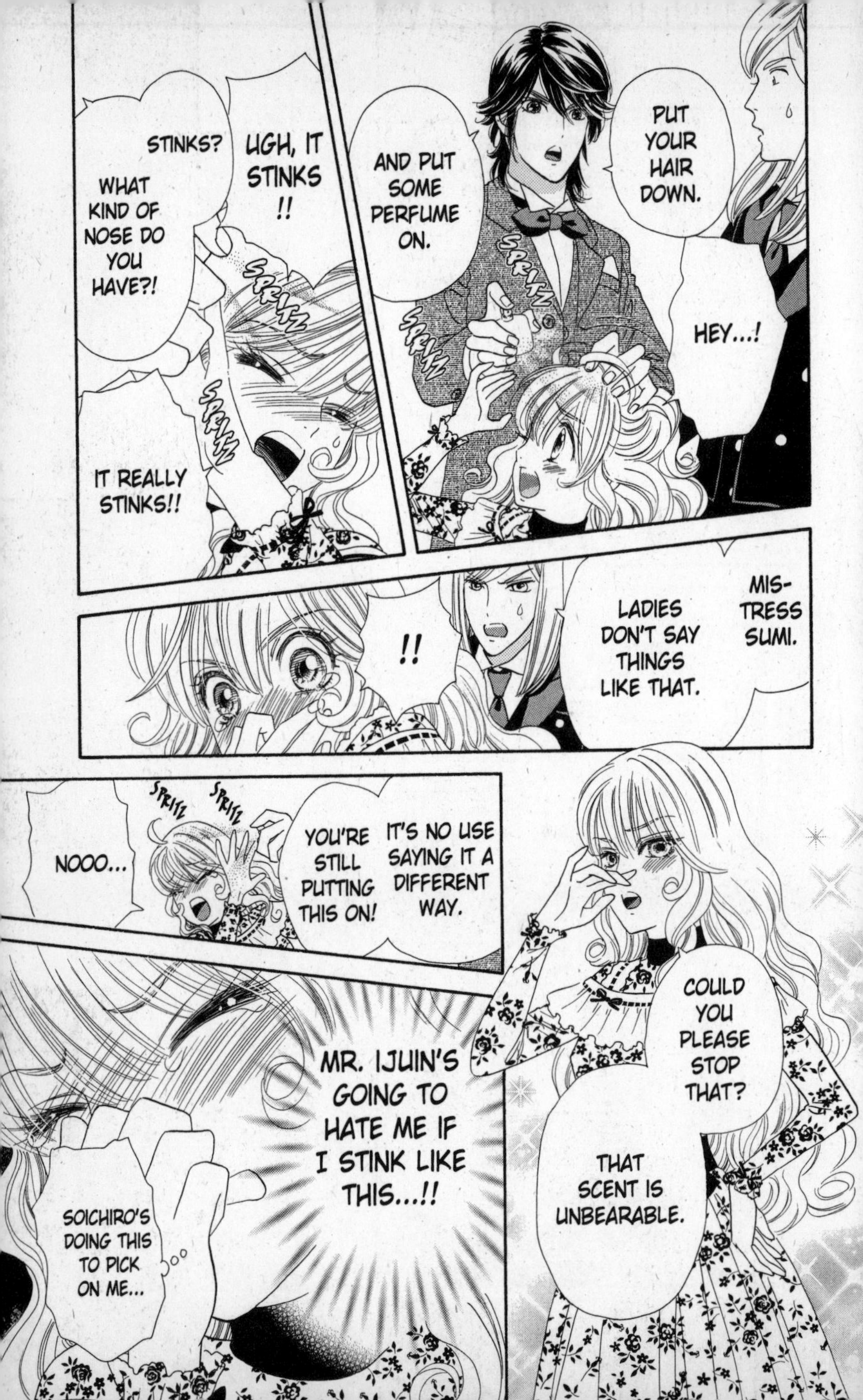
PUT YOUR HAIR DOWN.
HEY...!
AND PUT SOME PERFUME ON.
SPRIZZ
SPRIZZ
UGH, IT STINKS !!
STINKS? WHAT KIND OF NOSE DO YOU HAVE?!
SPRIZZ
SPRIZZ
IT REALLY STINKS!!
MIS-TRESS SUMI.
LADIES DON'T SAY THINGS LIKE THAT.
!!
COULD YOU PLEASE STOP THAT?
THAT SCENT IS UNBEARABLE.
IT'S NO USE SAYING IT A DIFFERENT WAY.
YOU'RE STILL PUTTING THIS ON!
SPRIZZ
SPRIZZ
NOOO...
MR. IJUIN'S GOING TO HATE ME IF I STINK LIKE THIS...!!
SOICHIRO'S DOING THIS TO PICK ON ME...

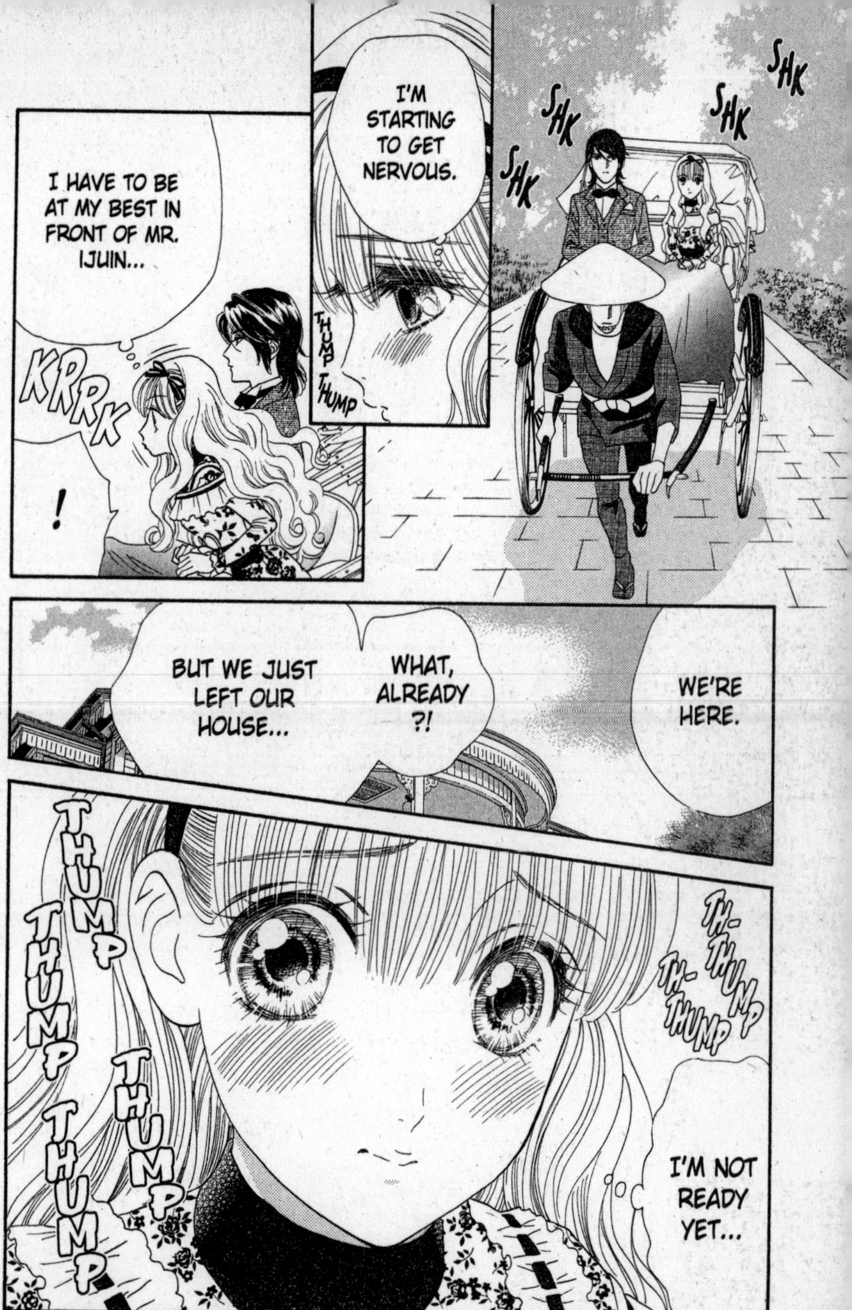
SHK
SHK
SHK
SHK
I'M STARTING TO GET NERVOUS.
THUMP THUMP
I HAVE TO BE AT MY BEST IN FRONT OF MR. IJUIN...
KRRRK
!
WE'RE HERE.
WHAT, ALREADY?!
BUT WE JUST LEFT OUR HOUSE...
TH-THUMP
TH-THUMP
I'M NOT READY YET...
THUMP
THUMP
THUMP
THUMP

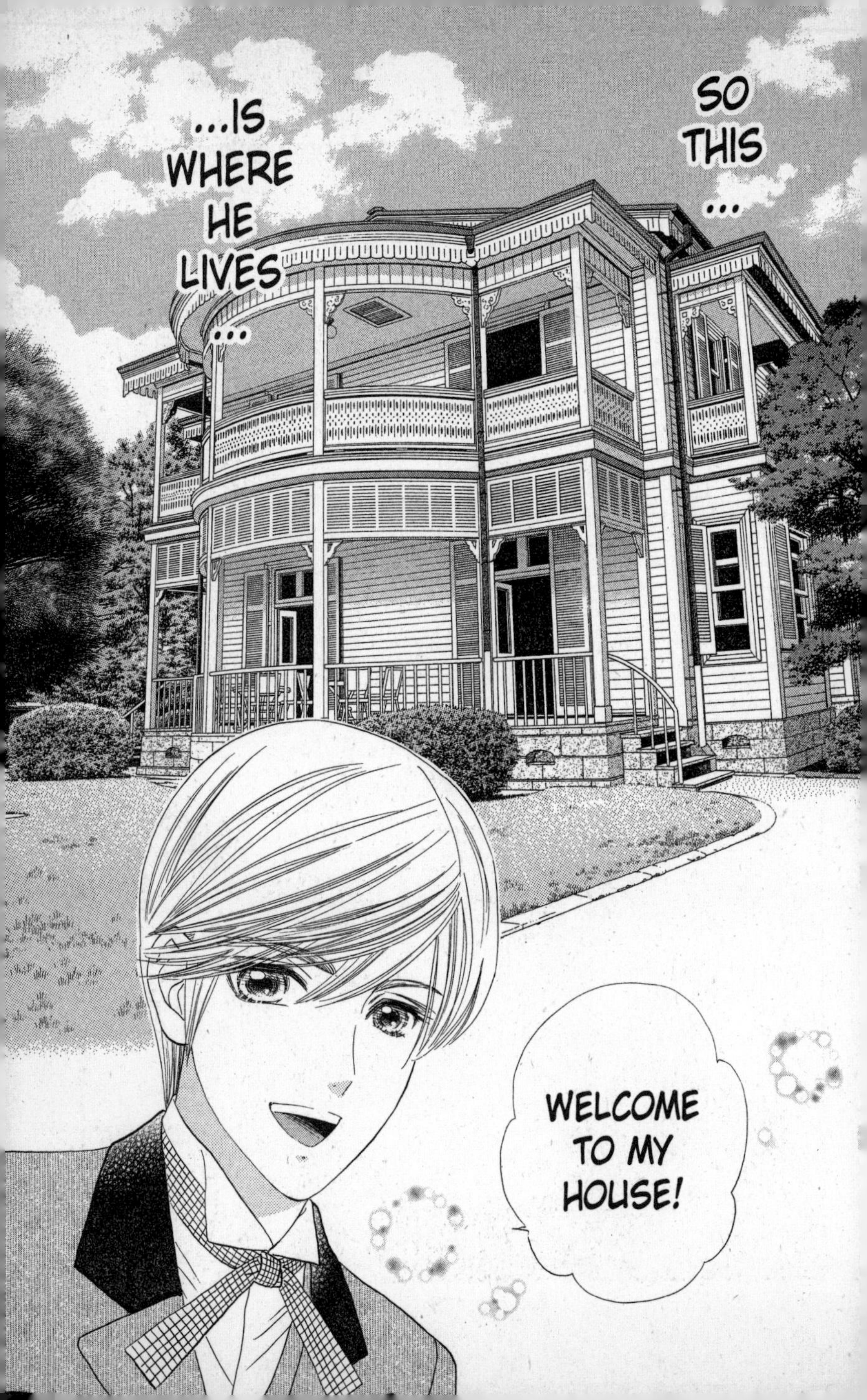
SO THIS ...
...IS WHERE HE LIVES ...
WELCOME TO MY HOUSE!

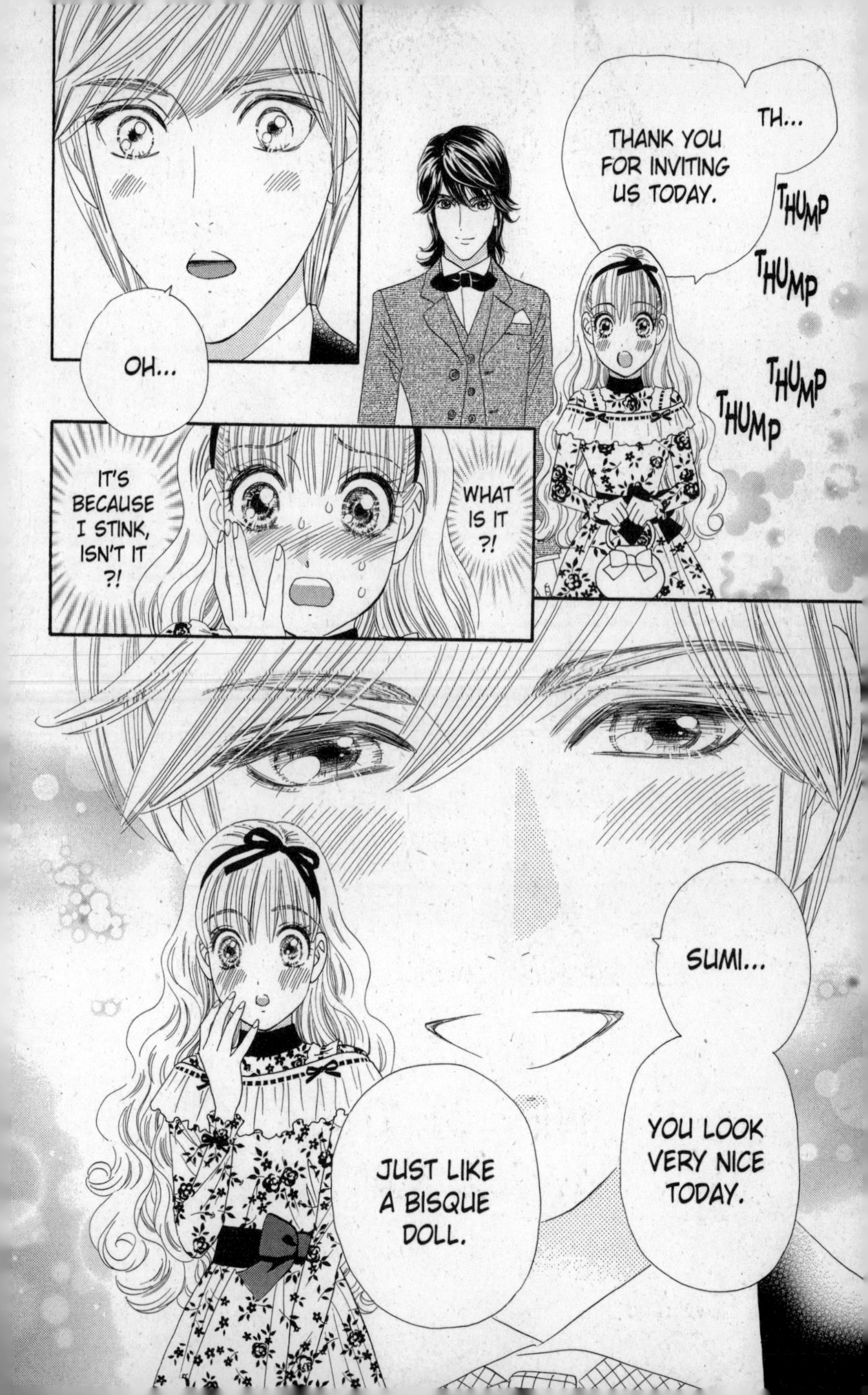
TH...
THANK YOU FOR INVITING US TODAY.
THUMP
THUMP
THUMP
THUMP
OH...
WHAT IS IT ?!
IT'S BECAUSE I STINK, ISN'T IT ?!
SUMI...
YOU LOOK VERY NICE TODAY.
JUST LIKE A BISQUE DOLL.

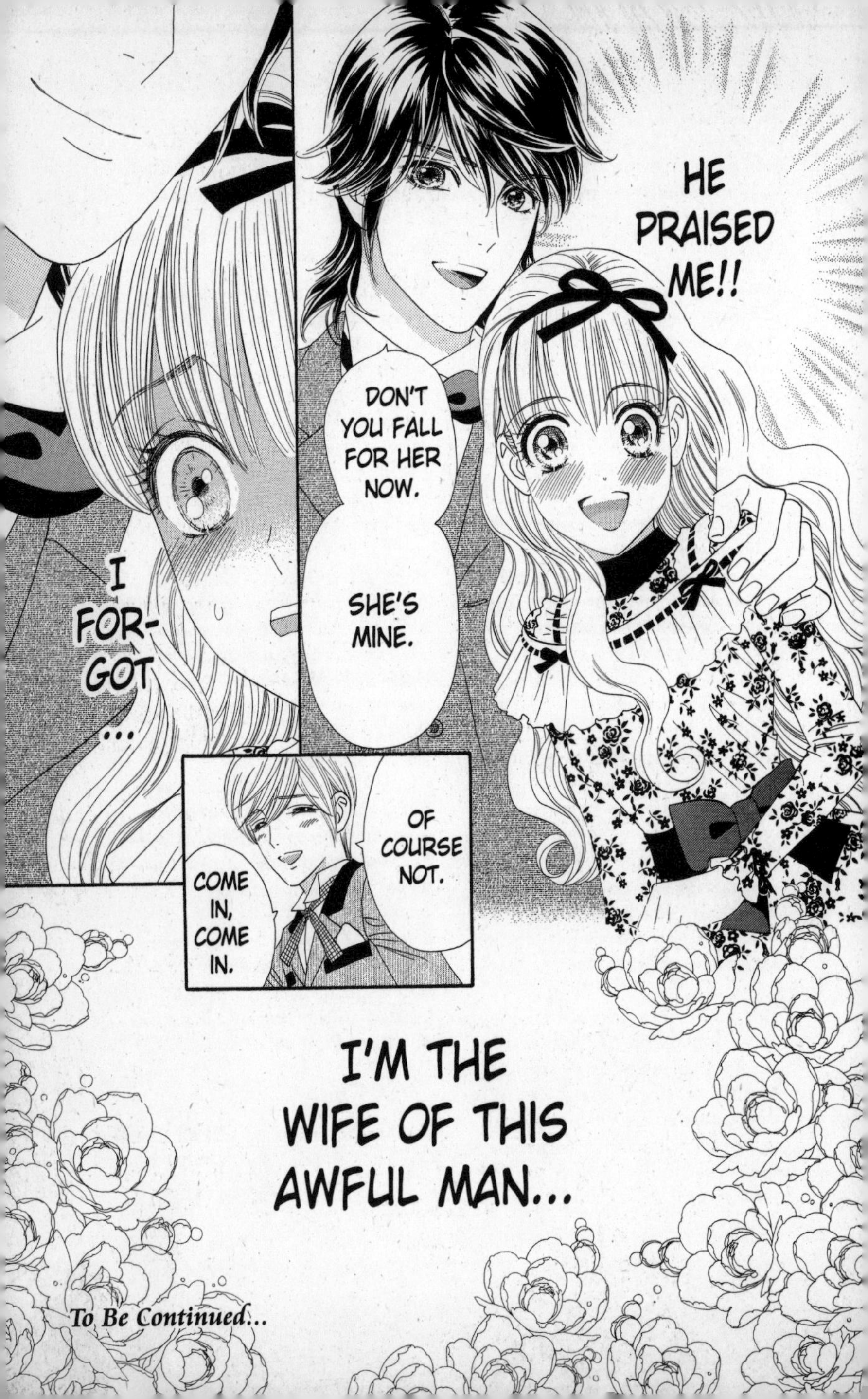
HE PRAISED ME!!
DON'T YOU FALL FOR HER NOW.
SHE'S MINE.
I FOR-GOT...
OF COURSE NOT.
COME IN, COME IN.
I'M THE WIFE OF THIS AWFUL MAN...
To Be Continued...

Glossary

The setting of *Stepping on Roses* plays an important part in the story, as it showcases a unique time of change and transformation in Japan. Check out the notes below to help enrich your reading experience.

**Page 116, panel 5:
Taking off shoes**
It is customary to take off one's shoes when entering a home in Japan. Sumi is used to this tradition, but the Western design of this house indicates that she should keep her shoes on.

Page 123, panel 7: Futon
Like most Japanese people during this time, Sumi is used to sleeping on a futon on the floor. She isn't accustomed to sleeping on a Western bed.

**Page 138, panel 1:
Beef hot pot**
The beef hot pot shown here is called *gyu-nabe*, a stewed dish that originated in Yokohama.

Page 165, panel 2: Kamakura
Kamakura is a coastal town in Kanagawa Prefecture and is located approximately 11 miles away from Yokohama.

Page 171, panel 1: Kneeling
Sumi is bowing to Nozomu in the formal kneeling position known as *seiza*. Though Sumi is doing this as a sign of respect, it looks a bit strange to her Western-minded guests.

Page 11, panel 2: Meiji Era
The Meiji Era (1868–1912) was a time of reform in Japan when Western models and technology were studied, borrowed and adapted for the sake of modernization. One of the slogans of this period was *bunmei kaika*, or "civilization and enlightenment."

Page 22, panel 3: Yokohama
A major port city located south of Tokyo, Yokohama is also the capital city of Kanagawa Prefecture. Yokohama's port was one of the first to be opened to foreign trade.

Page 33, panel 2: Hand towel
Sumi calls the item Nozomu gives her a *tenugui* (hand towel) because she doesn't know the term "handkerchief."

Page 112, panel 5: Hayama
Hayama is located about 31 miles south of Tokyo and is located in the northwest region of Miura Peninsula.

Creating a new story isn't easy.
No matter how much experience
I get, I can never figure out what
will be interesting to readers. But
I always have and always will like
formulaic stories, so I created a
pretty formulaic manga here. I do
hope you will all enjoy the story
with me.

-Rinko Ueda

Rinko Ueda is from Nara
Prefecture. She enjoys listening
to the radio, drama CDs and
Rakugo comedy performances.
Her works include *Ryo*, a series
based on the legend of Gojo
Bridge; *Home*, a story about love
crossing national boundaries; and
Tail of the Moon (*Tsuki no Shippo*),
a romantic ninja comedy.

STEPPING ON ROSES
Vol. 1
Shojo Beat Edition

STORY AND ART BY
RINKO UEDA

Translation & Adaptation/Tetsuichiro Miyaki
Touch-up Art & Lettering/Mark McMurray
Design/Yukiko Whitley
Editor/Amy Yu

VP, Production/Alvin Lu
VP, Sales & Product Marketing/Gonzalo Ferreyra
VP, Creative/Linda Espinosa
Publisher/Hyoe Narita

 A CIP catalogue record for this book is available from the British Library.

Printed in the U.S.A.

Published by VIZ Media, LLC
P.O. Box 77010
San Francisco, CA 94107

10 9 8 7 6 5 4 3 2 1
First printing, April 2010

www.viz.com
www.shojobeat.com

RATED T+ FOR OLDER TEEN
PARENTAL ADVISORY
STEPPING ON ROSES is rated T+ for Older Teen and is recommended for ages 16 and up. This volume contains brief nudity and sexual themes.
ratings.viz.com

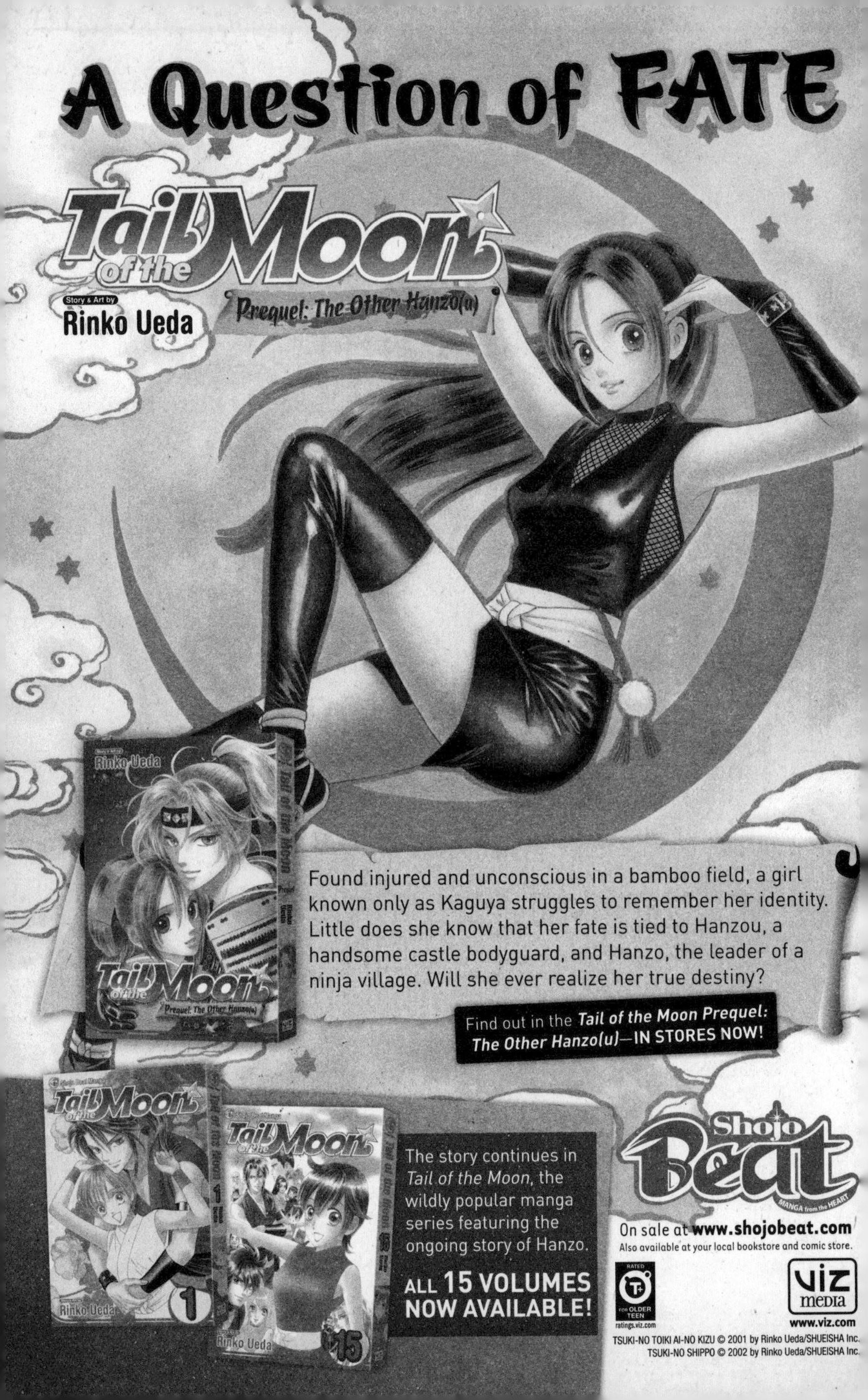
A Question of FATE
Tail of the Moon
Story & Art by
Rinko Ueda
Prequel: The Other Hanzo(u)
Found injured and unconscious in a bamboo field, a girl known only as Kaguya struggles to remember her identity. Little does she know that her fate is tied to Hanzou, a handsome castle bodyguard, and Hanzo, the leader of a ninja village. Will she ever realize her true destiny?
Find out in the Tail of the Moon Prequel: The Other Hanzo(u)—IN STORES NOW!
The story continues in Tail of the Moon, the wildly popular manga series featuring the ongoing story of Hanzo.
ALL 15 VOLUMES NOW AVAILABLE!
Shojo Beat
MANGA from the HEART
On sale at www.shojobeat.com
Also available at your local bookstore and comic store.
RATED T+ FOR OLDER TEEN
ratings.viz.com
VIZ media
www.viz.com
TSUKI-NO TOIKI AI-NO KIZU © 2001 by Rinko Ueda/SHUEISHA Inc.
TSUKI-NO SHIPPO © 2002 by Rinko Ueda/SHUEISHA Inc.

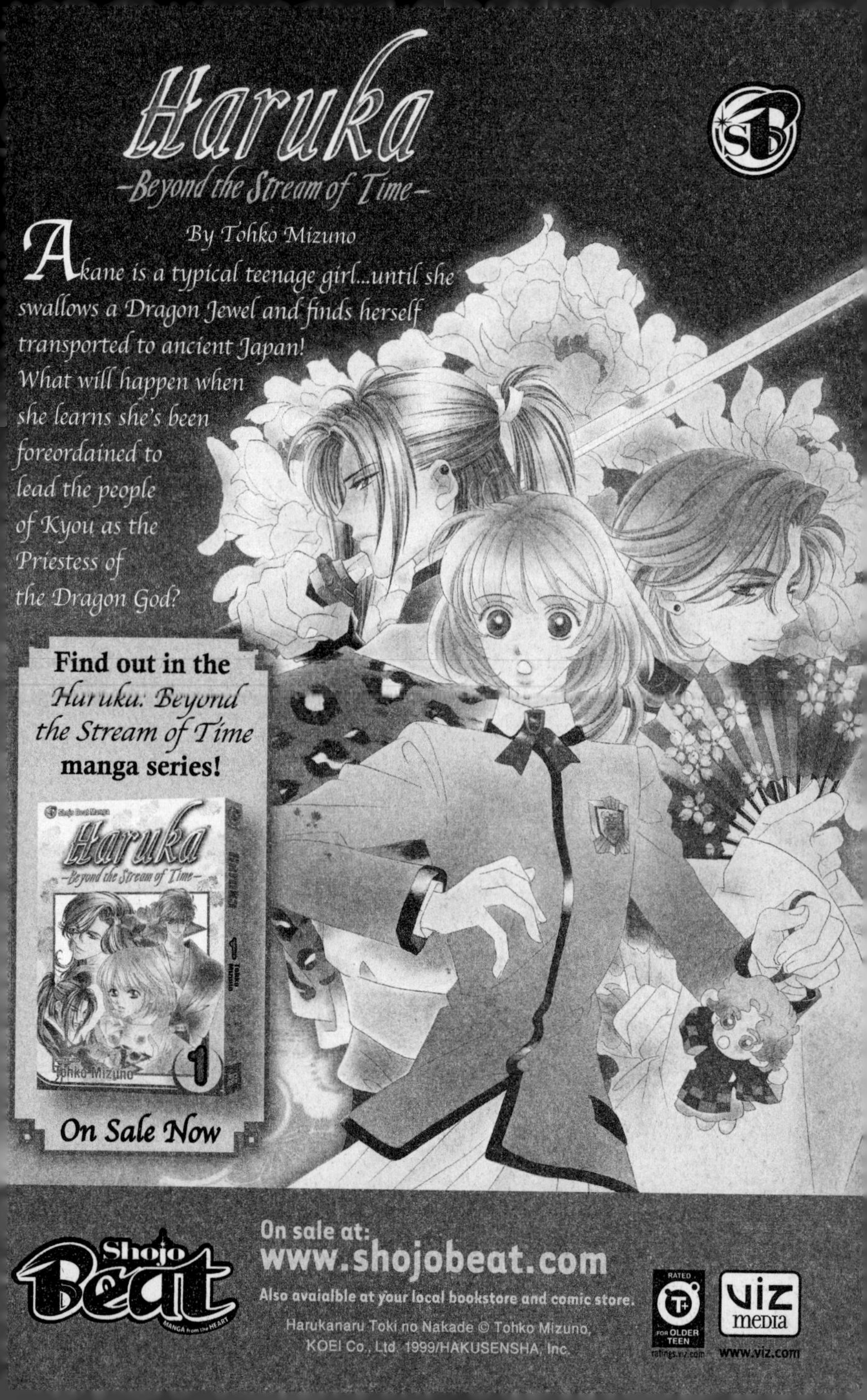
Haruka
-Beyond the Stream of Time-
By Tohko Mizuno
Akane is a typical teenage girl...until she swallows a Dragon Jewel and finds herself transported to ancient Japan! What will happen when she learns she's been foreordained to lead the people of Kyou as the Priestess of the Dragon God?
Find out in the Haruka: Beyond the Stream of Time manga series!
Haruka -Beyond the Stream of Time-
Tohko Mizuno
1
On Sale Now
Shojo Beat
MANGA from the HEART
On sale at:
www.shojobeat.com
Also avaialble at your local bookstore and comic store.
Harukanaru Toki no Nakade © Tohko Mizuno, KOEI Co., Ltd. 1999/HAKUSENSHA, Inc.
RATED T+ FOR OLDER TEEN
ratings.viz.com
VIZ media
www.viz.com

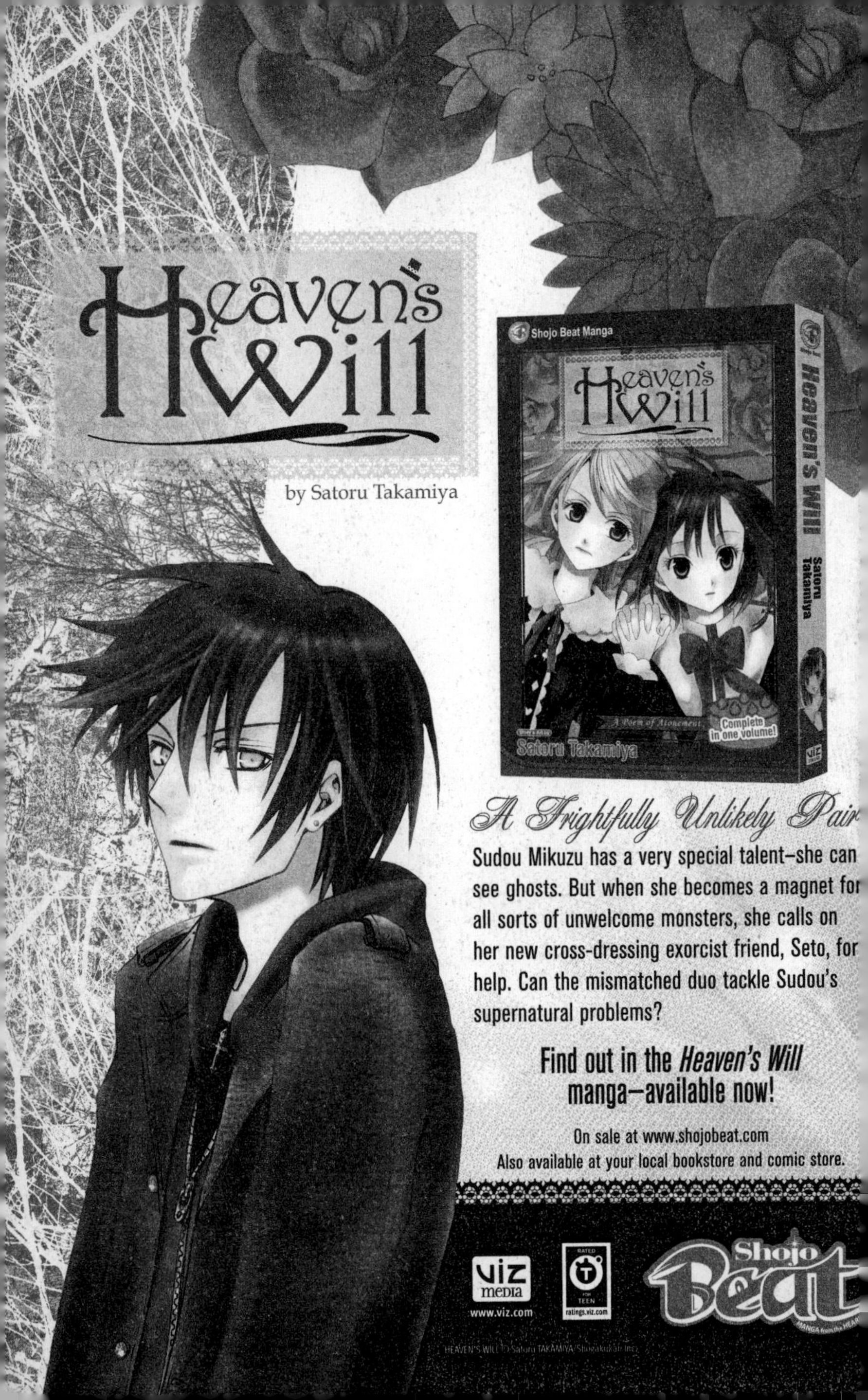
Heaven's Will
by Satoru Takamiya
Shojo Beat Manga
Heaven's Will
Satoru Takamiya
A Poem of Atonement
Complete in one volume!
A Frightfully Unlikely Pair
Sudou Mikuzu has a very special talent–she can see ghosts. But when she becomes a magnet for all sorts of unwelcome monsters, she calls on her new cross-dressing exorcist friend, Seto, for help. Can the mismatched duo tackle Sudou's supernatural problems?
Find out in the *Heaven's Will* manga—available now!
On sale at www.shojobeat.com
Also available at your local bookstore and comic store.
VIZ media
www.viz.com
RATED T FOR TEEN
ratings.viz.com
Shojo Beat
HEAVEN'S WILL © Satoru TAKAMIYA/Shogakukan Inc.

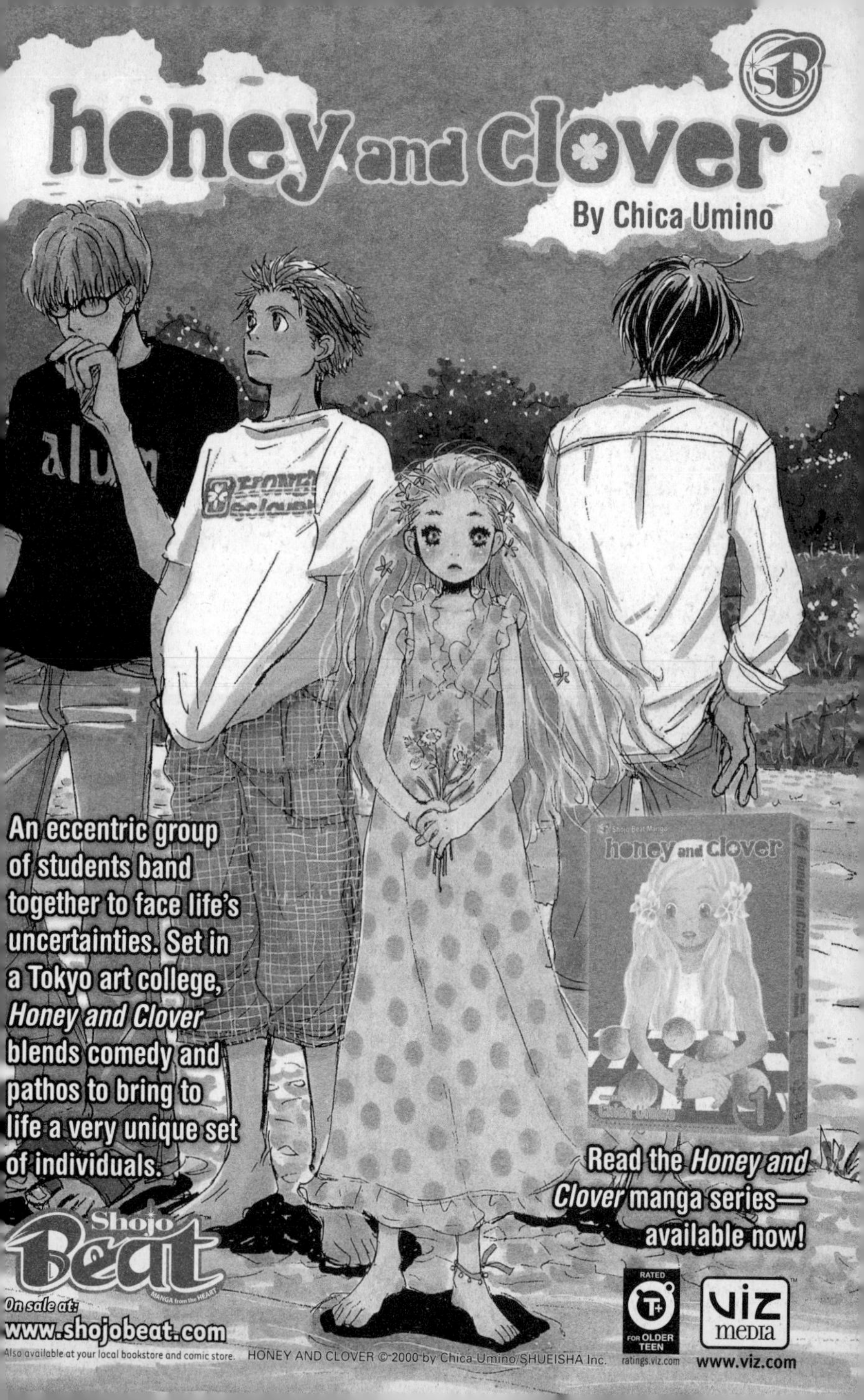
honey and clover
By Chica Umino
An eccentric group of students band together to face life's uncertainties. Set in a Tokyo art college, *Honey and Clover* blends comedy and pathos to bring to life a very unique set of individuals.
Read the *Honey and Clover* manga series—available now!
Shojo Beat
On sale at:
www.shojobeat.com
Also available at your local bookstore and comic store.
HONEY AND CLOVER © 2000 by Chica Umino/SHUEISHA Inc.
RATED T+ FOR OLDER TEEN
ratings.viz.com
VIZ media
www.viz.com

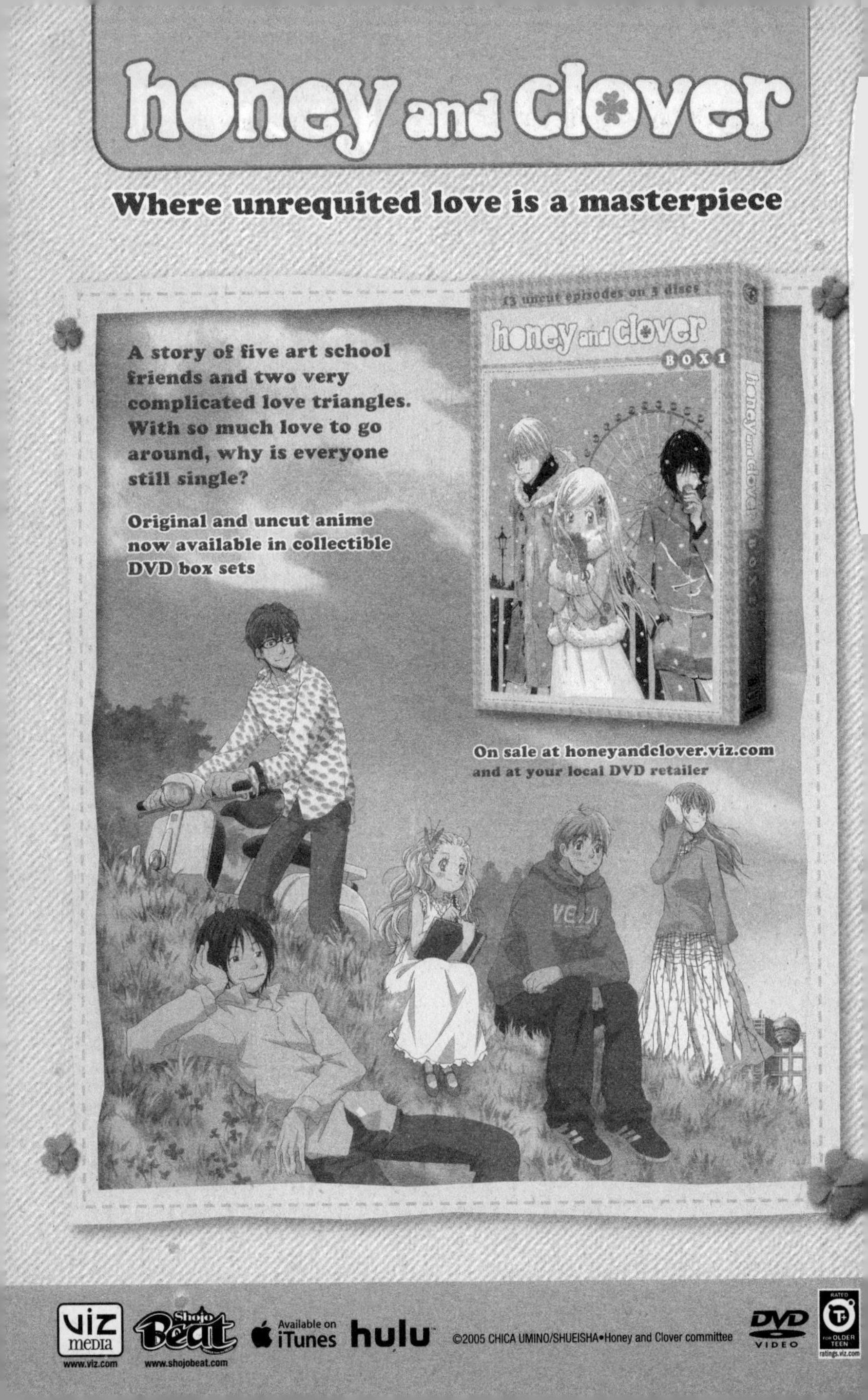
honey and clover
Where unrequited love is a masterpiece
A story of five art school friends and two very complicated love triangles. With so much love to go around, why is everyone still single?
Original and uncut anime now available in collectible DVD box sets
13 uncut episodes on 3 discs
honey and clover
BOX 1
On sale at honeyandclover.viz.com
and at your local DVD retailer
viz media
www.viz.com
Shojo Beat
www.shojobeat.com
Available on iTunes
hulu
©2005 CHICA UMINO/SHUEISHA•Honey and Clover committee
DVD VIDEO
RATED T FOR OLDER TEEN
ratings.viz.com

Shojo Beat

MANGA from the HEART

OTOMEN

STORY AND ART BY
AYA KANNO

VAMPIRE

Natsume's
BOOK of FRIENDS

RY AND ART BY
KI MIDORIKAWA

Want to see more of what you're looking for?

Let your voice be heard!

jobeat.com/mangasurvey

Help us give you more manga from the heart!

USENSHA, Inc.
2004/HAKUSENSHA, Inc.
awa 2005/HAKUSENSHA, Inc.